Modern
MANDARIN CHINESE
Grammar

Routledge Modern Grammars

Series concept and development – Sarah Butler

Other books in the series:

Modern Spanish Grammar, Second Edition
Modern Spanish Grammar Workbook, Second Edition

Modern French Grammar, Second Edition
Modern French Grammar Workbook, Second Edition

Modern German Grammar, Second Edition
Modern German Grammar Workbook, Second Edition

Modern Italian Grammar, Second Edition
Modern Italian Grammar Workbook, Second Edition

Modern MANDARIN CHINESE Grammar

A practical guide

Claudia Ross
and Jing-heng Sheng Ma

 Routledge
Taylor & Francis Group

LONDON AND NEW YORK

First published 2006
by Routledge
2 Park Square, Milton Park, Abingdon, Oxon OX14 4RN

Simultaneously published in the USA and Canada
by Routledge
270 Madison Ave, New York, NY 10016

Routledge is an imprint of the Taylor & Francis Group, an informa business

Typeset in Stone Serif and Akzidenz Grotesk by
Graphicraft Limited, Hong Kong
Printed and bound in Great Britain by
TJ International Ltd, Padstow, Cornwall

British Library Cataloguing in Publication Data
A catalogue record for this book is available from the British Library

Library of Congress Cataloging in Publication Data
Ross, Claudia.
    Modern Mandarin Chinese grammar : a practical guide / Claudia Ross and
Jing-heng Sheng Ma.
        p. cm. – (Routledge modern grammars)
        ISBN 0-415-70009-4 (hbk.) – ISBN 0-415-70010-8 (pbk.)   1. Chinese language – Grammar.
    I. Ma, Jing-heng Sheng.   II. Title.   III. Series.
    PL1107.R65 2006
    495.1′82421–dc22

                                                                                                    2005030422

ISBN10: 0-415-70009-4 (hbk)
ISBN10: 0-415-70010-8 (pbk)
ISBN10: 0-203-79993-3 (ebk)

ISBN13: 978-0-415-70009-2 (hbk)
ISBN13: 978-0-415-70010-8 (pbk)
ISBN13: 978-0-203-79993-2 (ebk)

Contents

Part A   Structures

Contents

Part B   Situations and functions

Contents

Contents

CONTENTS

Contents

Acknowledgements

We are grateful to the many people who have assisted us in the preparation of this book. We particularly thank Baozhang He for his careful reading of the entire manuscript and for his many useful suggestions, and Anne Shuqing Guo for providing some of the examples we use to illustrate the structures and functions of Mandarin. We thank our Routledge editor Sarah Butler for her detailed and timely feedback and for her patience. We thank our family members for their encouragement and help, Lester Ross, Jocelyn Ross, Adam Ross, and Weiyi Ma.

References consulted

Chapter 1
The classification of finals in Chapter 1 is from John Defrancis, *Beginning Chinese*, 2nd revised edition, New Haven: Yale University Press, 1976.

Chapter 3
Yuen-ren Chao, *A Grammar of Spoken Chinese*, Berkeley: University of California Press, 1968.
John DeFrancis (ed.) *ABC Chinese–English Dictionary*, Honolulu: University of Hawaii Press, 1996.
John DeFrancis, *Beginning Chinese*, 2nd revised edition, New Haven: Yale University Press, 1976.
Jerry Norman, *Chinese*, Cambridge: Cambridge University Press, 1988.
L. Wieger, *Chinese Characters*, New York: Paragon Book Reprint Corp., 1965.

Chapter 12
The source of the legal example in Chapter 12 is the Child Welfare Law of the Republic of China, Section 1, article 3.

Chapter 17
The information on names is based on a survey published in the 香港星島日報 **xiānggǎng xīng dǎo rìbào** (*Hong Kong and Singapore Daily News*) in 2002 and reported in 大參考总 **dà cān kǎo zǒng** (*VIP Reference*) vol. 1640, July 28, 2002.

Chapter 46
The source of the legal examples in Chapter 46 is the Economic Contract Law of the PRC (as amended 1993) as cited in Claudia Ross and Lester Ross, 'Language and Law,' in Karen G. Turner, James V. Feinerman, and R. Kent Guy (eds) *The Limits of the Rule of Law in China*, Seattle: University of Washington Press, 2000, pp. 221–70.

Claudia Ross and Jing-heng Sheng Ma

Introduction

This book is divided into two sections: 'Structures' and 'Situations and functions.'

Part A 'Structures' is a concise grammar of Mandarin Chinese organized in the familiar and traditional way, providing an overview of the Chinese writing system and describing the major features of Mandarin grammar. This section should be used for reference when you want to know something about a form or structure. For example, if you want to review the structure of the noun phrase, or how to form numbers, or the structure of the passive form, you should consult this section.

Part B 'Situations and functions' is organized in terms of how to do things with language, and it is the longer of the two sections. For example, if you want to know how to address someone, how to say 'no,' how to make comparisons, or how to apologize, you should consult this section.

Often, the same ground is covered in both parts of this book, although the emphasis is different in each section. Related sections are linked by cross-referencing, indicated by arrows in the margin of the page directing you to another section. Related functions are also cross-referenced throughout the book. You should always follow the cross-reference links so that you have a complete picture of the expression that you are exploring and can use it correctly and accurately.

Topics covered in this book are listed in the table of contents and in the index, and you should use them to help you find words and topics quickly and easily. Notice that the index is an alphabetical listing that includes keywords in English and in Pinyin romanization. For example, if you want to know how to indicate that you have had an experience in the past you can look in the index for the English expression 'experience in the past' or for the Pinyin word **guo**.

In this book, we use traditional grammatical terms to explain the structures of Mandarin. The terms are presented in the glossary at the beginning of this book. Once you are familiar with the grammatical terms you will find them helpful in understanding the grammar and in expressing yourself accurately.

We hope that you will find this book useful and informative. We look forward to learning how you use the book, and to receiving your suggestions on how it can be improved.

Claudia Ross and Jing-heng Sheng Ma

How to use this book

This book brings together two different types of resources to help you to understand Mandarin Chinese. They are presented in two parts: Part A: 'Structures' and Part B: 'Situations and functions.'

When you want to review some aspect of Mandarin grammar such as how to describe a noun or where to put the prepositional phrase in a sentence, you should consult Part A. On the other hand, when you want to know how to apologize, or how to address someone, or how to emphasize something, you should consult Part B. Some topics are covered in more than one chapter of the book. For example, the verb suffix 过/過 **guò** is included in 'Structures' in the chapters on verbs (Chapters 11–13), and also in 'Situations and functions' in Chapter 33, 'Indicating completion and talking about the past.' Arrows in the left-hand margin of each page indicate additional sections of the book in which a topic is discussed. You should follow the cross-references and read everything about the topic that you are exploring in order to get a full picture of its structure and functions.

Some topics can be expressed differently depending upon the level of formality in a specific situation. Where appropriate, we have indicated the level of formality associated with expressions. See for example, 'Prepositions and prepositional phrases' (Chapter 14, section 14.2.8) and 'Greetings and goodbyes' (Chapter 20, section 20.3).

This book provides the most common ways of expressing the major structures and functions in Mandarin. Native speakers of Mandarin differ in their use of some expressions, and we have tried to note standard variations. In your study of Mandarin, you will come across structures and expressions that are not included in this book. You should add them to your repertoire as you continue to strengthen your language skills.

To help you to consolidate your overall knowledge of Chinese, we begin this book with a brief overview of Mandarin pronunciation and an introduction to the Chinese writing system. For a more detailed coverage of pronunciation, consult a beginning level Mandarin textbook. For more information about the Chinese writing system, consult the references cited in the Acknowledgements.

Claudia Ross and Jing-heng Sheng Ma, 2005

Glossary of grammatical terms

Adverbs

Adverbs are words that precede and modify a verb or verb phrase.

他们都很忙。
他們都很忙。
Tāmen *dōu* hěn máng.
They are *all* very busy.

弟弟已经回家了。
弟弟已經回家了。
Dìdi *yǐjing* huí jiā le.
Younger brother *already* went home.

⇨ | 15, 27, 30, 31, 32, 33, 34, 35, 36, 42, 43

Classifiers

Classifiers are words that occur after a number and/or specifier and before a noun. Some grammars refer to classifiers as 'measure words.' Classifiers often need not be translated into English.

一杯水	那本书	这两个人
	那本書	這兩個人
yī *bēi* shuǐ	**nà *běn* shū**	**zhè liǎng *gè* rén**
one [*glass of*] water	that [*volume of*] book	these two [*classifier*] people

⇨ | 8

Clauses

Clauses are dependent sentences, that is, sentences that occur within a larger sentence.

Some verbs take clauses as their objects:

她说她今天很忙。
她説她今天很忙。
Tā shuō *tā jīntiān hěn máng*.
She said *she is very busy today*.

我知道他没有钱。
我知道他沒有錢。
Wǒ zhīdao *tā méi yǒu qián*.
I know *he doesn't have any money*.

Clauses may also serve as subjects:

> 她昨天跟你说话并不表示她愿意当你的女朋友。
> 她昨天跟你説話並不表示她願意當你的女朋友。
> **Tā zuótiān gēn nǐ shuō huà bìng bù biǎoshì tā yuànyi dāng nǐ de nǚ péngyou.**
> (The fact that) *she spoke with you yesterday* does not mean that she is willing to be your girlfriend.

Complements
Complements are verb phrases that serve as the object of a verb. Modal verbs require complements, as do many other verbs.

> 她会说中国话。
> 她會説中國話。
> **Tā huì *shuō Zhōngguó huà*.**
> She can *speak Chinese.*

> 她叫我回家。
> **Tā jiào wǒ *huí jiā*.**
> She told me *to go home.*

Conjunctions
Conjunctions are words that connect two nouns or noun phrases to form a noun phrase.

> 妈妈和爸爸都会说中国话。
> 媽媽和爸爸都會説中國話。
> **Māma *hé* bàba dōu huì shuō Zhōngguó huà.**
> Mom *and* dad can both speak Chinese.

⇨ 16

Demonstratives see **Specifiers and demonstratives**

Direct objects see **Objects**

Final particles
Final particles are syllables that occur at the end of the sentence and indicate a speech act or speaker perspective.

> 我们吃饭吧！
> 我們吃飯吧！
> **Wǒmen chī fàn *ba*!**
> Let's eat! (suggestion)

> 我得走了。再不走就晚咯。
> **Wǒ děi zǒu le. Zài bù zǒu jiù wǎn *lo*.**
> I'd better go now. If I don't go I will be late. (obviousness)

⇨ 24.1.1, 24.5, 30.3, 34.1, 46, 52.2

Grammatical particles
Grammatical particles are syllables that convey grammatical meaning, for example 的 **de** (noun modification), 得 **de** (postverbal adverbial modification), 地 **de** (preverbal adverbial modification), 了 **le** (completed action), 着/著 **zhe** (duration).

⇨ 9, 27, 33, 35

Indirect objects see Objects

Intensifiers
Intensifiers are words that precede and modify stative verbs, adjectival verbs, and modal verbs.

我很喜欢他。	那本书太贵。	你真会跳舞。
我很喜歡他。	那本書太貴。	你真會跳舞。
Wǒ *hěn* xǐhuan tā.	**Nà běn shū *tài* guì.**	**Nǐ *zhēn* huì tiào wǔ.**
I like him *a lot*.	That book is *too* expensive.	You can *really* dance.

⇨ 10.3, 11.2, 12.6.3

Nouns
Nouns are words that can be directly preceded by a specifier and/or number + classifier.

一本书	那本书
一本書	那本書
yī běn *shū*	**nà běn *shū***
one *book*	that *book*

Noun phrases
Noun phrases are nouns and their modifiers.

⇨ 9

Numbers
Number words.

⇨ 6

Objects
There are two different types of objects, *direct* and *indirect*.

The direct object is generally the noun phrase affected by or created by the action of the verb. The direct object generally follows the verb, though it may also be topicalized (see **Topics**).

我每天在图书馆看书。
我每天在圖書館看書。
Wǒ měitiān zài túshūguǎn kàn *shū*.
I read *books* in the library every day.

我已经吃了晚饭。
我已經吃了晚飯。
Wǒ yǐjing chī le *wǎnfàn*.
I have already eaten *dinner*.

The indirect object refers to the recipient of the object noun phrase. In Mandarin, only a small number of verbs take a direct and indirect object. These include 给/給 **gěi** 'to give' and 送 **sòng** 'to present as a gift.' In all cases, the indirect object precedes the direct object.

我不要给他钱。
我不要給他錢。
Wǒ bù yào gěi *tā* qián.
I don't want to give *him* money.

For most verbs, the recipient is expressed as the object of a preposition and not as an indirect object.

> 我给她写了一封信。
> 我給她寫了一封信。
> **Wǒ gěi *tā* xiě le yī fēng xìn.**
> I wrote *her* a letter. (I wrote a letter to *her*.)

Predicates

The predicate of a sentence includes a verb and any object(s) or complements of the verb. It may also include negation, adverbs, prepositional phrases, and phrases that indicate time when, duration, or frequency.

Prepositional phrases

Prepositional phrases consist of a preposition and its following noun phrase. In Mandarin, the prepositional phrase always precedes the verb phrase.

> 我在家吃饭。
> 我在家吃飯。
> **Wǒ *zài jiā* chī fàn.**
> I eat *at home*.

> 我到图书馆去了。
> 我到圖書館去了。
> **Wǒ *dào túshūguǎn* qù le.**
> I went *to the library*.

Prepositions

Prepositions are words that indicate the relationship of a noun phrase to a verb, for example 在 **zài** 'at,' 到 **dào** 'to,' 给/給 **gěi** 'to/for,' 替 **tì** 'for.'

⇨ 14

Pronouns

Pronouns are words that take the place of a noun or noun phrase.

王明是学生。	他是学生。
王明是學生。	他是學生。
***Wáng Míng* shì xuésheng.**	***Tā* shì xuésheng.**
Wang Ming is a student.	*He* is a student.
我不认识那两个人。	我不认识他们。
我不認識那兩個人。	我不認識他們。
Wǒ bù rènshi *nà liǎng gè rén*.	**Wǒ bù rènshi *tāmen*.**
I don't know *those two people*.	I don't know *them*.

⇨ 5.2

Sentences

Normally, a full sentence includes a subject and a predicate. The sentence may begin with a topic.

topic + subject + predicate

那个孩子，脾气很坏。
那個孩子，脾氣很壞。
Nàge háizi, píqi hěn huài.
That child has a bad temper. (lit. 'That child, the temper is bad.')

Specifiers and demonstratives

Specifiers are words that translate as 'this/these' or 'that/those' and describe a noun.

这本书很有意思。
這本書很有意思。
***Zhè** bĕn shū hěn yŏu yìsi.*
This book is very interesting.

These same words, when used to 'point' to an object, are 'demonstratives.'

这是中国毛笔。
這是中國毛筆。
***Zhè** shì Zhōngguó máobĭ.*
This is a Chinese writing brush.

⇨ 7

Subjects

The subject is the noun or noun phrase about which information is provided in the predicate. In Mandarin, the subject of a sentence occurs before the verb phrase. It can be omitted if it is understood from the overall context of the sentence. Typically, a subject is omitted if it is identical in reference to the subject of the preceding sentence.

我看了电影。( )九点钟就回家了。
我看了電影。( )九點鐘就回家了。
Wŏ kàn le diànyĭng. ( ) jiŭdiăn zhōng jiù huí jiā le.
I saw a movie. At nine o'clock *I* returned home.

Topics

Generally speaking, the topic is the noun or noun phrase that the sentence, paragraph, or narrative is about. The topic occurs at the beginning of a sentence, and is often distinct from the subject.

中国菜，我特别喜欢吃家常豆腐。
中國菜，我特別喜歡吃家常豆腐。
***Zhōngguo cài**, wŏ tèbié xĭhuan chī jiācháng dòufu.*
(As for) *Chinese food*, I especially like to eat homestyle beancurd.

In Mandarin, the object of the verb may sometimes occur in 'topic' position, at the beginning of the sentence, before the subject.

羊肉，我不太喜欢吃。
羊肉，我不太喜歡吃。
***Yángròu**, wŏ bù tài xĭhuan chī.*
Mutton, I don't particularly like to eat (it).

A sentence need not begin with a topic.

Verbs

Verbs are words that can be directly negated, or modified by an adverb, or that can serve as the 'yes' answer to yes–no questions. Verbs are the main word in the predicate, and a Mandarin sentence must include a verb. Verbs that take one or more objects are called transitive, and verbs that do not take an object are called intransitive. Mandarin has the following types of verbs.

Adjectival verbs

Adjectival verbs are verbs that can be translated as adjectives in English, for example 大 **dà** 'big,' 好 **hǎo** 'good,' 贵/貴 **guì** 'expensive.' Adjectival verbs are usually intransitive. Note that adjectival verbs do not occur with 是 **shì** 'to be.'

Say this	*Not this*
他很高。	*他是很高。
Tā hěn _gāo_.	**Tā shì hěn gāo.**
He is very *tall*.	

⇨ 10

Stative verbs

(a) Stative verbs are verbs that express states, for example 喜欢/喜歡 **xǐhuan** 'to like,' 像 **xiàng** 'to resemble.'

我喜欢他。
我喜歡他。
Wǒ xǐhuan tā.
I *like* him.

(b) Stative verbs are linking verbs, for example 是 **shì** 'to be,' 姓 **xìng** 'to be family named,' 有 **yǒu** 'to have, to exist.'

她有很多朋友。
Tā _yǒu_ hěn duō péngyou.
She *has* many friends.

⇨ 11

Modal verbs

Modal verbs are verbs that express ability, permission, or obligation, for example 会/會 **huì** 'can' (mentally able), 能 **néng** 'can' (physically able), 可以 **kéyǐ** 'may' (have permission), 得 **děi** 'must/have to.' Modal verbs can serve as the one word answer to yes–no questions, but in complete sentences they are always followed by a verb phrase complement.

⇨ 12

Action verbs

Action verbs are verbs that refer to events. There are two kinds of action verbs:

• Open-ended action verbs express open-ended actions such as 跑 **pǎo** 'to run,' 写/寫 **xiě** 'to write,' and 听/聽 **tīng** 'to listen.' Most open-ended action verbs in Mandarin are transitive.

- Change-of-state action verbs express actions that refer to a change of state and have no duration such as 坐 **zuò** 'to sit (down),' 忘 **wàng** 'to forget,' and 放 **fàng** 'to put (down), to place.'

⇨ 13

Verb phrases
The verb phrase is the verb and its noun phrase objects and/or verb phrase complement clauses.

他每天看电视。
他每天看電視。
Tā měitiān _kàn diànshì_.
He _watches television_ every day.

爸爸给我钱。
爸爸給我錢。
Bàba _gěi wǒ qián_.
Dad _gives me money_.

他会开车。
他會開車。
Tā _huì kāi chē_.
He _can drive (a car)_.

我请你吃晚饭。
我請你吃晚飯。
Wǒ _qǐng nǐ chī wǎnfàn_.
I _invite you to eat dinner_.

A note on grammatical categories and grammatical category shift

In Mandarin, a word may belong to more than one grammatical category. For example, some words may serve as both a verb and a preposition.

		Verb	_Preposition_
给/給	**gěi**	to give	to/for
到	**dào**	to arrive	to
在	**zài**	to be located	at

Out of context, it is not possible to say whether the word 给/給 **gěi** or 到 **dào** or 在 **zài** is a preposition or a verb. However, in the context of a sentence or phrase, the category of the word is clear:

Preposition

我想到中国去。
我想到中國去。
Wǒ xiǎng _dào Zhōngguó_ qù.
I want _to China_ go
I want to go _to China_.

Verb

你什么时候到?
你甚麼時候到?
Nǐ shénme shíhòu *dào*?
When are you *arriving*?

Some textbooks and grammars provide special labels for words that can function as more than one category of word. For example, the label 'coverb' is used in many textbooks for words that can be both prepositions and verbs.

⇨ 13.5, 14.3

A note on Chinese characters

Certain traditional characters have more than one standard form. Here are some examples. This book uses the characters in the first column. An overview of the origin, structure, and systems of Chinese characters is presented in Chapter 3.

裏	裡	**lǐ**
着	著	**zhè**
叫	呌	**jiào**
為	爲	**wèi**
没	沒	**méi**

Part A

Structures

1

Overview of pronunciation and Pinyin romanization

1.1 **The Mandarin syllable**

The syllable in Mandarin Chinese can be made up of three parts: an initial consonant, a final, and a tone. For example, the syllable **má** 麻 is made up of the intial **m**, the final **a**, and the rising tone [/]. Syllables need not have an initial consonant. The syllable **è** 餓 is made up of the final **e** and the falling tone [\]. In addition, a syllable may lack a tone. Syllables that do not have a tone are referred to as having *neutral tone*.

This section presents a brief overview of the initials, finals, and tones of Mandarin. Initials and finals are presented in Pinyin romanization. For a guide to their pronunciation, please consult a beginning level Mandarin textbook.

1.1.1 **Initials**

The Mandarin initials are presented here in the traditional recitation order:

	Type of sound	Initial			
1	bilabial	b	p	m	f
2	alveolar	d	t	n	l
3	velar	g	k		h
4	palatal	j	q		x
5	retroflex	zh	ch	sh	r
6	alveolar affricate/fricatives	z	c	s	

1.1.2 **Finals**

Finals are listed by initial vowel.

a finals	a an ang ai ao
o/e finals	o e en eng ei ou ong er
u finals	u ua uo uai ui uan un uang ueng
i finals	i ia iao ie iu ian in iang ing iong
ü finals	ü üe üan ün

1.1.3   Tones

Tone is the pitch contour of the syllable. Mandarin has four contour tones and a neutral tone. In most romanization systems of Mandarin, the tone is indicated by a diacritic over a vowel, or as a number following the syllable.

The following chart illustrates the contour of the four Mandarin tones when a syllable is spoken in *isolation*, that is, when it is neither preceded nor followed by another syllable.

1 level pitch   ‾
2 rising pitch   ˊ
3 falling-rising pitch   ˇ
4 falling pitch   ˋ

Syllables whose isolation tone is the third tone change their contour in certain contexts as follows.

When a third tone occurs before another third tone, it is pronounced as a rising (second) tone.

> *3 + 3 → 2 + 3*
>
> **hěn hǎo → hén hǎo**   很好   very good

When a third tone occurs before any other tone, it is often pronounced as a low tone.

In this book, we indicate the change of a third tone to a second tone within a single word. For example, we write 所以 as **suóyǐ** and not as **suǒyǐ**. We do not indicate tone changes that occur across words in the Pinyin spelling. For example, **hěn hǎo** will be written as **hěn hǎo** and not as **hén hǎo**.

Tone is an inherent part of the Mandarin syllable, and Mandarin uses tones to distinguish meaning in the same way that the choice of a consonant or a vowel distinguishes meaning. Notice how tone determines the meaning of the following syllable.

Tone

1	**mā** (ma1) 妈/媽	mother
2	**má** (ma2) 麻	numb
3	**mǎ** (ma3) 馬	horse
4	**mà** (ma4) 骂/罵	scold
neutral	**ma** (ma5) 吗/嗎	question particle

1.2   Pinyin romanization

Mandarin is written with Chinese characters, but characters do not provide consistent information about pronunciation. Therefore, Mandarin is typically studied via a transcription. Many transcription systems have been devised for Mandarin Chinese in China and in the West. Most of these are based on the Roman alphabet, and are therefore termed 'romanization' systems. In 1958, the People's Republic of China established *Hanyu Pinyin* (usually referred to as Pinyin) as its standard romanization system. Because of the widespread use of this system of Pinyin in Chinese language teaching around the world, it is used to transcribe the Chinese words in this book.

1.2.1 Placement of tone mark in Pinyin

If a final includes three vowels, or two vowels and a final consonant, the tone mark is written over the second vowel:

    kuài   huán   biān   qióng

If a final includes two vowels and no final consonant, the tone mark is placed over the first vowel, unless the first vowel is **i** or **u**:

    āi   áo   ěi   òu

        iā   ié   iǔ

    uà   ué   uǐ   uò

1.2.2 Some additional Pinyin conventions

- 'u' after the initials **j**, **q**, and **x** is pronounced **ü** but is written as **u**.
- When 'i' and 'ü' begin a syllable, they are written as **yi**, and **yu**.
- When 'u' begins a syllable it is written as **w**.
- In two syllable words, when the boundary between syllables is not clear from the Pinyin spelling and more than one interpretation of the boundary is possible, an apostrophe is used to separate the syllables. For example, if the second syllable begins with a vowel, an apostrophe is used: **Xī'ān** vs. **xiān**.

2

Syllable, meaning, and word

2.1 ## The special status of the Mandarin syllable

2.1.1 ### The syllable and meaning

One of the features of Chinese is that each syllable is associated with a meaning. For example, the Mandarin word for bus station/train station or bus stop/train stop is **chēzhàn**. The syllable **chē** means vehicle and the syllable **zhàn** means stand. Occurring together as a word, **chēzhàn** is very nearly the sum of its parts: vehicle stand.

Some words in English have the kind of structure that Mandarin has, but for most English words, syllables need not have independent meaning. For example, the English word lettuce consists of two syllables *let* and *tuce*. These individual syllables do not have meaning on their own, and it makes no sense to ask about the meaning of 'let' or of 'tuce' in the word lettuce. In contrast, with very few exceptions, the individual syllables of Mandarin words have identifiable meanings, and when learning new words, it makes good sense to note the meanings of the individual syllables.

NOTES

1 In Chinese, a small number of syllables are not associated with a meaning. The most common is the noun suffix 子 **zǐ**. See **2.2.1.1**.
2 A multi-syllable Mandarin word is not always simply the sum of its parts. For example, the word 故事 **gùshì** 'story' is composed of the syllables 故 **gù** 'former, previous' and 事 **shì** 'situation, incident.'

2.1.2 ### The syllable and Chinese characters

In Chinese, the syllable is associated with a Chinese character as well as a meaning. When a syllable is associated with more than one meaning, it is generally the case that each meaning is written with a different character. For example, Mandarin has a number of meanings associated with the pronunciation **zhàn**. Each meaning is written with a different character:

蘸	**zhàn**	dip in liquid (like a pen in ink)
占/佔	**zhàn**	occupy
战/戰	**zhàn**	fight
栈/棧	**zhàn**	storehouse
绽/綻	**zhàn**	to split; to burst open
站	**zhàn**	to stand; a stop, a stand

Because of these differences, the status of the syllable is much more important in Chinese than in English. Conversely, the status of the word is less important in Chinese than in English.

Multi-syllable tendency in Mandarin words

Although Mandarin syllables have meanings, they often combine to form words. Here is a short list of Mandarin syllables and words that they form.

Syllable				*Word*		
学/學	**xué**	study, study of				
生	**shēng**	give birth to; grow		学生/學生	**xuésheng**	student
出	**chū**	go out, produce		出生	**chūshēng**	to be born, birth
口	**kǒu**	mouth, opening		出口	**chūkǒu**	export; exit
版	**bǎn**	printing block/printing		出版	**chūbǎn**	publish
校	**xiào**	school		学校/學校	**xuéxiào**	school
长/長	**zhǎng**	head, one in charge		校长/校長	**xiàozhǎng**	principal
中	**zhōng**	middle		中学/中學	**zhōngxué**	middle school
图/圖	**tú**	chart				
片	**piàn**	a slice, a part		图片/圖片	**túpiàn**	picture
地	**dì**	earth		地图/地圖	**dìtú**	map
书/書	**shū**	book				
馆/館	**guǎn**	place (for activities)		图书馆/圖書館	**túshūguǎn**	library
饭/飯	**fàn**	rice		饭馆/飯館	**fànguǎn**	restaurant

Strategies that create and maintain the two syllable word

The most common length of Mandarin words is two syllables, and a number of common word formation strategies exist which help to create and maintain the two syllable word.

The suffix 子 *zǐ*

One syllable words may be turned into two syllable words by the addition of the suffix 子 **zǐ**. This suffix adds little or no meaning to the word. It usually occurs in neutral tone (**zi**).

Some nouns occur in contemporary Mandarin only with the 子 **zi** suffix, for example 孩子 **háizi** 'child,' 房子 **fángzi** 'house,' 屋子 **wūzi** 'room,' 本子 **běnzi** 'notebook,' 袜子/襪子 **wàzi** 'socks.'

Some words can occur with or without the suffix. These include 车/車 **chē** → 车子/車子 **chēzi** 'car,' 鞋 **xié** → 鞋子 **xiézi** 'shoe(s),' 盘/盤 → 盘子/盤子 **pánzi** 'plate(s),' 票 **piào** → 票子 **piàozi** 'ticket.'

NOTE In the Beijing dialect of Mandarin, the suffix 儿/兒 **(é)r** is routinely added to words in many categories, especially to nouns and classifiers. 儿/兒 **r** suffixation adds a retroflex **(r)** sound but no additional syllable to the word. If a word ends in a final consonant, the 儿/兒 **r** suffix replaces the final consonant: **fēn → fēr** 'a portion,' **wán → wár** 'to play,' **diànyǐng → diànyǐr** 'movie,' etc. The suffix may also replace a vowel in the final: **hái → hár** 'child.'

In this book, we write **-r** suffixed words in terms of their changed pronunciation. That is, we write **wár** and not **wánr** or **wán'er**.

2.2.1.2 | **Location suffixes**

Location words may be suffixed with 头/頭 **tóu**, 面 **miàn**, or 边/邊 **biān** to make them two syllable words: 下头/下頭 **xiàtou** 'below,' 外面 **wàimian** 'outside,' 左边/左邊 **zuǒbiān** 'left side,' etc.

In Mandarin spoken in southern China and Taiwan, the specifiers 这/這 **zhè**, 那 **nà**, **nèi** and 哪 **nǎ**, **něi** are suffixed with 里/裏 when they are used as location words: 这里/這裏 **zhèlǐ** 'here,' 那里/那裏 **nàlǐ** 'there,' and 哪里?/哪裏? **nálǐ?** 'where?'

⇨ | 7.3, 43.1

2.2.1.3 | **Abbreviation**

Words and phrases that are longer than two syllables are often abbreviated to two syllables. The two syllables that form the new, abbreviated word are typically the first syllable of each of the words in the phrase or the first two syllables of the first word in the phrase, though other combinations occur.

超级市场/超級市場	**chāojí shìchǎng**	supermarket →	超市 **chāoshì**
公共汽车/公共汽車	**gōnggòng qìchē**	public bus →	公车/公車 **gōngchē**
飞机场/飛機場	**fēijīchǎng**	airport →	机场/機場 **jīchǎng**

2.3 | # Word-specific tone changes

In addition to the tone changes mentioned in Chapter 1 for all third-tone syllables, there are certain tone changes that occur in specific words.

2.3.1 | ## Tone change in the word 不 *bù*

不 **bù** changes to **bú** when it occurs before another fourth-toned syllable in the same word, phrase, or breath group:

	4–4	→	*2–4*
不对/不對 not correct	**bù duì**	→	**bú duì**
不必 need not	**bù bì**	→	**bú bì**

2.3.2 | ## Tone change in the numbers 一 *yī* 1, 七 *qī* 7, and 八 *bā* 8

The tone of the numbers 一 **yī** 1, and, less commonly, 七 **qī** 7, and 八 **bā** 8 may change to second tone **yí**, **qí**, and **bá** before a fourth-toned syllable in the same word, phrase, or breath group:

	1–4	→	*2–4*
一共 altogether	**yīgòng**	→	**yígòng**
一定 certainly	**yīdìng**	→	**yídìng**
一辈子 a lifetime	**yī bèizi**	→	**yí bèizi**

| 七块钱/七塊錢
seven dollars | **qī kuài qián** | → | **qí kuài qián** |
| 八倍
eightfold | **bā bèi** | → | **bá bèi** |

In addition, 一 **yī** changes to fourth tone before syllables with first, second, or third tone.

	1–1	→	*4–1*
一张/一張 one sheet (e.g. of paper)	**yī zhāng**	→	**yì zhāng**
	1–2	→	*4–2*
一条/一條 one thin strip (e.g. of news)	**yī tiáo**	→	**yì tiáo**
	1–3	→	*4–3*
一碗 one bowl	**yī wǎn**	→	**yì wǎn**

2.4 Change to neutral tone

In Beijing and northern China, certain syllables lose their original tone and are pronounced as neutral tone. This tone change does not occur in Taiwan, where all syllables retain their original tones.

⇨ 1.1.3

The complete conditions for change to neutral tone are complex, but here are some general rules for the change of a second syllable to neutral tone.

• The second syllable is a repetition of the first syllable:

	tone-tone	→	*tone-neutral*
太太 Mrs	**tàitài**	→	**tàitai**
弟弟 younger brother	**dìdì**	→	**dìdi**

• The second syllable is a suffix that does not contribute a meaning to the word. This includes the suffix 子 **zǐ**, and the directional suffixes 头/頭 **tóu**, 面 **miàn**, and 边/邊 **biān**:

	tone-tone	→	*tone-neutral*
孩子 child	**háizǐ**	→	**háizi**
里头/裏頭 inside	**lǐtóu**	→	**lǐtou**

• The meaning of the second syllable is the same as or overlaps with the meaning of the first syllable:

	tone-tone	→	*tone-neutral*
衣服 clothing	**yīfú**	→	**yīfu**

衣 **yī**
clothing

服 **fú**
clothing

事情 matter/situation	**shìqíng**	→	**shìqing**

事 **shì**
situation

情 **qíng**
situation

The second syllable retains its tone when it adds to and expands the meaning of the first syllable. Examples include:

学期/學期	学/學	期
xuéqī	**xué**	**qī**
semester	study	interval
作法	作	法
zuòfǎ	**zuò**	**fǎ**
method of doing	do	method
看完	看	完
kànwán	**kàn**	**wán**
finish reading	read	finish

2.5 Incorporating foreign words and naming foreign objects

Chinese has not borrowed freely from other languages. However, when it incorporates foreign words into the language, it typically uses the following strategies:

• Adapting the foreign pronunciation to conform to the syllable structure of Chinese.

Names

罗斯福/羅斯福	**Luósīfú**	Roosevelt
加缪/加繆	**Jiāmóu**	Camus
邱吉尔/邱吉爾	**Qiūjí'ěr**	Churchill
拿破仑/拿破崙	**Nápòlún**	Napoleon
莎士比亚/莎士比亞	**Shāshìbǐyà**	Shakespeare

Objects

比萨/比薩	**bǐsà**	pizza
汉堡包/漢堡包	**hànbǎobāo**	hamburger

⇨ 1.1

- Forming new words based on meaning or function.
  When new items enter China, they often lose their foreign pronunciation and get new Chinese names that reflect their meaning or function. Here are some examples:

电视/電視	**diànshì**	television (electric vision)
电脑/電腦	**diànnǎo**	computer (electric brain)
电传/電傳	**diànchuán**	fax (electric transmission)
手机/手機	**shǒujī**	cell phone/mobile phone (hand machine)
热狗/熱狗	**règǒu**	(lit.) hot dog
卫星/衛星	**wèixīng**	satellite (protection star)

- Forming new words based on meaning while preserving the foreign pronunciation.

万维网/萬維網	**wàn wéi wǎng**	the world wide web (a net of 10,000 connections)
可乐/可樂	**kělè**	cola (it can make you happy)
拖拉机/拖拉機	**tuōlājī**	tractor (drag pull machine)
摩托车/摩托車	**mótuō chē**	motorcycle (a vehicle you touch and support with your hands)
信用卡	**xìnyòng kǎ**	credit card (trust card)
吉普车/吉普車	**jípǔchē**	jeep (lucky widely used vehicle)

Foreign companies often follow this principle when translating the names of their companies and their products into Chinese.

可口可乐/可口可樂	**Kěkǒukělè**	Coca Cola [soft drink] (pleasant to drink and it can make you happy)
福特/福特	**Fútè**	Ford [automobiles] (happiness – exceptional)
汰渍/汰漬	**Tàizì**	Tide [laundry detergent] (eliminate stains and sludge)

3

The Chinese writing system: an overview

Although transcription systems can be used to write Chinese, Chinese characters are the basis of written communication in China. This chapter presents an overview of Chinese characters.

3.1 Traditional and simplified characters

There are two standard systems of characters in current use: traditional characters and simplified characters. Simplified characters are the official characters used in mainland China and Singapore. Traditional characters are the official characters used in Taiwan and other parts of the Chinese speaking world.

Most characters in the traditional and simplified systems are identical. However, in the simplified character system, many frequently used characters have been simplified from their traditional, more complex form. Here are some examples.

Traditional	Simplified	Pronunciation	Meaning
國	国	**guó**	country
東	东	**dōng**	east
車	车	**chē**	car
買	买	**mǎi**	buy
寫	写	**xiě**	write

A simplified way of writing characters has existed for hundreds of years. Simplified characters were used in informal documents and in some forms of calligraphy before they were adopted by mainland China as the official form. Therefore, although the two forms now have some political significance, you may encounter simplified characters in use in Taiwan and traditional characters in use in mainland China.

3.2 The structure of Chinese characters: the radical and the phonetic

3.2.1 The radical

All Chinese characters contain a *radical*, a sequence of strokes that broadly categorize the character in terms of meaning.

In the set of traditional characters, there are 214 radicals. In the set of simplified characters, there are 189 radicals. Some radicals may occur as independent characters. Others only occur as part of a character.

Here is a list of some of the most common radicals, including their simplified form if there is one.

Traditional radical	Alternate form	Radicals with simplified forms	Meaning
人	亻		person
刀	刂		knife
力			energy
水	氵		water
門		门	door
土			earth
竹	⺮		bamboo
口			mouth
囗			enclosure
心	忄		heart
火	⺗		fire
木			wood
日			sun
食		饣	eat, food
	⺍		grass
言		讠	language
金		钅	metal/gold

When a radical is simplified, the simplified form is used in all of the characters in which it occurs. Here are some examples.

Traditional	Simplified	Pronunciation	Meaning
話	话	**huà**	speech
錢	钱	**qián**	money
鋼	钢	**gāng**	steel
飯	饭	**fàn**	rice
餓	饿	**è**	hungry

3.2.2 The phonetic

Some characters are radicals by themselves. Examples include:

水	**shuǐ**	water
木	**mù**	wood
人	**rén**	person

However, most characters include a radical and additional strokes. Often, these additional strokes provide a hint at the pronunciation of the character. When they do, they are called the *phonetic*.

Here are examples of characters with phonetics. As you can see, the pronunciation of the phonetic may be identical with or similar to the pronunciation of the character.

Character	Phonetic: the character sounds like . . .
问/問 **wèn** to ask	门/門 **mén** door
间/間 **jiān** between	
简/簡 **jiǎn** simple	
们/們 **men** plural marker	
清 **qīng** clear	青 **qīng** blue or green
情 **qíng** situation, sentiment	
请/請 **qǐng** to request	
河 **hé** river	可 **kě** approve, can
哥 **gē** older brother	

Noting phonetic information is a helpful way to remember characters. However, the phonetic rarely provides complete information about the pronunciation of a character.

3.3 The traditional classification of characters

Chinese characters originated during the early Shang dynasty or the late Xia dynasty, in the seventeenth century BC. One of the earliest Chinese dictionaries, the *Shuowen Jiezi*, compiled in AD 121, established a classification of characters that is still used today. The classification identified the following six categories based on structure and representation of meaning.

3.3.1 Pictographs 象形 *xiàngxíng*

Pictographs originated as pictures of objects. They represent only a small portion of Chinese characters. The modern forms are stylized versions of the ancient forms. Here are comparisons of the Shang Dynasty forms with the modern forms of the same characters.

Shang form	Modern form	Meaning
⅏	水 **shuǐ**	water
☉	日 **rì**	sun
⬦	目 **mù**	eye

3.3.2   Ideographs 指事 *zhǐ shì*

Ideographs represent abstract meanings, often having to do with spatial orientation. Only a small number of characters are ideographs. Examples are presented here.

Shang form	Modern form	Meaning
二	上 **shàng**	above
二	下 **xià**	below
中	中 **zhōng**	middle (picture of a target hit by an arrow)

3.3.3   Associative compounds 会意/會意 *huì yì*

The meaning of these characters is reflected in the meaning of their component parts.

Character			Composed of					
好	**hǎo**	good	女	**nǚ**	woman +	子	**zǐ**	child
话/話	**huà**	speech	言	**yán**	language +	舌	**shé**	tongue

3.3.4   Phonetic compounds 形声/形聲 *xíngshēng*

Phonetic compounds are the most common type of Chinese character and are discussed in 3.2.2 above.

3.3.5   False borrowings 假借 *jiǎjiè*

False borrowings involve the use of a character to refer to another word with identical pronunciation but different meaning. For example, the word for wheat, written as 来/來, a picture of the wheat plant, was 'borrowed' to write the abstract concept 'come,' which, at the time, had the same pronunciation as the word for wheat. The character for wheat was later revised to distinguish it from the character for come. In present day writing, 'wheat' is written as 麦/麥 **mài** and 'come' is written as 来/來 **lái**. The similarity in the characters can be seen in the traditional form of the characters. Note that the pronunciation of the two words is no longer identical, though they still rhyme.

3.3.6   Semantic derivations 转注/轉注 *zhuǎnzhù*

Characters are considered 转注/轉注 **zhuǎnzhù** when they are used to represent a meaning that is derived from the original meaning of the character. For example, the character 网/網 **wǎng**, originally a picture of a fishing net, is used to refer to networks in general. It is the character used in one of the Chinese translations of the World Wide Web: 万维网/萬維網 **wàn wéi wǎng**. The simplified character for net, 网, is the older form of the character.

3.4   Character stroke order: 笔顺/筆順 *bǐshùn*

3.4.1   Basic rules of stroke order

Each Chinese character contains a precise number of strokes written in a fixed order. Below are the basic rules of stroke order for the writing of Chinese characters.

Rule   *Example*

1 Horizontal (横 **héng**) precedes vertical (竖/豎 **shù**).   十
2 Left falling stroke (撇 **piě**) precedes right falling stroke (捺 **nà**). 人
3 First top, then bottom.   三
4 First left, then right.   他
5 First outside, then inside.   月
6 First complete the inside of a box, then seal the box.   日
7 First center, then sides.   小
8 First horizontal (横 **héng**), then left falling stroke (撇 **piě**), then
   right falling stroke (捺 **nà**).   大

3.4.2 Special stroke order rules

Rule   *Example*

1 Write the dot (点/點 **diǎn**) last if it is positioned at the top right
   corner of a character.   我
2 Write the dot (点/點 **diǎn**) last if it is positioned inside a character. 太
3 If the character includes the curved left-falling stroke (横折撇/橫摺撇
   héng zhé piě) and one other component, write the curved left-falling
   stroke last.   建
4 If the character consists of more than one horizontal stroke (横 **héng**)
   and vertical stroke (竖/豎 **shù**), write the vertical stroke first, and
   the horizontal stroke at the bottom last.   上
5 If a character has a horizontal stroke (横 **héng**) in the middle,
   write the horizontal stroke last.   女

4

Phrase order in the Mandarin sentence

Basic phrase order

The basic order of the Mandarin sentence is

> *topic + subject + predicate*

A sentence need not have an overt topic. In addition, if the subject is understood from the context of the sentence, it is often omitted from the sentence.

The predicate consists of everything in the sentence except for the topic and subject, including the verb, its objects, negation, adverbial modifiers, and prepositional phrases. The following sections present the order of these constituents.

⇨ 4.1, 8.3, 15.2.2, 17.6, 21.11, 35.1.2, 36.3, 42.1.1, 53.1, 53.1.2.2, Glossary

The position of direct and indirect objects

In the neutral sentence in which nothing is emphasized, the direct and indirect objects of the verb follow the verb. We refer to the verb and its objects as the verb phrase.

If there is an indirect object, it precedes the direct object.

> *subject + verb + indirect object + direct object*
>
> 他给我一本书。
> 他給我一本書。
> **Tā gěi wǒ yī běn shū.**
> He gave (gives) me one book.

Most verbs take only a direct object.

> *subject + verb + direct object*
>
> 我看了那些书。
> 我看了那些書。
> **Wǒ kàn le nà xiē shū.**
> I read those books.

The object may also occur before the subject for emphasis. In this position it is *topicalized*.

➪ 53

4.3 The position of prepositional phrases

Prepositional phrases always occur right before the verb and its objects.

> *subject + prepositional phrase + verb + direct object*
>
> 他跟他的女朋友吃晚饭。
> 他跟他的女朋友吃晚飯。
> **Tā gēn tā de nǚ péngyou chī wǎnfàn.**
> He eats dinner with his girlfriend.

➪ 14

4.4 The position of location phrases

The location phrase is a type of preposition phrase. It always occurs before the verb phrase.

> *subject + location phrase + verb phrase*
>
> 我在家吃饭。
> 我在家吃飯。
> **Wǒ zài jiā chī fàn.**
> I eat at home.

Within the location phrase, the order of constituents is from the largest to the smallest. Letters are addressed following this principle.

> 中国北京潮阳区建国门外大街一号
> 中國北京潮陽區建國門外大街一號
> **Zhōngguó Běijīng Cháoyáng qū Jiànguó mén wài dà jiē yī hào**
> China Beijing Chaoyang District Jianguo Gate Outer Road Number 1 →
> Number 1, Jianguo Gate Outer Road, Chaoyang District, Beijing, China

➪ 18.7

4.5 The position of 'time when' phrases

A phrase that indicates the 'time when' a situation takes place occurs at the beginning of the predicate.

> *subject + time when + predicate*
>
> | 我 | 每天 | 喝咖啡。 |
> |---|---|---|
> | **Wǒ** | **měitiān** | **hē kāfēi.** |
> I drink coffee every day.

subject + time when + predicate

| 他 | 每天 | 跟他的女朋友吃晚饭。 |
| 他 | 每天 | 跟他的女朋友吃晚飯。 |

Tā **měitiān** **gēn tā de nǚ péngyou chī wǎnfàn.**
He eats dinner every day with his girlfriend.

If 'time when' is emphasized or contrasted with another time, it may occur before the subject:

昨天我不太舒服。今天已经没问题了。
昨天我不太舒服。今天已經沒問題了。
Zuótiān wǒ bù tài shūfu. Jīntiān yǐjing méi wèntí le.
Yesterday I was a bit uncomfortable. Today it is no longer a problem.

Within the 'time when' phrase, the order of constituents is from the largest block of time to the smallest block of time:

一九九八年二月十五日
yī jiǔ jiǔ bā nián èryuè shíwǔ rì
1998   year February 15 → February 15, 1998

昨天晚上八点钟
昨天晚上八點鐘
zuótiān wǎnshang bā diǎn zhōng
yesterday evening 8 o'clock → 8 o'clock last night.

4.6 The relative order of the 'time when' phrase and the location phrase

When a sentence includes both a 'time when' phrase and a location phrase, 'time when' generally occurs before location.

subject + time when + location + verb phrase

我每天在家吃饭。
我每天在家吃飯。
Wǒ měitiān zài jiā chī fàn.
I eat at home every day.

4.7 The position of adverbs

Adverbs occur at the beginning of the predicate, before the verb and any prepositional phrase. Adverbs usually occur after the 'time when' phrase.

我上个月只看了一个电影。
我上個月只看了一個電影。
Wǒ shàng gè yuè *zhǐ* kàn le yī gè diànyǐng.
Last month I *only* saw one movie.

⇨ 15

4.8 The position of negation

Negation occurs before the verb and any prepositional phrase. It usually occurs after an adverb, though certain adverbs may either precede or follow negation.

⇨ | 15, 23.2

4.9 The position of duration phrases

Duration phrases are time phrases that indicate the length of time that an action occurs. Duration phrases directly follow the verb. Unlike English, there is no preposition associated with the expression of duration in Mandarin.

我在中国住了三年。
我在中國住了三年。
Wǒ zài Zhōngguó zhù le *sān nián*.
I in China lived *three years*. → I lived in China *for three years*.

我昨天晚上睡了八个钟头。
我昨天晚上睡了八個鐘頭。
Wǒ zuótiān wǎnshang shuì le *bā gè zhōngtóu*.
I yesterday evening slept *eight hours*. → I slept *for eight hours* yesterday.

⇨ | 35

4.10 Order within the noun phrase

The main noun in the noun phrase, the *head noun*, occurs as the last word in the phrase. All phrases that describe or *modify* the head noun occur before the head noun.

那本很有意思的书
那本很有意思的書
nà běn hěn yǒu yìsi de *shū*
that very interesting *book*

⇨ | 9

4.11 Phrase order in questions

In Mandarin, the order of phrases in questions is identical to the order of phrases in statements. Unlike English and many European languages, Mandarin questions are not characterized by a special question word order.

Statement

我喜欢他。
我喜歡他。
Wǒ xǐhuan *tā*.
I like *him*.

Content question

你喜欢谁？
你喜歡誰？
Nǐ xǐhuan *shéi*?
Who do you like?

Yes–no question

你喜欢他吗？
你喜歡他嗎？
Nǐ xǐhuan *tā* ma?
Do you like *him*?

⇨ 24

5

Nouns

In Mandarin, the same form of the noun is used in subject and object position.

Subject	*Object*
猫吃鱼。	我养猫。
貓吃魚。	我養貓。
Māo chī yú.	**Wǒ yǎng māo.**
Cats eat fish. (or) *The cat* eats fish.	I raise *cat/cats*.
他学中文。	我喜欢他。
他學中文。	我喜歡他。
Tā xué Zhōngwén.	**Wǒ xǐhuan tā.**
He studies Chinese.	I like *him*.

With the exception of the written form of the third person pronoun, **tā** (see below), Mandarin nouns are not marked for gender, and there is not the distinction between masculine, feminine and neuter found in many European languages. The properties of Mandarin nouns are described here.

5.1 Common nouns

Most nouns are common nouns. Their referents may be concrete (纸/紙 **zhǐ** 'paper,' 桌子 **zhuōzi** 'table,' 水 **shuǐ** 'water') or abstract (思想 **sīxiǎng** 'thought,' 原则/原則 **yuánzé** 'principle,' 自由 **zìyóu** 'freedom'). Mandarin makes no grammatical distinction between 'mass' and 'count' nouns.

Mandarin common nouns have a single, invariant form. They do not reflect number, and the same form of the noun is used whether the noun is singular or plural. When no number is used with a noun, the noun is understood to be neither singular nor plural, but simply unspecified for number. In addition, nouns that occur without any modifiers or descriptions have a general rather than a specific reference. For example, 书/書 **shū** refers to 'book' in general and not to any specific book.

When it is necessary to indicate the number of a noun, the noun is modified by a *number + classifier* phrase. The classifier is *required* after the number. *Number + noun* without an intervening classifier is ungrammatical. Compare the following:

Say this	*Not this*
一本书/一本書	*一书/一書
yì běn shū	**yì shū**
one book	

	Say this	*Not this*
	三个人/三個人	*三人
	sān gè rén	**sān rén**
	three people	

⇨ 6, 8

When a specifier 这/這 **zhè, zhèi** 'this/these,' 那 **nà, nèi** 'that/those,' or the question specifier 哪 **nǎ, něi** 'which' modifies the noun, it also must be followed by a classifier or number + classifier. If the number is *one*, the number may be omitted.

这(一)本书	那两本书	哪三本书?
這(一)本書	那兩本書	哪三本書?
zhè (yì) běn shū	**nà liǎng běn shū**	**nǎ sān běn shū?**
this book	those two books	which three books?

⇨ 7

A small number of common nouns referring to people can be suffixed by -们/們 **men**, the suffix that also marks the plural form of pronouns (see section 5.2 below).

同志们/同志們	**tóngzhìmen**	comrades
孩子们/孩子們	**háizimen**	children
学生们/學生們	**xuéshengmen**	students

This use of -们/們 **men** with common nouns is relatively rare. It conveys a sense of inclusion and is sometimes used when addressing an audience.

> 同学们，今天我们听马老师作报告。
> 同學們，今天我們聽馬老師作報告。
> **Tóngxuémen, jīntiān wǒmen tīng Mǎ lǎoshī zuò bàogào.**
> Fellow students, today we are going to listen to a report by teacher Ma.

When a noun is suffixed with 们/們 **men** it cannot be further modified with any kind of modifying phrase, including a *number + classifier* phrase.

	Say this	*Not this*
	我们的同学	*我们的同学们
	我們的同學	我們的同學們
	wǒmen de tóngxué	**wǒmen de tóngxuémen**
	our fellow students	
	三个孩子	*三个孩子们
	三個孩子	三個孩子們
	sān gè háizi	**sān gè háizimen**
	three children	

⇨ 9

Pronouns

Mandarin has first, second, and third person pronouns and has a reflexive pronoun.

Mandarin pronouns have the following properties:

- Pronouns are not distinguished in terms of grammatical role. The same pronouns are used for subject, object, possession, etc.
- Pronouns have singular and plural forms. The suffix -们/們 **men** is added to the singular form to make it the plural form.
- Gender is not reflected in the spoken language. The written language has distinctions for the second and third person pronouns, though only the third person gender distinction is commonly used.

	Singular	*Plural*
First person	我 **wǒ** I/me	我们/我們 **wǒmen** we/us (exclusive or neutral) 咱们/咱們 **zánmen** we (inclusive)
Second person	你 **nǐ** (masculine or neutral) 妳 **nǐ** (feminine) you	你們 **nǐmen** you
Third person	他 **tā** (masculine or neutral) 她 **tā** (feminine) 它/牠 **tā** (non-human or inanimate)	他们/他們 **tāmen** (masculine or non-specific for gender) 她们/她們 **tāmen** (feminine) they/them
Reflexive	自己 **zìjǐ** self	

The reflexive pronoun 自己 *zìjǐ* 'self'

Mandarin has only one reflexive pronoun, and it is not marked for person or gender. To indicate person, the reflexive may optionally be preceded by the relevant personal pronoun.

我自己 **wǒ zìjǐ** myself	我们自己/我們自己 **wǒmen zìjǐ** ourselves
你自己 **nǐ zìjǐ** yourself	你们自己/你們自己 **nǐmen zìjǐ** yourselves
他自己/她自己 **tā zìjǐ** himself, herself	他们自己/他們自己 **tāmen zìjǐ** themselves

自己 **zìjǐ** 'self' is also used without a personal pronoun. When it occurs in object position, it is understood to refer to the subject:

你在中国一定得把自己照顾好。
你在中國一定得把自己照顧好。
Nǐ zài Zhōngguó yīdìng děi bǎ zìjǐ zhàogù hǎo.
When *you* are in China you certainly should take good care of your*self*.

没有人不喜欢自己的。
沒有人不喜歡自己的。
Méi yǒu *rén* bù xǐhuan *zìjǐ* de.
No *one* doesn't like *him/herself.*

自己 **zìjǐ** 'self' may be used to indicate contrast with another noun phrase or pronoun:

我希望他们结婚，可是我自己不想结婚。
我希望他們結婚，可是我自己不想結婚。
Wǒ xīwàng tāmen jiéhūn, kěshì wǒ *zìjǐ* bù xiǎng jiéhūn.
I hope they will get married, but I *myself* don't plan to get married.

这是我自己的事。你不用管。
這是我自己的事。你不用管。
Zhè shì wǒ zìjǐ de shì. Nǐ bù yòng guǎn.
This is my affair. You need not be concerned with it.

5.2.2 The inclusive pronoun 咱们/咱們 *zánmen* 'we'

The inclusive pronoun 咱们/咱們 **zánmen** 'we' is used in northern dialects of Mandarin. 咱们/咱們 **zánmen** 'we' refers to the speaker, other people associated with the speaker, and to the addressee. When a speaker uses 咱们/咱們 **zánmen** 'we' as the subject, he or she includes *you* in the remarks.

咱们都是自己人。
咱們都是自己人。
Zánmen dōu shì zìjǐ rén.
We are all family. (We, including you, are all one family.)

'Inclusive' 咱们/咱們 **zánmen** contrasts with an 'exclusive' use of 'we' that is associated with 我们/我們 **wǒmen**. In the exclusive sense, 我们/我們 **wǒmen** refers to the speaker and others associated with the speaker but not to the addressee.

我们欢迎你。
我們歡迎你。
Wǒmen huānyíng nǐ.
We welcome you.

咱们/咱們 **zánmen** only has the inclusive meaning. In addition, 咱们/咱們 **zánmen** is only used as subject, and never as object.

我们/我們 **wǒmen** can have either inclusive or exclusive meaning and it occurs as subject and object. It is much more commonly used than 咱们/咱們 **zánmen**.

5.2.3 Modification of pronouns

Pronouns represent an entire noun phrase. Therefore, in general, they are not further modified. However, Mandarin has a small number of literary expressions in which the pronoun is modified:

可怜的我
可憐的我
kělián de wǒ
poor me

美丽的她
美麗的她
měilì de tā
pretty her

善良的高老师
善良的高老師
shànliáng de Gāo lǎoshī
good hearted professor Gao

5.2.4 Possession involving pronouns

Mandarin does not have possessive pronouns. The meaning of possessive pronouns is conveyed by *pronoun* + 的 *de*.

我的朋友
wǒ de péngyou
my friend

他的小狗
tā de xiáogǒu
his puppy

Here is a table showing the Mandarin equivalent of English possessive pronouns.

Singular		*Plural*	
my	我的 **wǒ de**	our	我们的/我們的 **wǒmen de** 咱们的/咱們的 **zánmen de**
your	你的 **nǐ de**	your	你们的/你們的 **nǐmen de**
his (hers)	他的 (她的) **tā de**	their	他们的/他們的 **tāmen de**
Reflexive ones	自己的 **zìjǐ de**		
Interrogative whose?	谁的?/誰的? **shéi de?**		

⇨ 9.2.1.2, 25.2.2

5.3 Proper nouns

Proper nouns include personal names, place names, names of companies, names of schools, etc.

牛津大学
牛津大學
Niújīn Dàxué
Oxford University

伦敦/倫敦
Lúndūn
London

长城/長城
Chángchéng
The Great Wall

喜玛拉雅山脉/喜瑪拉雅山脈
Xǐmǎlāyǎ shān mài
Himalayan Mountains

Proper nouns, like pronouns, typically occur without additional modification. As is the case with pronouns, Mandarin has a small number of literary expressions in which the proper noun may be modified. Here are some examples.

可爱的王美玲
可愛的王美玲
kě'ài de Wáng Měilíng
Charming Wang Meiling

山清水秀的台湾
山清水秀的臺灣
shānqīng shuǐxiù de Táiwān
Taiwan of green hills and clear streams → beautiful Taiwan

地大物博的美国
地大物博的美國
dìdà wùbó de Měiguó
America vast in territory and rich in resources

⇨ 5.2.3

6

Numbers

6.1 **Mandarin numbers 0–99**

6.1.1 **Numbers 0–10**

0	○ or 零 **líng**			
1	一 **yī**		6	六 **liù**
2	二 **èr**, 两/兩 **liǎng**		7	七 **qī**
3	三 **sān**		8	八 **bā**
4	四 **sì**		9	九 **jiǔ**
5	五 **wǔ**		10	十 **shí**

The number 2 occurs in two forms.

- When counting without a classifier, the number 2 is always 二 **èr**.

  一　二　三　四　五
  yī - èr - sān - sì - wǔ
  1　2　3　4　5

- When it occurs in a phrase with a classifier, the number 2 is 两/兩 **liǎng**.

  两本书
  兩本書
  liǎng běn shū
  two books

  两个人
  兩個人
  liǎng gè rén
  two people

⇨ 9.1

Telephone numbers are recited as a series of single digits from zero to 9. When reciting a telephone number, the number 2 is always 二 **èr**.

  我的电话号码是八六二二五六○二。
  我的電話號碼是八六二二五六○二。
  Wǒ de diànhuà hàomǎ shì bā liù èr èr wǔ liù líng èr.
  My phone number is 8 6 2 2 5 6 0 2.

⇨ 22.5

6.1.2 ## Numbers 11–19

Numbers 11–19 consist of the number 10 [十 **shí**] followed by the number 1 [一 **yī**] through 9 [九 **jiǔ**] as follows. Note that the number 12 is 十二 **shí'èr** and not *十两/十兩 **shí liǎng**.

11	十一	**shíyī**	16	十六	**shíliù**
12	十二	**shí'èr**	17	十七	**shíqī**
13	十三	**shísān**	18	十八	**shíbā**
14	十四	**shísì**	19	十九	**shíjiǔ**
15	十五	**shíwǔ**			

6.1.3 ## Numbers 20–90

Numbers 20, 30, 40, etc. consist of the numbers 2 [二 **èr**] through 9 [九 **jiǔ**] followed by the number 10 [十 **shí**] as follows:

20	二十	**èrshí**	60	六十	**liùshí**
30	三十	**sānshí**	70	七十	**qīshí**
40	四十	**sìshí**	80	八十	**bāshí**
50	五十	**wǔshí**	90	九十	**jiǔshí**

The numbers 21, 22, etc. are formed as follows:

21	二十一	**èrshíyī**	57	五十七	**wǔshíqī**
22	二十二	**èrshí'èr**	68	六十八	**liùshíbā**
35	三十五	**sānshíwǔ**	74	七十四	**qīshísì**
46	四十六	**sìshíliù**	99	九十九	**jiǔshíjiǔ**

6.2 # Number 100 and higher

6.2.1 ## 100, 1000, 10,000 and 100,000,000

Chinese has distinct words for multiples of 100, 1000, 10,000, and 100,000,000 as follows:

Hundreds	百 **bǎi**	100	一百 **yī bǎi**
Thousands	千 **qiān**	1000	一千 **yī qiān**
Ten thousands	万/萬 **wàn**	10,000	一万/一萬 **yī wàn**
Hundred millions	亿/億 **yì**	100,000,000	一亿/一億 **yī yì**

These number words function as classifiers. Therefore, the number 2 is usually 两/兩 **liǎng** when it occurs immediately before the word for 'hundred,' 'thousand,' or 'ten-thousand': 两百/兩百 **liǎng bǎi**, 两千/兩千 **liǎng qiān**, 两万/兩萬 **liǎng wàn**, etc. In many regional dialects of Mandarin, 二百 **èr bǎi**, 二千 **èr qiān**, 二万/二萬 **èr wàn**, etc. is also acceptable.

6.2.2 ## Forming numbers through 9,999

Numbers up to 9,999 follow the same pattern as in English:

352	三百	五十	二
	sān bǎi	**wǔshí**	**èr**

1,670	一千 yī qiān	六百 liù bǎi	七十 qīshí	
3,482	三千 sān qiān	四百 sì bǎi	八十 bāshí	二 èr
9,222	九千 jiǔ qiān	二百 or 两百/兩百 èr bǎi or liǎng bǎi	二十 èrshí	二 èr

6.2.3 'Zero' as a placeholder

The word 〇/零 **líng** may be used when the 'hundreds' place or the 'tens' place is empty, provided there is a number before and after 〇/零 **líng**. For example, it can be used to mark the 'hundreds' place when thousands and tens are filled, as in the following number.

| 7,066 | 七千
qī qiān | 零
líng | 六十
liù shí | 六
liù |

It can be used to mark the 'tens' place when hundreds and single numbers are filled, as in the following number.

| 9,102 | 九千
jiǔ qiān | 一百
yī bǎi | 〇
líng | 二
èr |

When two consecutive places are empty, 〇/零 **líng** occurs only once.

| 6,006 | 六千
liù qiān | 零
líng | | 六
liù |

6.2.4 Forming numbers 10,000 to 100,000,000

Languages read numbers in terms of the categories that they distinguish. English distinguishes tens, hundreds, thousands, millions, and up. Numbers between one thousand and one million are read in terms of the numbers of thousands that they contain.

Chinese distinguishes the categories of tens, hundreds, thousands, ten-thousands, and hundred millions. Numbers between ten thousand and one-hundred million are read in terms of the number of *ten-thousands* that they contain. Compare the way that English and Chinese read the following numbers.

	English	*Chinese*
1,000	one thousand	一千 **yī qiān** one thousand
10,000	ten thousand	一万/一萬 **yī wàn** one ten-thousand
100,000	one hundred thousand	十万/十萬 **shí wàn** ten ten-thousands
1,000,000	one million	百万/百萬 **bǎi wàn** one hundred ten-thousands
10,000,000	ten million	千万/千萬 **qiān wàn** one thousand ten-thousands
100,000,000	one hundred million	亿/億 **yì**
1,000,000,000	one billion	十亿/十億 **shí yì** ten one hundred-millions

Observe how these numbers are read in Chinese.

	亿/億 *yì*	万/萬 ***wàn***		千 ***qiān***	百 ***bǎi***	十 ***shí***
25,250		两万 兩萬 **liǎng wàn**		五千 **wǔqiān**	二百 **èrbǎi**	五十 **wǔshí**
225,250		二十二万 二十二萬 **èrshí'èr wàn**		五千 **wǔqiān**	二百 **èrbǎi**	五十 **wǔshí**
2,225,250		两百二十二万 兩百二十二萬 **liǎngbǎi èrshí'èr wàn**		五千 **wǔqiān**	二百 **èrbǎi**	五十 **wǔshí**
22,225,250		两千二百二十二万 兩千二百二十二萬 **liǎngqiān èrbǎi èrshí'èr wàn**		五千 **wǔqiān**	二百 **èrbǎi**	五十 **wǔshí**
522,225,250	五亿 五億 **wǔ yì**	两千二百二十二万 兩千二百二十二萬 **liǎngqiān èrbǎi èrshí'èr wàn**		五千 **wǔqiān**	二百 **èrbǎi**	五十 **wǔshí**

6.3   Formal characters for numbers

To discourage forgery, Chinese numbers are sometimes written using the following special set of characters. The numerals on Chinese currency are written with these special characters.

	Ordinary form	*Special form*	
1	一	壹	yī
2	二	貳	èr
3	三	叁	sān
4	四	肆	sì
5	五	伍	wǔ
6	六	陸	liù
7	七	柒	qī
8	八	捌	bā
9	九	玖	jiǔ
10	十	拾	shí
100	百	佰	bǎi
1000	千	仟	qiān

Chapter 8 presents the words and phrases associated with money.

⇨ 8.5

6.4 Ordinal numbers

To make a number ordinal, add the prefix 第 **dì** before the number:

1st	第一	**dì yī**	20th	第二十	**dì èrshí**
2nd	第二	**dì èr**	50th	第五十	**dì wǔshí**
3rd	第三	**dì sān**	77th	第七十七	**dì qīshíqī**
4th	第四	**dì sì**	83rd	第八十三	**dì bāshí sān**
5th	第五	**dì wǔ**	95th	第九十五	**dì jiǔshíwǔ**
6th	第六	**dì liù**	100th	第一百	**dì yìbǎi**
10th	第十	**dì shí**	1000th	第一千	**dì yíqiān**

NOTE In ordinal numbers, 'second' is always 第二 **dì èr** and never 第两/第兩 **dì liǎng**.

6.5 Estimates and approximations

To indicate that a quantity is 'more or less' than the stated number, use the phrase 左右 **zuǒyòu** 'more or less,' as follows:

number + classifier (+ noun) + 左右 zuǒyòu

五十个(人)左右
五十個(人)左右
wǔshí gè (rén) zuǒyòu
about 50 (people) (50 people more or less)

一百块钱左右
一百塊錢左右
yībǎi kuài qián zuǒyòu
around $100 ($100 more or less)

To indicate that a quantity is almost but not quite the stated amount, use 差不多 **chàbuduō** + number 'almost number.'

差不多 + number + classifier (+ noun)

差不多五十个(人)
差不多五十個(人)
chàbuduō wǔshí gè (rén)
almost 50 people

差不多一百块(钱)
差不多一百塊(錢)
chàbuduō yībǎi kuài (qián)
almost $100

To indicate that a quantity is greater than or equal to the stated number use 以上 **yǐshàng** 'or more.' For a more formal expression of the same meaning, use 之上 **zhī shàng**.

number (+ classifier + noun) + 以上 yǐshàng/之上 zhī shàng

五十(个人)以上　　　　　五十(个人)之上
五十(個人)以上　　　　　五十(個人)之上
wǔshí (gè rén) yǐshàng　　**wǔshí (gè rén) zhī shàng**
50 (people) or more　　　　50 (people) or more

To indicate that the actual number is less than or equal to the stated number, use 以下 **yǐxià** 'or fewer.' For a more formal expression of the same meaning, use 之下 **zhī xià**.

> *number (+ classifier + noun) +* 以下 *yǐxià/*之下 *zhī xià*
>
> 五十(个人)以下   五十(个人)之下
> 五十(個人)以下   五十(個人)之下
> **wǔshí (gè rén) yǐxià**   **wǔshí (gè rén) zhī xià**
> 50 (people) or less   50 (people) or less
> 50 or fewer (people)   50 or fewer (people)

To indicate that the actual time lies within the specified period of time, use 以內 **yǐnèi**. For a more formal expression of the same meaning, use 之內 **zhī nèi**.

> 一年以内   一年之內
> **yì nián yǐnèi**   **yì nián zhī nèi**
> within one year   within one year

To indicate the actual number is more than the stated number, use 多 **duō** 'more than.'

> *number +* 多 *duō + classifier (+ noun)*
>
> 五十多个人
> 五十多個人
> **wǔshí duō gè rén**
> more than 50 people

To indicate an approximation within a small range, use two numbers in a sequence as follows:

> 我一两天就回来。
> 我一兩天就回來。
> **Wǒ yì liǎng tiān jiù huí lai.**
> I'll come back in a day or two.
>
> 这个东西卖三四块钱。
> 這個東西賣三四塊錢。
> **Zhège dōngxi mài sān sì kuài qián.**
> This thing sells for three or four dollars.

This expression can be used together with 左右 **zuǒyòu**:

> 这个东西卖三四块钱左右。
> 這個東西賣三四塊錢左右。
> **Zhège dōngxi mài sān sì kuài qián zuǒyòu.**
> This thing sells for around three or four dollars.

6.6 Fractions, percentages, decimals, half, and multiples

6.6.1 Fractions

To indicate fractions, use the pattern:

X 分 之 Y
  fēn zhī

三分之一
sān fēn zhī yī
one-third (1/3)

Note that the 'whole' is expressed first and the 'part of the whole' is expressed second.

1/4	四分之一	sì fēn zhī yī
2/5	五分之二	wǔ fēn zhī èr
9/10	十分之九	shí fēn zhī jiǔ
7/9	九分之七	jiǔ fēn zhī qī
1/15	十五分之一	shíwǔ fēn zhī yī

6.6.2 | **Percentages**

Percentages are expressed as *parts of 100*. The expression used for percentages is the same as for fractions, but the 'whole' is always 百 **bǎi** '100':

百 分 之 number
bǎi fēn zhī number

10%	百分之十	bǎi fēn zhī shí
25%	百分之二十五	bǎi fēn zhī èrshíwǔ
37%	百分之三十七	bǎi fēn zhī sānshíqī
66%	百分之六十六	bǎi fēn zhī liùshíliù
99%	百分之九十九	bǎi fēn zhī jiǔshíjiǔ

6.6.3 | **Decimals**

Decimals are recited as a series of single digits and zeros after a decimal point. The decimal point is read as 点/點 **diǎn**:

1.1	一点一/一點一	yī diǎn yī
2.5	(二 or) 两点五/(二 or) 兩點五	(èr or) liǎng diǎn wǔ
14.56	十四点五六/十四點五六	shísì diǎn wǔ liù
30.808	三十点八零八/三十點八零八	sānshí diǎn bā líng bā
8.06	八点〇六/八點〇六	bā diǎn líng liù

If there is no number before the decimal point, the fraction may optionally be recited as 〇点/點 (XXX) **líng diǎn** (XXX):

| .35 | 〇点三五/〇點三五 | líng diǎn sān wǔ |
| .27 | 〇点二七/〇點二七 | líng diǎn èr qī |

NOTE | Chinese often omits the final zero after a decimal point. For example, $8.60 may also be written as $8.6.

6.6.4 | **Indicating 'half'**

The word 半 **bàn** means 'half.'

To indicate *half of something*, place 半 **bàn** before the classifier associated with the thing.

半碗饭/半碗飯
bàn wǎn fàn
half a bowl of rice

半本书/半本書
bàn běn shū
half a book

半杯水
bàn bēi shuǐ
half a glass of water

⇨ 8

To indicate *one or more things and a half*, place 半 **bàn** immediately after the classifier associated with the thing: *number + classifier +* 半 ***bàn***

三碗半(饭)/三碗半(飯)
sān wǎn bàn (fàn)
three and a half bowls (of rice)

三本半(书)/三本半(書)
sān běn bàn (shū)
three and a half volumes (of books)

三杯半(水)
sān bēi bàn (shuǐ)
three and a half cups (of water)

To indicate 'half' in time expressions, see

⇨ 45.1.3, 45.1.4, 45.1.5

6.6.5 Indicating multiples of a quantity with 倍 *bèi*

倍 **bèi** is a classifier and is always preceded by a number: 一倍 **yī bèi**, 两倍/兩倍 **liǎng bèi**, 三倍 **sān bèi**, etc.

一倍 **yī bèi** means 'one fold,' or 'one time more than a given quantity.' 两倍/兩倍 **liǎng bèi** means 'twofold,' 三倍 **sān bèi** means 'threefold,' etc.

倍 **bèi** often occurs with expressions that imply an increase:

价格都增加了一倍了。
價格都增加了一倍了。
Jiàgé dōu zēngjiā le yī bèi le.
Prices have all doubled (increased by one-fold).

今年这本书比去年贵了一倍。
今年這本書比去年貴了一倍。
Jīnnián zhè běn shū bǐ qùnián guì le yī bèi.
This year this book is twice as expensive as it was last year.

倍 **bèi** also occurs in equational sentences such as the following:

我的书是你的书的两倍。
我的書是你的書的兩倍。
Wǒ de shū shì nǐ de shū de liǎng bèi.
I have twice as many books as you.
(lit. 'My books are the equivalent of two times your books.')

If 半 **bàn** 'half' occurs, it follows 倍 **bèi**:

> 今年学中文的学生是去年的一倍半。
> 今年學中文的學生是去年的一倍半。
> **Jīnnián xué Zhōngwén de xuésheng shì qùnián de yī bèi bàn.**
> The number of students studying Chinese this year is 1¹/₂ times greater than last year.

⇨ 6.6.4, 26.1

6.6.6 ## Discounts, sales, and percentage off the price

The expression for discount or sale is the verb phrase 打折 **dǎ zhé**.

Discounts are expressed as a percentage of the original or full price.

九折 **jiǔ zhé** is 90% of the original price, or 10% off. 七点五折/七點五折 **qīdiǎn wǔ zhé** is 75% of the original price, or 25% off. Here are additional examples of discounts. Discounts are written with either Chinese or Arabic numerals.

8 折 **bā zhé**	80% of original price	20% off
5折 **wǔ zhé**	50% of original price	50% off
or	or	
半折 **bàn zhé**	half of original price	
二折 **èr zhé**	20% of original price	80% off
一折 **yī zhé**	10% of original price	90% off

To find out if an item is discounted or on sale, you can ask:

打折吗?	or	打不打折?	or	有折吗?
打折嗎?				有折嗎?
Dǎ zhé ma?		**Dǎ bù dǎ zhé?**		**Yǒu zhé ma?**
Do you discount?		Do you discount?		Is there a discount?

To find out how much of a discount there is, you can ask:

> 打几折?/打幾折?
> **Dǎ jǐ zhé?**
> How much discount is there?

⇨ 24

6.7 ## Lucky and unlucky numbers

Some numbers have special significance in Chinese based on their value in traditional Chinese numerology or because they are near-homophones with a word with positive or negative connotations. Here some numbers with special significance.

Numbers with negative connotations – unlucky numbers

> 四 **sì** (near homophone with 死 **sǐ** 'to die')
> 五 **wǔ** (near homophone with 无/無 **wú** 'nothing')

Numbers with positive connotations – lucky numbers

六 **liù** (near homophone with 留 **liú** 'remain, leftover/excess')
八 **bā** (near homophone with 发/發 **fā** 'prosperity')

The special significance of odd and even numbers

- 单号/單號 **dānhào** 'odd numbers.' Odd numbered items are appropriate for funerals and other sad occasions.
- 双号/雙號 **shuānghào** 'even numbers.' Even numbered items (except for the number 4) are appropriate for weddings and other happy occasions.

6.8 Numbers used in phrases and expressions

Numbers, especially sequential numbers, are often used in Chinese phrases.

1's and 2's

一清二楚
yī qīng èr chǔ
perfectly clearly

他说得一清二楚。
他說得一清二楚。
Tā shuō de yī qīng èr chǔ.
He said it perfectly clearly.

3's and 4's

张三李四
張三李四
Zhāng Sān Lǐ Sì
John Doe and Mary Smith (ordinary people)

不三不四
bù sān bù sì
neither here nor there, questionable, no good

7's and 8's

乱七八糟
亂七八糟
luàn qī bā zāo
a mess/disorganized

七上八下
qī shàng bā xià
to be in an unsettled state of mind

6.9 一 *yī* as a marker of sequence

In addition to functioning as a number, the word 一 **yī** is also used to indicate sequence in the following structure:

一 **yī** + verb as soon as verb occurs . . .

他一看见他孩子就很高兴。

他一看見他孩子就很高興。

Tā yī kànjian tā háizi jiù hěn gāoxìng.

As soon as he sees (his) children he is happy.

⇨ 38.3.3

6.10 Numbers that are used as words

Numbers that are homophonous or near homophones with words may be used as abbreviations for words. This kind of substitution is particularly common on the internet and in written advertisements and signs. Examples include:

530 五三零
wǔ sān líng
(我想你)
(**wǒ xiǎng nǐ**)
I'm thinking of you – I miss you.

520 五二〇
wǔ èr líng
(我爱你)
(**wǒ ài nǐ**)
I love you

88 八八
bā bā
(拜拜)
(**bàibài**)
bye bye

7

Specifiers and demonstratives

这/這 **zhè** and 那 **nà** have two functions.

They can be used as *demonstratives*, or words that are used to point out an item:

> 那是汉语词典。
> 那是漢語辭典。
> ***Nà* shì Hànyǔ cídiǎn.**
> *That* is a Chinese language dictionary.

They can be used as *specifiers*, or words that occur as part of a noun phrase and that identify specific items:

> 这三本书
> 這三本書
> ***zhè* sān běn shū**
> *these* three books

When used as specifiers, these words each have an alternative pronunciation. 这/這 may be pronounced **zhè** or **zhèi**. 那 may be pronounced **nà** or **nèi**. The choice of pronunciation varies by speaker and region of China.

7.1 这/這 *zhè* 'this' and 那 *nà* 'that' as demonstratives

As demonstratives, 这/這 **zhè** 'this' and 那 **nà** 'that' refer to an entire noun phrase, either a concrete object or an abstract concept. They always occur at the beginning of the sentence, and they serve as the subject of the sentence. They can occur in statements or in questions.

> 那是中文字典。
> **Nà shì Zhōngwén zìdiǎn.**
> That is a Chinese dictionary.

> 这是我的书。
> 這是我的書。
> **Zhè shì wǒ de shū.**
> This is my book.

> 那是什么？
> 那是甚麼？
> **Nà shì shénme?**
> What is that?
> (lit. 'That is what?')

这是什么意思？
這是甚麼意思？
Zhè shì shénme yìsi?
What is the meaning of this?
(lit. 'This is what meaning?')

这/這 *zhè*, *zhèi* 'this/these' and 那 *nà*, *nèi* 'that/those' as specifiers

When they are used as specifiers, 这/這 **zhè**, **zhèi** 'this/these' and 那 **nà**, **nèi** 'that/those' are part of a noun phrase. They occur before the number if there is one, and before the classifier and the noun in this order:

specifier + (number) + classifier + noun

⇨ | 6, 8, 9

Here are examples of noun phrases that begin with specifiers. Following each noun phrase there is an example showing how the noun phrase is used in a sentence.

Noun phrase that begins with a specifier	*Sample sentence with the noun phrase*
这三本书 這三本書 **zhè sān běn shū** these three books	这三本书都很贵。 這三本書都很貴。 ***Zhè sān běn shū** dōu hěn guì.* *These three books are all expensive.*
这种音乐 這種音樂 **zhè zhǒng yīnyuè** this type of music	我很喜欢这种音乐。 我很喜歡這種音樂。 *Wǒ hěn xǐhuan **zhè zhǒng yīnyuè**.* *I like this kind of music very much.*
那个人 那個人 **nàge rén** that person	那个人很聪明。 那個人很聰明。 ***Nàge rén** hěn cōngming.* *That person is very intelligent.*
那个电影 那個電影 **nàge diànyǐng** that movie	我要看那个电影。 我要看那個電影。 *Wǒ yào kàn **nàge diànyǐng**.* *I want to see that movie.*

Notice that 这/這 **zhè**, **zhèi** and 那 **nà**, **nèi** do not have separate singular and plural forms.

这儿/這兒 *zhèr* and 这里/這裏 *zhèlǐ* 'here;' 那儿/那兒 *nàr* and 那里/那裏 *nàlǐ* 'there'

这儿/這兒 **zhèr** (这里/這裏 **zhèlǐ**) 'here' and 那儿/那兒 **nàr** (那里/那裏 **nàlǐ**) 'there' indicate location. 这儿/這兒 **zhèr** 'here' and 那儿/那兒 **nàr** 'there' are used in the north of China, including Beijing. 这里/這裏 **zhèlǐ** and 那里/那裏 **nàlǐ** are used in the south of China, including Taiwan. The meaning and use of 这儿/這兒 **zhèr** and 这里/這裏 **zhèlǐ** is the same, as is the meaning and use of 那儿/那兒 **nàr** and 那里/那裏

nàlǐ. Each member of the pair is interchangeable in our examples here and throughout this book.

这儿/這兒 **zhèr** 'here' and 那儿/那兒 **nàr** 'there' may occur at the beginning of the sentence as the subject. As subjects, they may optionally be preceded by the location preposition 在 **zài** 'at.'

> (在)这儿有很多书店。
> (在)這兒有很多書店。
> **(Zài) zhèr yǒu hěn duō shūdiàn.**
> Here (in this location) are a lot of bookstores.

> (在)那儿没有停车场。
> (在)那兒沒有停車場。
> **(Zài) nàr méi yǒu tíngchē cháng.**
> There (in that location) there aren't any parking lots.

When they are not the subject they must be preceded by the location preposition 在 **zài** 'at.'

> 我在这儿工作。
> 我在這兒工作。
> **Wǒ zài zhèr gōngzuò.**
> I work here.

> 我在那儿买东西。
> 我在那兒買東西。
> **Wǒ zài nàr mǎi dōngxi.**
> I shop there.

⇨ 14

People cannot serve as location nouns. To make a person into a location, follow it with a location specifier.

> 请到我这儿来。
> 請到我這兒來。
> **Qǐng dào wǒ zhèr lái.**
> Please come to me. [to my location]

> 我们今天晚上去小王那儿吃饭。
> 我們今天晚上去小王那兒吃飯。
> **Wǒmen jīntiān wǎnshang qù Xiǎo Wáng nàr chī fàn.**
> Tonight we'll go to Xiao Wang's to eat.

7.4 Question words that correspond to specifiers

- 哪 **nǎ/něi** 'which?' is the question word that corresponds to the specifier 那 **nà**.

Question	Answer
你要哪本书?	(我要)那本(书)。
你要哪本書?	(我要)那本(書)。
Nǐ yào nǎ běn shū?	**(Wǒ yào) nà běn (shū).**
Which book do you want?	(I want) that (book).
(lit. 'You want which book?')	

- 哪儿/哪兒 **nǎr** 'where?' is the question word that corresponds to the location words 这儿/這兒 **zhèr** 'here' and 那儿/那兒 **nàr** 'there.'

Question	*Answer*
哪儿有书店?	那儿有书店。
哪兒有書店?	那兒有書店。
***Nǎr** yǒu shūdiàn?*	***Nàr** yǒu shūdiàn.*
Where is there a bookstore?	*There is a bookstore there.*
你在哪里工作?	我在这里工作。
你在哪裏工作?	我在這裏工作。
*Nǐ zài **nálǐ** gōngzuò?*	*Wǒ zài **zhèlǐ** gōngzuò.*
Where do you work?	*I work here.*

⇨ 24.6

8

Classifiers

8.1 The structure of phrases involving classifiers

A classifier is a word that occurs between the specifier and/or number and the noun. In Chinese, a classifier always occurs between a specifier or number and a noun in this order:

> *specifier + number + classifier + noun*

Specifier and/or number + classifier + noun forms a *noun phrase*.

NOTE
1 Classifiers are sometimes referred to as 'measure words.'
2 In English, mass nouns such as 'coffee' and 'rice' and 'sand' occur with classifiers. In Chinese, all nouns occur with classifiers when they are preceded by a specifier and/or number.

⇨ 6, 7, 9

Here are examples of noun phrases with specifiers, numbers, classifiers, and nouns. The classifier is emphasized in each example. The classifier is often omitted when a Mandarin noun phrase is translated into English.

Specifier + classifier + noun	*Number + classifier + noun*	*Specifier + number + classifier + noun*
这个人	三本书	这两碗饭
這個人	三本書	這兩碗飯
zhège **rén**	**sān** *běn* **shū**	*zhè liǎng* **wǎn** **fàn**
this person	three books	these two *bowls* of rice
那个学校	三杯咖啡	那三本书
那個學校	三盃咖啡	那三本書
nàge **xuéxiào**	**sān** *bēi* **kāfēi**	**nà sān** *běn* **shū**
that school	three *cups* of coffee	those three books

8.2 Choosing the classifier

8.2.1 Nouns and associated classifiers

Most nouns are associated with a particular classifier. Classifiers are often not predictable from the noun so they must be memorized. Some dictionaries indicate the classifier associated with a noun.

Noun	Classifier	Noun phrase
书/書 **shū** book	本 **běn** volume	三本书/三本書 **sān běn shū** three books
纸/紙 **zhǐ** paper	张/張 **zhāng** sheet	一张纸/一張紙 **yì zhāng zhǐ** one piece of paper
钢笔/鋼筆 **gāngbǐ** pen	枝 **zhī** branch	这枝钢笔/這枝鋼筆 **zhè zhī gāngbǐ** this pen
房子 **fángzi** house	所 **suǒ** building	一所房子 **yī suǒ fángzi** one house
猫/貓 **māo** cat	只/隻 **zhī** classifier for animals	两只猫/兩隻貓 **liǎng zhī māo** two cats
车/車 **chē** car	辆/輛 **liàng** classifier for cars	三辆车/三輛車 **sān liàng chē** three cars
椅子 **yǐzi** chair	把 **bǎ** classifier for things with handles	一把椅子 **yì bǎ yǐzi** one chair
桌子 **zhuōzi** table	张/張 **zhāng** sheet	那张桌子/那張桌子 **nà zhāng zhuōzi** that table
照片 **zhàopiàn** photograph	张/張 **zhāng** sheet	这张照片/這張照片 **zhè zhāng zhàopiàn** this photograph
电影/電影 **diànyǐng** movie	部 **bù** classifier for film	一部电影/一部電影 **yí bù diànyǐng** one movie
衣服 **yīfu** clothing	件 **jiàn** classifier for items	这件衣服/這件衣服 **zhè jiàn yīfú** this article of clothing
树/樹 **shù** tree	棵 **kē** classifier for trees	一棵树/一棵樹 **yì kē shù** a tree
人 **rén** person	个/個 **gè** classifier for people and many other nouns	一个人/一個人 **yī gè rén** one person

位 **wèi** is a polite classifier for people. When it is used, the noun typically does not occur:

一位	**yī wèi**	one person
两位/兩位	**liǎng wèi**	two people

8.2.2 | Classifiers that indicate a property of the noun

Some classifiers indicate a property of the noun. These classifiers are often translated into English:

Shape of noun	张/張	一张纸/一張紙
	zhāng	**yì zhāng zhǐ**
	a flat sheet	a sheet of paper
The shape of the container of the noun	杯/盃	一杯茶/一盃茶
	bēi	**yì bēi chá**
	cup	a cup of tea
The weight of the noun	斤	一斤苹果
	jīn	**yì jīn píngguǒ**
	·5 kilograms	½ kilo of apples
The value of the noun	毛	一毛钱/一毛錢
	máo	**yì máo qián**
	dime	a dime's worth of money

Different classifiers may be used to describe a noun in different ways.

Noun	*Classifier*	*Noun phrase*
饭/飯	碗	一碗饭/一碗飯
fàn	**wǎn**	**yì wǎn fàn**
rice	bowl	one bowl of rice
饭/飯	斤	两斤饭/兩斤飯
fàn	**jīn**	**liǎng jīn fàn**
rice	½ kilo	one kilo of rice
面包/麵包	条/條	一条面包/一條麵包
miànbāo	**tiáo**	**yì tiáo miànbāo**
bread	loaf	a loaf of bread
面包/麵包	块/塊	一块面包/一塊麵包
miànbāo	**kuài**	**yí kuài miànbāo**
bread	slice/piece	a slice of bread
水	瓶	一瓶水
shuǐ	**píng**	**yì píng shuǐ**
water	bottle	a bottle of water
水	杯/盃	一杯水/一盃水
shuǐ	**bēi**	**yì bēi shuǐ**
water	glass	a glass of water
水	壶/壺	一壶水/一壺水
shuǐ	**hú**	**yì hú shuǐ**
water	pot/vase	a pot/vase of water

Noun	Classifier	Noun phrase
花	瓶	一瓶花/一瓶花
huā	**píng**	**yì píng huā**
flower	bottle	a vase of flowers
花	束	一束花
huā	**shù**	**yí shù huā**
flower	bouquet	a bouquet of flowers

8.2.3 个/個 *gè*, the general classifier

The most commonly used classifier is 个/個 **gè**. It is used with many different nouns including people and things. It does not contribute any meaning to the noun phrase in which it occurs. It is generally pronounced with neutral tone.

一个人/一個人
yí gè rén
a person

一个问题/一個問題
yí gè wèntí
a problem/a question

一个东西/一個東西
yí gè dōngxi
a thing (a physical object)

In mainland China, in informal speech, 个/個 **gè** can be used as the classifier for almost any noun, even those with an established classifier. This phenomenon is sometimes referred to as 个化/個化 **gè huà** 'ge-ization.'

一个车/一個車
yí gè chē
(compare with 一辆车/一輛車 **yí liàng chē**) a car

一个房子/一個房子
yí gè fángzi
(compare with 一所房子 **yì suǒ fángzi**) a house

8.3 Omission of the head noun

In modern Mandarin, if a noun phrase includes a specifier and/or a number, the classifier may not be omitted. However, the head noun may be omitted from the noun phrase.

Say this	Not this
三本书 [or] 三本	*三书
三本書	三書
sān běn shū [or] **sān běn**	**sān shū**
three books [or] three	
那个学校 [or] 那个	*那学校
那個學校 [or] 那個	那學校
nàge xuéxiào [or] **nà ge**	**nà xuéxiào**
that school [or] that one	

⇨ 7, 9

8.4 Classifiers that occur without a noun

The words for day and year are classifiers. They may be preceded by a number, and they are never followed by a noun.

天 **tiān** day	一天 **yì tiān** one day	两天/兩天 **liǎng tiān** two days
年 **nián** year	一年 **yì nián** one year	两年/兩年 **liǎng nián** two years

⇨ 45.2

8.5 Money and prices

In Chinese, money and prices are expressed as noun phrases. The units of money, dollars, dimes, and cents, are expressed by classifiers. The word for money, 钱/錢 **qián**, sometimes occurs at the end of the noun phrase.

In informal and spoken contexts, the classifiers for money are as follows:

块/塊	**kuài**	dollar
毛	**máo**	dime
分	**fēn**	cent

分 **fēn** represents 1 cent to 9 cents. Multiples of 10 cents are represented by 毛 **máo**.

五块/五塊	三毛	八分	钱/錢	= $5.38
wǔ kuài	**sān máo**	**bā fēn**	**qián**	

四十八块/塊	九毛	六分	钱/錢	= $48.96
sìshíbā kuài	**jiǔ máo**	**liù fēn**	**qián**	

The number 2 in the phrase 2 dollars, 2 dimes (20 cents) or 2 cents may be either 二 **èr** or 两/兩 **liǎng**.

三块/三塊	四毛	二分	钱/錢	= $3.42
sān kuài	**sì máo**	**èr fēn**	**qián**	
		or		
		两分/兩分		
		liǎng fēn		

The noun 钱/錢 **qián** 'money' need not occur in a money phrase. If it is absent, the classifier that immediately precedes it may also be absent.

四十八块/塊	九毛	六	= $48.96
sìshíbā kuài	**jiǔ máo**	**liù**	

If the classifier is absent, the number 2 can only be represented as 二 **èr** and not as 两/兩 **liǎng**.

三块/三塊	四毛	二	= $3.42
sān kuài	**sì máo**	**èr**	

Chinese also has the following formal written classifiers for dollars and dimes.

元/圓	**yuán**	dollar
角	**jiǎo**	dime

These are the classifiers used on currency and in formal financial transactions.

For the formal characters for numbers, see

⇨ | 6.3

When 元/圓 **yuán** and 角 **jiǎo** are used, the noun 钱/錢 **qián** does not occur in the money phrase. 元/圓 **yuán** and 角 **jiǎo** are often not used together in the same price. 角 **jiǎo** tends to occur only when the denomination is smaller than one 元/圓 **yuán**.

		Formal/written
$3.00	三元/圓	**sān yuán**
$.60	六角	**liù jiǎo**

9

Noun phrases

A noun phrase consists of a noun and any words that describe or 'modify' the noun. Here is an example of a noun phrase with the noun emphasized.

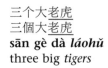

三个大老虎
三個大老虎
sān gè dà *láohǔ*
three big *tigers*

Additional examples of noun phrases are presented below.

In this chapter, we refer to the noun that is being described or modified as the *head noun* and to the words or phrases that describe or modify the head noun as the *modifier*.

In Mandarin Chinese, the relative position of modifier and noun is constant:

> **In Chinese, all noun modifiers occur before the head noun.**

9.1 Modifying a noun with a specifier and/or number

Nouns can be modified by

a specifier ('this,' 'that,' 'which?')
or a number ('four,' 'twenty'),
or a specifier and number together ('these four,' 'those twenty,' 'which two?')

In Mandarin, the classifier associated with the noun being modified must be included in the modifying phrase. The entire phrase precedes the head noun as follows:

specifier + classifier + noun

那	本	书
那	本	書
nà	**běn**	**shū**
that		book

number + classifier + noun

两	本	书
兩	本	書
liǎng	**běn**	**shū**
two		books

specifier + number + classifier + noun

那	三	个	人
那	三	個	人
nà	**sān**	**gè**	**rén**
those	three		people

哪	三	个	人
哪	三	個	人
nǎ	**sān**	**gè**	**rén**
which	three		people?

➪ 6, 7, 8

9.2 Modifying a noun with all other modifiers: modification with 的 *de*

Noun modifiers may also be nouns, pronouns, verbs, or phrases that include a verb. These kinds of modifiers are typically followed by the particle 的 **de**, and the noun phrase has the following form:

modifier + 的 de + head noun

➪ 5

NOTE In English, when a modifier includes a verb, the modifier occurs after the head noun as a relative clause introduced by a relative pronoun ('who,' 'whom,' 'which') or a complementizer ('that'). In these examples, the modifier of the noun is presented in square brackets.

> that book [that I bought]
> the people [who spoke to you]

In Mandarin, *all* modifiers precede the head noun. In addition, Mandarin has no words that correspond to relative pronouns or complementizers. Do not attempt to translate them into Chinese.

9.2.1 Examples of noun phrases with different types of modifiers

9.2.1.1 Modifiers that are nouns

Modifier	*Head noun*	*Noun phrase*
孩子	衣服	孩子的衣服
háizi	**yīfu**	**háizi de yīfu**
child	clothing	children's clothing
车/車	速度	车的速度
		車的速度
chē	**sùdù**	**chē de sùdù**
car	speed	the speed of a/the car
马老师	学生	马老师的学生
馬老師	學生	馬老師的學生
Mǎ lǎoshī	**xuésheng**	**Mǎ lǎoshī de xuésheng**
Professor Ma	student(s)	Professor Ma's student(s)

Modifier	Head noun	Noun phrase
美国 美國 **Měiguó** America	城市 **chéngshì** city	美国的城市 美國的城市 **Měiguó de chéngshì** America's city (cities)/ a city (cities) in America.

9.2.1.2 Modifiers that are pronouns

Modifier	Head noun	Noun phrase
我 **wǒ** I (my)	车/車 **chē** car	我的车 我的車 **wǒ de chē** my car
他 **tā** he (his)	家 **jiā** home	他的家 **tā de jiā** his home
你们 你們 **nǐmen** you (your)	书 書 **shū** book(s)	你们的书 你們的書 **nǐmen de shū** your book(s)

Notice that *pronoun* + 的 *de* serves the same function as a possessive pronoun in English and other languages. There are no possessive pronouns in Mandarin.

See Chapter 5 for a table showing the Mandarin equivalent of English possessive pronouns.

⇨ 5.2.4, 25.2.2

9.2.1.3 Modifiers that are adjectival verbs

Modifier	Head noun	Noun phrase
很贵 很貴 **hěn guì** a very expensive	车/車 **chē** car	很贵的车 很貴的車 **hěn guì de chē** a very expensive car

⇨ 10

9.2.1.4 Modifiers that are stative verbs

Modifier	Head noun	Noun phrase
喜欢 喜歡 **xǐhuan** like	车/車 **chē** car	我喜欢的车 我喜歡的車 **wǒ xǐhuan de chē** a car that I like

⇨ 11

9.2.1.5 Modifiers that are action verbs

Modifier	Head noun	Noun phrase
写	字	写的字
寫		寫的字
xiě	**zì**	**xiě de zì**
write	character	a character that is written
来	人	来的人
來		來的人
lái	**rén**	**lái de rén**
come	people/person	the people who have come/ the person who has come

 13

9.2.1.6 Modifiers that are *verb + object*

Modifier	Head noun	Noun phrase
唱歌儿	女孩子	唱歌儿的女孩子
唱歌兒		唱歌兒的女孩子
chàng gēr	**nǚ háizi**	**chàng gēr de nǚ háizi**
sing song	girl	the girl who is singing
卖书	人	卖书的人
賣書		賣書的人
mài shū	**rén**	**mài shū de rén**
sell book	person	the person who sells books

9.2.1.7 Modifiers that are *prepositional phrase + verb*

Modifier	Head noun	Noun phrase
在公园里玩	人	在公园里玩的人
在公園裏玩		在公園裏玩的人
zài gōngyuán lǐ wán	**rén**	**zài gōngyuán lǐ wán de rén**
play in the park	people/person	people who are playing in the park
从日本来	学生	从日本来的学生
從日本來	學生	從日本來的學生
cóng Rìběn lái	**xuésheng**	**cóng Rìběn lái de xuésheng**
come from Japan	student	a student who has come from Japan

14

9.2.1.8 Modifiers that are *subject + verb* sequences

Modifier	Head noun	Noun phrase
他喜欢	东西	他喜欢的东西
他喜歡	東西	他喜歡的東西
tā xǐhuan	**dōngxi**	**tā xǐhuan de dōngxi**
he likes	things	the things that he likes

Modifier	Head noun	Noun phrase
我们看	电影	我们看的电影
我們看	電影	我們看的電影
wǒmen kàn	**diànyǐng**	**wǒmen kàn de diànyǐng**
we see/we saw	movie	the movie that we saw

9.2.1.9 **Modifiers that are question words**

Modifier	Head noun	Noun phrase
谁	书	谁的书?
誰	書	誰的書?
shéi	**shū**	**shéi de shū?**
who	book	whose book?
哪儿	饭馆	哪儿的饭馆?
哪兒	飯館	哪兒的飯館?
nǎr	**fànguǎn**	**nǎr de fànguǎn?**
where	restaurant	a restaurant located where?

⇨ | 24.6, 26.4.2

9.3 ## Omission of the particle 的 *de*

The particle 的 **de** is sometimes omitted from the modifier.

的 **de** may be omitted:

- when the modifier is an unmodified one syllable adjectival verb.

  > 贵的车/貴的車 **guì de chē** → 贵车/貴車 **guì chē**
  > expensive car
  > *but not*
  > 很贵的车/很貴的車 **hěn guì de chē** → *很贵车/*很貴車 **hěn guì chē**

- when the modifier is closely associated with the noun, describing, for example, nationality:

  > 美国的人/美國的人 **Měiguó de rén** → 美国人/美國人 **Měiguó rén**
  > American person

  or a close personal relationship in which the modifier is a pronoun:

  > 我的爸爸 **wǒ de bàba** → 我爸爸 **wǒ bàba** my father

9.4 ## Noun modifiers in a series

In Mandarin Chinese, a noun may be modified by any number of modifiers.

- The modifiers occur in a series before the head noun.
- A modifier that is a specifier and/or a number ends with a classifier. All other modifiers may end in the particle 的 **de**.
- The head noun occurs only once, at the end of the series of modifiers.

Here are examples of noun phrases in which the head noun is modified by a series of modifiers. Each modifying phrase is included in [square brackets].

> 我们 [昨天看的] [刚出来的] [中国的] 电影
> 我們 [昨天看的] [剛出來的] [中國的] 電影
> **wǒmen [zuótiān kàn de] [gāng chūlái de] [Zhōngguo de] diànyǐng**
> we　　　[yesterday see]　　[just come out]　　[China]　　*movie*
> the Chinese *movie* that just came out that we saw yesterday

> [你给我介绍的] [那两个] [很聪明的] 留学生
> [你給我介紹的] [那兩個] [很聰明的] 留學生
> **[nǐ gěi wǒ jièshào de] [nà liǎng gè] [hěn cōngming de] liúxuéshēng**
> [you introduced to me] [those two]　　[very smart] *exchange students*
> those two very smart *exchange students* who you introduced me to

Modifiers may occur in any order. However, modifiers involving inherent personal characteristics often occur closer to the head noun.

> [穿毛衣的] [很可爱的] 小孩子
> [穿毛衣的] [很可愛的] 小孩子
> **[chuān máoyī de] [hěn kě'ài de] xiǎo háizi**
> the very cute child who is wearing a sweater

Noun modifiers involving specifiers and numbers often occur first in a sequence of modifiers, though they may also occur closer to the head noun for emphasis or contrast.

> [那个] [戴眼镜的] [很高的] 人
> [那個] [戴眼鏡的] [很高的] 人
> **[nàge] [dài yǎnjìng de] [hěn gāo de] rén**
> **[that] [wear glasses] [very tall]** *person*
> that very tall *person* who wears glasses

> [很高的] [戴眼镜的] [那个] 人
> [很高的] [戴眼鏡的] [那個] 人
> **[hěn gāo de] [dài yǎnjìng de] [nàge] rén**
> that very tall *person* who wears glasses

9.5 Omission of the head noun

When the head noun is predictable from the context, it may be omitted. The presence of 的 **de** or a classifier at the end of a phrase identifies the phrase as a noun phrase modifier. When the head noun is omitted, 的 **de** cannot be omitted.

> 这是谁做的菜？　　　　　　　　这是马老师做的(__)。
> 這是誰做的菜？　　　　　　　　這是馬老師做的(__)。
> **Zhè shì shéi zuò de cài?**　　　**Zhè shì Mǎ lǎoshī zuò de (__).**
> This is food cooked by whom?　　This is (food) cooked by Professor Ma.

> 你喜欢什么样的菜？　　　　　　我特别喜欢红烧的(__)。
> 你喜歡甚麼樣的菜？　　　　　　我特別喜歡紅燒的(__)。
> **Nǐ xǐhuan shénme yàng de cài?**　**Wǒ tèbié xǐhuan hóngshāo de (__).**
> What kind of dishes do you like?　I especially like red cooked (ones).

你要买哪本书?   我要那本(书)。
你要買哪本書?   我要那本(書)。
Nǐ yào mǎi nǎ běn shū?   **Wǒ yào nà běn (shū).**
Which book do you want to buy?   I want that (one).

多少钱?   三块(钱)。
多少錢?   三塊(錢)。
Duōshǎo qián?   **Sān kuài (qián).**
How much money?   Three dollars.

9.6   Modification with 之 *zhī*

之 **zhī** is the marker of noun modification in literary Chinese, and it is used for this purpose in certain literary expressions in modern Chinese, including the following. These instances of 之 **zhī** are not interchangeable with 的 **de**.

Percentages and fractions

> 三分之一
> **sān fēn zhī yī**
> one-third (1/3)

> 百分之十
> **bǎi fēn zhī shí**
> 10%

⇨   6.6.1, 6.6.2

Time phrases and sequence

之后/之後 **zhīhòu** *'after'* (以后/以後 **yǐhòu**)

> 三年之后
> 三年之後
> **sān nián zhīhòu**
> three years afterward/after three years

之前 **zhīqián** *'before, previous'* (以前 **yǐqián**)

> 第二次世界战争之前
> 第二次世界戰爭之前
> **dì èrcì shìjiè zhànzhēng zhīqián**
> before the Second World War

⇨   38.1, 38.2

之内 **zhīnèi** *'within, including'* (cf. 以内 **yǐnèi**)

> 我三天之内一定作得完。
> **wǒ sāntiān zhīnèi yīdìng zuòdewán.**
> I will definitely be able to finish within three days.

⇨   6.5

10

Adjectival verbs

Adjectival verbs translate into adjectives in English. They include 高 **gāo** 'to be tall,' 贵/貴 **guì** 'to be expensive,' 小 **xiǎo** 'to be small,' 大 **dà** 'to be big,' 好 **hǎo** 'to be good,' etc.

Mandarin adjectival verbs, unlike English adjectives, are *not* preceded by a linking verb such as the verb 是 **shì** be.

Say this	*Not this*
他高。	*他是高。
Tā gāo.	**Tā shì gāo.**
He is tall.	
那本书贵。	*那本书是贵。
那本書貴。	那本書是貴。
Nà běn shū guì.	**Nà běn shū shì guì.**
That book is expensive.	
那个学校大。	*那个学校是大。
那個學校大。	那個學校是大。
Nàge xuéxiào dà.	**Nàge xuéxiào shì dà.**
That school is big.	

The properties of adjectival verbs are discussed below.

10.1 Negation of adjectival verbs

Adjectival verbs are negated by 不 **bù**. They are never negated by 没 **méi**.

他不高。	*他没高。
Tā bù gāo.	**Tā méi gāo.**
He is not tall.	
那本书不贵。	*那本书没贵。
那本書不貴。	那本書沒貴。
Nà běn shū bù guì.	**Nà běn shū méi guì.**
That book is not expensive.	
那个人不好。	*那个人没好。
那個人不好。	那個人沒好。
Nàge rén bù hǎo.	**Nàge rén méi hǎo.**
That person is not good.	

10.2 Yes–no questions with adjectival verbs

Adjectival verbs can occur in yes–no questions formed by 吗/嗎 **ma** or the *verb-not-verb* structure.

那个学校大吗？
那個學校大嗎？
Nàge xuéxiào dà ma?
Is that school big?

那个学校大不大？
那個學校大不大？
Nàge xuéxiào dà bù dà?
Is that school big?

⇨ 24.1

10.3 Modification by intensifiers

Adjectival verbs can be modified by intensifiers. Most intensifiers precede the adjectival verb.

Intensifier		*Intensifier + adjectival verb*	
很 **hěn**	very	很好 **hěn hǎo**	to be very good
真 **zhēn**	really	真好 **zhēn hǎo**	to be really good
比较/比較 **bǐjiào**	rather	比较好/比較好 **bǐjiào hǎo**	to be rather good
相当/相當 **xiāngdāng**	quite	相当好/相當好 **xiāngdāng hǎo**	to be quite good
特别 **tèbié**	especially	特别好 **tèbié hǎo**	to be especially good
非常 **fēicháng**	extremely	非常好 **fēicháng hǎo**	to be extremely good
尤其 **yóuqí**	especially	尤其好 **yóuqí hǎo**	to be especially good
极其/極其 **jíqí**	extremely	极其好/極其好 **jíqí hǎo**	to be extremely good
太 **tài**	too	太好 **tài hǎo**	to be too good
更 **gèng**	more	更好 **gèng hǎo**	to be even better
最 **zuì**	most	最好 **zuì hǎo**	to be best

The intensifiers 得很 **de hěn** 'very,' 极了/極了 **jíle** 'extremely,' and 得不得了 **de bùdéliǎo** 'extremely' follow the adjectival verb:

> 好得很
> **hǎo de hěn**
> to be very good

> 好极了
> 好極了
> **hǎojíle**
> to be terrific

> 好得不得了
> **hǎo de bùdéliǎo**
> to be terrific

Stative verbs and the modal verbs 会/會 **huì** and 能 **néng** can also be modified by intensifiers.

⇨ | 11.2, 12.6.3

10.4 Two syllable preference

Adjectival verbs generally occur in two syllable phrases. In affirmative form, when no special emphasis is intended, one syllable adjectival verbs are usually preceded by 很 **hěn**. When negated, 不 **bù** provides the second syllable.

> 他很高。
> **Tā hěn gāo.**
> He is tall.

> 他不高。
> **Tā bù gāo.**
> He is not tall.

> 那本书很贵。
> 那本書很貴。
> **Nà běn shū hěn guì.**
> That book is expensive.

> 那本书不贵。
> 那本書不貴。
> **Nà běn shū bù guì.**
> That book is not expensive.

10.5 Comparative meaning

Adjectival verbs do not have a distinct comparative form. However, in certain contexts they have comparative meaning.

They have comparative meaning when the context implies a comparison:

> Q: 谁高？誰高？
> **Shéi gāo?**
> Who is tall?
> or
> Who is taller?

> A: 他高。
> **Tā gāo.**
> He is tall.
> or
> He is taller.

They have comparative meaning when they occur in comparison structures:

> 他比你高。
> **Tā bǐ nǐ gāo.**
> He is taller than you.

⇨ 26.6, 29.3

They also have comparative meaning when they occur in structures that indicate change.

⇨ 10.9

To explicitly express comparative meaning, precede the adjectival verb with the intensifier 更 **gèng** or the expression 还(要)/還(要) **hái (yào)**.

他更高。	他还(要)高。
	他還(要)高。
Tā gèng gāo.	**Tā hái (yào) gāo.**
He is (even) taller.	He is (even) taller.

⇨ 29.5

10.6 Superlative meaning

Adjectival verbs do not have a distinct superlative form. To express the superlative meaning, precede the adjectival verb with the intensifier 最 **zuì** 'most.'

他最高。	那本书最贵。
	那本書最貴。
Tā zuì gāo.	**Nà běn shū zuì guì.**
He is the tallest.	That book is the most expensive.

⇨ 29.6

10.7 Adjectival verbs and comparison structures

Adjectival verbs are used in comparison structures.

Comparison structures involving 比 **bǐ** 'more than' and 没有 **méi yǒu** 'less than' typically end with an adjectival verb or a modified adjectival verb.

我比你高。
Wǒ bǐ nǐ gāo.
I am taller than you.

我没有你高。
Wǒ méi yǒu nǐ gāo.
I am not as tall as you.

⇨ 29

10.8 Linking adjectival verbs

The adverb 又 **yòu** can be used to link adjectival verbs as follows. The structure is used to convey the meaning 'both . . . and . . .'

那个男的又高又大。
那個男的又高又大。
Nàge nán de *yòu gāo yòu dà*.
That guy is *both big and tall.*

那双鞋子很好。又便宜又舒服。
那雙鞋子很好。又便宜又舒服。
Nà shuāng xiézi hěn hǎo. *Yòu piányi yòu shūfu*.
That pair of shoes is really good. They are *both cheap and comfortable.*

⇨ 36.9

10.9 Adjectival verbs and expressions that indicate change over time

10.9.1 越来越 *yuè lái yuè* adjectival verb 'more and more' adjectival verb

东西越来越贵。
東西越來越貴。
Dōngxi yuè lái yuè guì.
Things are more and more expensive.

10.9.2 越 *yuè* action verb 越 *yuè* adjectival verb 'the more' (action), 'the more' (adjectival verb)

他越说越快。
他越說越快。
Tā yuè shuō yuè kuài.
The more he speaks, the faster he speaks.

⇨ 34.3

10.10 Adjectival verbs and sentence final -了 *le*

Sentence final -了 le may occur at the end of a sentence with an adjectival verb to indicate change.

你高了。
Nǐ gāo le.
You have gotten taller.

⇨ 34.1

11

Stative verbs

Stative verbs describe situations that do not involve action. Examples of stative verbs include 喜欢/喜歡 **xǐhuan** 'to like,' 爱/愛 **ài** 'to love,' 像 **xiàng** 'to resemble,' 想 **xiǎng** 'to want,' 要 **yào** 'to want,' 需要 **xūyào** 'to need,' 怕 **pà** 'to fear,' 尊敬 **zūnjìng** 'to respect,' 感谢/感謝 **gǎnxiè** 'to appreciate,' 懂 **dǒng** 'to understand,' 信 **xìn** 'to believe,' and 想念 **xiǎngniàn** 'to miss.' Certain stative verbs have special meanings and properties and will be discussed separately below. They include the equational verbs 是 **shì** 'to be' and 姓 **xìng** 'to be family named,' and the verb 有 **yǒu** 'to have,' 'to exist.'

Stative verbs are similar to adjectival verbs in their form of negation, their occurrence with intensifiers, and their use in comparison structures.

⇨ 10.1, 10.3, 29.

11.1 Negation of stative verbs

Most stative verbs may only be negated by 不 **bù**. The stative verb 有 **yǒu** 'to have' may only be negated by 没 **méi**.

不 *bù negates most stative verbs*	没 *méi only negates* 有 *yǒu*
他不像他爸爸。 **Tā bù xiàng tā bàba.** He doesn't resemble his dad.	
他不怕狗。 **Tā bù pà gǒu.** He is not afraid of dogs.	
我不要钱。 我不要錢。 **Wǒ bù yào qián.** I don't want money.	
	他没有车。 他沒有車。 **Tā méi yǒu chē.** He doesn't have a car.

⇨ 23

11.2 Modification by intensifiers

Stative verbs, like adjectival verbs, can be preceded and modified by intensifiers. The intensifiers are emphasized in each of the following sentences.

> 我们很尊敬他。
> 我們很尊敬他。
> **Wǒmen *hěn* zūnjìng tā.**
> We all respect him *a lot*.

> 我很想念你。
> **Wǒ *hěn* xiǎngniàn nǐ.**
> I miss you *a lot*.

> 我真怕这种人。
> 我真怕這種人。
> **Wǒ *zhēn* pà zhè zhǒng rén.**
> I'm *really* afraid of this kind of person.

> 他特别需要你的支持。
> **Tā *tèbié* xūyào nǐ de zhīchí.**
> He *especially* needs your support.

For a complete list of intensifiers, see section 10.3.

⇨ 10.3, 12.6.3

11.3 Indicating completion, past time, and change of state

The verb suffixes 了 **le** or 过/過 **guo** cannot be used to indicate the *completion* or *past time* of a stative verb. To indicate that a state existed in the past, use a time expression or adverb that refers to the past.

> 我小的时候怕狗。
> 我小的時候怕狗。
> **Wǒ *xiǎo de shíhou* pà gǒu.**
> *When I was small* I was afraid of dogs.

> 我以前很喜欢吃口香糖。
> 我以前很喜歡吃口香糖。
> **Wǒ *yǐqián* hěn xǐhuan chī kǒuxiāngtáng.**
> I *used to* like to chew gum. (lit. '*Before*, I liked to chew gum.')

When a stative verb is followed by 了 **le**, it indicates *change of state*.

> 我懂了！
> **Wǒ dǒng le!**
> I understand (now)!

⇨ 33.8, 34

| NOTE | Some verbs can function as a stative verb and as an action verb. |

有 *yǒu* as a stative verb   有 *yǒu* as an action verb

她很有钱。   她有了一笔钱。
她很有錢。   她有了一筆錢。
Tā hěn yǒu qián.   **Tā yǒu le yī bǐ qián.**
She has a lot of money.   She has acquired a sum of money.
She is rich.

⇨   Glossary

11.4   The equational verb 是 *shì* 'to be'

是 **shì** 'to be' joins two noun phrases and indicates an equational relationship between them.

她是大学生。
她是大學生。
Tā shì dàxuésheng.
She is a college student.

王老师是英国人。
王老師是英國人。
Wáng lǎoshī shì Yīngguó rén.
Professor Wang is English (an English person).

The negation of 是 **shì** is 不是 **bù shì**.

她不是大学生。
她不是大學生。
Tā bù shì dàxuésheng.
She is not a college student.

王老师不是英国人。
王老師不是英國人。
Wáng lǎoshī bù shì Yīngguó rén.
Professor Wang is not English (an English person).

是 **shì** is used less often than the English verb 'to be.' In particular, in Mandarin, 是 **shì** is ordinarily not used with adjectival verbs or stative verbs. In most circumstances,

Say this	*Not this*
我的弟弟很高。	我的弟弟是很高。
Wǒ de dìdi hěn gāo.	**Wǒ de dìdi shì hěn gāo.**
My younger brother is very tall.	
他很聪明。	他是很聪明。
他很聰明。	他是很聰明。
Tā hěn cōngming.	**Tā shì hěn cōngming.**
He is very intelligent.	

是 **shì** is only used with adjectival verbs or stative verbs for special emphasis, especially contrastive emphasis.

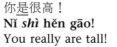

你是很高！
Nǐ *shì* hěn gāo!
You really are tall!

那本书是很贵。
那本書是很貴。
Nà běn shū *shì* hěn guì.
That book *is* expensive, despite what you claim.

他是很聪明。
他是很聰明。
Tā *shì* hěn cōngming.
He really is intelligent (despite what you may think).

是 **shì** can be used for contrastive emphasis with action verbs.

我是明天走，不是今天走。
Wǒ shì míngtiān zǒu, bù shi jīntiān zǒu.
I am leaving tomorrow. I am not leaving today.

⇨ | 53.3

是 **shì** is not used to indicate location or existence.

⇨ | 11.6.3, 11.7

When the object of 是 **shì** includes a number (for example, when it refers to money, age, time, etc.) 是 **shì** can be omitted in affirmative form.

那本书(是)五块钱。
那本書(是)五塊錢。
Nà běn shū (shì) wǔ kuài qián.
That book is $5.00

我妹妹(是)十八岁。
我妹妹(是)十八歲。
Wǒ mèimei (shì) shíbā suì.
My younger sister is 18 years old.

现在(是)八点钟。
現在(是)八點鐘。
Xiànzài (shì) bādiǎn zhōng.
It is now 8 o'clock.

However, when the object is negated, 是 **shì** cannot be omitted.

Say this	*Not this*
那本书不是五块钱。 那本書不是五塊錢。 **Nà běn shū bù shì wǔ kuài qián.** That book is not $5.00	*那本书不五块钱。 那本書不五塊錢。 **Nà běn shū bù wǔ kuài qián.**
我妹妹不是十八岁。 我妹妹不是十八歲。 **Wǒ mèimei bù shì shíbā suì.** My younger sister is not 18 years old.	*我妹妹不十八岁。 我妹妹不十八歲。 **Wǒ mèimei bù shíbā suì.**

Say this	Not this
现在不是八点钟。	*现在不八点钟。
現在不是八點鐘。	現在不八點鐘。
Xiànzài bù shì bādiǎn zhōng.	**Xiànzài bù bādiǎn zhōng.**
It is not 8 o'clock now.	

是 **shì** is used to focus on some detail of a situation, for example the time, place, or participants in a situation, or the material that something is made from.

> 他是昨天来的。
> 他是昨天來的。
> **Tā shì zuótiān lái de.**
> It was yesterday that he came. (He came *yesterday*.)

> 我是在大学学中文。
> 我是在大學學中文。
> **Wǒ shì zài dàxué xué Zhōngwén.**
> It is at the university where I study Chinese. (I study Chinese *at university*.)

> 我的耳环是(用)金子作的。
> 我的耳環是(用)金子作的。
> **Wǒ de ěrhuán shì (yòng) jīnzi zuò de.**
> My earrings are made of gold.

⇨ | 33.9, 53.2.4

11.5 The equational verb 姓 *xìng* 'to be family named'

To tell someone your family name or to indicate the family name of another person, use 姓 **xìng**.

> 我姓罗。
> 我姓羅。
> **Wǒ xìng Luó.**
> My family name is Luo.

> 她姓马。
> 她姓馬。
> **Tā xìng Mǎ.**
> Her family name is Ma.

The negation of 姓 **xìng** is 不姓 **bù xìng**.

> 我不姓李。我姓罗。
> 我不姓李。我姓羅。
> **Wǒ bù xìng Lǐ. Wǒ xìng luó.**
> My family name isn't Li. My family name is Luo.

To ask someone's family name, say:

> 你姓什么？
> 你姓甚麼？
> **Nǐ xìng shénme?**
> What is your family name?

The very polite way to ask someone's family name is:

> 你贵姓?
> 你貴姓?
> **Nǐ guì xìng?**
> (What is) your honorable family name?

⇨ 18

11.6 The verb of possession and existence: 有 *yǒu* 'to have,' 'to exist'

有 **yǒu** has two meanings: 'to have' and 'to exist.'

11.6.1 有 *yǒu* used to express possession

有 **yǒu** means 'to have' when the subject is something that can have possessions. This includes people, animals, or any other noun that can be described as 'having' things:

> 我有一個弟弟。
> **Wǒ yǒu yī gè dìdi.**
> I have a younger brother.

> 那个书店有很多旧书。
> 那個書店有很多舊書。
> **Nàge shūdiàn yǒu hěn duō jiù shū.**
> That bookstore has many old books.

> 中国有很多名胜古迹。
> 中國有很多名勝古跡。
> **Zhōngguó yǒu hěn duō míng shèng gǔ jì.**
> China has many scenic spots and historical sites.

⇨ 25.2.1

11.6.2 有 *yǒu* used to express existence

有 **yǒu** indicates existence when the subject is a location. The most common English translation of this meaning is 'there is' or 'there are.'

> 房子后头有一个小湖。
> 房子後頭有一個小湖。
> **Fángzi hòutou yǒu yī gè xiǎo hú.**
> Behind the house there is a small lake.

> 那儿有很多人排队。
> 那兒有很多人排隊。
> **Nàr yǒu hěn duō rén pái duì.**
> There are a lot of people there waiting in line.

⇨ 43.1

11.6.3 **Possession vs. existence**

The meanings of possession and existence are closely related, and often a Chinese sentence with 有 **yǒu** can be interpreted as conveying either possession or existence. The difference in interpretation typically depends upon whether the subject is understood to be a possessor or a location.

> 美国大学有很多留学生。
> 美國大學有很多留學生。
> **Měiguó dàxué yǒu hěn duō liúxuéshēng.**
> American universities have many exchange students.
> There are many exchange students in American universities.

> 这个图书馆有很多中文书。
> 這個圖書館有很多中文書。
> **Zhège túshūguǎn yǒu hěn duō Zhōngwén shū.**
> This library has a lot of Chinese books.
> There are a lot of Chinese books in this library.

11.6.4 **Negation of 有 *yǒu***

The negation of 有 **yǒu** is always 没有 **méi yǒu**.

> 我没有弟弟。
> **Wǒ méi yǒu dìdi.**
> I do not have a younger brother.

> 房子后头没有湖。
> 房子後頭沒有湖。
> **Fángzi hòutou méi yǒu hú.**
> There is no lake behind the house.

> 这个图书馆没有很多中文书。
> 這個圖書館沒有很多中文書。
> **Zhège túshūguǎn méi yǒu hěn duō Zhōngwén shū.**
> This library does not have a lot of Chinese books.
> There aren't a lot of Chinese books in this library.

⇨ 23.1.2

11.7 **The location verb 在 *zài* 'to be located at'**

To indicate location, use 在 **zài**.

> 他在家。
> **Tā zài jiā.**
> He is at home.

> 图书馆在公园的北边。
> 圖書館在公園的北邊。
> **Túshūguǎn zài gōngyuán de běibiān.**
> The library is north of the park.

Notice that English uses the verb 'to be' and the preposition 'at' to express this meaning.

The negation for 在 **zài** is 不在 **bù zài**.

> 他不在家。
> **Tā bù zài jiā.**
> He is not at home.

> 图书馆不在公园的北边。
> 圖書館不在公園的北邊。
> **Túshūguǎn bù zài gōngyuán de běibiān.**
> The library is not to the north of the park.

在 **zài** also functions as a preposition. As a preposition, it indicates the location where an action occurs. Depending upon the sentence, it may be translated into English as 'at,' or 'in,' or 'on.'

> 他在家吃饭。
> 他在家吃飯。
> **Tā zài jiā chī fàn.**
> He eats at home.

> 孩子在公园里玩。
> 孩子在公園裏玩。
> **Háizi zài gōngyuán lǐ wán.**
> The children play in the park.

⇨ 14, 43.1

12

Modal verbs

Modal verbs occur before a verb and express the meanings of possibility, ability, permission, obligation, and prohibition.

12.1 Expressing possibility: 会/會 *huì*

明天会下雨。
明天會下雨。
Míngtiān huì xià yǔ.
It may rain tomorrow.

我希望我们将来会有机会再见。
我希望我們將來會有機會再見。
Wǒ xīwàng wǒmen jiānglái huì yǒu jīhuì zài jiàn.
I hope that in the future we will have the chance to meet again.

Notice that this meaning of 会/會 **huì** also implies future time.

⇨ 32.3

12.2 Expressing ability

12.2.1 会/會 *huì*

会/會 **huì** expresses innate ability or ability based on learning and knowledge. The negative is 不会/不會 **bù huì**.

她会说中文。
她會說中文。
Tā huì shuō Zhōngwén.
She can speak Chinese.

我不会写那个字。
我不會寫那個字。
Wǒ bù huì xiě nàge zì.
I can't write that character.

⇨ 48.1, 50.1

12.2.2 能 *néng*

能 **néng** expresses physical ability or the unobstructed ability to perform some action. 不能 **bù néng** is used when performance is obstructed.

> 你能不能把桌子搬到那边去?
> 你能不能把桌子搬到那邊去?
> **Nǐ néng bù néng bǎ zhuōzi bān dào nàbiān qù?**
> Can you move this table over there?
> (lit: Can you take this table and move it over there?)

> 他的嗓子疼,不能说话。
> 他的嗓子疼,不能説話。
> **Tā de sǎngzi téng, bù néng shuō huà.**
> His throat is sore. He can't speak.

> 现在在修路。不能过。
> 現在在修路。不能過。
> **Xiànzài zài xiū lù. Bù néng guò.**
> The road is being repaired now. You can't cross it.

⇨ 48.1.3

12.2.3 可以 *kéyǐ*

可以 **kéyǐ** is sometimes used to express knowledge-based or physical ability. The negative is 不可以 **bù kéyǐ**.

> 你可以不可以写你的名字?
> 你可以不可以寫你的名字?
> **Nǐ kéyǐ bù kéyǐ xiě nǐ de míngzi?**
> Can you write your name?

> 她已经八十岁了,可是还可以骑自行车。
> 她已經八十歲了,可是還可以騎自行車。
> **Tā yǐjing bāshí suì le, kěshì hái kéyǐ qí zìxíngchē.**
> She is already eighty years old but can still ride a bicycle.

12.3 Expressing permission: 可以 *kéyǐ*

The primary use of 可以 **kéyǐ** is to express permission to perform an action. The negative is 不可以 **bù kéyǐ**.

> 妈妈说我可以跟你去看电影。
> 媽媽説我可以跟你去看電影。
> **Māma shuō wǒ kéyǐ gēn nǐ qù kàn diànyǐng.**
> Mom said I can go with you to see a movie.

> 你才十六岁。不可以喝酒。
> 你才十六歲。不可以喝酒。
> **Nǐ cái shíliù suì. Bù kéyǐ hē jiǔ.**
> You are only 16 years old. You cannot drink alcohol.

⇨ 47.2

12.4 **Expressing obligations**

Obligations may be strong (*must*) or weak (*should*). In Mandarin, as in English, negation often changes the force of the words used to express obligation. This section presents a brief overview of the use of modal verbs to express obligations. For more on expressing obligations, see Chapter 46.

12.4.1 **Strong obligation: must, have to**

The Mandarin words used to indicate strong obligation (*must*) in Mandarin are 必须/必須 **bìxū**, 必得 **bìděi**, and 得 **děi**. 必得 **bìděi** and 必须/必須 **bìxū** are more formal than 得 **děi**. 必须/必須 **bìxū** is used in legal pronouncements and in other formal spoken and written contexts.

必须/必須 *bìxū*

> 婚前必须做健康检查。
> 婚前必須做健康檢查。
> **Hūn qián bìxū zuò jiànkāng jiǎnchá.**
> Before you get married you must have a physical exam.

必得 *bìděi*

> 医生说我每天必得吃药。
> 醫生説我每天必得吃藥。
> **Yīshēng shuō wǒ měitiān bìděi chī yào.**
> The doctor says I must take medicine every day.

得 *děi*

> 住院以前得先付钱。
> 住院以前得先付錢。
> **Zhù yuàn yǐqián děi xiān fù qián.**
> Before being admitted to the hospital you must first pay a fee.

⇨ 46.1.1

12.4.2 **'Weak obligations' – Socal and moral obligation: should, ought to**

The modal verbs used to express weak obligations (*should*) associated with social or moral responsibilities include 应该/應該 **yīnggāi**, 该/該 **gāi**, 应当/應當 **yīngdāng**, and 当/當 **dāng**. 应当/應當 **yīngdāng** is more formal than 应该/應該 **yīnggāi** and can be used in formal texts including legal documents. 该/該 **gāi** is used in informal speech. 应/應 **yīng** is used in formal texts including legal documents. For illustrations of legal uses, see

⇨ 46.1.2

应该/應該 *yīnggāi*

> 学生应该认真地学习。
> 學生應該認真地學習。
> **Xuésheng yīnggāi rènzhēn de xuéxí.**
> Students should study conscientiously.

该/該 **gāi**

> 你该早一点睡觉。
> 你該早一點睡覺。
> **Nǐ gāi zǎo yīdiǎn shuì jiào.**
> You should go to sleep a little earlier.

应当/應當 **yīngdāng**

> 孩子应当尊敬父母。
> 孩子應當尊敬父母。
> **Háizi yīngdāng zūnjìng fùmǔ.**
> Children should respect their parents.

⇨ 46.1.2

12.4.3 Using modal verbs to express negative obligations: need not, do not have to

不必 **bù bì** expresses negative obligations using the syllable 必 **bì** that occurs in the strong obligation modal verbs 必得 **bìděi** and 必须/必須 **bìxū**. For additional ways to express negative obligations, see 46.1.3.

> 你去看朋友的时候不必送礼物。
> 你去看朋友的時候不必送禮物。
> **Nǐ qù kàn péngyou de shíhou bù bì sòng lǐwù.**
> When you visit friends it is not necessary to bring a gift.

12.5 Expressing prohibitions

The following phrases involving modal verbs are used to express prohibitions. For additional phrases used in expressing prohibitions, see

⇨ 46.2

不可以 **bù kéyǐ** 'not allowed to'

> 考试的时候不可以说话。
> 考試的時候不可以說話。
> **Kǎoshì de shíhou bù kéyǐ shuō huà.**
> During the test you cannot speak.

不能 **bù néng** 'cannot'

> 这些书都是内部刊物。你不能借。
> 這些書都是內部刊物。你不能借。
> **Zhè xiē shū dōu shì nèi bù kānwù. Nǐ bù néng jiè.**
> Those books are all restricted publications. You can't borrow them.

> 这件事情，我不能告诉你。
> 這件事情，我不能告訴你。
> **Zhè jiàn shìqing, wǒ bù néng gàosu nǐ.**
> (As for) this matter, I can't tell you about it.

不许/不許 **bù xǔ** *'must not, not allowed'*

不许/不許 **bù xǔ** is used in formal speech and writing.

> 图书馆里不许抽烟、吃东西。
> 圖書館裏不許抽菸、吃東西。
> **Túshūguǎn lǐ bù xǔ chōu yān, chī dōngxi.**
> You are not allowed to smoke or eat (things) in the library.

⇨ 46.2.1

12.6 Grammatical properties of modal verbs

12.6.1 Negation of modal verbs

Modal verbs are always negated with 不 **bù** and never with 没 **méi**.

Say this	*Not this*
他不会说中文。	*他没会说中文。
他不會説中文。	他沒會説中文。
Tā bù huì shuō Zhōngwén.	**Tā méi huì shuō Zhōngwén.**
He can't speak Chinese.	
你不应该抽烟。	*你没应该抽烟。
你不應該抽菸。	你沒應該抽菸。
Nǐ bù yīnggāi chōu yān.	**Nǐ méi yīnggāi chōu yān.**
You shouldn't smoke.	

Modal verbs indicating weak obligation, 会/會 **huì**, 可以 **kéyǐ**, 能 **néng**, 应该/應該 **yīnggāi**, and 应当/應當 **yīngdāng**, have the properties of stative verbs.

⇨ 11

12.6.2 Questions with modal verbs

Modal verbs can occur as the short, one word answers to yes–no questions.

Question	*Response*
你会不会说中文?	会。
你會不會説中文?	會。
Nǐ huì bù huì shuō Zhōngwén?	**Huì.**
Can you speak Chinese?	(I) can.
我可以不可以借你的车?	可以。
我可以不可以借你的車?	
Wǒ kéyǐ bù kéyǐ jiè nǐ de chē?	**Kéyǐ.**
Can I borrow your car?	(You) can.
你能不能帮助我?	能。
你能不能幫助我?	
Nǐ néng bù néng bāngzhù wǒ?	**Néng.**
Can you help me?	(I) can.

Question	Response
我们该不该交作业?	该。
我們該不該交作業?	該。
Wǒmen gāi bù gāi jiāo zuòyè?	**Gāi.**
Should we hand in our homework?	(We) should.

They can serve as the verb in *verb-not-verb* questions:

你会不会说中文?
你會不會説中文?
Nǐ huì bù huì shuō Zhōngwén?
Can you speak Chinese?

你能不能帮助我?
你能不能幫助我?
Nǐ néng bù néng bāngzhù wǒ?
Can you help me?

你可以不可以在图书馆说话?
你可以不可以在圖書館説話?
Nǐ kéyǐ bù kéyǐ zài túshūguǎn shuō huà?
Can you speak in the library? (Are you allowed to . . .)

我们该不该请他吃饭?
我們該不該請他吃飯?
Wǒmen gāi bù gāi qǐng tā chī fàn?
Should we invite him to dinner?

⇨ 24

12.6.3 Modification by intensifiers

会/會 **huì** and 能 **néng** can be modified by intensifiers.

那个人很会跳舞。
那個人很會跳舞。
Nàge rén hěn huì tiào wǔ.
That person can really dance.

中国人很能吃苦。
中國人很能吃苦。
Zhōngguórén hěn néng chī kǔ.
Chinese people can endure a lot of hardship.

For a complete list of intensifiers, see **10.3**.

⇨ 10.3, 11.2

12.6.4 Modal verbs and expressions that indicate change over time

会/會 **huì**, 能 **néng**, and 可以 **kéyǐ** can be used in the structures 越来越 **yuè lái yuè** and 越 verb 越 verb **yuè** verb **yuè** verb to indicate change over time.

他越来越会说话。
他越來越會說話。
Tā yuè lái yuè huì shuō huà.
He is becoming more and more elegant (diplomatic) in his speech.

他越来越能适应英国的生活了。
他越來越能適應英國的生活了。
Tā yuè lái yuè néng shìyìng Yīngguó de shēnghuó le.
Little by little he is getting used to English life.

中国人越来越可以有谈话的自由了。
中國人越來越可以有談話的自由了。
Zhōngguórén yuè lái yuè kéyǐ yǒu tán huà de zìyóu le.
Little by little, Chinese people are able to have freedom of speech.

➪ 34.3

12.6.5 Modal verbs and adverbs

The modal verbs that indicate strong obligation, 必须/必須 **bìxū**, 必得 **bìděi**, 得 **děi**, are similar to adverbs.

They cannot serve as the verb in *verb-not-verb* questions:

Say this	*Not this*
你必须马上回家吗？	*你必须不必须马上回家？
你必須馬上回家嗎？	你必須不必須馬上回家？
Nǐ bìxū mǎshàng huí jiā ma?	**Nǐ bìxū bù bìxū mǎshàng huí jiā?**
Do you have to go right home?	
我们得在这儿注册吗？	*我们得不得在这儿注册？
我們得在這兒註冊嗎？	我們得不得在這兒註冊？
Wǒmen děi zài zhèr zhù cè ma?	**Wǒmen děi bù děi zài zhèr zhù cè?**
Do we have to register here?	

The modal 得 **děi** cannot be used as the one-word answer to yes–no questions:

Question	*Respond with this*	*Do not respond with this*
今天得注册吗？	今天得注册。	*得。
今天得註冊嗎？	今天得註冊。	
Jīntiān děi zhù cè ma?	**Jīntiān děi zhù cè.**	**Děi**
Do we have to register today?	We have to register today.	
	or	
	对。	
	對。	
	Duì.	
	Correct.	

13

Action verbs

Action verbs are verbs that describe doing things. They include 买/買 **mǎi** 'to shop,' 学/學 **xué** 'to study,' 看 **kàn** 'to look at,' 'watch,' 'read,' 吃 **chī** 'to eat,' 睡 **shuì** 'to sleep,' 去 **qù** 'to go,' 唱 **chàng** 'to sing,' 洗 **xǐ** 'to wash,' etc.

This chapter shows you how to talk about completed, past, and ongoing actions, and introduces the overall properties of action verbs. There are two kinds of action verbs, those that describe open-ended actions, and those that describe actions that cause a change. The last two sections of this chapter present the characteristics of these two types of verbs.

13.1 Indicating that an action is completed or past

To indicate that an action is completed or past, follow the action verb with the verb suffix 了 **le**.

> 她买了东西。
> 她買了東西。
> **Tā mǎi le dōngxi.**
> She bought things.

> 她到图书馆去了。
> 她到圖書館去了。
> **Tā dào túshūguǎn qù le.**
> She went to the library.

If the action verb takes an object and the object is one syllable in length, 了 **le** generally follows the object.

> 她上课了。
> 她上課了。
> **Tā shàng kè le.**
> She attended class.

⇨ 33.1

13.2 Indicating that an action has been experienced in the past

To indicate that the subject had the experience of performing some action in the past, follow the action verb with the verb suffix 过/過 **guo**. The verb suffix 过/過 **guo** is used when talking about actions that the subject does not perform on a regular basis or for actions that happened in the remote past.

> 我看过那个电影。
> 我看過那個電影。
> **Wǒ kànguo nàge diànyǐng.**
> I've seen that movie before.

> 我来过这里。
> 我來過這裏。
> **Wǒ láiguo zhèlǐ.**
> I've been here before.

➡ 33.6

13.3 Negating actions

13.3.1 Indicating that an action does not occur or will not occur

To indicate that an action does not occur or will not occur, negate the action verb with 不 **bù**.

> 我不吃肉。
> **Wǒ bù chī ròu.**
> I don't eat meat.

> 台北从来不下雪。
> 臺北從來不下雪。
> **Táiběi cónglái bù xià xuě.**
> It does not snow in Taipei.

> 明天是星期六。我们不上课。
> 明天是星期六。我們不上課。
> **Míngtiān shì xīngqīliù. Wǒmen bù shàng kè.**
> Tomorrow is Saturday. We don't attend class.

13.3.2 Indicating that an action did not occur in the past

To indicate that an action did not occur in the past, negate the action verb with 没 (有) **méi (yǒu)**.

> 我今天没(有)吃早饭。
> 我今天沒(有)吃早飯。
> **Wǒ jīntiān méi (yǒu) chī zǎofàn.**
> I didn't eat breakfast today.

> 我没买电脑。
> 我沒買電腦。
> **Wǒ méi mǎi diànnǎo.**
> I didn't buy a computer.

➡ 23.1.2, 33.3

When a verb is negated with 没 (有) **méi (yǒu)**, it cannot be suffixed with 了 **le**. It can, however, be suffixed with 过/過 **guo**.

Say this	*Not this*
我没吃过日本菜。	*我没吃了日本菜。
我沒吃過日本菜。	**Wǒ méi chī le Rìběn cài.**
Wǒ méi chīguo Rìběn cài.	
I have never eaten Japanese food before.	

⇨ 33.6

13.4 Open-ended action verbs

Open-ended action verbs refer to actions that can have duration and can be performed for a period of time. Examples of open-ended action verbs include 念 **niàn** 'to study/read aloud,' 买/買 **mǎi** 'to shop,' 写/寫 **xiě** 'to write,' 学/學 **xué** 'to study,' 跑 **pǎo** 'to run,' 吃 **chī** 'to eat,' 玩 **wán** 'to play,' and 唱 **chàng** 'to sing.'

13.4.1 Duration of open-ended actions

To indicate the duration of an open-ended action verb, follow the verb with a duration expression. In the following examples, the verb is emphasized.

> 他在中国住了一年。
> 他在中國住了一年。
> **Tā zài Zhōngguó *zhù* le yīnián.**
> He *lived* in China for a year.

> 他每天看一个钟头的报。
> 他每天看一個鍾頭的報。
> **Tā měitiān *kàn* yī gè zhōngtou de bào.**
> He *reads* a newspaper for one hour every day.

⇨ 35.1

To emphasize the ongoing action of an open-ended action verb without specifying the length of the duration, follow the verb with the suffix 着/著 **zhe**. 在 **zài** and 呢 **ne** often occur with 着/著 **zhe**. 在 **zài** occurs before the verb and 呢 **ne** occurs at the end of the sentence.

> 他在说着话呢。
> 他在説著話呢。
> **Tā zài shuōzhe huà ne.**
> He is speaking.

⇨ 35.2

13.4.2 Open-ended action verbs and obligatory objects

Open-ended action verbs are typically followed by an *obligatory object*, a noun phrase that serves as the direct object of the verb. Many open-ended action verbs have a *default object*, an object that automatically occurs with the verb.

Default objects contribute little or no meaning to the *verb + object* phrase and are typically not translated into English.

Open-ended action verb	Default object	Verb + object	Example sentence
说	话	说话	他们在说话呢。
説	話	説話	他們在説話呢。
shuō	**huà**	**shuō huà**	**Tāmen zài shuō huà ne.**
speak	speech	speak	They are speaking.
睡	觉	睡觉	她没睡觉。
	覺	睡覺	她沒睡覺。
shuì	**jiào**	**shuì jiào**	**Tā méi shuì jiào.**
sleep	sleep	sleep	She didn't sleep.
看	书	看书	我喜欢看书。
	書	看書	我喜歡看書。
kàn	**shū**	**kàn shū**	**Wǒ xǐhuan kàn shū.**
read	book	read	I like to read.
吃	饭	吃饭	我们吃饭吧！
	飯	吃飯	我們吃飯吧！
chī	**fàn**	**chī fàn**	**Wǒmen chī fàn ba!**
eat	rice	eat	Let's eat!
写	字	写字	他不会写字。
寫		寫字	他不會寫字。
xiě	**zì**	**xiě zì**	**Tā bù huì xiě zì.**
write	character	write	He can't write.
画	画儿	画画儿	他会画画儿。
畫	畫兒	畫畫兒	他會畫畫兒。
huà	**huàr**	**huà huàr**	**Tā huì huà huàr.**
paint	picture	paint	He can paint.
唱	歌儿	唱歌儿	他周末跟朋友唱歌儿。
	歌兒	唱歌兒	他週末跟朋友唱歌兒。
chàng	**gēr**	**chàng gēr**	**Tā zhōumò gēn péngyou chàng gēr.**
sing	song	sing	He sings with friends on the weekend.
洗	澡	洗澡	孩子不喜欢洗澡。
			孩子不喜歡洗澡。
xǐ	**zǎo**	**xǐ zǎo**	**Háizi bù xǐhuan xǐ zǎo.**
wash	bathe	wash; bathe	Children do not like to bathe.
睡	觉	睡觉	你几点钟睡觉？
	覺	睡覺	你幾點鐘睡覺？
shuì	**jiào**	**shuì jiào**	**Nǐ jǐdiǎn zhōng shuì jiào?**
sleep	a sleep	sleep	What time do you go to sleep?

When an object with fuller meaning is used, it replaces the default object.

For example:

- 'to eat' is 吃饭/吃飯 **chī fàn**
  'to eat *dumplings*' is 吃饺子/吃餃子 **chī jiǎozi** and not
  *吃饭饺子/吃飯餃子 **chī fàn jiǎozi**.

- 'to write' is 写字/寫字 **xiě zì**
  'to write *English*' is 写英文/寫英文 **xiě Yīngwén** and not
  *写字英文/寫字英文 **xiě zì Yīngwén**
- 'to read' is 看书/看書 **kàn shū**
  'to read *a newspaper*' is 看报/看報 **kàn bào** and not
  *看书报/看書報 **kànshū bào**.

The direct object may be absent when it can be inferred from the context of the
sentence.

Q: 你吃了晚饭吗？   A: 吃了。
你吃了晚飯嗎？
Nǐ chī le wǎnfàn ma?   **Chī le.**
Did you eat dinner?   I ate (dinner).

When it receives special emphasis, the direct object may occur at the beginning of
the sentence as the topic, instead of after the verb.

那个电影我还没看过。
那個電影我還沒看過。
Nàge diànyǐng wǒ hái méi kànguo.
That movie, I still haven't seen (it).

⇨ 53.1.2.1

13.5 Change-of-state action verbs

Change-of-state verbs describe events in which the action of the verb results in a
change. Here are some examples of change-of-state verbs.

坐	**zuò**	to sit (a change from standing to sitting)
站	**zhàn**	to stand (a change from sitting to standing)
放	**fàng**	to put/place (a change of location)
挂/掛	**guà**	to hang (a change of location)
离开 離開	**líkāi**	to depart (a change of location)
穿	**chuān**	to put on (clothing – on the torso and legs)
戴	**dài**	to put on (clothing – on the head, neck, and hands)
病	**bìng**	to become sick (a change of health)
到	**dào**	to arrive (a change of location from 'not here' to 'here')
去	**qù**	to go (a change of location from 'here' to 'not here')

13.5.1 Change-of-state verbs and duration

Change-of-state verbs have no duration so they cannot be suffixed with the duration
suffix 着/著 **zhe** and they cannot occur in other patterns that focus on the duration
of an event.

13.5.2 Change-of-state verbs and stative verbs

Many change-of-state verbs also function as stative verbs.

		Change-of-state verb	*Stative verb*
坐	**zuò**	to sit down	to be seated
站	**zhàn**	to stand up	to be standing
戴	**dài**	to put on (clothing)	to wear
病	**bìng**	to become sick	to be sick
挂/掛	**guà**	to hang (something up)	to be hanging

⇨ Glossary

14

Prepositions and prepositional phrases

Prepositions occur before a noun phrase and indicate some relationship between the noun phrase and the main verb of the sentence. The preposition plus its noun phrase forms a prepositional phrase.

The grammar of the prepositional phrase in the Mandarin sentence

Here are the two rules to follow when using prepositional phrases.

Rule 1. **In Mandarin, the prepositional phrase occurs immediately before the verb phrase.**

Compare this with English, in which the prepositional phrase occurs immediately *after* the verb phrase.

他们	[给弟弟]	[买了冰淇淋]。
他們	[給弟弟]	[買了冰淇淋]。
Tāmen	**[gěi dìdi]**	**[mǎi le bīngqilín].**
They	[for younger brother]	[buy ice cream]

They bought ice cream for younger brother.

她	[跟同学]	[聊天]。
她	[跟同學]	[聊天]。
Tā	**[gēn tóngxué]**	**[liáo tiān].**
She	[with classmates]	[chat]

She chats with classmates.

Rule 2. **Nothing occurs between the preposition and its noun phrase object.**

- The suffixes 了 **le**, 着/著 **zhe**, and 过/過 **guo** follow verbs, but not prepositions:

Say this	*Not this*
他在中国住过一年。	*他在过中国住一年。
他在中國住過一年。	他在過中國住一年。
Tā zài Zhōngguó zhùguo yīnián.	**Tā zàiguo Zhōngguo zhù yīnián.**
He lived in China for a year.	

Say this	*Not this*
我昨天跟他说话了。	*我昨天跟了他说话。
我昨天跟他說話了。	我昨天跟了他說話。
Wǒ zuótiān gēn tā shuō huà le.	**Wǒ zuótiān gēn le tā shuō huà.**
I spoke with him yesterday.	

- Adverbs occur before the prepositional phrase. They do not occur between the prepositional phrase and the main verb.

Say this	*Not this*
请你马上到我家来。	*请你到我家马上来。
請你馬上到我家來。	請你到我家馬上來。
Qǐng nǐ *mǎshàng* dào wǒ jiā lái.	**Qǐng nǐ dào wǒ jiā *mǎshàng* lái.**
Please come to my home *immediately*.	
我一定跟你去看电影。	*我跟你一定去看电影。
我一定跟你去看電影。	我跟你一定去看電影。
Wǒ *yīdìng* gēn nǐ qù kàn diànyǐng.	**Wǒ gēn nǐ *yīdìng* qù kàn diànyǐng.**
I will *definitely* go with you to see a movie.	

⇨ 15.1

14.2 Basic functions of prepositions

Here are the most common Mandarin prepositions, arranged according to function. The prepositional phrase is emphasized in each example. The last category includes prepositions that are only used in formal speech and writing.

14.2.1 Prepositions that indicate location in time or space – no movement involved

在 *zài* 'at, in, on'

他每天晚上在家吃饭。
他每天晚上在家吃飯。
Tā měitiān wǎnshang *zài jiā* chī fàn.
He eats *at home* every evening.

他们每天在公园里玩。
他們每天在公園裏玩。
Tāmen měitiān *zài gōngyuán lǐ* wán.
They play *in the park* every day.

在 **zài** is optional in time expressions

我(在)两点钟来找你，行吗?
我(在)兩點鐘來找你，行嗎?
Wǒ *(zài) liǎng diǎn zhōng* lái zhǎo nǐ, xíng ma?
I'll come looking for you at *2 o'clock*, okay?

14.2.2 **Prepositions that indicate an action performed towards a reference point – no movement involved**

对/對 *duì* 'to, towards'

> 他对你说了什么话?
> 他對你説了甚麼話?
> **Tā *duì nǐ* shuō le shénme huà?**
> What did he say *to you*?

向 *xiàng* 'towards'

> 他一直向外面看。
> **Tā yīzhí *xiàng wàimian* kàn.**
> He keeps looking *(to the) outside*.

14.2.3 **Prepositions that indicate joint performance of an action**

跟 *gēn* 'with'

> 她每天跟他朋友吃午饭。
> 她每天跟他朋友吃午飯。
> **Tā měitiān *gēn tā péngyou* chī wǔfàn.**
> She eats lunch every day *with her friends*.

This use of 跟 **gēn** overlaps with that of the conjunction 跟 **gēn**.

⇨ | 16.1

14.2.4 **Prepositions that indicate movement of the subject**

从/從 *cóng* 'from': *movement from a location*

> 他慢慢地从宿舍走出来了。
> 他慢慢地從宿舍走出來了。
> **Tā mànmān de *cóng sùshè* zǒuchūlái le.**
> He slowly walked *out of the dormitory*.

到 *dào* 'to': *movement to a location that is the destination*

> 他想到餐厅去找朋友。
> 他想到餐廳去找朋友。
> **Tā xiǎng *dào cāntīng* qù zhǎo péngyou.**
> He's thinking about going *to the cafeteria* to look for his friends.

往 *wǎng*, 'towards' *a location*

> 往西边走。
> 往西邊走。
> ***Wǎng xībian* zǒu.**
> Go *(towards the) west*.

进/進 *jìn* 'into' a location

> 他进城去了。
> 他進城去了。
> **Tā *jìn chéng* qù le.**
> He went *into the city*.

从/從 **cóng** and 到 **dào** may occur in sequence in the same sentence:

> 从宿舍 到邮局 怎么走？
> 從宿舍 到郵局 怎麼走？
> ***Cóng sùshè dào yóujú* zěnme zǒu?**
> How do you go *from the dormitory to the post office*?

Prepositions that indicate transfer of something from one noun phrase to another

给/給 *gěi* 'to, for'

> 她给我买书了。
> 她給我買書了。
> **Tā *gěi wǒ* mǎi shū le.**
> She bought a book *for me*.

跟 *gēn* 'from'

> 他跟我借书了。
> 他跟我借書了。
> **Tā *gēn wǒ* jiè shū le.**
> He borrowed a book *from me*.

向 *xiàng* 'from'

> 他向我借书了。
> 他向我借書了。
> **Tā *xiàng wǒ* jiè shū le.**
> He borrowed a book *from me*.

Prepositions that indicate the beneficiary of an action performed by another

给/給 *gěi* 'for, on behalf of'

> 她给我写信了。
> 她給我寫信了。
> **Tā *gěi wǒ* xiě xìn le.**
> She wrote a letter *for me* (on my behalf).
> (This can also mean: She wrote a letter *to me*.)

替 *tì* 'for, on behalf of'

> 明天请你替我教书。
> 明天請你替我教書。
> **Míngtiān qǐng nǐ *tì wǒ* jiāo shū.**
> Please teach *for me* tomorrow.

14.2.7 **Prepositions that mark the agent in passive sentences**

被 *bèi* 'by'

> 我的皮包被人家偷走了。
> **Wǒ de píbāo *bèi* rénjiā tōuzǒu le.**
> My wallet was stolen *by* someone.

叫 *jiào* 'by'

> 我的课本叫朋友弄丢了。
> 我的課本叫朋友弄丟了。
> **Wǒ de kèběn *jiào* péngyou nòngdiū le.**
> My textbook was lost *by* my friend.

让/讓 *ràng* 'by'

> 他们的房子让火烧了。
> 他們的房子讓火燒了。
> **Tāmen de fángzi *ràng* huǒ shāo le.**
> Their house was burned down *by* the fire.

⇨ 17

NOTE The preposition is part of the following fixed expressions:

> 跟 (someone) 开玩笑
> 跟 (someone) 開玩笑
> **gēn (someone) kāi wánxiào**
> to play a joke on (someone)

>> 他哥哥喜欢跟他开玩笑。
>> 他哥哥喜歡跟他開玩笑。
>> **Tā gēge xǐhuan gēn tā kāi wánxiào.**
>> His older brother likes to play jokes on him.

> 对 (something) 有兴趣
> 對 (something) 有興趣
> **duì (something) yǒu xìngqù**
> to be interested in (something)

>> 我对科学有兴趣。
>> 我對科學有興趣。
>> **Wǒ duì kēxué yǒu xìngqù.**
>> I am interested in science.

14.2.8 **Prepositions used in formal speech and formal written language**

To indicate beneficiary or recipient

为/為 *wèi* 'for/on behalf of'

> 我们应该为人民服务。
> 我們應該為人民服務。
> **Wǒmen yīnggāi *wèi* rénmín fúwù.**
> We should serve the people.
> (serve *for the people*)

To indicate the source (no movement)

由 *yóu* 'from'

> <u>由此</u>可见，人民都喜欢自由。
> <u>由此</u>可見，人民都喜歡自由。
> ***Yóu cǐ* kě jiàn, rénmín dōu xǐhuan zìyóu.**
> You can see *from* this that everyone likes freedom.

To indicate location in time or space

于/於 *yú* '*at, in, on*'

> 谨定<u>于三月十五日</u>在人民大会堂开会。
> 謹定<u>於三月十五日</u>在人民大會堂開會。
> **Jǐndìng *yú sānyuè shíwǔ rì* zài rénmín dàhuìtáng kāi huì.**
> The meeting is respectfully set at March 15 in the Great Hall of the People.

To indicate a point in time (no movement)

自从/自從 **zìcóng** '*from, (ever) since*'

> <u>自从中国开放以后</u>，人民的生活水平提高了。
> <u>自從中國開放以後</u>，人民的生活水平提高了。
> ***Zìcóng Zhōngguó kāifàng* yǐhòu, rénmín de shēnghuó shuǐpíng tígāo le.**
> *Ever since China began to open up*, the standard of living of its people has improved.

14.3 Prepositions that also function as verbs

Many prepositions also function as verbs.

	As a preposition	*As a verb*
在 **zài**	*at*	*exist; be located at*
	他<u>在</u>家吃饭。	他<u>在</u>家。
	他<u>在</u>家吃飯。	
	Tā *zài* jiā chī fàn.	**Tā *zài* jiā.**
	He eats *at* home.	He is *at* home.
给/給 **gěi**	*to/for*	*give*
	他<u>给</u>我买了毛衣。	她<u>给</u>了我这件毛衣。
	他<u>給</u>我買了毛衣。	她<u>給</u>了我這件毛衣。
	Tā *gěi* wǒ mǎi le máoyī.	**Tā *gěi* le wǒ zhè jiàn máoyī.**
	He bought a sweater *for* me.	She *gave* me this sweater.
到 **dào**	*to*	*arrive*
	你什么时候到图书馆去？	他什么时候到？
	你甚麼時候<u>到</u>圖書館去？	他甚麼時候<u>到</u>？
	Nǐ shénme shíhòu *dào* túshūguǎn qù?	**Tā shénme shíhòu *dào*?**
	When are you going *to* the library?	What time does he *arrive*?

		As a preposition	*As a verb*
对/對	**duì**	*to, towards*	*correct*

对/對 **duì** *to, towards*

你应该对客人很客气。
你應該對客人很客氣。

Nǐ yīnggāi *duì* kèren hěn kèqi.

You should be polite *to* guests.

correct

Q: 你是英国人，对吗？
你是英國人，對嗎？

Nǐ shì Yīngguórén, *duì* ma?

You are English, *right*?

A: 对。
對。

***Duì*.**

Correct.

跟 **gēn** *with*

他每天跟朋友聊天。

Tā měitiān *gēn* péngyou liáo tiān.

He chats *with* friends every day.

follow

不要老跟着我。
不要老跟著我。

Bù yào lǎo *gēn*zhe wǒ.

Don't *follow* me all the time.

You can identify a word as either a preposition or a verb by observing the other words with which it occurs.

- Prepositions are always followed by an object noun phrase and a verb phrase. If a word is not followed by both an object noun phrase and a verb phrase, it is not a preposition.

Verb: followed by a noun phrase but no verb phrase

她给我这件毛衣了。
她給我這件毛衣了。

Tā *gěi* wǒ zhè jiàn máoyī le.

She *gave* me this sweater.

他在家。

Tā *zài* jiā.

He *is at* home.

Preposition: followed by a noun phrase and a verb phrase

她给我买了这件毛衣了。
她給我買了這件毛衣了。

Tā *gěi* wǒ mǎi le zhè jiàn máoyī le.

She bought this sweater *for* me.

他在家吃饭。
他在家吃飯。

Tā *zài* jiā chī fàn.

He is eating *at* home.

⇨ Glossary

15

Adverbs

Adverbs are words that modify the verb or verb phrase.

15.1 General properties of adverbs

In Mandarin, adverbs occur at the beginning of the verb phrase, before the verb and any prepositional phrase.

Most adverbs must precede negation, but some adverbs may occur before or after negation.

她一定不去。	*and also*	她不一定去。
Tā yīdìng bù qù.		**Tā bù yīdìng qù.**
She's definitely not going.		She's may not go.
		(She is not definitely going.)
她也许不去。	*but not*	*她不也许去。
她也許不去。		她不也許去。
Tā yéxǔ bù qù.		**Tā bù yěxǔ qù.**
Perhaps she won't go.		
她并不喜欢我。	*but not*	*她不并喜欢我。
她並不喜歡我。		她不並喜歡我。
Tā bìng bù xǐhuan wǒ.		**Tā bù bìng xǐhuan wǒ.**
She doesn't like me at all.		

⇨ | 23.2

Unlike verbs, adverbs typically cannot be the one word answer to a yes–no question.

Question	*Respond with this*	*Not this*
他们经常在那个饭馆吃饭吗?	对。	*经常。
他們經常在那個飯館吃飯嗎?	對。	經常。
Tāmen jīngcháng zài nàge fànguǎn chī fàn ma?	**Duì.**	**Jīngcháng.**
Do they often eat at that restaurant?	Correct.	
	or	
	他们 经常在那儿吃饭。	
	他們 經常在那兒吃飯。	
	Tāmen jīngcháng zài nàr chī fàn.	
	They often eat there.	

Question	Respond with this	Not this
你已经吃了吗?	对。	*已经。
你已經吃了嗎?	對。	已經。
Nǐ yǐjing chī le ma?	**Duì.**	**Yǐjing.**
Have you already eaten?	Correct.	
	or	
	我已经吃了。	
	我已經吃了。	
	Wǒ yǐjing chī le.	
	I have already eaten.	

Mandarin has a number of structures that are *adverbial* in function in that they describe an action in some way. These structures are presented in the chapter on adverbial modification.

⇨ 27

Adjectival verbs, stative verbs, and modal verbs may be modified by intensifiers such as 很 **hěn** 'very,' 太 **tài** 'too,' and 真 **zhēn** 'really.' A list of intensifiers is presented in **10.3**.

⇨ 10.3, 11.2, 12.6.3

Adverbs add many different kinds of meaning to a sentence. This chapter presents adverbs that have *logical* functions. Other adverbs are presented throughout this book in chapters that focus on the meanings associated with the specific adverbs.

⇨ 23, 30, 31, 32, 33, 34, 36, 37, 38, 40, 42, 46, 48, 49, 52, 53

15.2 Adverbs with logical function: 也 *yě*, 都 *dōu*, 还/還 *hái*, 就 *jiù*, 只 *zhǐ*, and 才 *cái*

15.2.1 也 *yě* 'also, in addition'

也 **yě** is used to introduce a second verb phrase. It never follows negation.

也 **yě** can be used to introduce a second verb phrase that adds additional information about the subject.

> 小王学中文。他也学日文。
> 小王學中文。他也學日文。
> **Xiǎo Wáng xué Zhōngwén. Tā yě xué Rìwén.**
> Little Wang studies Chinese. He also studies Japanese.

When the subjects are identical in reference, the second subject may be omitted:

> 小王学中文，也学日文。
> 小王學中文，也學日文。
> **Xiǎo Wáng xué Zhōngwén, yě xué Rìwén.**
> Little Wang studies Chinese and also studies Japanese.

也 **yě** can be used to indicate that two different subjects share similar properties or perform the same action.

小王很高。小李也很高。
Xiǎo Wáng hěn gāo. Xiǎo Lǐ yě hěn gāo.
Little Wang is very tall. Little Li also is very tall.

小王上大学。小李也上大学。
小王上大學。小李也上大學。
Xiǎo Wáng shàng dàxué. Xiǎo Lǐ yě shàng dàxué.
Little Wang attends college. Little Li also attends college.

⇨ | 36.1

Since 也 **yě** introduces additional information it can sometimes be translated by 'and' in English. However, it is very different from English 'and.' 'And' can connect almost any kind of phrase. 也 **yě** can only occur before verbs or verb phrases.

Compare this Mandarin example and its English translation.

我学中文，也学中国历史。
我學中文，也學中國歷史。
Wǒ xué Zhōngwén, yě xué Zhōngguó lìshǐ.
I study Chinese and I also study Chinese history.

Chinese conjunctions that join noun phrases and convey the meaning of the English 'and' include 和 **hé** and 跟 **gēn**.

我学中文和中国历史。
我學中文和中國歷史。
Wǒ xué Zhōngwén hé Zhōngguó lìshǐ.
I study Chinese and Chinese history.

⇨ | 36.7

15.2.2 都 *dōu* 'all, both'

都 **dōu** can indicate that a verb phrase is true for the entire subject.

我们都学中文。
我們都學中文。
Wǒmen dōu xué Zhōngwén.
We all study Chinese.

小王和小李都学中文。
小王和小李都學中文。
Xiǎo Wáng hé Xiǎo Lǐ dōu xué Zhōngwén.
Little Wang and Little Li both study Chinese.

都 **dōu** can indicate that a verb is true for multiple objects. Typically, when 都 **dōu** refers to objects, the objects occur before the verb as the topic of the sentence.

中文，日文，他都学。
中文，日文，他都學。
Zhōngwén, Rìwén, tā dōu xué.
Chinese, Japanese, he studies them both.

⇨ | 53.1.2.1

都 **dōu** before a verb without an object can be used to express the meaning 'completely.'

> 我都懂。
> **Wǒ dōu dǒng.**
> I understand everything.

都 **dōu** can occur with a question word to indicate that something is universally true.

> 她什么都会。
> 她甚麼都會。
> **Tā shénme dōu huì.**
> She can do everything.

> 她什么时候都很忙。
> 她甚麼時候都很忙。
> **Tā shénme shíhòu dōu hěn máng.**
> She is always busy.

⇨ | 42.4

都 **dōu** can occur before or after negation. The relative position of negation and 都 **dōu** reflects a difference in meaning.

The sequence 都 **dōu** + *Negation* conveys the meaning 'all not.'

都 **dōu** before negation may indicate that the negated verb phrase is true for the entire subject.

> 他们都没学中文。
> 他們都沒學中文。
> **Tāmen dōu méi xué Zhōngwén.**
> They all have not studied Chinese.

都 **dōu** before negation can also indicate that the negated verb is true for the entire object. Often, when 都 **dōu** refers to the object, the object is topicalized.

> 猪肉，牛肉我都不吃。
> 豬肉，牛肉我都不吃。
> **Zhūròu, niúròu wǒ dōu bù chī.**
> Pork, beef, I don't eat either.

都 **dōu** after negation indicates that negation is not true for the entire subject or that it is not true for the entire object. The sequence *negation* + 都 **dōu** can often be translated into English as 'not all.'

> 我们不都是中国人。她是美国人，他是英国人。只有我是中国人。
> 我們不都是中國人。她是美國人，他是英國人。只有我是中國人。
> **Wǒmen bù dōu shì Zhōngguó rén. Tā shì Měiguó rén, tā shì Yīngguó rén.**
> **Zhǐ yǒu wǒ shì Zhōngguó rén.**
> We are not all Chinese. She is American, he is English. Only I am Chinese.

> 美国人不都有钱。有的有钱，有的没有钱。
> 美國人不都有錢。有的有錢，有的沒有錢。
> **Měiguó rén bù dōu yǒu qián. Yǒu de yǒu qián, yǒu de méi yǒu qián.**
> Americans don't all have money. Some have money, some don't have money.

15.2.3 还/還 *hái* 'in addition, still, also, else'

还/還 **hái** marks the continuation of a situation or introduces additional actions performed by the subject. It can never follow negation.

> 他们还在这儿。
> 他們還在這兒。
> **Tāmen hái zài zhèr.**
> They are still here.

> 你还学中文吗？
> 你還學中文嗎？
> **Nǐ hái xué Zhōngwén ma?**
> Are you still studying Chinese?

> 我要买书，还要买纸。
> 我要買書，還要買紙。
> **Wǒ yào mǎi shū, hái yào mǎi zhǐ.**
> I want to buy books. (I) also want to buy paper.

> 你还要买什么？
> 你還要買甚麼？
> **Nǐ hái yào mǎi shénme?**
> What else do you want to buy?

还/還 **hái** may introduce additional information about a noun phrase. In this function it is similar to 也 **yě** 'also.'

> 他会说中文，还会说日文。
> 他會説中文，還會説日文。
> **Tā huì shuō Zhōngwén, hái huì shuō Rìwén.**
> He can speak Chinese (and) can also speak Japanese.

还没(有)/還沒(有) **hái méi (yǒu)** translates into English as 'not yet' or 'still.'

> 他还没回来呢。
> 他還沒回來呢。
> **Tā hái méi huí lái ne.**
> He hasn't returned yet. (He still hasn't returned.)

➡ 36.2

NOTE 还有/還有 **hái yǒu** is a phrase that occurs at the beginning of a sentence or clause and introduces additional information. It can be translated into English as 'in addition.'

> 她的男朋友很和气。还有，他很帅！
> 她的男朋友很和氣。還有，他很帥！
> **Tā de nán péngyou hěn héqi. Hái yǒu, tā hěn shuài!**
> Her boyfriend is very friendly. In addition, he is really cute!

➡ 35.2.2, 36.3

15.2.4 就 *jiù* 'only, uniqueness'

When 就 **jiù** precedes a verb phrase that is not linked to another verb phrase, it conveys the meaning of uniqueness.

In some sentences, this meaning is best translated by the English word 'only':

> 我就有一块钱。
> 我就有一塊錢。
> **Wǒ jiù yǒu yī kuài qián.**
> I only have one dollar.

In some contexts, 就 **jiù** conveys precise identification of a noun phrase. If the noun phrase is a person or place, there may be no English equivalent for 就 **jiù**.

> 王: 你找谁？　　　　林: 我找王美玲。　　　　王: 我就是。
> 　　你找誰？
> Wáng: **Nǐ zhǎo shéi?**　Lín: **Wǒ zhǎo Wáng Měilíng.**　Wáng: **Wǒ jiù shì.**
> Wang: Who are you　　Lin: I am looking　　　　Wang: That's me.
> 　　　looking for?　　　　for Wang Meiling.

If the noun phrase is a specifier or a directional expression, 就 **jiù** may be translated as 'right' or 'precisely.'

> Q: 赵经理的办公室在哪儿？　　　　A: 她的办公室就在这儿。
> 　　趙經理的辦公室在哪兒？　　　　　　她的辦公室就在這兒。
> **Zhào jīnglǐ de bàngōngshì zài nǎr?**　**Tā de bàngōngshì jiù zài zhèr.**
> Where is Manager Zhao's office?　　　　Her office *is right here*.

> Q: 图书馆在哪儿？　　　　A: 就在火车站的对面。
> 　　圖書館在哪兒？　　　　　就在火車站的對面。
> **Túshūguǎn zài nǎr?**　**Jiù zài huǒchēzhàn de duìmiàn.**
> Where is the library?　　*Right across from the train station.*

就 **jiù** is also used to link two verb phrases and to signal a relationship of sequence between them.

> 我看了报以后就睡觉。
> 我看了報以後就睡覺。
> **Wǒ kàn le bào yǐhòu jiù shuì jiào.**
> After I read the newspaper I will go to sleep.

> 她很聪明。一学就会。
> 她很聰明。一學就會。
> **Tā hěn cōngming. Yī xué jiù huì.**
> She is really smart. As soon as she studies it she gets it.

⇨ 38.2.2.1

就 **jiù** usually precedes negation, but it may also follow negation.

> 这件事情不就是我一个人知道。
> 這件事情不就是我一個人知道。
> **Zhè jiàn shìqing bù jiù shì wǒ yī gè rén zhīdao.**
> (As for) this matter, it is not just I who knows.

15.2.5　只 *zhǐ* 'only'

只 **zhǐ** can be used interchangeably with 就 **jiù** to express the meaning 'only.'

我只有一块钱。
我只有一塊錢。
Wǒ zhǐ yǒu yī kuài qián.
I only have one dollar.

Like 就 **jiù**, 只 **zhǐ** typically precedes negation, but may also follow it.

这件事情不只是我一个人知道。
這件事情不只是我一個人知道。
Zhè jiàn shìqing bù zhǐ shì wǒ yī gè rén zhīdao.
(As for) this matter, it is not just I who knows.

15.2.6   才 *cái* 'only, only then'

才 **cái** indicates that something is less than expected. In sentences in which there is only a single verb, 才 **cái** may be translated into English as 'only.'

他才认识五个字。
他才認識五個字。
Tā cái rènshi wǔ gè zì.
He only knows (recognizes) five characters [and that is fewer than one would expect].

那个孩子才一岁。当然还不会说话。
那個孩子才一歲。當然還不會說話。
Nàge háizi cái yīsuì. Dāngrán hái bù huì shuō huà.
That child is only one year old. Of course s/he can't speak yet.

我今天才挣了三百元。
Wǒ jīntiān cái zhèng le sānbǎi yuán.
Today I only earned 300 yuan (300 dollars).

When 才 **cái** is used to link two verb phrases as in the following sentences, it may be translated as 'only then.'

她做完了功课才睡觉。
她做完了功課才睡覺。
Tā zuòwán le gōngkè cái shuì jiào.
She finishes doing her homework and only then goes to sleep.

那本书我看了两次才懂。
那本書我看了兩次才懂。
Nà běn shū wǒ kàn le liǎng cì cái dǒng.
That book, I read it two times and only then understood (it).

⇨ | 38.2.2.2

才 **cái** never follows negation.

15.2.7   而已 *éryǐ* 'and that is all'

In Taiwan, the sentence final expression 而已 **éryǐ** 'and that is all' is commonly used to reinforce the sense of *only* contributed by 就 **jiù**, 只 **zhǐ**, and 才 **cái**.

我只有五块钱而已。
我只有五塊錢而已。
Wǒ zhǐ yǒu wǔ kuài qián éryǐ.
I only have five dollars (and that is all.)

他就写了一个字而已。
他就寫了一個字而已。
Tā jiù xiě le yī gè zì éryǐ.
He only wrote one character (and that is all.)

The meaning 'only if' is expressed with the sentence initial phrase 除非 **chúfēi**.

⇨ 41.4

16

Conjunctions

Conjunctions are words that join phrases belonging to the same grammatical category and indicate a relationship between them. Mandarin conjunctions include the following.

16.1 Conjunctions that indicate an 'additive' or 'and' relationship

16.1.1 和 *hé*

王明和李安是大学生。
王明和李安是大學生。
Wáng Míng hé Lǐ Ān shì dàxuéshēng.
Wang Ming and Li An are college students.

16.1.2 跟 *gēn*

北京跟上海都是很值得去看的地方。
Běijīng gēn Shànghǎi dōu shì hěn zhíde qù kàn de dìfang.
Beijing and Shanghai are both places worth seeing.

跟 gēn also functions as a preposition.

⇨ 14

16.1.3 同 *tóng*

我同他的关系很不错。
我同他的關係很不錯。
Wǒ tóng tā de guānxi hěn bù cuò.
The relationship between him and me is not bad (really good).

16.1.4 与/與 *yǔ*

我们对中国的文化与历史都很有兴趣。
我們對中國的文化與歷史都很有興趣。
Wǒmen duì Zhōngguó de wénhuà yǔ lìshǐ dōu hěn yǒu xīngqù.
We are really interested in Chinese culture and history.

NOTE 同 **tóng** is used in southern China and is not common in the north. 与/與 **yǔ** is used in literary phrases.

16.2 Conjunctions that indicate a disjunctive or 'or' relationship

16.2.1 还是/還是 *háishi* 'or'

还是/還是 **háishi** is used in questions that ask the addressee to choose between two alternatives, only one of which can be true or possible. It conveys the sense of 'either . . . or'.

Q: 你是来旅游的还是来学习的?
你是來旅遊的還是來學習的?
Nǐ shì lái lǚyóu de háishi lái xuéxí de?
Did you come for vacation or to study?

A: 我是来学习的。
我是來學習的。
Wǒ shì lái xuéxí de.
I came to study.

Q: 你要喝红茶还是喝花茶?
你要喝紅茶還是喝花茶?
Nǐ yào hē hóng chá háishi hē huā chá?
Do you want to drink black tea
or jasmine tea?
(In Chinese: red tea or jasmine tea?)

A: 我要喝红茶。
我要喝紅茶。
Wǒ yào hē hóng chá.
I want to drink black tea.

还是/還是 **háishi** is sometimes included in an answer to a 还是/還是 **háishi** question to mark the preferred alternative. In this usage, 还是/還是 **háishi** functions as an adverb and not as a conjunction.

Q: 你想这个问题，是现在讨论好
还是以后再讨论好?
你想這個問題，是現在討論好
還是以後再討論好?
**Nǐ xiǎng zhège wèntí, shì xiànzài tǎolùn
hǎo háishi yǐhòu zài tǎolùn hǎo?**
(As for) this question, do you think
we should talk about it now or later?

A: 我想还是以后再讨论好。

我想還是以後再討論好。
**Wǒ xiǎng háishi yǐhòu
zài tǎolùn hǎo.**
I think we should
talk about it later.

⇨ 15, 24.3

16.2.2 或者 *huòzhě* 'or'

或者 **huòzhě** 'or' is used in statements to present two alternatives, both of which are possible.

Q: 你要今天去长城还是明天去长城?
你要今天去長城還是明天去長城?
**Nǐ yào jīntiān qù chángchéng
háishi míngtiān qù chángchéng?**
Do you want to go to the Great Wall
today or tomorrow?

A: 今天去或者明天去都行。

**Jīntiān qù huòzhě
míngtiān qù dōu xíng.**
Today and tomorrow
are both okay.

Mandarin conjunctions are much more restricted than English conjunctions in the grammatical categories that they join. In Mandarin, the 'and' conjunctions only join noun phrases. The 'or' conjunctions only join verb phrases.

Most Mandarin connecting words are adverbs. They are presented in the relevant chapters on sentence connection.

⇨ | 28, 37, 38, 39, 40, 41

17

The passive

The structure of the Mandarin passive

In active sentences, the subject is typically the *agent*, the noun phrase that initiates the action, and the object of the verb is the noun phrase *affected by* the action of the verb.

> *subject + verb +* *object*
>
> *agent* *affected object*
>
> 他 偷走了 我的车。
> 他 偷走了 我的車。
> **Tā tōuzǒu le wǒ de chē.**
> He stole my car.

In Mandarin passive sentences, the affected noun phrase occurs as the subject of the verb, and the agent occurs as the object of a passive marking preposition. As in all sentences with prepositional phrases, the prepositional phrase occurs before the verb:

> *subject + prepositional phrase + verb*

⇨ 14

Mandarin has three passive marking prepositions (*passive markers*): 被 **bèi**, 叫 **jiào**, and 让/讓 **ràng**, all of which may be translated with the English 'by.'

> *subject* *+ passive NP* *+ verb*
>
> *affected NP* *agent*
>
> 我的车 [被/叫/让] 他 偷走了。
> 我的車 [被/叫/讓] 他 偷走了。
> **Wǒ de chē [bèi/jiào/ràng] tā tōuzǒu le.**
> My car was stolen by him.

In passive structures, the word 给/給 **gěi** is sometimes placed before the verb.

> 那本字典 [被/叫/让] 小李 给借走了。
> 那本字典 [被/叫/讓] 小李 给借走了。
> **Nà běn zìdiǎn [bèi/jiào/ràng] Xiǎo Lǐ gěi jièzǒu le.**
> That dictionary was borrowed by Little Li.

The presence of 给/給 **gěi** before the verb indicates that the sentence is passive, even when the passive markers 被 **bèi**, 叫 **jiào**, and 让/讓 **ràng** do not occur.

那个坏人被/给抓住了。
那個壞人被/給抓住了。
Nàge huàirén bèi/gěi zhuāzhù le.
That bad person was arrested.

The agent of a passive sentence need not be an animate entity. An inanimate entity, a force, or a situation may also function as the agent. For example:

他们的房子[被/叫/让]火烧了。
他們的房子[被/叫/讓]火燒了。
Tāmen de fángzi [bèi/jiào/ràng] huǒ shāo le.
Their house was burned down by fire.

他被学校撤职了。
他被學校撤職了。
Tā bèi xuéxiào chèzhí le.
He was fired by the school.

An agent is obligatory when using the passive markers 叫 **jiào** and 让/讓 **ràng**. An agent is optional for the marker 被 **bèi**.

他被撤职了。
他被撤職了。
Tā bèi chèzhí le.
He was fired.

When the passive marker is followed by an object, all of the passive markers are interchangeable. Therefore, all remaining examples in this chapter will be illustrated with only one passive marker.

17.2 The passive and negation

Sentences in passive form typically refer to situations that occurred in the past. Therefore, negation in passive sentences is typically 没(有) **méi (yǒu)**. 没(有) **méi (yǒu)** must occur before the passive marking preposition, and never before the verb.

Say this	*Not this*
你的车没有被警察拖走。	*你的车被警察没有拖走。
你的車沒有被警察拖走。	你的車被警察沒有拖走。
Nǐ de chē méi yǒu bèi jǐngchá tuōzǒu.	**Nǐ de chē bèi jǐngchá méi yǒu tuōzǒu.**
The policeman didn't tow your car away.	

⇨ 23.1, 33.3

The passive form can also be used when expressing prohibitions and warnings.

别被你的朋友骗了。
別被你的朋友騙了。
Bié bèi nǐ de péngyou piàn le.
Don't let your friend cheat you.

我们作的事不要被别人知道。
我們作的事不要被別人知道。
Wǒmen zuò de shì bù yào bèi biéren zhīdao.
We shouldn't let other people know what we did.

47.1.2

17.3 Conditions for using the passive in Mandarin

The Mandarin passive is used under the following circumstances:

*   To express adversity
    To indicate that the event has negative consequences or is in some way 'bad news' for the narrator, addressee, or affected noun:

    我的钱被小偷偷走了。
    我的錢被小偷偷走了。
    Wǒ de qián bèi xiǎotōu tōuzǒu le.
    My money was stolen by a thief.

*   To express surprise or astonishment

    我们的秘密被政府发现了。
    我們的祕密被政府發現了。
    Wǒmen de mìmì bèi zhèngfǔ fāxiàn le.
    Our secret was discovered by the government.

*   To emphasize the affected noun phrase rather than the agent

    这儿的树都被人砍了。
    這兒的樹都被人砍了。
    Zhèr de shù dōu bèi rén kǎn le.
    The trees here were all cut down by people.

*   To describe an action when the agent is unknown

    昨天银行被抢了。
    昨天銀行被搶了。
    Zuótiān yínháng bèi qiǎng le.
    The bank was robbed yesterday.

*   To avoid mentioning the agent of an action

    我女儿被骗了。
    我女兒被騙了。
    Wǒ nǚ'ér bèi piàn le.
    My daughter was cheated.

17.4 **Differences between the passive markers 被 *bèi*, 叫 *jiào*, and 让/讓 *ràng***

- Frequency: 被 **bèi** occurs more frequently in written or formal contexts than the other passive markers. In colloquial speech, 叫 **jiào** and 让/讓 **ràng** are more commonly used. Dialects differ in the preferred passive marker.
- Adversity: 被 **bèi** connotes stronger adversity than the other three passive markers.

17.5 **Additional functions of 让/讓 *ràng*, 叫 *jiào*, and 给/給 *gěi***

In addition to their role in passive sentences, 让/讓 **ràng**, 叫 **jiào**, and 给/給 **gěi** have other functions.

- 叫 **jiào** is also used as a verb meaning 'to call,' or 'to order.'
- 让/讓 **ràng** is also used as a verb meaning 'to let' or 'to allow.'
- 给/給 **gěi** is also used as a verb meaning 'to give,' and as a preposition meaning 'to' or 'for/on behalf of.'

When the verb is not followed by an object noun phrase, 叫 **jiào** and 让/讓 **ràng** may sometimes be interpreted as either a passive marker or as a verb, and the sentence may be ambiguous.

> 教授让学生批评了。
> 教授讓學生批評了。
> **Jiàoshòu ràng xuéshéng pīpíng le.**
> The professor was criticized by the students.
> (让/讓 **ràng** = passive marker: by the students)
> *or*
> The professor now allows the students to criticize.
> (让/讓 **ràng** = allow: allows the students)

In most cases, however, the context will make clear the function of 叫 **jiào**, or 让/讓 **ràng**, or 给/給 **gěi**, and only one interpretation will make sense. For example, the following sentence only makes sense if 让/讓 **ràng** is interpreted as 'to allow' or 'to let' and not as the passive marker 'by.'

> 妈妈让孩子吃饼干。
> 媽媽讓孩子吃餅乾。
> **Māma ràng háizi chī bǐnggān.**
> Mom let the children eat cookies. (*by the children . . .)

17.6 **English passives and their Mandarin equivalents**

The association of Mandarin passives with the sense of adversity or bad news makes the passive structure more restricted and less common in Mandarin than in English. Compare the following:

Acceptable use of the passive in English	Inappropriate use of the passive in Mandarin
The book was written by my professor.	*这本书被我教授写了。 這本書被我教授寫了。 **Zhè běn shū bèi wǒ jiàoshòu xiě le.**
The check has already been received by the bank.	*支票已经被银行收到了。 支票已經被銀行收到了。 **Zhīpiào yǐjing bèi yínháng shōudào le.**
The fruit was sent as a gift by a friend.	*水果被朋友送来了。 水果被朋友送來了。 **Shuíguǒ bèi péngyou sònglai le.**

Mandarin has several different patterns that are used to emphasize an affected object or to avoid mentioning the agent that do not convey adversity. These include the following:

• Topicalization

支票，银行已经收到了。
支票，銀行已經收到了。
Zhīpiào, yínháng yǐjing shōudào le.
(As for) the check, the bank has already received it.

⇨ 53.1.2.1

• The 把 **bǎ** construction

朋友把水果送来了。
朋友把水果送來了。
Péngyou bǎ shuíguǒ sònglai le.
A friend sent the fruit as a gift.
(A friend took the fruit and sent it as a gift.)

⇨ 53.2.1

• The 是 **shì** ... 的 **de** construction

这本书是我教授写的 。
這本書是我教授寫的 。
Zhè běn shū shì wǒ jiàoshòu xiě de.
This book was written by my professor.
(This book, it was my professor who wrote it.)

⇨ 53.2.4

Part B

Situations and functions

18

Names, kinship terms, titles, and terms of address

Names: 姓名 *xìngmíng*

The order of a Chinese name is:

family name + given name

姓	名字
xìng	**míngzi**
王	莉花
Wáng	**Lìhuā**
张/張	伟明/偉明
Zhāng	**Wěimíng**

In this book we translate Chinese names using Chinese word order. That is, 王莉花 **Wáng Lìhuā** is translated as 'Wang Lihua' and not 'Lihua Wang.'

18.1.1 Family names

There are over 3500 Chinese family names. However, of these, only about 100 are widely occurring. This is probably the basis of the expression 老百姓 **lǎobǎixìng** 'the old 100 family names,' which is used to refer to 'the people' or 'the common man.'

The three most common Chinese family names are 李 **Lǐ**, 王 **Wáng**, and 张/張 **Zhāng**. The next most common family names, representing the overwhelming majority of Chinese people, are 刘/劉 **Liú**, 陈/陳 **Chén**, 杨/楊 **Yáng**, 赵/趙 **Zhào**, 黄 **Huáng**, 周 **Zhōu**, 吴/吳 **Wú**, 徐 **Xú**, 孙/孫 **Sūn**, 胡 **Hú**, 朱 **Zhū**, 高 **Gāo**, 林 **Lín**, 何 **Hé**, 郭 **Guō**, and 马/馬 **Mǎ**.

Most family names are a single character/single syllable in length. However, there are a small number of two character/two syllable Chinese family names. The most common are 司马/司馬 **Sīmǎ**, 司徒 **Sītú**, 欧阳/歐陽 **Oūyáng**, and 皇甫 **Huángfǔ**.

18.1.2 Given names

A given name consists of one or two characters/syllables. There is no fixed inventory of given names in Chinese as there is in English such as Ruth, Michael, Lisa, and Mark. Instead, names express meaning, and families select as names, words or phrases with positive connotations that they wish to associate with their child. While this method of naming is also used in the West, it is the exception rather than the rule.

In the traditional naming process, the first character of a given name is a generational name: all children in the family who are of the same gender and in the same generation share the same first character in their given name. The second character reflects some other positive characteristic. Thus, brothers might be named 亦豪 **Yì Háo** (talent) and 亦強 **Yì Qiáng** (strength). Sisters might be named 颖怡/穎怡 **Yǐng Yí** (joyful) and 颖美/穎美 **Yǐng Měi** (beautiful).

Modern naming practice often does not include a generational name. This is especially common in mainland China. Instead, given names reflect positive attributes, and may be one or two syllables in length.

Given names are personal and somewhat private. In general, they are only used as terms of address by good friends and close acquaintances, and in closed settings such as a family, classroom, or office, where people are members of a well-defined group. Often, people use kinship terms and titles rather than names when addressing and referring to others.

18.2 Kinship terms

Here are the most commonly used kinship terms and the distinctions that they reflect.

18.2.1 Kinship terms for immediate family

Male				*Female*		
父亲/父親	**fùqin**	father		母亲/母親	**mǔqīn**	mother
爸爸	**bàba**	dad		妈妈/媽媽	**māma**	mom
哥哥	**gēge**	brother older than self		姐姐	**jiéjie**	sister older than self
弟弟	**dìdi**	brother younger than self		妹妹	**mèimei**	sister younger than self

The reference point for siblings is oneself. For example, an older brother is a brother older than oneself. If you are male and have an older brother and a younger brother, then your younger brother has two older brothers.

Your family from your perspective

> 我有一个哥哥、一个弟弟。
> 我有一個哥哥、一個弟弟。
> **Wǒ yǒu yī gè gēge, yī gè dìdi.**
> I have one older brother, one younger brother.

Your family from your younger brother's perspective

> 我有两个哥哥，没有弟弟。
> 我有兩個哥哥，沒有弟弟。
> **Wǒ yǒu liǎng gè gēge, méi yǒu dìdi.**
> I have two older brothers and no younger brother.

18.2.2 **Kinship terms for extended family**

		Paternal				Maternal
爷爷/爺爺	**yéye**	grandfather (father's father)		外公	**wàigōng**	grandfather (mother's father)
奶奶	**nǎinai**	grandmother (father's mother)		外婆	**wàipó**	grandmother (mother's mother)
叔叔	**shūshu**	uncle (on father's side)		舅舅	**jiùjiu**	uncle (on mother's side)
姑姑	**gūgu**	aunt (on father's side)		阿姨	**āyí**	aunt (on mother's side)
堂哥	**tánggē**	male cousin older than self		表哥	**biǎogē**	male cousin older than self
堂弟	**tángdì**	male cousin younger than self		表弟	**biǎodì**	male cousin younger than self
堂姐	**tángjiě**	female cousin older than self		表姐	**biǎojiě**	female cousin older than self
堂妹	**tángmèi**	female cousin younger than self		表妹	**biǎomèi**	female cousin younger than self
婆婆	**pópo**	mother-in-law (husband's mother)				

18.3 **Titles**

Titles refer to gender and marital status, education, or occupation. When a name includes a title, the order of information is as follows:

family name	(+ given name)	+	title
王	莉花		博士
Wáng	**Lìhuā**		**bóshì**
			Ph.D. (Dr.)

Dr. Wang Lihua

Chinese people often use titles when addressing others or when talking about others. Titles may also be used alone or with the family name and given name.

18.3.1 **Titles that indicate gender and marital status**

The most common titles used to reflect gender and marital status are:

先生	王先生
xiānsheng	**Wáng xiānsheng**
Mr.	Mr. Wang

太太	王太太
tàitai	**Wáng tàitai**
夫人	王夫人
fūren	**Wáng fūren**
Mrs.	Mrs. Wang

小姐	王小姐
xiǎojie	**Wáng xiǎojie**
女士	王女士
nǚshì	**Wáng nǚshì**
Miss	Miss Wang

18.3.2 Professional titles

Commonly used professional titles include:

医生/醫生	大夫
yīshēng	**dàifu**
doctor	doctor

护士/護士	师傅/師傅
hùshì	**shīfu**
nurse	master (skilled person)

老师/老師	教授
lǎoshī	**jiàoshòu**
teacher	professor

律师/律師	法官
lùshī	**fǎguān**
lawyer	judge, justice

主席	校长/校長
zhǔxí	**xiàozhǎng**
chairperson of a government, political party, etc.	principal

警察	公关/公關
jǐngchá	**gōngguān**
police officer	receptionist

秘书/祕書	秘书长/祕書長
mìshū	**mìshūzhǎng**
secretary	secretary general

主任	司机/司機
zhǔrèn	**sījī**
director of a department, chairperson of a department	driver; chauffeur

大使	总统/總統
dàshǐ	**zǒngtǒng**
ambassador	president, chief of state

经理/經理	总经理/總經理
jīnglǐ	**zǒngjīnglǐ**
manager	general manager (abbreviated to 总/總 **zǒng** 王总/王總 **Wáng zǒng** General Manager Wang)

博士 **bóshì**
doctor of philosophy (Ph.D.)

18.4 Addressing others

18.4.1 Addressing friends

Close friends may address each other using family name and given name together, or, if they are very close, by given name alone.

> 王莉花，早。
> **Wáng Lìhuā, zǎo.**
> Wang Lihua, good morning.

> 莉花，最近怎么样？
> 莉花，最近怎麼樣？
> **Lìhuā, zuì jìn zěnmeyàng?**
> Lihua, how have you been recently?

Friends or close acquaintances may also address each other using the prefix 老 **lǎo** 'old' or 小 **xiǎo** 'small' before the family name as follows:

老高	**Lǎo Gāo**	Old Gao	小高	**Xiǎo Gāo**	Little Gao
老王	**Lǎo Wáng**	Old Wang	小王	**Xiǎo Wáng**	Little Wang

老 **lǎo** or 小 **xiǎo** do not literally mean 'old' and 'little' here. 老 **lǎo** is used for those older than oneself, and 小 **xiǎo** is used for those younger than oneself.

18.4.2 Addressing family and others with kinship terms

In China, people use kinship terms rather than names to address relatives. Kinship terms are also used in informal contexts to address people who are not relatives. The term that is used depends upon the age and gender of the person whom you are addressing. Here are the kinship terms most commonly used when talking with people who are not your relatives.

大哥 **dà gē**
older brother (title for man near your age but older than you)

大姐 **dà jiě**
older sister (title for woman near your age but older than you)

叔叔 **shūshu**
uncle (title for man who is about your father's age)

阿姨 **āyí**
aunt (title for woman who is about your mother's age or older)

爷爷/爺爺 **yéye**
grandfather (title for man who is about your grandfather's age)

奶奶 **nǎinai**
grandmother (title for woman who is about your grandmother's age)

18.4.3 Colloquial terms of address used with strangers

The following terms are used in informal contexts to address strangers

小伙子	**xiǎo huǒzi**	young fellow (used to address young boys – very colloquial)
小朋友	**xiǎo péngyǒu**	little friend (commonly used to address children)
朋友	**péngyou**	friend (often used by shopkeepers to address customers)

18.4.4   **Using titles as terms of address**

Titles are commonly used as terms of address. The titles 先生 **xiānsheng** 'Mr.,' 太太 **tàitai** 'Mrs.,' 小姐 **xiǎojie** 'miss,' and 师傅/師傅 **shīfu** 'master' are used alone without any additional name to address strangers in a polite way. 师傅/師傅 **shīfu** 'master' is often used in mainland China as a polite way to address a man in relatively informal contexts. 小姐 **xiǎojie** is used to address young women in service positions such as in restaurants and shops. 夫人 **fūren** 'Mrs.' and 女士 **nǚshì** 'Miss' are very formal and their use is restricted to formal contexts such as speeches and formal events. The titles presented in 18.3.2 can all be used as terms of address. For occupations that are not used as titles or terms of address, see

⇨   19.3

18.5   **Addressing new acquaintances and negotiating terms of address**

When you meet someone for the first time, you need to determine how to address them. Since given names are not freely used, and family names are generally not used by themselves, an initial conversation usually includes some negotiation about terms of address. The most common expressions are as follows.

The neutral and most common way to inquire about someone's family name is:

> 你姓什么？
> 你姓甚麼？
> **Nǐ xìng shénme?**
> What is your family name? (neutral question)

A more formal and polite way to inquire about someone's family name is:

> 你貴姓？/你贵姓
> **Nǐ guì xìng?**
> What is your family name? (polite, formal)

The most common way to reply to either of these questions is:

> 我姓王。
> **Wǒ xìng Wáng.**
> My family name is Wang.

A very polite and humble response to the formal question is:

> 敝姓(王)。
> **Bì xìng (Wáng).**
> My humble family name is (Wang).

While the polite form of the question is fairly common, the polite humble form of the response is rarely used.

The neutral and most common way to inquire about someone's family name and given name is:

你姓什么，叫什么名字？
你姓甚麼，叫甚麼名字？
Nǐ xìng shénme, jiào shénme míngzi?
What is your family name and what is your given name?

The neutral and most common way to respond to this question is:

我姓王，叫莉花。
Wǒ xìng Wáng, jiào Lìhuā.
My family name is Wang, my given name is Lihua.

The very polite way to inquire about someone's family name and given name is:

请问，尊姓大名？
請問，尊姓大名？
Qǐng wèn, zūnxìng dàmíng?
Excuse me, What is your (honorable) family name and your (great) given name?

The polite, humble response to this question is:

敝姓王，小名建国。
敝姓王，小名建國。
Bì xìng Wáng, xiǎo míng Jiànguó.
My humble family name is Wang, and my small name is Jianguo.

People often do not inquire about given names when they first meet. When you have established a friendship, you may inquire about a given name by asking:

你叫什么名字？
你叫甚麼名字？
Nǐ jiào shénme míngzi?
What is your name?

The reply to this question is either the family name plus the given name, or the given name alone:

我叫王玫玲。
Wǒ jiào Wáng Měilíng.
I am called Wang Meiling. (My name is Wang Meiling.)

To make a general inquiry about someone's identity, ask:

你是谁？
你是誰？
Nǐ shì shéi?
Who are you?

你是。。。？
Nǐ shì . . . ?
You are . . . ?

你是哪位？
Nǐ shì něi wèi?
Who are you? (polite)

To learn how someone prefers to be addressed by you, ask:

> 我应该怎么称呼你?
> 我應該怎麼稱呼你?
> **Wǒ yīnggāi zěnme chēnghu nǐ?**
> How should I address you?

18.6 Name cards and business cards

Name cards and business cards are widely used in China, and people often exchange name cards when they meet for the first time. The information on a person's name card will help you to determine how to address him or her.

When handing your card to someone, use both hands, and give it to the person so that the writing is facing him or her. Receive a card with both hands, read the card, and thank the person who gave you the card or comment on the information on the card so that it is clear that you have read it. If business cards are exchanged during a meeting or a meal, it is customary to place the cards you receive on the table arranged according to hierarchy so that you can refer to them as you talk.

The organization of the Chinese name card or business card is typically as follows:

```
┌─────────────────────────────────────────────────┐
│  Business Organization                          │
│                                                 │
│  Title                                          │
│                                                 │
│                                                 │
│              NAME education degree              │
│                                                 │
│                      (Contact information)      │
│                                                 │
│                      Address                    │
│                                                 │
│                      Telephone number           │
│                                                 │
│                      Mobile phone number        │
│                                                 │
│                      Fax number                 │
│                                                 │
└─────────────────────────────────────────────────┘
```

XX中文系

主任教授

张惟康

电话：8666-8686

地址：中山南路10号

电传：8666-8687

手机：13058886666

In mainland China, cards written in Chinese are usually printed horizontally. In Taiwan, cards may also be printed vertically.

Business

Title

NAME

FAX NUMBER   PHONE NUMBER   MOBILE PHONE   ADDRESS

18.7 Addressing letters and envelopes

18.7.1 Special terms for the recipient (addressee) and the sender

The name of the recipient is typically followed by recipient's title, or the title plus the expression 收 **shōu**, 启/啟 **qǐ**, or 大启/大啟 **dà qǐ**. 启/啟 **qǐ** and 大启/大啟 **dà qǐ** are more formal than 收 **shōu**. All three expressions mean *recipient*.

The name of the sender may be followed by the expression 寄 **jì** or 缄/緘 **jiān**. 缄/緘 **jiān** is more formal than 寄 **jì**. Both expressions mean *sender*.

18.7.2 **The format of a horizontal envelope (commonly used in mainland China).**

☐☐☐☐☐☐   stamp

Address of the recipient

Name of Recipient 启/啟 (收)

Address of the sender, name of sender 缄/緘 **jiān**

☐☐☐☐☐☐   stamp

北京市新街口南大街十号

王建国先生大 启

南京中山路五号孙古缄

18.7.3 **The format of a vertical envelope (commonly used in Taiwan)**

stamp		□ □ □
Sender Address & name 緘/緘 □ □ □	Recipient Name 启/ 啟	Recipient Address

In vertical format, addresses are written from top to bottom.

18.7.4 Terms used in addresses and their order of presentation

Addresses in China are presented from the largest unit to the smallest. If the postal code is included in the address, it occurs before the name of the city.

The major regional distinctions used in addresses in order of size are as follows:

州	县/縣	市	乡/鄉	镇/鎮
zhōu	**xiàn**	**shì**	**xiāng**	**zhèn**
prefecture/state	county	city	village	town/township

The terms used to refer to the units in street addresses differ somewhat in Taiwan and in mainland China. Here is a summary of the most common terms. The term 胡同 **hútòng** 'alley' is used in Beijing, though as streets are restructured, alleys are being eliminated.

Terms used in Taiwan				*Terms used in mainland China*		
段	**duàn**	section		区/區	**qū**	district
区/區	**qū**	district		(大)街	**(dà)jiē**	street
巷	**xiàng**	alley		路	**lù**	road, street
弄	**lòng**	alley, lane		胡同	**hútòng**	alley
里	**lǐ**	neighborhood		号/號	**hào**	number
路	**lù**	road, street				
号/號	**hào**	number				

Two sample addresses in Beijing:

北京市西城区红星胡同18号
北京市西城區紅星胡同18號
Běijīng shì xīchéng qū hóngxīng hútóng 18 hào
18 Red Star Alley, West District, Beijing

北京市新街口南大街十号
北京市新街口南大街十號
Běijīng shì xīn jiē kǒu nán dà jiē shí hào
10 South Xinjiekou Street, Beijing

In Beijing, street names often make reference to their location inside or outside of a traditional city gate. Here is an example:

建国门外大街
建國門外大街
Jiànguó mén wài dà jiē
The big street outside of the Jianguo Gate.

Three sample addresses in Taiwan:

台北市和平东路一段162号
臺北市和平東路一段162號
Táiběi shì Hépíng dōng lù yī duàn 162 hào
162 Section 1 Hoping East Road, Taipei

40744 台中市西屯区台中港路三段181号
40744 臺中市西屯區臺中港路三段181號
40744 Táizhōng shì xī tún qū Táizhōng gǎng lù sān duàn 181 hào
181 Section 3, Taichung Harbor Road, Xitun district, Taichung, 40744

高雄县清水镇永康乡，镇南里冈山南路42号
高雄縣清水鎮永康鄉，鎮南裏岡山南路42號
Gāoxióng xiàn qīngshuǐ zhèn yǒngkāng xiāng, zhèn nán lǐ gāng shān nán lù 42 hào
42 South Gangshan Road, Zhennan Neighborhood, Yongkang Village, Qingshui Township, Gaoxiong (County)

For greetings and goodbyes in letters, see

⇨ 20.3

19

Introductions

The general format of introductions

Formal introductions use the polite classifier for people, 位 **wèi**.

> 这位是刘晓东。这位是王玫玲。
> 這位是劉曉東。這位是王玫玲。
> **Zhè wèi shì Liú Xiǎodōng. Zhè wèi shì Wáng Méilíng.**
> This (person) is Liu Xiaodong. This (person) is Wang Meiling.

Neutral introductions have the following format.

> 这是刘晓东。这是王玫玲。
> 這是劉曉東。這是王玫玲。
> **Zhè shì Liú Xiǎodōng. Zhè shì Wáng Méilíng.**
> This is Liu Xiaodong. This is Wang Meiling.

The most common and neutral response to an introduction is:

> 你好。
> **Nǐ hǎo.**
> Hello. (lit. 'How are you?')

More formal responses to an introduction include:

> 很高兴认识你。
> 很高興認識你。
> **Hěn gāoxìng rènshi nǐ.**
> I'm very happy to meet you.

> 久仰。
> **Jiǔ yǎng.**
> I have wanted to make your acquaintance for a long time.

久仰 **jiǔ yǎng** is often said twice.

> 久闻大名。
> 久聞大名。
> **Jiǔ wén dà míng.**
> I have heard so much about you.

19.2   Sample introductions

The following conversations illustrate informal and formal introductions. It is appropriate to include information about a person's work or field of study in an introduction. Following the conversations are the Mandarin terms for many common occupations and fields of study.

conversation 1 (neutral level of formality)

> A: 这是李小姐，我的同学。她学地质学。
>
> 這是李小姐，我的同學。她學地質學。
>
> **Zhè shì Lǐ xiǎojie, wǒ de tóngxué. Tā xué dìzhìxué.**
>
> 这是我哥哥，张大年。他学语言学。
>
> 這是我哥哥，張大年。他學語言學。
>
> **Zhè shì wǒ gēge, Zhāng Dànián. Tā xué yǔyánxué.**
>
> This is Miss Li, my classmate. She studies geology.
>
> This is my older brother, Zhang Danian. He studies linguistics.
>
> B: 你好。
>
> **Nǐ hǎo.**
>
> Hello.
>
> C: 你好。
>
> **Nǐ hǎo.**
>
> Hello.

conversation 2 (more formal)

> A: 我给你们介绍介绍，这位是唐教授。这位是从美国来的司密斯先生。
>
> 我給你們介紹介紹，這位是唐教授。這位是從美國來的司密斯先生。
>
> **Wǒ gěi nǐmen jièshào jièshào, zhè wèi shì Táng jiàoshòu. Zhè wèi shì cóng Měiguó lái de Sī Mìsī xiānsheng.**
>
> Allow me to introduce the two of you. This is Professor Tang. This is Mr. Smith from America.
>
> B: 久仰，久仰。
>
> **Jiǔ yǎng, jiǔ yǎng.**
>
> I have wanted to make your acquaintance for a long time now.

conversation 3 (formal)

> A: 这位是有名的音乐家，马友友，这位是名导演，张艺谋。
>
> 這位是有名的音樂家，馬友友，這位是名導演，張藝謀。
>
> **Zhè wèi shì yǒu míng de yīnyuè jiā, Mǎ Yǒu-yǒu, zhè wèi shì míng dáoyǎn, Zhāng Yìmóu.**
>
> This is the famous musician, Ma You-you. This is the famous film Director, Zhang Yimou.
>
> B: 久仰大名。
>
> **Jiǔ yǎng dàmíng.**
>
> I have heard your name and have wanted to meet you for a long time.
>
> C: 彼此，彼此。
>
> **Bícǐ, bícǐ.**
>
> The feeling is mutual. (in reply to someone well-known)

19.3 Common occupations and fields of study

Common professions

科学家/科學家 **kēxuéjiā** scientist	作者 **zuòzhě** writer
画家/畫家 **huàjiā** artist	音乐家/音樂家 **yīnyuè jiā** musician
记者/記者 **jìzhě** reporter	会计/會計 **kuàijì** accountant
农民/農民 **nóngmín** farmer	工人 **gōngrén** worker
牙医/牙醫 **yá yī** dentist	救火员/救火員 **jiùhuǒyuán** fireman
木匠 **mùjiang** carpenter	水工 **shuǐgōng** plumber
化工 **huàgōng** chemical engineer	电工/電工 **diàngōng** electrical engineer; electrician
业主/業主 **yèzhǔ** owner of a business	小贩/小販 **xiǎofàn** street vendor

NOTE   These are not used as titles or as terms of address. For professions that are also used as titles and terms of address, see

⇨ | 18.3.2

Fields of study

会计学/會計學 **kuàijì xué** accounting	人类学/人類學 **rénlèixué** anthropology
人文科学/人文科學 **rénwén kēxué** art (includes all performing arts)	亚洲学系/亞洲學系 **yàzhōu xuéxì** Asian Studies
生物学/生物學 **shēngwù xué** biology	化学/化學 **huàxué** chemistry

资讯/資訊
zīxùn
computer science

地理学/地理學
dìlǐ xué
geography

地质学/地質學
dìzhì xué
geology

经济学/經濟學
jīngjì xué
economics

历史/歷史
lìshǐ
history

数学/數學
shùxué
math

医学/醫學
yīxué
medicine

音乐学/音樂學
yīnyuè xué
music

哲学/哲學
zhé xué
philosophy

物理学/物理學
wùlǐ xué
physics

政治学/政治學
zhèngzhì xué
political science

心理学/心理學
xīnlǐ xué
psychology

宗教学/宗教學
zōngjiào xué
religious studies

社会学/社會學
shèhuì xué
sociology

戏剧学/戲劇學
xìjù xué
theater

语言学/語言學
yǔyán xué
linguistics

20

Greetings and goodbyes

This chapter contains the most common expressions used by Mandarin Chinese speakers when greeting others and saying goodbye in different contexts. The expressions here are those used by the majority of Mandarin speakers, but differences between mainland and Taiwan Mandarin are noted where relevant. In Chinese, greetings and goodbyes are typically not accompanied by body contact such as a handshake, hug, or kiss, though handshakes are becoming more common in cities.

Greetings are used to acknowledge the presence of another person. Chinese uses different kinds of greetings depending upon the relationship of speaker and addressee, the time of day in which the greeting is made, and whether or not contact is face-to-face. Greetings that take the form of questions typically need no response.

20.1 Greetings in conversations

20.1.1 Basic greeting

To greet casual acquaintances or to greet others in a shopping or business environment, or when meeting someone for the first time, or when answering the telephone, say:

> 你好。
> **Nǐ hǎo.**
> Hi. (How are you?)

The response to this greeting is:

> 你好
> **Nǐ hǎo.**
> Hi. (How are you?)

or

> 好。谢谢。你呢?
> 好。謝謝。你呢?
> **Hǎo. Xièxie. Nǐ ne?**
> Fine. Thanks. And you?

NOTE | Until recently, the expression 你好 **nǐ hǎo** was primarily used when greeting foreigners, but in Chinese cities it is now widely used between native speakers of Chinese.

A more formal variation of this greeting uses the polite pronoun 您 **nín** 'you':

毛： 王经理，您好？
毛： 王經理，您好？
Máo: **Wáng jīnglǐ, nín hǎo?**
Mao: Manager Wang, how are you?

王： 好。
Wáng: **Hǎo.**
Wang: Fine.

20.1.2 Greetings with reference to time of day

The most common morning greeting is:

早。
Zǎo.
Good morning.

The response is:

早
Zǎo.
Good morning.

An alternative form of this greeting is:

早安。
Zǎo'ān.
Good morning.

or

早上好。
Zǎoshang hǎo.
Good morning.

There is no greeting associated with any other time of day.

20.1.3 Greeting people by calling them (叫 jiào)

In China, it is very common to greet others by making eye contact and calling them by name, title, or appropriate kinship term. To greet others in this way is to 叫 **jiào** 'call' them. This greeting can include 好 **hǎo** or 你好 **nǐ hǎo**.

罗老师！/羅老師！	张萌！/張萌！
Luó lǎoshī!	**Zhāng Méng!**
Professor Ross!	Zhang Meng!
王经理！/王經理！	阿姨好！
Wáng jīnglǐ!	**Āyí hǎo!**
Manager Wang!	How are you auntie!
小王！	老张你好！/老張你好！
Xiǎo Wáng!	**Lǎo Zhāng nǐ hǎo!**
Little Wang!	How are you Old Zhang!

20.1.4 Greeting others by referring to their present activity

Relatives, friends, or close acquaintances may greet each other by referring to their present activity. Here are some examples.

吃饭去。
吃飯去。
Chī fàn qù.
(I see that you are) Going off to eat.

上课吧！
上課吧！
Shàng kè ba!
Going to class, I assume.

回家呢?
Huí jiā ne?
Are you going home?

上班呢。
Shàng bān ne.
Going to work, right?

A variation of this kind of greeting is to ask about present activity.

你上哪儿去?
你上哪兒去?
Nǐ shàng nǎr qù?
Where are you going?

你到哪儿去?
你到哪兒去?
Nǐ dào nǎr qù?
Where are you going?

你去哪儿?
你去哪兒?
Nǐ qù nǎr?
Where are you going?

你今天去哪儿玩了?
你今天去哪兒玩了?
Nǐ jīntiān qù nǎr wán le?
Where are you heading off to play?

干吗(呢)?   (informal/casual)
幹嗎(呢)?
Gànmá (ne)?
What are you up to?

忙什么呢?
忙甚麼呢?
Máng shénme ne?
What are you busy doing?

20.1.5 Greeting by asking about eating a meal

When greeting others around normal meal times, you can ask if they have eaten.

(你)吃了吗?
Nǐ chī le ma?
Have you eaten yet?

(你)吃了没有?
Nǐ chī le méi yǒu
Have you eaten yet?

20.1.6 Telephone greetings

The most common phone greetings are:

喂?
Wèi/Wéi. (It may be spoken in a rising or falling tone.)
Hello.

喂，你好。
Wéi, nǐ hǎo.
Hello, how are you?

20.2 Saying goodbye in conversations

20.2.1 Basic goodbyes

The most general way to say goodbye and to end a conversation is:

再見。
Zài jiàn.
Goodbye. (lit. 'again see' → 'see you again')

In Taiwan, and increasingly in mainland China, people also say:

拜拜。
Báibái. (also pronounced **bàibài**)
Bye bye. (borrowed from English 'bye bye')

If the participants in a conversation expect to see each other in the near future, they may use variations of 再見 **zàijiàn** to say goodbye. These include:

一会儿见。
一會兒見。
Yīhuìr jiàn.
See you in a moment.

回头见。
回頭見。
Huí tóu jiàn.
See you in a moment. (lit. 'See you in the turn of a head.')

明天见。
明天見。
Míngtiān jiàn.
See you tomorrow.

后天见。
後天見。
Hòutiān jiàn.
See you the day after tomorrow.

Other expressions indicating future time can be used before 见/見 **jiàn.**

20.2.2 Saying goodbye to a guest

To say goodbye to a guest, use one of these expressions:

慢走。
Màn zǒu.
Don't hurry off.

再来玩。
再來玩。
Zài lái wán.
Come again. (informal)

有空再来。
有空再來。
Yǒu kòng zài lái.
Come again when you have time.

(请)好走。
(請)好走。
(Qǐng) hǎo zǒu.
(Please) take care.

To respond to a host when taking leave, use one of these expressions:

别送。
Bié sòng.
Don't see me off.

请留步。
請留步。
Qǐng liú bù.
Please do not bother to see me off. (more formal)

⇨ | 54.4.2

20.2.3 Saying goodbye to someone who is leaving on a trip

To say goodbye to someone who is leaving on a trip, say:

一路顺风。	or	一路平安。
一路順風。		
Yī lù shùn fēng.		**Yī lù píng'ān.**
Have a good trip.		Have a good trip.
(Have a smooth wind for the entire road.)		(Have peace for the entire road.)

20.2.4 Saying goodbye with reference to time of day

晚安。
Wǎn'ān.
Goodnight.

___

NOTE   晚安 **wǎn'ān** can only be used as a goodbye, and not as a greeting.

___

20.3 Greetings and goodbyes in letters

20.3.1 Greetings and salutations in letters

Letters begin with the name of the addressee.

In informal letters to someone with whom you have a close relationship, you may use the recipient's given name, or family name and given name. Sometimes these are followed by these kinship terms:

兄	**xiōng**	elder brother, a form of address used by males of the same generation
弟	**dì**	younger brother, a form of address used to a younger male
姊	**zǐ**	elder sister or 姐 **jiě**, a form of address used by female of the same generation
or		
妹	**mèi**	younger sister, a form of address used to a younger female

建国兄：
建國兄：
Jiànguó xiōng:
Elder brother Jianguo:

美英姊：
Měiyīng zǐ:
Elder sister Meiying:

A more formal letter may begin with the addressee's family name or family name and given name followed by his or her title.

王建国先生：
王建國先生：
Wáng Jiànguó xiānsheng:
Mr. Wang Jianguo:

More formal letters may also begin with the name and title of the addressee following by a standard salutation. Note that the use of the family name makes the greeting more formal than the use of the given name alone.

The following phrases may also be used after the name and title of the addressee.

Polite and formal

钧鉴/鈞鑒 *jūnjiàn* 'for your perusal'

王先生钧鉴：
王先生鈞鑒：
Wáng xiānsheng jūnjiàn:
Mr. Wang for your perusal:

王校长钧鉴：
王校長鈞鑒：
Wáng xiàozhǎng jūnjiàn:
Principal Wang for your perusal:

Polite but less formal

如晤 *rúwù* 'as if talking to you face-to-face'

建国兄如晤：
建國兄如晤：
Jiànguó xiōng rúwù:
Elder brother Jianguo, it is as if I were talking to you face-to-face:

惠鉴/惠鑒 *huìjiàn* 'please be kind enough to read the following letter'

美英姊惠鉴：
美英姊惠鑒：
Měiyīng zǐ huìjiàn:
Elder sister Meiying, please be kind enough to read the following letter:

The use of a formal title makes this salutation more formal:

> 美英女士惠鉴：
> 美英女士惠鑒：
> **Měiyīng nǚshì huìjiàn:**
> Ms. Meiying, please be kind enough to read the following letter:

This salutation is used in letters from a government department or organization to an individual.

台端 *táiduān 'for your gracious perusal'*

> 王先生台端：
> 王先生臺端：
> **Wáng xiānsheng táiduān:**
> Mr. Wang, for your gracious perusal:

20.3.2 Goodbyes in letters

The following expressions are used to close the letter. They occur after the body of the letter, before the name of the sender.

Expressions used to extend good wishes to the addressee

These expressions occur immediately after the body of the letter, before any additional greetings.

顺颂/順頌	**shùn sòng**	I take this opportunity to send regards and wish your well-being
祝	**zhù**	expressing good wishes
敬祝	**jìng zhù**	respectfully extending (good) wishes to you
敬颂/敬頌	**jìng sòng**	(I) extend good wishes
敬请/敬請	**jìng qǐng**	(I) respectfully extend (good) wishes
此颂/此頌	**cǐ sòng**	(I) extend good wishes

Wishes for good health and well being

The following phrases are standard expressions of good wishes. They occur after one of the previous phrases, before the name of the sender. Note that many are linked to a specific season or to the new year.

春安	**chūn'ān**	a peaceful spring
夏安	**xià'ān**	your health, your well-being in the summer season
秋安	**qiū'ān**	your welfare in this autumn season
冬安	**dōng'ān**	your well-being in this winter season
祺	**qí**	good fortune
教祺	**jiào qí**	(instructing you to have) good fortune [for teachers or educators]
岁祺/歲祺	**suìqí**	good fortune at the New Year
新禧	**xīnxǐ**	Happy New Year
道安	**dào'ān**	asking about your well-being
钧安	**jūn'ān**	your well-being
文安	**wén'ān**	your health

Expressions included with the signature

The following expressions are included after the name of the sender.

For letters written to someone of the same generation as oneself:

Less formal

手	**shǒu**	written by

More formal

敬上	**jìng shàng**	respectfully presented
拜上	**bài shàng**	respectfully yours
拜启/拜啟	**bài qǐ**	respectfully report
再拜	**zài bài**	bow twice (a polite closing to a letter)

For very formal letters written to a superior

谨启/謹啟	**jǐn qǐ**	cautiously and prudently respectfully present
谨禀/謹稟	**jǐn bǐng**	respectfully submitted

In addition, if the addressee is referred to as 兄 **xiōng**, 弟 **dì**, 姊 **zǐ**, or 妹 **mèi** in the salutation, the writer typically prefixes the reciprocal generation term to his or her name in the closing. In other words, a male writer who greets his addressee with 兄 **xiōng** typically closes the letter by prefixing his name with 弟 **dì**. A female writer who greets her addressee with 姊 **zǐ** typically closes the letter by prefixing her name with妹 **mèi**.

In the body of a letter, the name of the sender and the date of the letter are placed at the end of the letter.

Sample letters illustrating the format and the use of these expressions are presented here.

20.3.3 Sample letter outlines

20.3.3.1 Informal letter to a friend

丽历姊如晤：
麗歷姊如晤：
Lìlì zǐ rúwù:
Older sister Lili as I talk to you face-to-face:
    [body of the letter]

               顺颂
               順頌
               Shùn sòng
    I take this opportunity to send regards and wish your well-being

夏安
Xià'ān
peace in this summer season
              妹　王嘉玲　上
                  一月十二日
             mèi　Wáng Jiālíng　shàng
                 yī yuè shí'èr rì
             Younger sister Wang Jialing
                 January 12

20.3.3.2 **Formal letter**

张老师钧鉴：
張老師鈞鑒：
Zhāng lǎoshī jūn jiàn:
Professor Zhang, for your perusal:
    [body of the letter]

          敬颂
          敬頌
          jìng sòng
          (I) extend good wishes

教祺
jiào qí
good fortune

        学生　王美丽　拜上
                 五月十七日
        學生　王美麗　拜上
                 五月十七日
        xuésheng　Wáng Měilì　bài shàng
                wǔ yuè shíqī rì
        (Your) student, Wang Meili, I bow to you
        May 17

20.3.3.3 **Very formal letter**

刘建安校长台端：
劉建安校長臺端：
Liú Jiàn'ān xiàozhǎng táiduān:
Principal Liu Jian'an, for your perusal:
    [body of the letter]

          此颂
          此頌
          Cǐ sòng
          (I) extend good wishes to

道安
dào'ān
Your health

        郭友情　谨禀
                 九月二十八日
        郭友情　謹稟
                 九月二十八日
        Guō Yǒuqíng　jǐn bǐng
                jiǔ yuè èrshí bā rì
        Guo Youqing　respectfully submitted
                September 28, 2004

For the format used in addressing envelopes, see

⇨　18.7

21

Basic strategies for communication

Languages have specific expressions that speakers use to start conversations and to keep them going. These expressions often reflect the degree of formality of the situation, the relationship of the participants in the conversation, and the attitudes of the speakers. This section presents the most commonly used expressions in Mandarin.

21.1 Attracting someone's attention

21.1.1 Attracting attention by using a name or title

In Mandarin, the most common way to attract someone's attention is to address them with their name or a title or kinship term.

⇨ 18.4

马教授/馬教授	王玫玲
Mǎ jiàoshòu	**Wáng Méilíng**
Professor Ma	Meiling Wang
先生	小姐
Xiānsheng	**Xiǎojie**
Mr./sir	Miss

In mainland China, to politely get the attention of a male whom you do not know, you can say:

师傅/師傅	**shīfu**	master (as in, master craftsman)

Taxi drivers are typically addressed as:

司机/司機	**sījī**	driver

An informal way to attract someone's attention is by using the interjection:

欸	**ē**	hey

21.1.2 Attracting attention by apologizing for the intrusion

麻烦你	对不起	劳驾
麻煩你	對不起	勞駕
máfan nǐ	**duìbuqǐ**	**láojià**
excuse me (I am bothering you)	excuse me (sorry for being rude)	excuse me (for creating extra work for you)

21.1.3 Attracting attention by indicating that you want to ask a question

请问	(我想)打听一下
請問	(我想)打聽一下
qǐng wèn	**(wǒ xiǎng) dǎting yí xià**
may I ask	I'd like to inquire for a moment

21.1.4 Attracting attention by asking for help

请帮(个)忙。	劳驾/勞駕
請幫(個)忙。	
Qǐng bāng (gè) máng.	**láojià**
Please help me.	excuse me (for creating extra work for you)

21.2 Responding to a call for attention

The most common way to respond to a call for attention is to use the phrase

什么事?
甚麼事?
Shénme shì?
What is the matter?/What do you want?

Other responses include

有事吗?	怎么了?
有事嗎?	怎麼了?
Yǒu shì ma?	**Zěnme le?**
Is something the matter?	What's the matter?

21.3 Checking whether people have understood you

清楚吗?	懂不懂?	懂吗?
清楚嗎?		懂嗎?
Qīngchu ma?	**Dǒng bù dǒng?**	**Dǒng ma?**
Is it clear?	Do you understand.	Do you understand?

21.4 Indicating understanding or lack of understanding

好。	行。	(我)懂(了)。
Hǎo.	**Xíng.**	**(Wǒ) dǒng (le).**
Okay.	Okay.	(I) understand (now).

我不懂。
Wǒ bù dǒng.
I don't understand.

21.5 Requesting repetition or clarification of spoken language

请你再说。
請你再說。
Qǐng nǐ zài shuō.
Please repeat./Please say it again.

(那是)什么意思?
(那是)甚麼意思?
(Nà shì) shénme yìsi?
What does that mean?

请你说慢一点。
請你說慢一點。
Qǐng nǐ shuō màn yīdiǎn.
Please speak a little slower.

21.6 Asking for assistance in identifying a Chinese character

怎么念?
怎麼唸?
Zěnme niàn?
How is it pronounced?

这个字怎么念?
這個字怎麼唸?
Zhège zì zěnme niàn?
How is this character pronounced?

怎么写?
怎麼寫?
Zěnme xiě?
How do you write it?

那个字怎么写?
那個字怎麼寫?
Nàge zì zěnme xiě?
How do you write that character?

'qīngchu' 怎么写?
'qīngchu' 怎麼寫?
'qīngchu' zěnme xiě?
How do you write the word 'qingchu'?

我不认识那个字。
我不認識那個字。
Wǒ bù rènshi nàge zì.
I don't recognize that character.

那个字是什么意思。
那個字是甚麼意思。
Nàge zì shì shénme yìsi.
What does that character mean?

21.7 Providing information about the identification of Chinese characters

The following strategies are commonly used to help a listener identify a character.

- Present a common word in which the character in question occurs

  「清楚」的「清」
  'qīngchu' de 'qīng'
  the 'qing' in 'qingchu'

  「朋友」的「友」
  'péngyou' de 'yǒu'
  the 'you' of 'pengyou'

- List the components of the character in question

  「三点水」的「清」
  「三點水」的「清」
  'sāndiǎn shuǐ' de 'qīng'
  the character 'qing' with the 'three dot water' radical

  「木子」「李」
  'mù' 'zǐ' 'Lǐ'
  the character '李 Lǐ' that consists of the character '木 mù' and the character
  '子 zǐ'

21.8 Signaling that you are following the speaker

To indicate that you are following a speaker, say:

是,是	**shì, shì**	yes, yes
嗯,嗯	**ng, ng**	yeh, yeh
对,对/對,對	**duì, duì**	right, right

21.9 Interrupting a speaker

To interrupt a speaker say:

对不起/對不起	**duìbuqǐ**	excuse me

21.10 Using fillers

A filler is an expression that fills a pause in a conversation and keeps the conversation going. English uses expressions such as 'well,' 'mmm,' 'uh.' Mandarin uses these expressions.

那么/那麼	**nàme**	well
嗯,嗯	**ng, ng**	yeh
这个,这个.../這個,這個...	**zhège, zhège**	this, this ...

21.11 Formal development of a topic

21.11.1 Opening remarks

To formally introduce a topic in a talk or written report, use the following expressions:

今天要谈到的问题是 . . .
今天要談到的問題是 . . .
Jīntiān yào tándào de wèntí shì . . .
The issue/problem we are going to discuss today is . . .

今天要讲的题目是 . . . (今天要讨论的题目是 . . .)
今天要講的題目是 . . . (今天要討論的題目是 . . .)
Jīntiān yào jiǎng de tímù shì . . . (jīntiān yào tǎolùn de tímù shì . . .)
The topic I am going to talk about today is . . . (The topic I am going to discuss today is . . .)

请各位多多指教。
請各位多多指教。
Qǐng gèwèi duōduō zhǐjiào.
I invite your comments and corrections. (used in formal speeches and written presentations)

⇨ | 53.1

21.11.2 Introducing further points

To introduce additional points in a discussion or in writing, say:

首先	**shǒuxiān**	in the first place
第一	**dì yī**	first
除了 (noun phrase) 以外	**chúle** (noun phrase) **yǐwài**	besides (noun phrase)
还有/還有	**hái yǒu**	also, in addition
请看/請看	**qǐng kàn** (+ noun phrase)	please look at (noun phrase)

⇨ | 6.4, 36.3

21.11.3 Establishing a sequence

第一	**dìyī**	first
第二	**dì èr**	second
第三	**dì sān**	third
然后/然後	**ránhòu**	afterwards
后来/後來	**hòulái**	afterwards (only used to describe sequence in the past)

⇨ | 6.4, 38

21.11.4 **Establishing references**

To refer to information that is relevant to the conversation, use these expressions:

关于/關於 **guānyú** *regarding (noun phrase)*

> 关于买飞机票的事，请你负责。
> 關於買飛機票的事，請你負責。
> **Guānyú mǎi fēijī piào de shì, qǐng nǐ fùzé.**
> As for buying the airplane tickets, please take charge.

至于/至於 **zhìyú** *in reference to (noun phrase)*

> 至于定旅馆的事，你不必费心。
> 至於定旅館的事，你不必費心。
> **Zhìyú dìng lǚguǎn de shì, nǐ bù bì fèixīn.**
> As for making the hotel reservations, you don't have to bother (doing that).

甚至于/甚至於 **shènzhì yú** *even, go so far as to (noun phrase or verb phrase)*

> 一切手续都办好了，甚至于你住的地方。
> 一切手續都辦好了，甚至於你住的地方。
> **Yīqiè shǒuxù dōu bànhǎo le, shènzhìyú nǐ zhù de dìfang.**
> All of the arrangements have been taking care of, even down to the place where you will live.

> 为什么有时候打开网页的速度很慢甚至于无法连接？
> 為什麼有時候打開網頁的速度很慢甚至於無法連接？
> **Wèishénme yǒu shíhòu dǎkāi wǎngyè de sùdù hěn màn shènzhìyú wúfǎ liánjie?**
> Why is it that sometimes it takes a very long time for a web page to open, sometimes not even connecting at all?

⇨ 53.1.1

21.11.5 **Giving examples**

To give examples, use these expressions to introduce your remarks:

比方说/比方説 **bǐfang shuō** *for example (+ sentence)*

> 中文跟英文不同。比方说，中文有四个声调，英文没有。
> 中文跟英文不同。比方説，中文有四個聲調，英文沒有。
> **Zhōngwén gēn Yīngwén bù tóng. Bǐfang shuō, Zhōngwén yǒu sì gè shēngdiào, Yīngwén méi yǒu.**
> Chinese and English are different. For example, Chinese has four tones, English doesn't have tones.

例如 **lìrú** *for example (+ sentence)*

> 请你说一下你是怎么学中文的，例如每天化多少时间，听多少时间录音，等等。
> 請你説一下你是怎麼學中文的，例如每天化多少時間，听多少時間錄音，等等。
> **Qǐng nǐ shuō yīxià nǐ shì zěnme xué Zhōngwén de, lìrú měitiān huā duōshao shíjiān, tīng duōshao shíjiān lùyīn, děng děng.**
> Please tell (me) how you study Chinese, for example, how many hours you spend every day, how long you listen to recordings, etc.

譬如 *pìrú* for example (used the same way as 例如 *lìrú*, but in more formal contexts)

举例来说/舉例來說 *jǔlì láishuō* to give an example (+ sentence)

> 中国话有很多词可以重叠，举例来说，走走，哥哥，天天，等。
> 中國話有很多詞可以重疊，舉例來說，走走，哥哥，天天，等。
> **Zhōngguó huà yǒu hěn duō cí kěyǐ chóngdié, jǔ lì lái shuō, zǒu zǒu, gēge, tiāntiān, děng.**
> Chinese language has a lot of words that can be reduplicated, for example, 'zou zou,' 'gege,' 'tiantian,' etc.

21.11.6 Summarizing and concluding

To summarize and conclude, use these expressions to introduce your remarks:

总而言之/總而言之 *zǒng'éryánzhī* in other words, to put it another way

> 这件事我们已经谈了很多次了。总而言之，希望我们能互相信任。
> 這件事我們已經談了很多次了。總而言之，希望我們能互相信任。
> **Zhè jiàn shì wǒmen yǐjing tán le hěn duō cì le. Zǒng'éryánzhī, xīwàng wǒmen néng hùxiāng xìnrèn.**
> We've talked about this matter many times before. To put it another way, I hope we can trust each other.

总括来说/總括來說 *zǒngkuò láishuō* to sum up

> 总括来说，中国文字太复杂，需要改革。
> 總括來說，中國文字太復雜，需要改革。
> **Zǒngkuò lái shuō, Zhōngguó wénzì tài fùzá, xūyào gǎigé.**
> To sum things up, the Chinese language is too comlicated and needs to be revised.

最后/最後 *zuì hòu* finally

> 以下是我的看法，最后希望各位能多提意见。
> 以下是我的看法，最後希望各位能多提意見。
> **Yǐxià shì wǒde kànfǎ, zuìhòu xīwàng gè wèi néng duō tí yìjian.**
> What follows is my opinion. Finally, I hope that everyone will provide feedback.

22

Telecommunications and e-communications: telephones, the internet, beepers, and faxes

Telecommunications and e-communications play a major role in communication in China. This chapter presents expressions associated with the use of these technologies.

22.1 ## Sending and receiving phone calls, faxes, email, and beeper messages

22.1.1 ### Telephone and mobile phone/cell phone

给 (someone) 打电话/給 (someone) 打電話
gěi (someone) *dǎ* diànhuà
make a phone call to someone

(请) 给我打电话。
(請) 給我打電話。
(Qǐng) gěi wǒ *dǎ* diànhuà.
(Please) call me.

请打我的手机。
請打我的手機。
Qǐng *dǎ* wǒ de shǒujī.
Please call my mobile.

接电话/接電話
***jiē* diànhuà**
receive a phone call

没人接电话。
沒人接電話。
Méi rén *jiē* diànhuà
No one is *answering* the phone.

发短信   或   发短消息
發短信   發短消息
***fā* duǎnxìn**   ***fā* duǎn xiāoxi**
send a text message

我给你发了短信。
我給你發了短信。
Wǒ gěi nǐ fā le duǎnxìn.
I sent you a text message.

收短信　　　　　　　or　　　　收短消息
shōu duǎnxìn　　　　　　　　　*shōu* duǎn xiāoxi
receive a text message

我收了你的短信。
Wǒ shōu le nǐ de duǎnxìn.
I received your text message.

发传真/發傳真
fā chuán zhēn
send a fax

收传真/收傳真
shōu chuánzhēn
receive a fax

我没收到你的传真。请你重发一次。
我沒收到你的傳真。請你重發一次。
Wǒ méi *shōudào* nǐ de chuánzhēn. Qǐng nǐ chóng *fā* yīcì.
I didn't *receive* your fax. Please *transmit* again.

电子信/電子信　　　　　or　　　(电子)邮件/(電子)郵件
diànzǐ xìn　　　　　　　　　　**(diànzǐ) yóujiàn**
email　　　　　　　　　　　　　email

发电子信　　　　　　　　or　　　送电子邮件
發電子信　　　　　　　　　　　　送電子郵件
fā diànzǐ xìn　　　　　　　　**sòng diànzǐ yóujiàn**
send an email　　　　　　　　　send an email

接电子邮件/接電子郵件
jiē diànzǐ yóujiàn
receive an email

添加附加件
tiānjiā fùjiā jiàn
add an attachment

打开附件/打開附件
dǎkāi fù jiàn
open an attachment

呼机/呼機　　　　or　　　寻呼机/尋呼機　　　or　　　BB 机/BB 機
hū jī　　　　　　　　　**xún hū jī**　　　　　　　**BB jī**
beeper　　　　　　　　　beeper　　　　　　　　　beeper

(请)呼我。 or 叩我。
(請)呼我。
(Qǐng) hū wǒ.   **Kòu wǒ.**
(Please) beep me.   (from English 'call me')

22.2 Dialing a number and entering a number

拨电话号码/撥電話號碼
bō diànhuà hàomǎ
dial a phone number

在你刚拨的电话号码前请加'○'。
在你剛撥的電話號碼前請加'○'。
Zài nǐ gāng bō de diànhuà hàomǎ qián qǐng jiā 'líng'.
Please add 'zero' in front of the telephone number that you just dialed.

输入号码/輸入號碼
shūrù hàomǎ
enter a phone number

请输入你的客户号码。
請輸入你的客戶號碼。
Qǐng shūrù nǐ de kèhù hàomǎ.
Please enter your customer (account) number.

22.3 Using the internet

Basic vocabulary

万维网/萬維網
wàn wéi wǎng
internet

(世界)网路/(世界)網路
(shìjiè) wǎng lù
internet

因特网/因特網
yīn tè wǎng
internet

互联网/互聯網
hùlián wǎng
internet

网站/網站
wǎng zhàn
website

网页/網頁
wǎng yè
webpage

网路专家/網路專家
wǎnglù zhuānjiā
webmaster

网吧/網吧
wǎng bā
internet cafe

上网(路)/上網(路)
shàng **wǎng (lù)**
surf the web

22.4 Telephone etiquette

Telephone calls are answered with the phrase:
喂？ **Wèi?** or **Wéi?**
喂？ **Wèi?** (in either tone) is the equivalent of 'Hello' in English.

NOTE 喂 **wèi** can be used more broadly as an interjection to attract somebody's attention. When used in answering a phone call, it is said in second or fourth tone. Second tone is more polite and more commonly used. Fourth tone conveys a sense of impatience.

Increasingly, in the cities of China, the phrase used to answer a phone call is:

> 喂? 你好。
> **Wéi? Nǐ hǎo.**
> Hello. How are you?

To ask to speak to someone say:

> (张老师)在吗?
> (張老師)在嗎?
> **(Zhāng lǎoshī) zài ma?**
> Is (Professor Zhang) in?

or

> 我找(张老师)。她在吗?
> 我找(張老師)。她在嗎?
> **Wǒ zhǎo (Zhāng lǎoshī). Tā zài ma?**
> I'm looking for (Professor Zhang). Is she in?

If the party in question is not in, say:

> (她) 不在。
> **(Tā) bù zài.**
> (She) is not in.

If you wish to leave a message say:

> 我要留言。
> **Wǒ yào liú yán.**
> I'd like to leave a message.

To arrange to get together with someone by phone say:

> 我们通电话。
> 我們通電話。
> **Wǒmen tōng diànhuà.**
> Let's be in touch by phone.

To describe problems reaching someone by phone say:

> (我)打不通。
> **(Wǒ) dǎbutōng.**
> (I am) unable to get through.

> 现在占线。
> 現在占線。
> **Xiànzài zhàn xiàn.**
> The line is busy.

22.5 Writing and reciting phone numbers, fax numbers, and beeper numbers

Phone, fax, and beeper numbers are recited as a list of single digits. In mainland China, when reciting numbers, the number 1 (一) is pronounced **yāo**. In Taiwan it is pronounced **yī**. Phone, fax, and beeper numbers are typically written with Arabic numerals and not with Chinese characters.

Sample numbers

Phone, fax, beeper

> 6 5   2 7 – 3   3   7 8
> liù wǔ èr qī sān sān qī bā

Cell phone

> 1   3   5   5   7 6   7 6   6   6   6
> yī   sān wǔ wǔ qī liù qī liù liù liù liù
> or
> yāo sān wǔ wǔ qī liù qī liù liù liù liù

⇨ 6.1.1

___

NOTE Phone numbers that include the numerals 6 or 8 are considered particularly good and lucky. Those with the numeral 4 are less desirable. In mainland China, cellphone customers select and purchase their numbers from a list. Those with 6s and 8s are more expensive. Those with 4s are less expensive.

___

23

Negating information

23.1 Negation of verbs and verb phrases

The words that are used to negate verbs and verb phrases in Mandarin are 不 **bù** and 没 **méi**. 不 **bù** and 没 **méi** immediately precede the verb or anything that precedes and modifies the verb, including an adverb, a location phrase, or any other prepositional phrase.

> 他不<u>喝</u>酒。[*negation + verb*]
> **Tā bù *hē* jiǔ.**
> He doesn't *drink* (alcohol).

> 他不<u>一定</u>考得好。[*negation + adverb*]
> **Tā bù *yīdìng* kǎodehǎo.**
> It is not *certain* that he will do well on the exam. (He may not do well on the exam.)

> 他不<u>在家</u>吃饭。[*negation + location prepositional phrase*]
> 他不<u>在家</u>吃飯。
> **Tā bù *zài jiā* chī fàn.**
> He doesn't eat *at home*.

> 她没<u>跟弟弟</u>说话。[*negation + prepositional phrase*]
> 她沒<u>跟弟弟</u>説話。
> **Tā méi *gēn dìdi* shuō huà.**
> She didn't speak *with younger brother*.

In addition to the primary role of 不 **bù** and 没 **méi** as markers of negation, they often serve to identify the aspect and time frame of events.

⇨ 13.3, 33.4

23.1.1 不 *bù*

不 **bù** is the marker of negation for

- adjectival verbs, stative verbs, and modal verbs:

> 妹妹不<u>高</u>。(*adjectival verb*)
> **Mèimei bù *gāo*.**
> Younger sister is not *tall*.

我不喜欢他。(*stative verb*)
我不喜歡他。
Wǒ bù *xǐhuan* tā.
I don't *like* him.

十六岁的孩子不可以喝酒。(*modal verb*)
十六歲的孩子不可以喝酒。
Shíliù suì de háizi bù *kéyǐ* hē jiǔ.
16-year-old children are not *allowed* to drink.

⇨ | 10.1, 11.1, 12.6.1

● action verbs describing present, future, or habitual events:

他不吃肉。
Tā bù *chī* ròu.
He does not *eat* meat.

我不学法语。
我不學法語。
Wǒ bù *xué* Fáyǔ.
I don't *study* French.

⇨ | 13.3

23.1.2 没 *méi* and 没有 *méi yǒu*

没 **méi** is the negation word that negates the verb 有 **yǒu**.

他没有钱。
他沒有錢。
Tā méi yǒu qián.
He doesn't have any money.

公园里没有人。
公園裏沒有人。
Gōngyuán lǐ méi yǒu rén.
There are no people in the park.

In addition, 没 **méi** (or 没有 **méi yǒu**) negates action verbs under the following conditions:

The action is not complete

我还没看完那本书。
我還沒看完那本書。
Wǒ hái méi kànwán nà běn shū.
I still haven't finished reading that book.

The action did not happen in the past

我昨天没吃晚饭。
我昨天沒吃晚飯。
Wǒ zuótiān méi chī wǎnfàn.
Yesterday, I didn't eat dinner.

我这个月都没看电影。
我這個月都沒看電影。
Wǒ zhège yuè dōu méi kàn diànyǐng.
This month I haven't seen a movie.

When negation occurs at the end of the sentence in *verb-not-verb* questions, 没 **méi** must be followed by 有 **yǒu**.

你看完了那本书没有？
你看完了那本書沒有？
Nǐ kànwán le nà běn shū méi yǒu?
Have you finished reading that book?

⇨ | 13.3, 33.3

23.2 The relative order of negation and adverbs

Here are some general rules for the relative order of negation and adverbs. The adverbs are emphasized in each example.

- Most adverbs occur before negation.

  那本书，我还没看完。
  那本書，我還沒看完。
  Nà běn shū, wǒ *hái* méi kànwán.
  That book, I have not *yet* finished reading it.

  我喜欢吃中国饭，就不喜欢吃海参。
  我喜歡吃中國飯，就不喜歡吃海參。
  Wǒ xǐhuan chī Zhōngguó fàn, *jiù* bù xǐhuan chī hǎishēn.
  I like to eat Chinese food; I *just* don't like to eat sea slugs.

  他也许不认识你妹妹。
  他也許不認識你妹妹。
  Tā *yéxǔ* bù rènshi nǐ mèimei.
  Perhaps he doesn't know your younger sister.

- A small number of adverbs may occur either before or after negation. The order of negation and adverb influences the meaning of the sentence.

  我们都不会开车。
  我們都不會開車。
  Wǒmen *dōu* bù huì kāi chē.
  We *all* cannot drive (a car).

  我们不都会开车。有的会，有的不会。
  我們不都會開車。有的會，有的不會。
  Wǒmen bù *dōu* huì kāi chē. Yǒu de huì, yǒu de bù huì.
  Not *all* of us can drive a car. Some can, some can't.

  我一定不去。
  Wǒ *yīdìng* bù qù.
  I am *definitely* not going.

我不<u>一定</u>去。
Wǒ bù *yīdìng* qù.
I am not *definitely* going. (I may not go.)

⇨ 15.1

23.3 Words that occur with negation

23.3.1 Adverbs that occur with negation

Certain adverbs always occur with negation or in negative contexts. These include:

从来/從來 *cónglái* (+ negation) 'never'

我从来没抽过烟。
我從來沒抽過菸。
Wǒ cónglái méi chōuguo yān.
I've never smoked cigarettes.

根本 *gēnběn* (+ negation) 'absolutely not'

那样的话根本没有道理。
那樣的話根本沒有道理。
Nà yàng de huà gēnběn méi yǒu dàoli.
That kind of talk makes no sense.

并/並 *bìng* (+ negation) 'absolutely (not)'

我并不愿意跟他一起住。
我並不願意跟他一起住。
Wǒ bìng bù yuànyi gēn tā yīqǐ zhù.
I am absolutely not willing to live with him.
(I am not at all willing to live with him.)

⇨ 31.3

23.3.2 The noun modifier 任何 *rènhé* and negation

任何 *rènhé* 'any'

我没告诉任何人。
我沒告訴任何人。
Wǒ méi gàosu rènhé rén.
I didn't tell anyone.

23.4 不 *bù* in resultative verb structures

不 **bù** occurs between the verb and the resultative suffix to indicate inability to achieve the result. Here are some examples.

吃完 *chīwán* 'finish eating'

我吃不完。
Wǒ chībuwán.
I am unable to finish eating (the food).

看見 **kànjian** *'see, perceive'*

> 这个电影的字幕太小。我根本看不见。
> 這個電影的字幕太小。我根本看不見。
> **Zhège diànyǐng de zìmù tài xiǎo. Wǒ gēnběn kànbujiàn.**
> The subtitles in this movie are too small. I can't see them at all.

听懂/聽懂 **tīngdǒng** *'understand by listening'*

> 他说得太快。我听不懂。
> 他說得太快。我聽不懂。
> **Tā shuōde tài kuài. Wǒ tīngbudǒng.**
> He speaks too quickly. I can't understand (by listening).

⇨ 28.2

Literary markers of negation: 無 **wú** and 非 **fēi**

The literary markers of negation 無 **wú** and 非 **fēi** occur in modern Mandarin as components of words. The following are commonly used words which include 無 **wú** and 非 **fēi**.

Expressions with 無 **wú**

无论/無論	**wúlùn**	no matter what
无论如何/無論如何	**wúlùn rú hé**	in any case, no matter what
无比/無比	**wúbǐ**	incomparable
无故/無故	**wúgù**	without reason; for no reason
无理/無理	**wúlǐ**	unreasonable; for no reason
毫无/毫無	**háowú**	not in the least, not at all

> 无论你去不去上课，我也不去。
> 無論你去不去上課，我也不去。
> **Wúlùn nǐ qù bù qù shàng kè, wǒ yě bù qù.**
> Whether or not you go to class, I am not going.

> 你无论如何得帮我这个忙。
> 你無論如何得幫我這個忙。
> **Nǐ wúlùn rúhé děi bāng wǒ zhège máng.**
> No matter what, you have to help me with this matter.

> 夏威夷的风景美丽无比。
> 夏威夷的風景美麗無比。
> **Xiàwēiyí de fēngjǐng měilì wúbǐ.**
> The scenery of Hawaii is so beautiful that no place can match it.

> 你为什么无缘无故打人？
> 你為甚麼無緣無故打人？
> **Nǐ wèi shénme wúyuán wúgù dǎ rén?**
> Why do you hit people for no reason at all?

> 你这真是无理取闹。
> 你這真是無理取鬧。
> **Nǐ zhè zhēn shì wúlǐ qǔnào.**
> You are really picking a fight for no reason.

毫无疑问，她是一个很好的学生。
毫無疑問，她是一個很好的學生。
Háowú yí wèn, tā shì yī gè hěn hǎo de xuésheng.
No doubt at all; she is a very good student.

Q: 你明天能来吗？ A: 毫无问题。
你明天能來嗎？ 毫無問題。
Nǐ míngtiān néng lái ma? **Háowú wèntí.**
Are you able to come tomorrow? No problem.

Expressions with 非 *fēi*

非 (verb phrase) 不可	**fēi** (verb phrase) **bù kě**	must (verb phrase)
非得	**fēiděi**	must
非凡	**fēifán**	outstanding
非法	**fēifǎ**	illegal
非常	**fēicháng**	extraordinary, extremely

我非把中文学好不可。
我非把中文學好不可。
Wǒ fēi bǎ Zhōngwén xué hǎo bù kě.
I must master Chinese.

你今天下午非得把功课做完。
你今天下午非得把功課做完。
Nǐ jīntiān xiàwǔ fēi děi bǎ gōngkè zuòwán.
You must finish your homework this afternoon.

这次的庆祝会隆重非凡。
這次的慶祝會隆重非凡。
Zhè cì de qìngzhù huì lóngzhòng fēifán.
This celebration was extraordinarily ceremonious.

非法的生意我不会作的。
非法的生意我不會作的。
Fēifǎ de shēngyì wǒ bù huì zuò de.
I will never do any illegal business.

他的英文非常好。
Tā de Yīngwén fēicháng hǎo.
His English is extremely good.

24

Asking questions and replying to questions

Questions are used to ask for information. Here are the most common question types in Mandarin.

24.1 Yes–no questions

Yes–no questions are questions that can be answered with 'yes' or 'no.' In Mandarin, there are several ways to ask yes–no questions. Notice that unlike English, the overall phrase order of statements and yes–no questions is the same. In addition, no helping word equivalent to 'do' is involved in yes–no questions in Chinese.

24.1.1 Yes–no questions with 吗/嗎 *ma*

When 吗/嗎 **ma** is added to the end of a statement, it turns the statement into a yes–no question.

Statement	*Yes–no question*
她是中国人。	她是中国人吗？
她是中國人。	她是中國人嗎？
Tā shì Zhōngguo rén.	**Tā shì Zhōngguo rén ma?**
She is a Chinese person.	Is she a Chinese person?
他们卖橘子。	他们卖橘子吗？
他們賣橘子。	他們賣橘子嗎？
Tāmen mài júzi.	**Tāmen mài júzi ma?**
They sell tangerines.	Do they sell tangerines?
他会说中文。	他会说中文吗？
他會説中文。	他會説中文嗎？
Tā huì shuō Zhōngwén.	**Tā huì shuō Zhōngwén ma?**
He can speak Chinese.	Can he speak Chinese?

24.1.2 Yes–no questions with verb-not-verb structure

Yes–no questions may also be formed by repeating the first verb of the verb phrase in affirmative and negative form. Here are examples with different types of verbs.

Modal verbs

> 他会不会说中文?
> 他會不會説中文?
> **Tā *huì* bù *huì* shuō Zhōngwén?**
> *Can* he speak Chinese?

⇨ | 12.6.2

The equational verb 是 **shì** *'to be'*

> 她是不是中国人?
> 她是不是中國人?
> **Tā *shì* bù *shì* Zhōngguo rén?**
> *Is* she a Chinese person?

⇨ | 11.5

Action verbs

> 他们卖不卖橘子?
> 他們賣不賣橘子?
> **Tāmen *mài* bù *mài* júzi?**
> Do they *sell* tangerines?

⇨ | 13

Stative verbs

> 你喜欢不喜欢他?
> 你喜歡不喜歡他?
> **Nǐ *xǐhuan* bù *xǐhuan* tā?**
> Do you *like* him?

or

> 你喜不喜欢他?
> 你喜不喜歡他?
> **Nǐ xǐ bù xǐhuan tā?**
> Do you like him?

⇨ | 11

Adjectival verbs

> 飞机票贵不贵?
> 飛機票貴不貴?
> **Fēijī piào *guì* bù *guì*?**
> Are airplane tickets *expensive*?

⇨ | 10.2

When the main verb of a sentence is 有 **yǒu**, the *verb-not-verb* question is 有没有 **yǒu méi yǒu**.

你有没有钱？
你有沒有錢？
Nǐ yǒu méi yǒu qián?
Do you have money?

➪ 11.6.4, 23.1.2

When the verb is followed by a direct object and no other phrase, *verb-not-verb* may be split. In this case, *not-verb* can occur immediately after the object.

他会说中文不会？
他會說中文不會？
Tā *huì* shuō Zhōngwén bù *huì*?
Can he speak Chinese?

她是中国人不是？
她是中國人不是？
Tā *shì* Zhōngguo rén bù *shì*?
Is she a Chinese person?

他们卖橘子不卖？
他們賣橘子不賣？
Tāmen *mài* júzi bù *mài*?
Do they sell tangerines?

你有钱没有？
你有錢沒有？
Nǐ *yǒu* qián méi *yǒu*?
Do you have money?

The *verb-not-verb* structure can be used to question whether an action is past or completed. In this case, *not* must be 没有 **méi yǒu**. 没有 **méi yǒu** occurs after the direct object, at the end of the sentence.

你吃饭了没有？
你吃飯了沒有？
Nǐ *chī* fàn le *méi yǒu*?
Have you eaten?

NOTE Native speakers differ in where they put 了 **le** in sentences like these. Some speakers prefer to put 了 **le** after the object of the verb as in the example above. Some speakers prefer to put 了 **le** after the verb itself, as in the following example

你吃了饭没有？
你吃了飯沒有？
Nǐ *chī* le fàn *méi yǒu*?
Have you eaten?

➪ 33.1

24.1.3 **Yes–no questions with 是否 *shìfǒu***

是否 **shìfǒu** before the verb turns a statement into a yes–no question. 是否 **shìfǒu** questions are more common in written Chinese than in the spoken language.

Statement	是否 *shìfǒu* question

你喜欢他。
你喜歡他。
Nǐ xǐhuan tā.
You like him.

你是否喜欢他?
你是否喜歡他?
Nǐ shìfǒu xǐhuan tā?
Do you like him (or not)?

他去过中国。
他去過中國。
Tā qùguò Zhōngguó.
He has been to China.

他是否去过中国?
他是否去過中國?
Tā shìfǒu qùguò Zhōngguó?
Has he been to China (or not)?

他会说汉语。
他會说漢語。
Tā huì shuō Hànyǔ.
He can speak Chinese.

他是否会说汉语?
他是否會说漢語?
Tā shìfǒu huì shuō Hànyǔ?
Can he speak Chinese (or not)?

24.1.4 Replying to yes–no questions

24.1.4.1 Replying 'yes'

There is no word 'yes' in Mandarin. To reply 'yes' to a yes–no question in 吗/嗎 **ma** form, in 是否 **shìfǒu** form, or in *verb-not-verb* form, repeat the verb.

吗/嗎 *ma* question	是否 *shìfǒu* question	Verb-not-verb question	Yes
她是中国人吗? 她是中國人嗎? **Tā *shì* Zhōngguo rén ma?** Is she a Chinese person?	她是否是中国人? 她是否是中國人? **Tā shìfǒu *shì* Zhōngguo rén?** Is she a Chinese person?	她是不是中国人? 她是不是中國人? **Tā *shì* bù *shì* Zhōngguo rén?** Is she a Chinese person?	是。 Shì. Yes.
他去过中国吗? 他去過中國嗎? **Tā *qùguò* Zhōngguó ma?** Has he *been* to China?	他是否去过中国? 他是否去過中國? **Tā shìfǒu *qùguò* Zhōngguó?** Has he *been* to China?	他去过中国没有? 他去過中國沒有? **Tā *qùguò* Zhōngguó méi yǒu?** Has he *been* to China?	去过。 去過。 Qùguò. Yes.
他会说中文吗? 他會说中文嗎? **Tā *huì* shuō Zhōngwén ma?** *Can* he speak Chinese?	他是否会说中文? 他是否會说中文? **Tā shìfǒu *huì* shuō Zhōngwén?** *Can* he speak Chinese?	他会不会说中文? 他會不會说中文? **Tā *huì* bù *huì* shuō Zhōngwén?** *Can* he speak Chinese?	会/會。 Huì. Yes.
你有钱吗? 你有錢嗎? **Nǐ *yǒu* qián ma?** Do you *have* money?	你是否有钱? 你是否有錢? **Nǐ shìfǒu *yǒu* qián?** Do you *have* money?	你有没有钱? 你有沒有錢? **Nǐ *yǒu* méi *yǒu* qián?** Do you *have* money?	有。 Yǒu. Yes.

24.1.4.2 Replying 'no'

If the question asks about non-past time and the main verb of the sentence is any verb except for 有 **yǒu**, the 'no' answer is 不 **bù** + the verb.

If the question asks about a past or completed event or if the main verb of the question is 有 **yǒu**, the 'no' answer is 没有 **méi yǒu**.

Yes–no question	是否 *shìfǒu* question	Verb-not-verb question	No
她是中国人吗? 她是中國人嗎? **Tā *shì* Zhōngguo rén ma?** *Is* she a Chinese person?	她是否是中国人? 她是否是中國人? **Tā shìfǒu *shì* Zhōngguo rén?** *Is* she a Chinese person?	她是不是中国人? 她是不是中國人? **Tā *shì* bù *shì* Zhōngguo rén?** *Is* she a Chinese person?	不是。 **Bù shì.** No.
他去过中国吗? 他去過中國嗎? **Tā *qùguo* Zhōngguó ma?** Has he *been* to China?	他是否去过中国? 他是否去過中國? **Tā shìfǒu *qùguo* Zhōngguó?** Has he *been* to China?	他去过中国没有? 他去過中國沒有? **Tā *qùguo* Zhōngguó méi yǒu?** Has he *been* to China?	没有。 **Méi yǒu.** No.
他会说中文吗? 他會説中文嗎? **Tā *huì* shuō Zhōngwén ma?** *Can* he speak Chinese?	他是否会说中文? 他是否會説中文? **Tā shìfǒu *huì* shuō Zhōngwén?** *Can* he speak Chinese?	他会不会说中文? 他會不會説中文? **Tā *huì* bù *huì* shuō Zhōngwén?** *Can* he speak Chinese?	不会/不會。 **Bù huì.** No.
你有钱吗? 你有錢嗎? **Nǐ *yǒu* qián ma?** Do you *have* money?	你是否有钱? 你是否有錢? **Nǐ shìfǒu *yǒu* qián?** Do you *have* money?	你有没有钱? 你有沒有錢? **Nǐ *yǒu* méi *yǒu* qián?** Do you *have* money?	没有。 **Méi yǒu.** No.

24.2 Asking for agreement

To ask a listener for agreement with a statement, follow the statement with one of these expressions.

对不对?/對不對? *duì bù duì?* 'correct?'

> 她是中国人,对不对?
> 她是中國人,對不對?
> **Tā shì Zhōngguo rén, duì bù duì?**
> She is a Chinese person, right?

好不好? *hǎo bù hǎo?* or 好吗?/好嗎? *hǎo ma?* 'okay?'

> 我们说中文,好不好?
> 我們説中文,好不好?
> **Wǒmen shuō Zhōngwén, hǎo bù hǎo?**
> Let's speak Chinese, okay?

行不行? *xíng bù xíng?* or 行吗?/行嗎? *xíng ma?* 'okay?'

> 我请小白跟我们一起吃饭,行不行?
> 我請小白跟我們一起吃飯,行不行?
> **Wǒ qǐng Xiǎo Bái gēn wǒmen yīqǐ chī fàn, xíng bù xíng?**
> I am inviting Little Bai to eat with us, okay?

可以吗?/可以嗎? *kéyǐ ma?* '*okay?*'

> 我跟你去看王老师，可以吗？
> 我跟你去看王老師，可以嗎？
> **Wǒ gēn nǐ qù kàn Wáng lǎoshī, kéyǐ ma?**
> I will go with you to see Professor Wang, okay?

To answer in the affirmative, repeat the verb.

To answer 'no,' say 不 **bù** + the verb.

Question	Affirmative	No
她是中国人，对不对？ 她是中國人，對不對？ **Tā shì Zhōngguo rén, duì bù duì?** She is a Chinese person, right?	对。 對。 **Duì.** Right.	不对。 不對。 **Bù duì.** Wrong.
我们说中文，好不好？ 我們説中文，好不好？ **Wǒmen shuō Zhōngwén, hǎo bù hǎo?** Let's speak Chinese, okay?	好。 好。 **Hǎo.** Okay.	不好。 不好。 **Bù hǎo.** No.

The expression 是不是? **shì bù shì?** 'right?' follows the subject.

> 她是不是会说中文？
> 她是不是會説中文？
> **Tā shì bù shì huì shuō Zhōngwén?**
> Does she speak Chinese?

To answer 'yes,' say 是 **shì**. To answer 'no,' say 不 **bù** + the main verb of the sentence.

Question	Affirmative	No
她是不是会说中文？ 她是不是會説中文？ **Tā shì bù shì huì shuō Zhōngwén?** Does she speak Chinese?	是。 是。 **Shì.** Yes.	不是。 不是。 **Bù shì.** No.
她是不是会说中文？ 她是不是會説中文？ **Tā shì bù shì huì shuō Zhōngwén?** Does she speak Chinese?	会。 會。 **Huì.** Yes.	不会。 不會。 **Bù huì.** No.

24.3 Choosing between alternatives with either–or questions

To ask a listener to choose between alternatives, use 还是/還是 **háishi**.

If the main verb of the sentence is 是 **shì**, 还是/還是 **háishi** can occur before a noun or noun phrase.

> 她是学生还是老师？
> 她是學生還是老師？
> **Tā shì xuésheng háishi lǎoshī?**
> Is she a student or a teacher?

Otherwise, 还是/還是 **háishi** occurs before the verb phrase.

> 你喝茶还是喝啤酒？
> 你喝茶還是喝啤酒？
> **Nǐ hē chá háishi hē píjiǔ?**
> Will you drink tea or beer?

When both alternatives are sentences, 还是/還是 **háishi** occurs before the second sentence.

> 你觉得中文难还是日文难？
> 你覺得中文難還是日文難？
> **Nǐ juéde Zhōngwén nán háishi Rìwén nán?**
> Which do you think is more difficult: Chinese or Japanese?
> (lit. '(Do) you think Chinese is difficult or Japanese is difficult?')

The first alternative may be preceded by 是 **shì**.

> (是)中国大还是俄国大？
> (是)中國大還是俄國大？
> **(Shì) Zhōngguó dà háishi Éguó dà?**
> Which is bigger, China or Russia?
> (lit. 'Is China big or is Russia big?')

To answer a 还是/還是 **háishi** question, select the alternative that you prefer. To indicate that a choice was made after careful consideration, it may be preceded by 是 **shì** or 还是/還是 **háishi**.

> 中国大。   or   是中国大。
> 中國大。   是中國大。
> **Zhōngguó dà.**   **Shì Zhōngguó dà.**
> China is bigger.   [I think] China is bigger.

> (我觉得)日文难。   or   (我觉得)还是日文难。
> (我覺得)日文難。   (我覺得)還是日文難。
> **(Wǒ juéde) Rìwén nán.**   **(Wǒ juéde) háishi Rìwén nán.**
> (I think) Japanese is   After careful consideration (I think)
> more difficult.   Japanese is more difficult.

⇨ 16.2.1

24.4 Rhetorical questions

To ask a question for which you think you know the answer, use 不是 **bù shì** +吗/嗎 **ma**. 不是 **bù shì** occurs immediately before the predicate.

> 他<u>不是</u>已经毕业了<u>吗</u>？
> 他<u>不是</u>已經畢業了<u>嗎</u>？
> **Tā *bù shì* yǐjing bì yè le *ma*?**
> Hasn't he already graduated? (Isn't it the case that he's already graduated?)

> 你<u>不是</u>已经看过那部电影了<u>吗</u>？
> 你<u>不是</u>已經看過那部電影了<u>嗎</u>？
> **Nǐ *bù shì* yǐjing kànguo nà bù diànyǐng le *ma*?**
> Haven't you already seen that movie?

24.5 Follow-up questions with 呢 *ne*

呢 **ne** is used to follow up a question with another question. It is used to ask the same question as the first one, but about another subject or object. 呢 **ne** follows the new subject or object.

呢 **ne** question to ask about a new subject:

> 小白：　<u>你(的)弟弟</u>上大学了吗？
> 小白：　<u>你(的)弟弟</u>上大學了嗎？
> **Xiǎo Bái: *Nǐ (de) dìdi* shàng dàxué le ma?**
> Little Bai: Does *your younger brother* attend college?

> 小高：　上了。
> **Xiǎo Gāo: Shàng le.**
> Little Gao: Yes. [(He) attends.]

> 小白：　<u>你(的)妹妹</u>呢？
> **Xiǎo Bái: *Nǐ (de) mèimei* ne?**
> Little Bai: (What about) *Your younger sister*?

> 小高：　她也上了。
> **Xiǎo Gāo: Tā yě shàng le.**
> Little Gao: She also attends.

呢 **ne** question to ask about a new object:

> 小白：　你会说<u>中文</u>吗？
> 　　　　你會说<u>中文</u>嗎？
> **Nǐ huì shuō *Zhōngwén* ma?**
> Little Bai: Can you speak *Chinese*?

> 小高：　会/會。
> **Huì.**
> Little Gao: Yes.

> 小白：　<u>日文</u>呢？
> ***Rìwén* ne?**
> Little Bai: *Japanese*?

> 小高：　不会/不會。
> **Bù huì.**
> Little Gao: No.

24.6 Content questions

Content questions are used to ask about the identify of a person, an object, a time, a location, or a quantity, or to seek an explanation or process. Mandarin content question words include the following:

Content question word	Meaning	What it questions	Example phrase
谁 誰 **shéi**	who?	person	他是谁？ 他是誰？ **Tā shì shéi?** Who is he?
什么 甚麼 **shénme**	what?	concrete or abstract object	那是什么？ 那是甚麼？ **Nà shì shénme?** What is that?
什么时候 甚麼時候 **shénme shíhòu**	when?	time (including clock time)	你什么时候开始学中文？ 你甚麼時候開始學中文？ **Nǐ shénme shíhòu kāishǐ xué Zhōngwén?** When will you begin to study Chinese?
几点钟 幾點鐘 **jǐdiǎn zhōng**	when?	clock time	你几点钟回家？ 你幾點鐘回家？ **Nǐ jǐdiǎn zhōng huí jiā?** When are you going home?
什么地方 甚麼地方 **shénme dìfang**	what place/ where?	location	你在什么地方工作？ 你在甚麼地方工作？ **Nǐ zài shénme dìfang gōngzuò?** Where do you work?
哪儿 哪兒 **nǎr** 哪里 哪裏 **nálǐ**	where?	location	你在哪儿工作？ 你在哪兒工作？ **Nǐ zài nǎr gōngzuò?** 你在哪里工作？ 你在哪裏工作？ **Nǐ zài nálǐ gōngzuò?** Where do you work?
为什么 為甚麼 **wèi shénme**	why?	reason	你为什么学中文？ 你為甚麼學中文？ **Nǐ wèi shénme xué Zhōngwén?** Why do you study Chinese?
凭什么 憑甚麼 **píng shénme**	on what basis/ by what right?	reason	你凭什么逮捕我？ 你憑甚麼逮捕我？ **Nǐ píng shénme dàibǔ wǒ?** On what grounds are you arresting me?
怎么 怎麼 **zěnme**	how?	process	怎么走？ 怎麼走？ **Zěnme zǒu?** How do you go?
哪 **nǎ**	which?	specifier	你要买哪本书？ 你要買哪本書？ **Nǐ yào mǎi nǎ běn shū?** Which book do you want to buy?

Content question word	Meaning	What it questions	Example phrase
几 幾 **jǐ**	how many? (usually 10 or less; used with countable nouns)	quantity	你想吃几个饺子? 你想吃幾個餃子? **Nǐ xiǎng chī jǐ gè jiǎozi?** How many dumplings do you want to eat?
多少 **duōshǎo**	how many? (larger number; used with mass nouns)	quantity	你有多少钱? 你有多少錢? **Nǐ yǒu duōshǎo qián?** How much money do you have?
多 **duō**	how? (used with adjectival verbs)	intensity	你多大? **Nǐ duō dà?** How old are you? 那本书有多贵啊? 那本書有多貴啊? **Nà běn shū yǒu duō guì a?** How expensive is that book?

The following content question words and phrases are more common in formal, literary texts than in spoken Mandarin.

Content question word	Meaning	What it questions	Example phrase
何必 **hébì**	why?	reason	你何必生那么大的气? 你何必生那麼大的氣? **Nǐ hébì shēng nàme dà de qì?** Why are you so angry?
何妨 **héfáng**	why not?	reason	如果你没事,何妨多坐一会儿。 如果你沒事,何妨多坐一會兒。 **Rúguǒ nǐ méi shì, héfáng duō zuò yīhuìr.** If you are not busy, why not sit for a while longer?
何时 何時 **héshí**	when?	time	飞机何时到达? 飛機何時到達? **Fēijī héshí dào dá?** What time is the plane arriving?
何故 **hégù**	why?	reason	他何故杀人? 他何故殺人? **Tā hégù shā rén?** Why did he kill someone?
为何 為何 **wéihé**	why?	reason	为何惊慌? 為何驚慌? **Wéihé jīnghuāng?** Why are (you) so frightened?

Content question word	Meaning	What it questions	Example phrase
何为 何為 **héwéi**	what is (noun phrase)?	identification	何为科学方法? 何為科學方法? **Héwéi kēxué fāngfǎ?** What is the scientific method?
何尝 何嘗 **hécháng**	how could (you) not (verb phrase)?	rhetorical request for reason	我何尝不想上大学? 我何嘗不想上大學? **Wǒ hécháng bù xiǎng shàng dàxué?** How could I not be thinking about going to university?

In Mandarin, questions and answers use the same phrase order.

In Mandarin, the content question word goes where the answer goes.

Question	Answer
你找谁? 你找誰? **Nǐ zhǎo *shéi*?** *Who* are you looking for?	我找王老师。 我找王老師。 **Wǒ zhǎo *Wáng lǎoshī*.** I am looking for *Professor Wang*.
这是什么? 這是甚麼? **Zhè shì *shénme*?** *What* is this?	这是手机。 這是手機。 **Zhè shì *shǒujī*.** This is *a cell phone*.
你今天喝什么茶? 你今天喝甚麼茶? **Nǐ jīntiān hē *shénme* chá?** *What* tea are you drinking today?	(我喝)龙井(茶)。 (我喝)龍井(茶)。 **(Wǒ hē) *lóngjǐng* (chá).** (I'm drinking) *Longjing* (tea).
你什么时候有空? 你甚麼時候有空? **Nǐ *shénme shíhòu* yǒu kōng?** *When* do you have free time?	我今天下午有空。 **Wǒ *jīntiān xiàwǔ* yǒu kōng.** I have free time *this afternoon*.
你在哪儿(哪里)学中文? 你在哪兒(哪裏)學中文? **Nǐ zài *nǎr (nǎlǐ)* xué Zhōngwén?** *Where* do you study Chinese?	我在大学学中文。 我在大學學中文。 **Wǒ zài *dàxué* xué Zhōngwén.** I study Chinese *in college/at university*.
你几点钟下课? 你幾點鐘下課? **Nǐ *jǐdiǎn zhōng* xià kè?** *What time* do you get out of class?	我四点钟下课。 我四點鐘下課。 **Wǒ *sìdiǎn zhōng* xià kè.** I get out of class *at 4 o'clock*.
你在什么地方吃午饭? 你在甚麼地方吃午飯? **Nǐ zài *shénme dìfang* chī wǔfàn?** *Where* do you eat lunch?	我在餐厅吃午饭。 我在餐廳吃午飯。 **Wǒ zài *cāntīng* chī wǔfàn.** I eat lunch *in the cafeteria*.

怎么/怎麼 **zěnme** 'how' asks for a process. It occurs right before the verb. The answer to a 怎么/怎麼 **zěnme** question is an explanation. It may be a short phrase or it may be a sentence or more in length. The long answer to 怎么/怎麼 **zěnme** 'how' questions involves a series of steps in which the process is described.

Question	*Answer*
这个字怎么写?	这个字这样写。
這個字怎麼寫?	這個字這樣寫。
Zhège zì zěnme xiě?	**Zhège zì zhèyàng xiě.**
How do you write this character?	You write this character *this way*.
从这儿到公园怎么走?	从这儿到公园往北走。
從這兒到公園怎麼走?	從這兒到公園往北走。
Cóng zhèr dào gōngyuán zěnme zǒu?	**Cóng zhèr dào gōngyuán wǎng běi zǒu.**
How do you go from here to the library?	From here to the park walk north.

The question expression 怎么样?/怎麼樣? **zěnmeyàng?** asks for a description:

那个饭馆怎么样?
那個飯館怎麼樣?
Nàge fànguǎn zěnmeyàng?
What is that restaurant like?

The expression 怎么了?/怎麼了? **zěnme le?** is used to ask how someone is when the speaker believes there is something the matter:

你怎么了?
你怎麼了?
Nǐ zěnme le?
What is the matter with you?

为什么/為甚麼 **wèi shénme** 'why' questions ask for reasons, and their responses typically require a sentence or more. 为什么/為甚麼 **wèi shénme** occurs after the subject of the sentence.

Replies to 为什么/為甚麼 **wèi shénme** questions often begin with the word 因为/因為 **yīnwéi** 'because.'

Question	*Answer*
你为什么学中文?	因为我想在中国找工作。
你為甚麼學中文?	因為我想在中國找工作。
Nǐ wèi shénme xué Zhōngwén?	**Yīnwéi wǒ xiǎng zài Zhōngguó zhǎo gōngzuò.**
Why do you study Chinese?	*Because* I want to look for a job in China.
你为什么喜欢他呢?	因为他特别帅!
你為甚麼喜歡他呢?	因為他特別帥!
Nǐ wèi shénme xǐhuan tā ne?	**Yīnwéi tā tèbié shuài!**
Why do you like him?	*Because* he's so handsome!

⇨ 40

In Mandarin, content question words are used in expressions that express the meanings 'any,' 'every,' 'none,' 'aways,' 'never,' etc.

> 谁都认识他。
> 誰都認識他。
> **Shéi dōu rènshi tā.**
> Everyone knows him.

> 我什么时候都忙。
> 我甚麼時候都忙。
> **Wǒ shénme shíhòu dōu máng.**
> I am always busy.

> 他什么酒都不喝。
> 他甚麼酒都不喝。
> **Tā shénme jiǔ dōu bù hē.**
> He doesn't drink any alcohol.

⇨ 42.4

25

Expressing identification, possession, and existence

25.1   Expressing identification

To identify a person, place, or thing, use the verb 是 **shì** 'to be.'

25.1.1 Identifying oneself and others

我是张明智。
我是張明智 。
Wǒ shì Zhāng Míngzhì.
I am Zhang Mingzhi.

这是我太太。
這是我太太。
Zhè shì wǒ tàitai.
This is my wife.

Q: 他们是谁？   A: 他们是我的朋友。
   他們是誰？   他們是我的朋友。
   Tāmen shì shéi?   **Tāmen shì wǒ de péngyou.**
   Who are they?   They are my friends.

Q: 你是经理吗？   A: 是。（我是经理。）
   你是經理嗎？   是。（我是經理。）
   Nǐ shì jīnglǐ ma?   **Shì. (Wǒ shì jīnglǐ.)**
   Are you the manager?   Yes. (I am the manager.)

⇨ 18.5

25.1.2 Identifying places

Q: 这是什么地方？   A: 这是北京饭店。
   這是甚麼地方？   這是北京飯店。
   Zhèi shì shénme dìfang?   **Zhè shì Běijīng fàndiàn.**
   What is this place?   This is the Beijing Hotel.

Q: 那是长安东路吗？ 那是長安東路嗎？ **Nà shì Cháng'ān dōng lù ma?** Is that East Chang'an Road?	A: 那不是长安东路；那是长安西路。 那不是長安東路；那是長安西路。 **Nà bù shì Cháng'ān dōng lù; nà shì Cháng'ān xī lù.** That is not East Chang'an Road; it is West Chang'an Road.
Q: 这是不是假日旅馆？ 這是不是假日旅館？ **Zhè shì bù shì Jiàrì Lǚguǎn?** Is this the Holiday Inn?	A: 是。 **Shì.** Yes, it is.
Q: 我们的房间是几号？ 我們的房間是幾號？ **Wǒmen de fángjiān shì jǐ hào?** What is our room number?	A: 你们的房间是479号。 你們的房間是479號。 **Nǐmen de fángjiān shì 479 hào.** Your room number is 479.

25.1.3 Identifying things

Chinese uses yes–no questions and content questions to ask about the identity of things.

⇨ 24.1, 24.6

Q: 这是我们的出租车吗？ 這是我們的出租車嗎？ **Zhè shì wǒmen de chūzūchē ma?** Is this our taxi?	A: 这不是你们的。 這不是你們的。 **Zhè bù shì nǐmen de.** This is not yours.
Q: 这是什么菜？ 這是甚麼菜？ **Zhè shì shénme cài?** What is this dish?	A: 这是清蒸鱼。 這是清蒸魚。 **Zhè shì qīngzhēng yú.** It is steamed fish.

25.2 Expressing possession

This section introduces the forms used by Chinese speakers to express possession and to inquire about possession.

25.2.1 Indicating 'having something'

To say that someone or something *has* something, use the verb 有 **yǒu** 'to have':

他有女朋友。
Tā yǒu nǚ péngyou.
He has a girlfriend.

你有弟弟吗？
你有弟弟嗎？
Nǐ yǒu dìdi ma?
Do you have a younger brother?

The negation of 有 **yǒu** is 没有 **méi yǒu**.

Q:	你有妹妹吗？		A:	没有。
	你有妹妹嗎？			
	Nǐ yǒu mèimei ma?			**Méi yǒu.**
	Do you have a younger sister?			No.

Q:	你有没有姐姐？		A:	我没有姐姐。
	Nǐ yǒu méi yǒu jiějie?			**Wǒ méi yǒu jiějie.**
	Do you have an older sister?			I do not have an older sister.

Q:	你现在有空吗？		A:	对不起。现在没有空。
	你現在有空嗎？			對不起。現在沒有空。
	Nǐ xiànzài yǒu kōng ma?			**Duìbuqǐ. Xiànzài méi yǒu kōng.**
	Do you have free time now?			Sorry. I don't have free time now.

⇨ 23.1.2

25.2.2 Expressing one's possession

To indicate one's possession, use the following structure:

possessor + 的 *de* + *possessed object*

哥哥的车	老师的书
哥哥的車	老師的書
gēgē de chē	**lǎoshī de shū**
older Brother's car	teacher's book

Mandarin does not have possessive pronouns. A *pronoun* + 的 *de* is equivalent in meaning to a possessive pronoun in English.

我的钥匙	谁的书？
我的鑰匙	誰的書？
wǒ de yàoshi	**shéi de shū?**
my key	whose book?

A table of English possessive pronouns and their Mandarin equivalents is presented in Chapter 5.

⇨ 5.2.4, 9.2.1.2

The *possessor* + 的 *de* may sometimes occur without the following 'possessed' noun. This is often the case when the noun is clear from the context of the sentence. In the following sentences, the noun in parentheses may be omitted.

这本书是你的(书)。
這本書是你的(書)。
Zhè běn shū shì nǐ de (shū).
This book is yours.

那个学校是他们的(学校)。
那個學校是他們的(學校)。
Nàge xuéxiào shì tāmen de (xuéxiào).
That school is theirs.

When there is a close relationship between the possessor and the possessed noun, 的 **de** may be omitted. 的 **de** is often omitted if the possessor is a pronoun.

我(的)母亲很忙。
我(的)母親很忙。
Wǒ (de) mǔqin hěn máng.
My mother is very busy.

他是我们(的)老师。
他是我們(的)老師。
Tā shì wǒmen (de) lǎoshī.
He is our teacher.

25.2.3 Expressing possession in formal written Chinese

属于/屬於 *shǔyú 'belong to, be affiliated with'*

这个幼儿园是属于北京大学的。
這個幼兒園是屬於北京大學的 。
Zhège yòu'éryuán shì shǔyú Běijīng Dàxué de.
This kindergarten is affiliated with Beijing University.

之 *zhī*

之 **zhī** is the formal written equivalent of 的 **de**, used in literary Chinese texts. Like 的 **de**, it occurs after the possessor and before the possessed noun.

钟鼓之声
鐘鼓之聲
zhōnggǔ zhī shēng
the sound of bells and drums

⇨ 9.6

25.3 Expressing existence

There are three verbs that are commonly used to express existence.

25.3.1 有 *yǒu* 'to exist'

In addition to its use in expressing possession, the verb 有 **yǒu** is also used to express existence.

昨天晚上有很大的雾。
昨天晚上有很大的雾。
Zuótiān wǎnshang yǒu hěn dà de wù.
Last night there was a very dense fog.

附近有三个旅馆。
附近有三個旅館。
Fùjìn yǒu sān gè lǚguǎn.
In this area there are three hotels.

To ask about existence, use the question form 有没有 **yǒu méi yǒu** or the yes–no question marker 吗/嗎 **ma**.

附近有没有旅馆？
附近有沒有旅館？
Fùjìn yǒu méi yǒu lǚguǎn?
Is there a hotel nearby?

昨天晚上有雾吗？
昨天晚上有霧嗎？
Zuótiān wǎnshang yǒu wù ma?
Was there fog last night? (Was it foggy last night?)

⇨ 24.1

To give a negative reply, say 没有 **méi yǒu**.

附近没有旅馆。
附近沒有旅館。
Fùjìn méi yǒu lǚguǎn.
There is no hotel nearby.

昨天晚上没有雾。
昨天晚上沒有霧。
Zuótiān wǎnshang méi yǒu wù.
There was no fog last night.

⇨ 23.1.2

25.3.2 The verb 是 *shì* 'to express existence'

是 **shì** can be used to express the existence of some object at a location. 是 **shì** is often used in this way when the object fills the location.

我们房子的屋顶上都是雪。
我們房子的屋頂上都是雪。
Wǒmen fángzi de wūdǐng shàng dōu shì xuě.
The roof of our house was covered with snow.

地上都是玩具。
地上都是玩具。
Dì shàng dōu shì wánjù.
Toys are all over the floor.

25.3.3 Expressing existence with placement verbs

Verbs that refer to placement such as 站 **zhàn** 'to stand,' 坐 **zuò** 'to sit,' 放 **fàng** 'to put, to place,' 躺 **tǎng** 'to lie,' etc. are often used in sentences that refer to existence. In these 'existential' sentences the verbs of placement are usually followed by the verb suffix 着/著 **zhe** to emphasize the ongoing duration of the situation.

街上站着很多人。
街上站著很多人。
Jiēshang zhànzhe hěn duō rén.
There are a lot of people standing in the street.

公共汽车上坐着很多人。
公共汽車上坐著很多人。
Gōnggòng qìchē shàng zuòzhe hěn duō rén.
There are a lot of people sitting on the bus.

书桌上放着一瓶花。
書桌上放著一瓶花。
Shūzhuō shàng fàngzhe yī píng huā.
There is a vase of flowers on the desk.

⇨ | 30.4, 35.2

26

Describing people, places, and things

26.1 Equational sentences: identifying or describing the subject with a noun phrase in the predicate

是 **shì** links the subject with a noun phrase in the predicate that identifies or describes it. Sentences with this form are *equational sentences*.

> *subject* 是 **shì** *noun or noun phrase*
>
> 赵玫玲是学生。
> 趙玫玲是學生。
> **Zhào Méilíng *shì* xuésheng.**
> Zhao Meiling *is* a student.
>
> 苏州是一个城市。
> 蘇州是一個城市。
> **Sūzhōu *shì* yī gè chéngshì.**
> Suzhou *is* a city.
>
> 奔驰是一种车。
> 奔馳是一種車。
> **Bēnchí *shì* yī zhǒng chē.**
> The Mercedes Benz *is* a type of car.

⇨ 11.4, 25.1

26.2 Describing the subject with a predicate that is an adjectival verb

Adjectival verbs may serve as the predicate of the sentence to describe the subject. The intensifier 很 **hěn** often occurs before the adjectival verb, especially if it is a one syllable adjectival verb. Notice that 是 **shì** is not used when the predicate is an adjectival verb.

> *subject (*很 **hěn***) adjectival verb*
>
> 赵玫玲很聪明。
> 趙玫玲很聰明。
> **Zhào Méilíng hěn cōngming.**
> Zhao Meiling is very smart.

苏州很漂亮。
蘇州很漂亮。
Sūzhōu hěn piàoliang.
Suzhou is very beautiful.

奔驰很贵。
奔馳很貴。
Bēnchí hěn guì.
The Mercedes Benz is very expensive.

⇨ 10

26.3 Identifying or describing a noun with a modifying phrase

Phrases that describe or 'modify' the noun always occur before the noun. The particle
的 **de** typically occurs right after the modifier and before the noun that is being
described. In the following examples, the *modifier* + 的 *de* is emphasized.

很聪明的女孩子
很聰明的女孩子
***hěn cōngming de* nǚháizi**
a very intelligent girl

很贵的车
很貴的車
***hěn guì de* chē**
a very expensive car

很有名的大学
很有名的大學
***hěn yǒu míng de* dàxué**
a very famous university

很安静的地方
***hěn ānjìng de* dìfang**
a very peaceful place

⇨ 9.2

26.4 Asking questions about the attributes of a person, place, or thing

26.4.1 Asking what someone or something is like

To ask what someone or something is like, say:

person/place/thing 怎么样？
　　　　　　　　怎麼樣？
　　　　　　　　zěnmeyàng?

What about this person/place/thing?
What is this person/place/thing like?

> 那个女孩子怎么样？
> 那個女孩子怎麼樣？
> **Nàge nǔ háizi zěnmeyàng?**
> What about that girl? (What is that girl like?)

> 那个大学怎么样？
> 那個大學怎麼樣？
> **Nàge dàxué zěnmeyàng?**
> What is that university like?

> 苏州怎么样？
> 蘇州怎麼樣？
> **Sūzhōu zěnmeyàng?**
> What is Suzhou like?

⇨ | 24.6

26.4.2 Asking for more information

To ask for more information about a person, place or thing, say:

什么/甚麼? **shénme** noun?
what person/place thing?

> 这是什么书？
> 這是甚麼書？
> **Zhè shì _shénme shū_?**
> _What book_ is this?

or

什么样的/甚麼樣的 **shénme yàng de** noun?
what kind of noun?

> 这是什么样的地方？
> 這是甚麼樣的地方？
> **Zhè shì _shénme yàng de dìfang_?**
> _What kind of place_ is this?

⇨ | 9.2.1.9, 24.6

26.5 Describing an item in terms of the material that it is made of

26.5.1 Describing what an item is made of

To describe an item in terms of the material that it is made of, say:

> (noun) 是 (用) ＿＿＿ 作的。
> **shì** (用) ＿＿＿ **zuò de.**

(noun) is made of _____.
那个桌子是用木头作的。
那個桌子是用木頭作的。
Nàge zhuōzi shì yòng mùtou zuò de.
That table is made of wood.

这个花瓶是(用)玻璃作的。
這個花瓶是(用)玻璃作的。
Zhège huāpíng shì (yòng) bōli zuò de.
This vase is made of glass.

我的耳环是(用)金子作的。
我的耳環是(用)金子作的。
Wǒ de ěrhuán shì (yòng) jīnzi zuò de.
My earrings are made of gold.

⇨ | 53.2.4

26.5.2 Asking what an item is made of

To ask what an item is made of, say:

(noun) 是用什么作的?
　　是用甚麼作的?
　　　shì yòng shénme zuò de?

What is (this object) made of?
这个花瓶是用什么作的?
這個花瓶是用甚麼作的?
Zhège huāpíng shì yòng shénme zuò de?
What is this vase made of?

你的耳环是用什么作的?
你的耳環是用甚麼作的?
Nǐ de ěrhuán shì yòng shénme zuò de?
What are your earrings made of?

26.6 Describing nouns in terms of attributes that imply comparison

In Mandarin, adjectival verbs imply comparison, even when they are not used in a comparison structure. Therefore, descriptions such as the following may be interpreted as simply descriptive or as comparative. The context usually makes it clear whether a simple description or a comparison is intended.

那本书贵。
那本書貴。
Nà běn shū guì.
That book is expensive.
or
That book is more expensive (than some other book).

王老师忙。
王老師忙。
Wáng lǎoshī máng.
Professor Wang is busy.
or
Professor Wang is busier (than some other people.)

⇨ | 10.5, 29

26.7 Describing people in terms of age

26.7.1 Describing age

To describe a person in terms of his or her age say:

王明(是)二十三岁。
王明(是)二十三歲。
Wáng Míng (shì) èrshísān suì.
Wang Ming is 23 (years old).

If it is clear from context, 岁/歲 **suì** 'years of age' may be omitted:

王明(是)二十三。
Wáng Míng (shì) èrshísān.
Wang Ming is 23.

The verb 是 **shì** is optional and is usually absent in statements.

我的弟弟十八岁。
我的弟弟十八歲。
Wǒ de dìdi shíbā suì.
My younger brother is 18 (years old).

However, when negation occurs in the sentence, 是 **shì** must also occur.

他不是十八岁。他只是十五岁。
他不是十八歲。他只是十五歲。
Tā bù shì shíbā suì. Tā zhǐ shì shíwǔ suì.
He is not 18 (years old). He is only 15 (years old).

When the adverb 已经/已經 **yǐjing** 'already' occurs, 是 **shì** may be absent.

他已经(是)两岁了。
他已經(是)兩歲了。
Tā yǐjing (shì) liǎng suì le.
He is already two (years old).

26.7.2 **Asking about age**

To ask the age of an adult, say:

> 你多大年纪？
> 你多大年紀？
> **Nǐ duō dà niánjì?**
> How old are you?

or

> 你多大岁数？
> 你多大歲數？
> **Nǐ duō dà suìshu?**
> How old are you?

To ask the age of a young person, say:

> 你多大？
> **Nǐ duō dà?**
> How old are you?

A formal and very polite way to inquire about the age of an older person is:

> 您今年高寿？
> 您今年高壽？
> **Nín jīnnián gāoshòu?**
> How old are you?

To ask the age of a child, you can say:

> 你几岁？
> 你幾歲？
> **Nǐ jǐ suì?**
> How old are you?

NOTE | 几/幾 jǐ is a classifier that is used to ask about small numbers. Therefore, it is appropriate to use when asking the age of young children, but not when asking the age of older people.

⇨ | 24.6

26.8 **Describing the weather**

26.8.1 **Statements that describe the weather**

Here are common Mandarin expressions used when discussing the weather. Notice that there is no word in Mandarin that is equivalent to the 'it' used in weather descriptions in English. Mandarin weather descriptions often begin with the verb and do not have a subject.

天气/天氣	舒服	凉快
tiān qì	**shūfu**	**liángkuai**
weather	comfortable	cool
闷热/悶熱	冷	暖和
mēn rè	**lěng**	**nuǎnhuo**
muggy; hot and humid	cold	warm

热/熱	多云/多雲	温和/溫和
rè	**duō yún**	**wēnhé**
hot	cloudy	mild

下雪	下雨	刮风/刮風
xià xuě	**xià yǔ**	**guā fēng**
snowing	raining	windy

今天的天气很好。
今天的天氣很好。
Jīntiān de tiānqì hěn hǎo.
Today's weather is very good.

昨天很闷热。
昨天很悶熱。
Zuótiān hěn mēnrè.
Yesterday was very humid and hot.

今天多云。
今天多雲。
Jīntiān duō yún.
Today it is cloudy. (used in weather reports)

昨天的天气很舒服。
昨天的天氣很舒服。
Zuótiān de tiānqì hěn shūfu.
Yesterday's weather was very comfortable.

昨天很凉快/冷/热/暖和。
昨天很凉快/冷/熱/暖和。
Zuótiān hěn liángkuai/lěng/rè/nuǎnhuo.
Yesterday's weather was cool/cold/hot/warm.

下雨了。
Xià yǔ le.
It's raining. (lit. 'falling the rain')

下雪了。
Xià xuě le.
It's snowing. (lit. 'falling the snow')

刮风了。
颳風了。
Guā fēng le.
It is windy. (lit. 'blowing the wind')

26.8.2 **Asking about the weather**

To ask about the weather or climate in general terms, use 怎么样/怎麼樣 **zěnmeyàng** 'what about it?' The following questions are followed by a typical answer.

Q: 这儿的天气怎么样?
這兒的天氣怎麼樣?
Zhèr de tiānqì zěnmeyàng?
What is the weather like here?

A: 这儿的天气很好。不冷也不热。
    這兒的天氣很好。不冷也不熱。
    Zhèr de tiānqì hěn hǎo. Bù lěng yě bù rè.
    The weather here is very nice, neither cold nor hot.

Q: 今年这儿的天气怎么样?
    今年這兒的天氣怎麼樣?
    Jīnnián zhèr de tiānqì zěnmeyàng?
    What was the weather like here this year?
A: 今年这儿的天气不太正常。
    今年這兒的天氣不太正常。
    Jīnnián zhèr de tiānqì bù tài zhèngcháng.
    The weather here was not normal this year.

Q: 杭州的气候怎么样?
    杭州的氣候怎麼樣?
    Hángzhōu de qìhòu zěnmeyàng?
    What is the climate like in Hangzhou?
A: 杭州的气候非常温和。
    杭州的氣候非常溫和。
    Hángzhōu de qìhòu fēicháng wēnhé.
    Hangzhou's climate is very mild.

Asking about temperature and describing temperature

Here are expressions associated with temperature.

温度/溫度	度	零下
wēndù	**dù**	**língxià**
temperature	degree	below zero

华氏/華氏	摄氏/攝氏	
huáshì	**shèshì**	
Fahrenheit	Celsius; centigrade	

Notice that when describing temperature, you can use the verb 是 **shì**. 是 **shì** is required with negation, but is otherwise usually absent. With the adverb 差不多 **chàbùduō** 'almost,' the verb may be 有 **yǒu**.

今天的温度是二十度。
今天的溫度是二十度。
Jīntiān de wēndù shì èrshí dù.
Today's temperature is 20 degrees.

Q: 今天的温度怎么样?
    今天的溫度怎麼樣?
    Jīntiān de wēndù zěnmeyàng?
    What is today's temperature?
A: 天气预报说今天的温度差不多有三十度。
    天氣預報說今天的溫度差不多有三十度。
    Tiānqì yùbào shuō jīntiān de wēndù chàbùduō yǒu sānshí dù.
    The weather report says today's temperature will be around 30 degrees.

Q: 你说的是华氏还是摄氏?
你説的是華氏還是攝氏?
Nǐ shuō de shì huáshì háishi shèshì?
Do you mean Fahrenheit or centigrade?

A: 在中国我们用的是摄氏。
在中國我們用的是攝氏。
Zài Zhōngguó wǒmen yòng de shì shèshì.
We use centigrade in China.

Q: 摄氏三十度是华氏多少度?
攝氏三十度是華氏多少度?
Shèshì sān shí dù shì huáshì duōshao dù?
Thirty degrees centigrade is how many degrees Fahrenheit?

A: 差不多是华氏九十度。
差不多是華氏九十度。
Chàbuduō shì huáshì jiǔshí dù.
It's about 90 degrees Fahrenheit.

今天很冷,零下五度。
Jīntiān hěn lěng, língxià wǔ dù.
It's really cold today, five degrees below zero.

26.9 Talking about illness and other medical conditions

26.9.1 Expressing general illness or allergy

Here are the most common ways to express having an illness or an allergy.

General illness	*Cold*	*Allergy*
(我)病了。	(我)感冒了。	(我)对(青霉素)过敏。
		(我)對(青黴素)過敏。
(Wǒ) bìng le.	**(Wǒ) gǎn mào le.**	**(Wǒ) duì (qīng méi sù) guòmǐn.**
(I) have become ill.	(I) have a cold.	(I) am allergic to (penicillin).
or		
(我)有病。		
(Wǒ) yǒu bìng.		
(I) have an illness.		

26.9.2 Describing symptoms

In English, symptoms are described as a possession of the patient: 'I have a headache'; 'you have a broken leg,' etc. Notice how symptoms are described in Mandarin.

Fever	*Cold symptoms*	*Sore throat*
(我)发烧了。	(我)流鼻涕。	(我)咳嗽。
(我)發燒了。		
(Wǒ) fā shāo le.	**(Wǒ) liú bíti.**	**(Wǒ) késou.**
(I) have fever.	(I) have a runny nose.	(I) have a cough.
(我)发高烧。	(我)打喷嚏。	(我)嗓子疼。
(我)發高燒。	(我)打噴嚏。	
(Wǒ) fā gāo shāo.	**(Wǒ) dǎ pēntì.**	**(Wǒ) sǎngzi téng.**
(I) have a high fever.	(I) am sneezing.	(I) have a sore throat.

General infection	*Earache*	*Headache*
(我)发炎。	(我)耳朵疼。	(我)头疼。
(我)發炎。		(我)頭疼。
(Wǒ) fāyán.	**(Wǒ) ěrduo téng.**	**(Wǒ) tóu téng.**
(I) have an infection.	(I) have an earache.	(I) have a headache.

Stomach ache	*Diarrhea*	*Broken bones*
(我)肚子疼。	(我)拉稀。	他骨头断了。
(Wǒ) dùzi téng.	**(Wǒ) lā xī.**	他骨頭斷了。
(I) have a stomach ache.	(I) have diarrhea.	**Tā gǔtou duàn le.**
		He has a broken bone.
		(Literally: His bone broke.)
我泻肚了。		他腿(手)断了。
我瀉肚了。	(我)拉肚子	他腿(手)斷了。
Wǒ xièdù le	**(Wǒ) lā dùzi**	**Tā tuǐ (shǒu) duàn le.**
I have diarrhea.	(I) have diarrhea.	He has a broken leg (arm).
(formal expression)		

26.9.3 Asking about symptoms

The following expressions are commonly used to ask about symptoms:

你什么地方不舒服？
你甚麼地方不舒服？
Nǐ shénme dìfang bù shūfu?
Where are you uncomfortable?

发不发烧？ 发烧吗？
發不發燒？ 發燒嗎？
Fā bù fā shāo? **Fā shāo ma?**
Do you have a fever? Do you have a fever?

(头)疼不疼？ (头)疼吗？
(頭)疼不疼？ (頭)疼嗎？
(Tóu) téng bù téng? **(Tóu) téng ma?**
Do you have a headache? Do you have a headache?

⇨ 24.1, 24.6

27

Describing how actions are performed

27.1 **Describing the general or past performance of an action with a manner adverbial phrase**

To describe how an action is generally performed or how it was performed in the past, use the following structure:

> *action verb* 得 ***de*** *adjectival verb*

Phrases that describe the performance of an action are often referred to as *manner adverbial* phrases. The word *adverbial* means they describe the verb.

> 他说得快。
> 他說得快。
> **Tā shuō de kuài.**
> He speaks fast.

> 她开得慢。
> 她開得慢。
> **Tā kāi de màn.**
> She drives slowly.

> 你们都考得好。
> 你們都考得好。
> **Nǐmen dōu kǎo de hǎo.**
> You all did well on the exam.

NOTE The suffixes 了 **le**, 过/過 **guo**, and 着/著 **zhe** do not occur after the action verb or the adjectival verb in manner adverbial phrases.

⇨ 33, 35

27.1.1 **Describing the performance of an action when the verb takes an object**

If the action verb takes an object, the verb is said twice, the first time followed by the object, and the second time followed by 得 ***de*** *adjectival verb*:

> *[action verb + object] [action verb* 得 ***de*** *adjectival verb]*

他说话说得快。
他説話説得快。
Tā shuō huà shuō de kuài.
He speaks fast.

他说中国话说得快。
他説中國話説得快。
Tā shuō Zhōngguó huà shuō de kuài.
He speaks Chinese fast.

她开车开得慢。
她開車開得慢。
Tā kāi chē kāi de màn.
She drives a car slowly.

你们考试都考得好。
你們考試都考得好。
Nǐmen kǎo shì dōu kǎo de hǎo.
You all did well on the exam.

27.1.2 Modifying the description of the action

27.1.2.1 Modifying with intensifiers

In these manner adverbial phrases, the adjectival verb may be preceded by an intensifier:

他说话说得很快。
他説話説得很快。
Tā shuō huà shuō de *hěn* kuài.
He speaks *very* quickly.

她开车开得太慢。
她開車開得太慢。
Tā kāi chē kāi de *tài* màn.
She drives a car *too* slowly.

你们考试都考得真好。
你們考試都考得真好。
Nǐmen kǎo shì dōu kǎo de *zhēn* hǎo.
You all did *really* well on the exam.

⇨ 10.3

27.1.2.2 Modifying with negation

In manner adverbial phrases, negation must occur before the adjectival verb, not before the action verb. Negation must be 不 **bù**:

他说得不快。
他説得不快。
Tā shuō de bù kuài.
He doesn't speak fast.

你们都考得不好。
你們都考得不好。
Nǐmen dōu kǎo de bù hǎo.
You all didn't do well on the exam.

⇨ 23.1.1

27.2 Asking about the performance of an action

To ask how an action is performed, say:

(subject) action verb 得怎么样?
得怎麼樣?
de zěnmeyàng?
How does the subject do the action?

他考得怎么样?
他考得怎麼樣?
Tā kǎode zěnmeyàng?
How did he do on the test?

她开车开得怎么样?
她開車開得怎麼樣?
Tā kāi chē kāi de zěnmeyàng?
How does she drive?

To ask if an action is performed in a particular way, form a yes–no question with the adjectival verb using:

- Verb-not-verb structure
   action verb 得 **de** adjective verb 不 **bù** adjective verb?

   你考试考得好不好?
   你考試考得好不好?
   Nǐ kǎo shì kǎo de hǎo bù hǎo?
   Did you do well on the test?

   他说得清楚不清楚?
   他說得清楚不清楚?
   Tā shuō de qīngchu bù qīngchu?
   Did he speak clearly?

- 吗/嗎 **ma** yes–no question structure

   你考得好吗?
   你考得好嗎?
   Nǐ kǎo de hǎo ma?
   Did you do well on the test?

   他说得清楚吗?
   他說得清楚嗎?
   Tā shuō de qīngchu ma?
   Did he speak clearly?

⇨ 24.1

27.3 **Describing the performance of an entire action with an adverbial modifier**

To describe how an entire action is performed on a specific occasion, precede the verb phrase (or prepositional phrase + verb phrase if there is a prepositional phrase) with an *adverbial verb modifier* + 地 *de* as follows. Note the tone changes on the second syllable of the modifier:

> *adverbial verb modifier* + 地 *de* + verb phrase

他偷偷儿地把钱拿走了。
他偷偷兒地把錢拿走了。
Tā *tōutōur de* bǎ qián názǒu le.
He secretly took away the money.

你们得好好儿地学。
你們得好好兒地學。
Nǐmen děi *hǎohāor de* xué.
You have to study *hard/well.*

他慢慢地把汉字学会了。
他慢慢地把漢字學會了。
Tā *mànmān de* bǎ Hàn zì xuéhuì le.
He *slowly* learned the Chinese characters.

快快地吃吧！
Kuàikuāi *de* chī ba!
Hurry up and eat!

孩子高高兴兴地在公园里玩。
孩子高高興興地在公園裏玩。
Háizi *gāo gāo xīng xīng de* zài gōngyuán lǐ wán.
The children are playing *happily* in the park.

他们静静地睡了一个晚上。
他們靜靜地睡了一個晚上。
Tāmen *jìngjìng de* shuì le yī gè wǎnshang.
They slept *peacefully* the whole night.

你得留心地听老师说话。
你得留心地聽老師説話。
Nǐ děi *liúxīn de* tīng lǎoshī shuō huà.
You should listen *attentively* to the teacher.

她急急忙忙地逃走了。
Tā *jíjí mángmáng de* táozǒu le.
She *hurriedly* ran away. (She ran away in a hurry.)

Phrases that frequently occur as adverbial modifiers of an entire action include the following:

慢慢地	**mànmān de**	slowly
快快地	**kuàikuāi de**	quickly
好好地	**hǎohāo de**	well
偷偷地	**tōutōu de**	secretly
静静地	**jìngjìng de**	peacefully

安静地	**ānjìng de**	peacefully/quietly
急忙地	**jímáng de**	hurriedly/hastily
匆忙地	**cōngmáng de**	hurriedly/hastily
兴奋地/興奮地	**xīngfèn de**	excitedly
大声地/大聲地	**dàshēng de**	loudly
悄悄地	**qiāoqiāo de**	quietly
严厉地/嚴厲地	**yánlì de**	sternly
残忍地/殘忍地	**cánrěn de**	cruelly
仔细地/仔細地	**zǐxì de**	meticulously
用心地	**yòngxīn de**	attentively, carefully
留心地	**liúxīn de**	attentively, cautiously
认真地/認真地	**rènzhēn de**	diligently, conscientiously
情愿地/情願地	**qíngyuàn de**	willingly
自愿地/自願地	**zìyuàn de**	willingly
使劲地/使勁地	**shǐjìn de**	using full strength/do with all one's might
渐渐地/漸漸地	**jiànjiàn de**	gradually
安安静静地	**ānānjìngjìng de**	peacefully
仔仔细细地/仔仔細細地	**zǐzǐxìxì de**	meticulously
急急忙忙地	**jíjí mángmáng de**	hurriedly
慌慌张张地/慌慌張張地	**huānghuāng zhāngzhāng de**	in a flustered manner

NOTE　These *adverbial modifiers* + 地 *de* occur in the same position in the predicate as other adverbs.

⇨　15

28

Indicating result, conclusion, potential, and extent

Indicating the result or conclusion of an action with resultative verbs

In Mandarin, action verbs refer to open-ended processes and not to their conclusions or results. For example, the verb 买/買 **mǎi** refers to *shopping*, not *buying*. The verb 找 **zhǎo** refers to *looking for* something, not *finding* it.

English sometimes uses two entirely different verbs to refer to a process and its result or conclusion. In Mandarin, processes and results are always expressed using the same verb. The process is expressed with an open-ended action verb. The result or conclusion is expressed by adding a resultative suffix to the open-ended action verb. Verbs that are formed by an action verb and a resultative suffix are often referred to as *resultative verbs*.

> Resultative verb structure: *action verb + resultative ending*

NOTE | Some grammars refer to the resultative suffix as a *complement of result*.

To read more about action verbs, see

⇨ | 13

28.1.1 Common resultative suffixes

Resultative suffixes that indicate the conclusion of the action:

Suffix	Meaning
完 **wán**	to finish
好 **hǎo**	to do to a successful conclusion

Resultative suffixes that indicate the result of an action:

Suffix	Meaning
见/見 **jiàn**	to perceive (used with verbs of perception: see, hear, smell)

Suffix	Meaning
到 **dào**	to attain a goal, to acquire (like 着/著 **zháo**)
着/著 **zháo**	to attain a goal, to acquire (like 到 **dào**)
错/錯 **cuò**	to do wrong, to be mistaken
饱/飽 **bǎo**	to be full
懂 **dǒng**	to understand
会/會 **huì**	to know
住 **zhù**	to stick
开/開 **kāi**	to open
够 **gòu**	enough
光 **guāng**	to use up
清楚 **qīngchu**	to be clear
干净/乾淨 **gānjìng**	to be clean

28.1.2 Common resultative verbs: action verbs + resultative ending

Action verb	Meaning	Resultative verb	Meaning
说/説 **shuō**	to say	说完/説完 **shuōwán**	to finish saying
吃 **chī**	to eat	吃完 **chīwán**	to finish eating
用 **yòng**	to use	用完 **yòngwán**	to use up (to use something until finished)
说/説 **shuō**	to say	说好/説好 **shuōhǎo**	to reach a successful conclusion through discussion; to reach an agreement
听/聽 **tīng**	to listen	听见/聽見 **tīngjian**	to hear something

187

Action verb	Meaning	Resultative verb	Meaning
看 **kàn**	to look	看見 **kànjian**	to see something
闻/聞 **wén**	to smell	闻见/聞見 **wénjian**	to smell something
听/聽 **tīng**	to listen	听到/聽到 **tīngdào**	to hear something
看 **kàn**	to look	看到 **kàndào**	to see something
闻/聞 **wén**	to smell	闻到/聞到 **wéndào**	to smell something
买/買 **mǎi**	to shop for	买到/買到 **mǎidào**	to buy/to purchase
找 **zhǎo**	to look for	找到 **zhǎodào**	to find
买/買 **mǎi**	to shop for	买着/買著 **mǎizháo**	to buy/to purchase
找 **zhǎo**	to look for	找着/找著 **zhǎozháo**	to find
睡/睡 **shuì**	to sleep	睡着/睡著 **shuìzháo**	to fall asleep
做 **zuò**	to do	做错/做錯 **zuòcuò**	to do wrong
写/寫 **xiě**	to write	写错/寫錯 **xiěcuò**	to write incorrectly
买/買 **mǎi**	to shop for	买错/買錯 **mǎicuò**	to buy wrong (to buy the wrong thing)
用 **yòng**	to use	用错/用錯 **yòngcuò**	to use wrong
吃 **chī**	to eat	吃饱/吃飽 **chībǎo**	to eat until full
看 **kàn**	to read	看懂 **kàndǒng**	to read to the point of understanding something
听/聽 **tīng**	to listen	听懂/聽懂 **tīngdǒng**	to listen to the point of understanding
学/學 **xué**	to study	学会/學會 **xuéhuì**	to study to the point of knowing something; to master by studying

Action verb	Meaning	Resultative verb	Meaning
记/記 **jì**	to record, to remember	记住/記住 **jìzhù**	to remember
打 **dǎ**	to hit (many idiomatic meanings)	打开/打開 **dǎkāi**	to open
吃 **chī**	to eat	吃够 **chīgòu**	to eat enough
问/問 **wèn**	to ask	问清楚 問清楚 **wènqīngchu**	to ask about something until you are clear about it
擦 **cā**	to wipe	擦干净 擦乾淨 **cāgānjìng**	to wipe something until it is clean
洗 **xǐ**	to wash	洗干净 洗乾淨 **xǐ gānjìng**	to wash something until it is clean

Here are example sentences with resultative verbs

Q: 你听到了那个声音吗？
你聽到了那個聲音嗎？
Nǐ tīngdào le nàge shēngyīn ma?
Did you hear that sound?

A: 没听到。
沒聽到。
Méi tīngdào.
I didn't hear it.

Q: 你吃饱了吗？
你吃飽了嗎？
Nǐ chībǎo le ma?
Did you eat until full?
(Are you full?)

A: 吃饱了。
吃飽了。
Chībǎo le.
I ate until full.
(I'm full.)

我把我自己的名字写错了。
我把我自己的名字寫錯了。
Wǒ bǎ wǒ zìjǐ de míngzi xiěcuò le.
I wrote my own name wrong.

Resultative suffixes may also refer to the direction of movement.

我们走进来了。
我們走進來了。
Wǒmen zǒujìnlái le.
We walked *in*.

猫跳上沙发去了。
貓跳上沙發去了。
Māo tiàoshàng shāfā qù le.
The cat jumped *onto* the sofa.

⇨ | 44.1

28.1.3 **Using the verb suffix 了 *le* with resultative verbs to indicate completion**

The verb suffix 了 **le** occurs at the end of resultative verbs, after the resultative suffix, to indicate that the action is completed or the desired result has been attained.

> 我做完了功课。
> 我做完了功課。
> **Wǒ zuòwán le gōngkè.**
> I finished my homework.

> 我吃饱了。
> 我吃飽了。
> **Wǒ chībǎo le.**
> I am full. (I've eaten until full.)

了 **le** never occurs between the action verb and the resultative ending.

Say this	*Not this*
你找到了你的皮包吗?	*你找了到你的皮包吗?
你找到了你的皮包嗎?	你找了到你的皮包嗎?
Nǐ zhǎodào le nǐ de píbāo ma?	**Nǐ zhǎo le dào nǐ de píbāo ma?**
Have you found your wallet?	

⇨ 13.1, 33.1

28.1.4 **Using 没 *méi* with resultative verbs to indicate lack of completion or result**

The negative marker 没 **méi** is used to indicate that an action has not been completed or that the desired result has not been attained. 没 **méi** occurs before the entire resultative verb.

> 我没看完。
> **Wǒ méi kànwán.**
> I haven't finished reading.

> 我没听懂。
> 我沒聽懂。
> **Wǒ méi tīngdǒng.**
> I didn't understand (by listening).

没 **méi** never occurs between the action verb and resultative suffix.

Say this	*Not this*
我没念错。	*我念没错。
我沒唸錯。	我唸没錯。
Wǒ méi niàncuò.	**Wǒ niàn méi cuò.**
I didn't read (it) wrong.	

⇨ 13.3.2, 33.3

28.2 ## Indicating the ability to reach a conclusion or result: the potential infixes 得 *de* and 不 *bu*

得 **de** and 不 **bu** may occur between the action verb and resultative suffix to indicate that it is possible or not possible to reach the result. When 得 **de** and 不 **bu** are used in this way, we refer to them as *potential infixes* and the form of the resultative verb as the *potential form*.

28.2.1 ### The potential infix 得 *de*

To indicate that *it is possible* to perform an action and reach a conclusion or result, add the potential infix 得 **de** into the middle of the resultative verb, between the action verb and the resultative suffix:

> *action verb* + 得 *de* + *resultative suffix*
>
> 我看得懂中国电影。
> 我看得懂中國電影。
> **Wǒ kàndedǒng Zhōngguó diànyǐng.**
> I can understand (by watching) Chinese movies.
>
> 你吃得完那么多东西吗?
> 你吃得完那麼多東西嗎?
> **Nǐ chīdewán nàme duō dōngxi ma?**
> Can you finish eating that many things?

28.2.2 ### The potential infix 不 *bu*

To indicate that *it is not possible* to reach a conclusion or result, add the potential infix 不 **bù** into the middle of the resultative verb, between the action verb and the resultative suffix:

> *action verb* + 不 *bu* + *resultative suffix*
>
> 王老师的话我都听不懂。
> 王老師的話我都聽不懂。
> **Wáng lǎoshī de huà wǒ dōu tīngbudǒng.**
> I can't understand (by listening) what Professor Wang says.
>
> 我找不到我的皮包。
> **Wǒ zhǎobudào wǒ de píbāo.**
> I can't find my wallet.

NOTE
: The infixes 得 **de** and 不 **bu** are the only things that can occur between the action verb and the resultative suffix.

28.2.2.1 #### Using resulative verbs to indicate that a result cannot be achieved no matter what

Resultative verbs in the negative potential form occur with the question word 怎么/怎麼 **zěnme** to indicate that a result cannot be achieved *no matter what* the subject does.

我怎么学也学不会。
我怎麼學也學不會。
Wǒ zěnme xué yě xuébuhuì.
No matter how I study I can't learn (it).

他怎么找也找不到。
他怎麼找也找不到。
Tā zěnme zhǎo yě zhǎobudào.
No matter how I look I can't find (it).

⇨   24.6, 42.4

28.3 Summary of the functions of resultative verbs

The functions of resultative verbs and their occurrence with 了 **le** and negation are summarized below:

The action occurred and the result was attained	*The action occurred but the result or conclusion was not attained*
resultative verb + 了 **le**	没 **méi** + resultative verb
我吃饱了。	我没吃饱。
我吃飽了。	我沒吃飽。
Wǒ chībǎo le.	**Wǒ méi chībǎo.**
I ate until full.	I did not eat until full.
	(I ate but was not full).
It is possible to attain the indicated result or conclusion by performing the verb	*It is impossible to attain the indicated result or conclusion by performing the verb*
action verb 得 **de** result/conclusion	action verb 不 **bu** result/conclusion
我吃得饱。	我吃不饱。
我吃得飽。	我吃不飽。
Wǒ chīdebǎo.	**Wǒ chībubǎo.**
I am able to eat until full.	I am unable to eat until full.

28.4 Indicating the ability to perform the verb: the potential suffixes 得了 *deliǎo* and 不了 *buliǎo*

Resultative suffixes indicate the result or conclusion of an action. To indicate that the subject is *able to* or *unable to* perform the action, add one of the following *potential suffixes* to the verb:

> *Verb* + 得了 *deliǎo* able to perform the action

> *Verb* + 不了 *buliǎo* unable to perform the action

28.4.1 The potential suffix 得了 *deliǎo*

Use this suffix to say that the subject is able to perform the action of the verb or that the subject is able to finish the action. In the latter sense, it is similar to the resultative suffix 完 **wán** 'to finish.'

他很聪明，一定做得了这件事情。
他很聰明，一定做得了這件事情。
Tā hěn cōngming, yīdìng zuòdeliǎo zhèjiàn shìqing.
He is very smart. He is certainly able to take care of this matter.

今天的功课这么多，我做不了。
今天的功課這麼多，我做不了。
Jīntiān de gōngkè zhème duō, wǒ zuòbuliǎo.
There is so much homework today. I can't do it. (can't finish it.)

你叫了这么多菜，我们吃得了吗？
你叫了這麼多菜，我們吃得了嗎？
Nǐ jiào le zhème duō cài, wǒmen chīdeliǎo ma?
You've ordered so many dishes. Will we be able to eat them? (finish eating them?)

28.4.2 The potential suffix 不了 *buliǎo*

Use this suffix to say that the subject is not able to do some action.

我用不了筷子。
Wǒ yòngbuliǎo kuàizi.
I am unable to use chopsticks.

他一定走不了那么远。
他一定走不了那麼遠。
Tā yīdìng zǒubuliǎo nàme yuǎn.
He is certainly unable to walk that far.

这是他的个性，他改不了。
這是他的個性，他改不了。
Zhè shì tā de gèxìng, tā gǎibùliǎo.
This is his nature. He can't change.

28.4.3 Asking about the ability to perform an action

To ask about the ability of a subject to perform an action, form a yes–no question with 吗/嗎 **ma** or with *verb-not-verb* structure.

- 吗/嗎 **ma**

  你吃得了这么多菜吗？
  你吃得了這麼多菜嗎？
  Nǐ chīdeliǎo zhème duō cài ma?
  Are you able to eat this many dishes?

- *Verb-not-verb* structure: *verb* 得了 *deliǎo verb* 不了 *bùliǎo*

  他做得了做不了这件事情？
  他做得了做不了這件事情？
  Tā zuòdeliǎo zuòbuliǎo zhè jiàn shìqing?
  Is he able to take care of this matter or not?

  这么多菜，你吃得了吃不了？
  這麼多菜，你吃得了吃不了？
  Zhème duō cài, nǐ chīdeliǎo chībuliǎo?
  This many dishes, are you able to eat them or not?

To answer 'yes' say *verb* 得了 *deliǎo*:

> 做得了。
> **Zuòdeliǎo.**
> He can do it.

> 吃得了。
> **Chīdéliǎo.**
> I can eat them.

To answer 'no' say *verb* 不了 *buliǎo*:

> 做不了。
> **Zuòbuliǎo.**
> He can't do it.

> 吃不了。
> **Chībuliǎo.**
> I can't eat them.

28.4.4 Resultative suffixes with special meanings or properties

掉 *diào*

掉 **diào** indicates completion, and often also carries negative connotations for the speaker. It may serve as a suffix on open-ended or change-of-state action verbs. It does not occur with the potential infixes 得 **de** and 不 **bu**.

甩掉 *shuǎidiào* 'to throw away, to discard'

> 他把那个孩子甩掉不管了。
> 他把那個孩子甩掉不管了。
> **Tā bǎ nàge háizi shuǎidiào bù guǎn le.**
> He abandoned that child.

扔掉 *rēngdiào* 'to throw away'

> 你怎么把我的信给扔掉了?
> 你怎麼把我的信給扔掉了?
> **Nǐ zěnme bǎ wǒ de xìn gěi rēngdiào le?**
> Why you throw away my letter?

死掉 *sǐdiào* 'to die'

> 我忘了浇水，花儿都死掉了。
> 我忘了澆水，花兒都死掉了。
> **Wǒ wàng le jiāo shuǐ, huār dōu sǐdiào le.**
> I forgot to water (them) and all of my flowers died.

忘掉 *wàngdiào* 'to forget completely'

> 你怎么能忘掉了这么要紧的事情?
> 你怎麼能忘掉了這麼要緊的事情?
> **Nǐ zěnme néng wàngdiào le zhème yàojǐn de shìqing?**
> How could you forget such an important thing?

丢掉 *diūdiào* 'to lose'

> 我的护照丢掉了。我得去报警。
> 我的護照丢掉了。我得去報警。
> **Wǒ de hùzhào diūdiào le. Wǒ děi qù bào jǐng.**
> I lost my passport. I have to report it to the police.

得及 *dejí*, 不及 *bují*

及 **jí** only occurs in potential form. It means to be able to do an action on time.

来得及/來得及 *láidejí* 'to be able to arrive on time'

来不及/來不及 *láibují* 'to be unable to arrive on time'

> Q: 我们现在去上课，来得及来不及？
> 我們現在去上課，來得及來不及？
> **Wǒmen xiànzài qù shàng kè, láidejí láibují?**
> If we go to class now will we get there on time?
> A: 还有五分钟。快点儿走来得及.
> 還有五分鐘。快點兒走來得及。
> **Hái yǒu wǔfēn zhōng. Kuài diǎr zǒu láidejí.**
> We still have five minutes. If we go fast we can get there on time.

得起 *deqǐ*, 不起 *buqǐ*

起 **qǐ** only occurs in potential form. Its most common meaning is to be able to afford to do the verb.

吃得起 *chīdeqǐ* 'to be able to afford to eat something'

吃不起 *chībuqǐ* 'to be unable to afford to eat something'

> Q: 天天在饭馆吃饭，吃得起吃不起？
> 天天在飯館吃飯，吃得起吃不起？
> **Tiāntiān zài fànguǎn chī fàn, chīdeqǐ chībuqǐ?**
> Can you afford to eat in a restaurant every day?
> A: 有的人吃得起，有的人吃不起。
> **Yǒude rén chīdeqǐ, yǒude rén chībuqǐ.**
> Some people can afford it, some can't.

住得起 *zhùdeqǐ* 'to be able to afford to live someplace'

住不起 *zhùbuqǐ* 'to be unable to afford to live someplace'

> Q: 现在北京房子那么贵，你们住得起住不起？
> 現在北京房子那麼貴，你們住得起住不起？
> **Xiànzài Běijīng fángzi nàme guì, nǐmen zhùdeqǐ zhùbuqǐ?**
> Houses in Beijing are so expensive now, can you afford to live there?
> A: 我们住得起，可是我们的孩子住不起。
> 我們住得起，可是我們的孩子住不起。
> **Wǒmen zhùdeqǐ, kěshì wǒmen de háizi zhùbuqǐ.**
> We can afford to live there, but our children cannot afford to live there.

得起 **deqǐ** and 不起 **buqǐ** also have idiomatic meanings when suffixed to certain verbs.

看不起 **kànbuqǐ** *'to look down on someone'*

> 你不应该看不起没有钱的人。
> 你不應該看不起沒有錢的人。
> **Nǐ bù yīnggāi kànbuqǐ méi yǒu qián de rén.**
> You should not look down on people who have no money.

对不起/對不起 **duìbuqǐ** *'to insult someone'* or *'show disrespect'*

对得起/對得起 **duìdeqǐ** *'to show respect to someone'*

> Q: 你不好好地念书对得起对不起你的父母?
> 　　你不好好地唸書對得起對不起你的父母?
> **Nǐ bù hǎohāo de niàn shū duìdeqǐ duìbuqǐ nǐ de fùmǔ?**
> If you do not study hard, how can you face your parents?
> A: 我一定要好好地念书才能对得起他们。
> 　　我一定要好好地唸書才能對得起他們。
> **Wǒ yīdìng yào hǎohāo de niànshū cái néng duìdeqǐ tāmen.**
> I certainly want to study hard so that I can show respect to them.

上 shàng

上 **shàng** has a special meaning when used in the resultative verb 考上 **kǎoshàng** *'to pass an entrance exam'* (especially a university entrance exam). The potential forms are:

考得上 **kǎodeshàng** *'able to pass the entrance exam'*

考不上 **kǎobushàng** *'unable to pass the entrance exam'*

> Q: 你想我今年考得上考不上北大?
> **Nǐ xiǎng wǒ jīnnián kǎodeshàng kǎobushàng Běi Dà?**
> Do you think I will be able to pass the exam for Beijing University this year?
> A: 我想你一定考得上。
> **Wǒ xiǎng nǐ yīdìng kǎodeshàng.**
> I think you will certainly pass the exam.

不定 budìng

不定 **budìng** has a restricted use as a resultative verb ending:

说不定/説不定 **shuōbudìng** *'perhaps'*

> 他现在还没来,说不定他不会来了。
> 他現在還沒來,説不定他不會來了。
> **Tā xiànzài hái méi lái, shuōbudìng tā bù huì lái le.**
> He hasn't come yet. Perhaps he won't come.

28.5 Indicating the extent or result of a situation

Resultative verbs indicate the result of actions. To indicate the result or extent of a situation, use the following structure:

verb 得 *de verb phrase/clause*

When the verb is an adjectival verb, 得 *de verb phrase/clause* introduces the extent of the situation: *so adjectival verb that* verb phrase/clause.

> 他累得抬不起头来了。
> 他累得抬不起頭來了。
> **Tā *lèi de* táibuqǐtóu lái le.**
> He was *so tired that* he could not pick up his head.

> 她高兴得说不出话来了。
> 她高興得説不出話來了。
> **Tā *gāoxìng de* shuōbuchū huà lái le.**
> She was *so happy that* she was unable to speak.

> 他冷得发抖了。
> 他冷得發抖了。
> **Tā *lěng de* fādǒu le.**
> He was so cold that he was shivering.

When the verb is an action verb, 得 *de verb phrase/clause* introduces the result of the action: *performed the action until* verb phrase/sentence.

> 妈妈哭得眼睛都红了。
> 媽媽哭得眼睛都紅了。
> **Māma *kū de* yǎnjing dōu hóng le.**
> Mom *cried until* her eyes were red.

> 他走得精疲力尽了。
> 他走得精疲力盡了。
> **Tā *zǒu de* jīngpí lìjìn le.**
> He *walked so much that* he was exhausted.

If the action verb takes an object, the sentence takes the following form:

> *[action verb + object] action verb* 得 *de verb phrase/clause*

> 他[走路]走得精疲力尽了。
> 他[走路]走得精疲力盡了。
> **Tā [zǒu lù] zǒu de jīngpí lìjìn le.**
> He walked so much that he was exhausted.

29

Making comparisons

Comparison structures are used to indicate that things are similar to or different from each other, or to indicate that something is more than or less than another thing in some way.

This chapter presents the structures used to make comparisons in Mandarin. It uses the following grammatical terms and abbreviations. Refer to the relevant chapters for more information about each grammatical category.

noun phrase (NP)			Chapter 9
adjectival verb (AV)	and	adjective verb phrase (AVP)	Chapter 10
stative verb (SV)	and	stative verb phrase (SVP)	Chapter 11
modal verb (MV)			Chapter 12
action verb (V)	and	action verb phrases (VP)	Chapter 13

29.1 Similarity

29.1.1 Indicating that noun phrases are identical

To indicate that two noun phrases are similar or equal, say:

NP₁	跟/和	NP₂	一样
NP₁	跟/和	NP₂	一樣
NP₁	**gēn/hé**	NP₂	**yīyàng**
NP₁	and	NP₂	identical/same

这本书跟/和那本书一样。
這本書跟/和那本書一樣。
Zhè běn shū gēn/hé nà běn shū yīyàng.
This book and that book are the same.

今天的天气跟/和昨天的一样。
今天的天氣跟/和昨天的一樣。
Jīntiān de tiānqì gēn/hé zuótiān de yīyàng.
Today's weather is the same as yesterday's.

NOTE The words 跟 **gēn** and 和 **hé** are equivalent in meaning. In all of the structures in this chapter in which they occur, 跟 **gēn** and 和 **hé** are interchangeable. In some dialects, 同 **tóng** occurs in this structure instead of 跟 **gēn** or 和 **hé**.

⇨ 16.1, 29.2.1

29.1.2 **Indicating that all noun phrases are the same**

When a noun phrase refers to multiple entities (for example, 'houses,' 'dogs,' 'two books,' etc.) use this pattern to say that all of the entities are the same.

> NP 一样
> NP 一樣
> NP **yīyàng**
> NP identical/same
> 这两本书一样。
> 這兩本書一樣。
> **Zhè liǎng běn shū yīyàng.**
> These two books are identical.
>
> 这三个菜一样吗?
> 這三個菜一樣嗎?
> **Zhè sān gè cài yīyàng ma?**
> Are these three dishes the same?

⇨ | 29.2.2

29.1.3 **Indicating that noun phrases share a property**

To indicate that two noun phrases are alike in a particular property, say the following.

> NP₁ 跟/和 NP₂ 一样 AV
> NP₁ 跟/和 NP₂ 一樣 AV
> NP₁ **gēn/hé** NP₂ **yīyàng** AV
> NP₁ and NP₂ identical/same AV
> 我儿子跟/和我女儿一样<u>高</u>。
> 我兒子跟/和我女兒一樣<u>高</u>。
> **Wǒ érzi gēn/hé wǒ nǚ'ér yīyàng *gāo*.**
> My son and my daughter are the same height. (equally *tall*)
>
> 小狗和小猫一样<u>可爱</u>。
> 小狗和小貓一樣<u>可愛</u>。
> **Xiǎogǒu hé xiǎomāo yīyàng *kě'ài*.**
> Puppies and kittens are equally *cute*.

⇨ | 29.2.3

29.1.4 **Indicating resemblance**

To indicate that one noun phrase resembles another noun phrase, say:

> NP₁ 像 NP₂
> NP₁ **xiàng** NP₂
> NP₁ looks like NP₂ (NP₁ resembles NP₂)
> 他像他爸爸。
> **Tā xiàng tā bàba.**
> He resembles his dad.
>
> 他像法国人吗?
> 他像法國人嗎?
> **Tā xiàng Fǎguórén ma?**
> Does he look like a French person?

or

NP₁	跟/和		NP₂	很像

NP₁	**gēn/hé**	NP₂	**hěn xiàng**

你儿子跟/和你女儿很像吗？

你兒子跟/和你女兒很像嗎？

Nǐ érzi gēn/hé nǐ nǚ'ér hěn xiàng ma?

Do your son and daughter look alike?

If the noun phrase refers to multiple entities, say:

NP	(很)	像

NP	**(hěn)**	**xiàng**

NP are very similar/very much alike.

他们很像。

他們很像。

Tāmen hěn xiàng.

They look very much alike.

⇨ 29.2.4

29.1.5 Indicating similarity in some property

To indicate that two noun phrases are similar enough to be considered equivalent, say:

NP₁	有	NP₂	那么/那麼	AV

NP₁	**yǒu**	NP₂	**nàme**	AV

他有他姐姐那么高。(AV)

他有他姐姐那麼高。

Tā yǒu tā jiějie nàme *gāo*.

He is as *tall* as his older sister.

他有他姐姐那么聪明吗？

他有他姐姐那麼聰明嗎？

Tā yǒu tā jiějie nàme *cōngming* ma?

Is he as *intelligent* as his older sister?

or

NP₁	有	NP₂	这么/這麼	AV

NP₁	有	NP₂	**zhème**	AV

NP₁ is as AV as NP₂

他有你这么高。AV

他有你這麼高。

Tā yǒu nǐ zhème *gāo*.

He is as *tall* as you.

A note on 那么/那麼 *nàme* and 这么/這麼 *zhème*

这么/這麼 **zhème** 'this/so' and 那么/那麼 **nàme** 'that/so' are used frequently in comparison structures. They may occur before an adjectival verb. It is often not necessary to translate 这么/這麼 **zhème** and 那么/那麼 **nàme** into English.

⇨ 29.4.1

29.1.6 Indicating identical performance of an action

To indicate that two noun phrases perform an action in a similar way, say:

NP₁   跟/和   NP₂   [verb 得]   一样   AV
NP₁   跟/和   NP₂   [verb 得]   一樣   AV
NP₁   **gēn/hé**   NP₂   [verb **de**]   **yīyàng**   AV
NP₁ and NP₂ perform the verb equally AV

> 我跟他吃得<u>一样</u>多。
> 我跟他吃得<u>一樣</u>多。
> **Wǒ gēn tā chī de *yīyàng duō*.**
> I eat *as much as* him.

> 弟弟跟妹妹写得<u>一样</u>快。
> 弟弟跟妹妹寫得<u>一樣</u>快。
> **Dìdi gēn mèimei xiě de *yīyàng kuài*.**
> Younger brother and younger sister write *equally fast.*

If the object of the action verb is included in the sentence, the action verb is said twice, once followed by the object, and once followed by 得 一样 de yīyàng (AV).

NP₁   跟/和   NP₂   [action verb + object] [action verb 得]   一样   AV
NP₁   跟/和   NP₂   [action verb + object] [action verb 得]   一樣   AV
NP₁   **gēn/hé**   NP₂   [action verb + object] [action verb **de**]   **yīyàng**   AV
NP₁ and NP₂ perform the action verb equally AV

> 我跟他吃<u>饭</u>吃得一样多。
> 我跟他吃<u>飯</u>吃得一样多。
> **Wǒ gēn tā *chī* fàn *chī* de yīyàng duō.**
> I eat as much as him.

> 弟弟跟妹妹写<u>字</u>写得一样快。
> 弟弟跟妹妹寫<u>字</u>寫得一樣快。
> **Dìdi gēn mèimei *xiě zì xiě* de yīyàng kuài.**
> Younger brother and younger sister write characters equally fast.

Here are several variations in this pattern. They differ in the order of the phrases. In all of these variations, [action verb + object] occurs before [action verb 得 **de**], and 一样/一樣 **yīyàng** AV occurs at the end of the sentence.

Variation 1

NP₁   [action verb + object] [action verb 得]   跟/和   NP₂   一样   AV
NP₁   [action verb + object] [action verb 得]   跟/和   NP₂   一樣   AV
NP₁   [action verb + object] [action verb **de**]   **gēn/hé**   NP₂   **yīyàng**   AV
NP₁ and NP₂ perform the action verb equally AV

> 我吃饭吃得跟他一样多。
> 我吃飯吃得跟他一樣多。
> **Wǒ chī fàn chī de gēn tā yīyàng duō.**
> I eat as much as him.

> 弟弟写字写得跟妹妹一样快。
> 弟弟寫字寫得跟妹妹一樣快。
> **Dìdi xiě zì xiě de gēn mèimei yīyàng kuài.**
> Younger brother and younger sister write characters equally fast.

Variation 2

NP₁ [action verb + object] 跟/和 NP₂ [action verb 得] 一样 AV
NP₁ [action verb + object] 跟/和 NP₂ [action verb 得] 一樣 AV
NP₁ [action verb + object] **gēn/hé** NP₂ [action verb **de**] **yīyàng** AV
NP₁ and NP₂ perform the action verb equally AV

我吃饭跟他吃得一样多。
我吃飯跟他吃得一樣多。
Wǒ chī fàn gēn tā chī de yīyàng duō.
I eat as much as him.

The verb 有 **yǒu** can be used instead of 跟 **gēn** or 和 **hé**.

NP₁ 有 NP₂ [action verb + object] [action verb 得] (那么/这么) AV
NP₁ 有 NP₂ [action verb + object] [action verb 得] (那麼/這麼) AV
NP₁ **yǒu** NP₂ [action verb + object] [action verb **de**] (**nàme/zhème**) AV
NP₁ and NP₂ perform the action verb equally AV

弟弟有爸爸写字写得那么漂亮。
弟弟有爸爸寫字寫得那麼漂亮。
Dìdi yǒu bàba xiě zì xiě de nàme piàoliang.
Younger brother writes characters as beautifully as dad.

or

NP₁ [action verb + object] [action verb 得] 有 NP₂ (那么/这么) AV
NP₁ [action verb + object] [action verb 得] 有 NP₂ (那麼/這麼) AV
NP₁ [action verb + object] [action verb **de**] **yǒu** NP₂ (**nàme/zhème**) AV
NP₁ performs the action verb as AV as NP₂

弟弟写字写得有爸爸那么漂亮。
弟弟寫字寫得有爸爸那麼漂亮。
Dìdi xiě zì xiě de yǒu bàba nàme piàoliang.
Younger brother writes characters as beautifully as dad.

Be careful to repeat the verb if you include the object of the verb.

Say this	*Not this*
我吃饭吃得跟他一样多。	*我吃饭得跟他一样多。
我吃飯吃得跟他一樣多。	我吃飯得跟他一樣多。
Wǒ chī fàn chī de gēn tā yīyàng duō.	**Wǒ chī fàn de gēn tā yīyàng duō.**
I eat as much as he does.	
弟弟写字写得有爸爸那么漂亮。	*弟弟写字得有爸爸那么漂亮。
弟弟寫字寫得有爸爸那麼漂亮。	弟弟寫字得有爸爸那麼漂亮。
Dìdi xiě zì xiě de yǒu bàba nàme piàoliang.	**Dìdi xiě zì de yǒu bàba nàme piàoliang.**
Younger brother writes characters as nicely as dad.	

⇨ | 27.1.2, 29.3.5, 29.4.3

29.2 Difference

29.2.1 Indicating that noun phrases are different

To indicate that two noun phrases are different, say:

NP₁   不   跟/和   NP₂   一样。
NP₁   不   跟/和   NP₂   一樣。
NP₁   **bù   gēn/hé   NP₂   yīyàng.**
NP₁ and NP₂ are not identical/the same.

> 这本书不跟/和那本书一样 。
> 這本書不跟/和那本書一樣 。
> **Zhè běn shū bù gēn/hé nà běn shū yīyàng.**
> This book is not the same as that book.

> 今天的天气不跟/和昨天的天气一样 。
> 今天的天氣不跟/和昨天的天氣一樣 。
> **Jīntiān de tiānqì bù gēn/hé zuótiān de tiānqì yīyàng.**
> Today's weather is not the same as yesterday's.

or

NP₁   跟/和   NP₂   不   一样。
NP₁   跟/和   NP₂   不   一樣。
NP₁   **gēn/hé   NP₂   bù   yīyàng.**
NP₁ and NP₂ are not identical/the same.

> 这个旅馆的价钱跟/和那个旅馆的价钱不一样。
> 這個旅館的價錢跟/和那個旅館的價錢不一樣。
> **Zhège lǚguǎn de jiàqian gēn/hé nàge lǚguǎn de jiàqian bù yīyàng.**
> The cost of this hotel is not the same as the cost of that hotel.

⇨ 29.1.1

29.2.2 Indicating that all noun phrases are not identical

When a noun phrase refers to more than one entity (for example 'houses,' 'dogs,' 'two books,' etc.) use this pattern to say that the entities are not identical.

NP   不   一样。
NP   不   一樣。
NP   **bù   yīyàng.**
NP are not identical/same

> 这两本书不一样。
> 這兩本書不一樣。
> **Zhè liǎng běn shū bù yīyàng.**
> These two books are not identical.

⇨ 29.1.2

29.2.3 Indicating that noun phrases are different in some property

To indicate that two noun phrases are different in a particular property, say:

NP₁	不	跟/和	NP₂	一	样	AV。
NP₁	不	跟/和	NP₂	一	樣	AV。
NP₁	**bù**	**gēn/hé**	NP₂	**yīyàng**		AV.

这个旅馆的房间不跟那个旅馆的房间一样干净。
這個旅館的房間不跟那個旅館的房間一樣乾淨。
Zhège lǘguǎn de fángjiān bù gēn nàge lǘguǎn de fángjiān yīyàng gānjìng.
The rooms in this hotel are not as *clean* as the rooms in that hotel.

我儿子不跟/和我女儿一样高。
我兒子不跟/和我女兒一樣高。
Wǒ érzi bù gēn/hé wǒ nǚ'ér yīyàng gāo.
My son is not the same *height* as my daughter.

or

NP₁	跟/和	NP₂	不	一	样	AV。
NP₁	跟/和	NP₂	不	一	樣	AV。
NP₁	**gēn/hé**	NP₂	**bù**	**yīyàng**		AV.

NP₁ and NP₂ are not identical/the same in some property.

这个旅馆的房间跟那个旅馆的房间不一样干净。
這個旅館的房間跟那個旅館的房間不一樣乾淨。
Zhège lǘguǎn de fángjiān gēn nàge lǘguǎn de fángjiān bù yīyàng gānjìng.
The rooms in this hotel are not as *clean* as the rooms in that hotel.

我儿子跟/和我女儿不一样高。
我兒子跟/和我女兒不一樣高。
Wǒ érzi gēn/hé wǒ nǚ'ér bù yíyàng gāo.
My son and my daughter are not the same height. (not equally *tall*)

⇨ 29.1.3

29.2.4 Indicating that one noun phrase does not resemble another

To indicate that one noun phrase does not resemble another noun phrase, say:

NP₁	不	像	NP₂
NP₁	**bù**	**xiàng**	NP₂

NP₁ does not look like NP₂/NP₁ does not resemble NP₂

他(一点也)不像法国人。
他(一點也)不像法國人。
Tā (yīdiǎn yě) bù xiàng Fǎguórén.
He doesn't look like a French person (at all).

⇨ 29.1.4

29.3 More than

'More than' comparisons indicate that some noun phrase has more of some property than another noun phrase. The property can be expressed as an adjectival verb, a stative verb, or a verb phrase with a modal verb.

29.3.1 Comparing noun phrases in terms of adjectival verbs

NP₁ 比 NP₂ AV
NP₁ **bǐ** NP₂ AV
NP₁ is more AV than NP₂

中国比日本大。
中國比日本大。
Zhōngguó bǐ Rìběn *dà*.
China is *bigger* than Japan.

我的身体比以前好了。
我的身體比以前好了。
Wǒ de shēntǐ bǐ yǐqián *hǎo* le.
My health is *better* than before.

吃饭比做饭容易。
吃飯比做飯容易。
Chī fàn bǐ zuò fàn *róngyì*.
Eating is *easier* than cooking.

写字比认字难。
寫字比認字難。
Xiě zì bǐ rèn zì *nán*.
Writing characters is *harder* than recognizing characters.

NOTE In the third and fourth example sentences in this section, the phrases that are being compared are a *verb + object*. In these sentences, the verb + object together function as a noun phrase, serving as the subject of the sentence or as the object of 比 **bǐ**.

29.3.2 Comparing noun phrases in terms of stative verbs

Stative verbs such as **ài** 'to love' and **xǐhuan** 'to like to,' 'to prefer' take noun phrase objects or verb phrase complements. The stative verb and its object or complement is a stative verb phrase (SVP). When comparing two noun phrases in terms of a stative verb phrase, say:

NP₁ 比 NP₂ SVP
NP₁ **bǐ** NP₂ SVP
NP₁ is more SVP than NP₂

他比我爱吃中国饭。
他比我愛吃中國飯。
Tā bǐ wǒ *ài chī Zhōngguó fàn*.
He *loves to eat Chinese food* more than I.

张先生比张太太喜欢买书。
張先生比張太太喜歡買書。
Zhāng xiānsheng bǐ Zhāng tàitai *xǐhuan mǎi shū*.
Mr. Zhang *likes to buy books* more than Mrs. Zhang.

⇨ 11

29.3.3 Comparing noun phrases in terms of modal verb phrase

To compare noun phrases in terms of verb phrases that begin with a modal verb, say:

> NP₁ 比 NP₂ MVP
> NP₁ **bǐ** NP₂ MVP
> NP₁ is more MVP than NP₂
> > 我姐姐比我哥哥会唱歌。(MV)
> > 我姐姐比我哥哥會唱歌。
> > **Wǒ jiějie bǐ wǒ gēgē *huì chàng gē*.**
> > My older sister *can sing* better than my older brother.

29.3.4 Indicating quantity in 'more than' comparisons

When comparing noun phrases, it is possible to indicate *how much more* one noun phrase is than the other. The phrase that indicates the quantity occurs at the end of the sentence, after the adjectival verb or stative verb.

29.3.4.1 Indicating a specific quantity

When the quantity is a specific number, say:

> NP₁ 比 NP₂ AV [number + classifier (+ noun)]
> NP₁ **bǐ** NP₂ AV [number + classifier (+ noun)]
> NP₁ is more AV than NP₂ by [number + classifier (+ noun)]
> > 她先生比她<u>大六岁</u>。
> > 她先生比她<u>大六歲</u>。
> > **Tā xiānsheng bǐ tā *dà liù suì*.**
> > Her husband is *six years older* than her.
>
> > 这个旅馆比那个旅馆贵<u>九十块钱</u>。
> > 這個旅館比那個旅館貴<u>九十塊錢</u>。
> > **Zhège lǚguǎn bǐ nàge lǚguǎn *guì jiǔ shí kuài qián*.**
> > This hotel is *ninety dollars more expensive* than that one.
>
> > 这个旅馆比那个旅馆贵<u>一倍</u>。
> > 這個旅館比那個旅館貴<u>一倍</u>。
> > **Zhège lǚguǎn bǐ nàge lǚguǎn *guì yī bèi*.**
> > This hotel is *twice as expensive* as that one.

The adjectival verbs 早 **zǎo** 'early,' 晚 **wǎn** 'late,' 多 **duō** 'more,' and 少 **shǎo** 'less' may be followed by an action verb. The *number + classifier and optional noun* sequence occurs after the *adjectival verb + action verb*.

> NP₁ 比 NP₂ AV action verb [number + classifier (+ noun)]
> NP₁ **bǐ** NP₂ AV action verb [number + classifier (+ noun)]
> NP₁ does verb more AV than NP₂ by [number + classifier (+ noun)]
> > 今天他比我早来了<u>五分钟</u>。
> > 今天他比我早來了<u>五分鐘</u>。
> > **Jīntiān tā bǐ wǒ zǎo lái le *wǔ fēn zhōng*.**
> > He came *five minutes* earlier than I did today.
>
> > 昨天我比老板晚走了<u>一个钟头</u>。
> > 昨天我比老闆晚走了<u>一個鐘頭</u>。
> > **Zuótiān wǒ bǐ lǎobǎn wǎn zǒu le *yí gè zhōngtou*.**
> > Yesterday I left *an hour* later than my boss did.

我今年比去年多挣了<u>两百块钱</u>。
我今年比去年多掙了<u>兩百塊錢</u>。
Wǒ jīnnián bǐ qùnián duō zhèng le *liǎng bǎi kuài qián*.
I earned *two hundred dollars* more this year than last year.

Noun phrase₁ is *much more* AV than noun phrase₂

To indicate that one noun phrase is *much more* AV than another noun phrase, say the following.

NP₁   比   NP₂   AV   得多
NP₁   **bǐ**   NP₂   AV   **de duō**
NP₁ is much more AV than NP₂

今天比昨天<u>冷得多</u>。
Jīntiān bǐ zuótiān *lěng de duō*.
Today is *much colder* than yesterday.

中文比英文<u>难得多</u>。
中文比英文<u>難得多</u>。
Zhōngwén bǐ Yīngwén *nán de duō*.
Chinese is *much more difficult* than English.

or

NP₁   比   NP₂   AV   多了
NP₁   **bǐ**   NP₂   AV   **duō le**
NP₁ is much more AV than NP₂

今天比昨天<u>冷多了</u>。
Jīntiān bǐ zuótiān *lěng duō le*.
Today is *much colder* than yesterday.

中文比英文<u>难多了</u>。
中文比英文<u>難多了</u>。
Zhōngwén bǐ Yīngwén *nán duō le*.
Chinese is *much more difficult* than English.

NOTE   Intensifiers cannot occur before the adjectival verb in the 比 **bǐ** comparison pattern.

Say this	*Not this*
今天比昨天冷得多。	*今天比昨天很冷。
Jīntiān bǐ zuótiān lěng de duō.	**Jīntiān bǐ zuótiān hěn lěng.**
Today is a lot colder than yesterday.	
他比我用功得多。	*他比我非常用功。
Tā bǐ wǒ yònggōng de duō.	**Tā bǐ wǒ fēicháng yònggōng.**
He is much more hardworking than I am.	

The following pattern with 真 **zhēn** conveys a very similar meaning to the above patterns.

NP₁   真   比   NP₂   AV
NP₁   **zhēn**   **bǐ**   NP₂   AV
NP₁ is really more AV than NP₂

今天<u>真</u>比昨天<u>冷</u>。
Jīntiān *zhēn* bǐ zuótiān *lěng*.
Today is *really much colder* than yesterday.

中文真比英文难。
中文真比英文難。
Zhōngwén *zhēn* bǐ Yīngwén *nán*.
Chinese is *really more difficult* than English.

29.3.4.3 Noun phrase₁ is *a little more* AV than noun phrase₂

To indicate that one noun phrase is *a little more* AV than another noun phrase, say the following.

NP₁ 比 NP₂ AV 一点儿/一點兒
NP₁ **bǐ** NP₂ AV **yīdiǎr**
NP₁ is a little more AV than NP₂

我们的房子比他们的小一点儿。
我們的房子比他們的小一點兒。
Wǒmen de fángzi bǐ tāmen de *xiǎo yīdiǎr*.
Our house is *a little smaller* than theirs.

哥哥比弟弟用功一点。
哥哥比弟弟用功一點。
Gēge bǐ dìdi *yònggōng yīdiǎn*.
Older brother is *a little more hardworking* than younger brother.

29.3.4.4 Noun phrase₁ is *more adjectival verb than* noun phrase₂ *by half*

To indicate that one noun phrase is *more* of some quality *by half*, put the phrase 一半 **yí bàn** 'one half' after the adjectival verb.

这两件衣服，哪一件便宜?
這兩件衣服，哪一件便宜?
Zhè liǎng jiàn yīfú, nǎ yí jiàn piányi?
Of these two dresses which one is cheaper?

这件衣服比那件便宜一半。
這件衣服比那件便宜一半。
Zhè jiàn yīfú bǐ nà jiàn piányi *yí bàn*.
This dress is half the price of that one.

29.3.4.5 Noun phrase₁ is more *adjectival verb than* noun phrase₂ *by a specific percent*

The phrase X 分 之 Y occurs after the adjectival verb.

今年学中文的学生比去年多四分之一。
今年學中文的學生比去年多四分之一。
Jīnnián xué Zhōngwén de xuésheng bǐ qùnián duō *sì fēn zhī yī*.
There are *25%* more students studying Chinese this year.

⇨ 6.6

29.3.5 Comparing the performance of an action

To indicate that one noun phrase does some action *more AV than* another noun phrase, say:

NP₁ 比 NP₂ [verb 得] AV
NP₁ **bǐ** NP₂ [verb **de**] AV
NP₁ performs the verb more AV than NP₂

他比我吃得多。

Tā bǐ wǒ *chī de duō*.

He *eats more* than me.

弟弟比妹妹写得快。
弟弟比妹妹寫得快。

Dìdi bǐ mèimei *xiě de kuài*.

Younger brother *writes faster* than younger sister.

If the object of the action verb is included in the sentence, the action verb must be said twice, once followed by the object, and once followed by AV.

NP₁ 比 NP₂ [action verb + object] [action verb 得] AV
NP₁ **bǐ** NP₂ [action verb + object] [action verb **de**] AV

NP₁ performs the action verb more AV than NP₂

他比我吃饭吃得多。
他比我吃飯吃得多。

Tā bǐ wǒ *chī* fàn *chī de duō*.

He *eats* more food than me.

弟弟比妹妹写字写得快。
弟弟比妹妹寫字寫得快。

Dìdi bǐ mèimei *xiě* zì *xiě de kuài*.

Younger brother *writes* characters faster than younger sister.

Here are several variations in this pattern. They differ in the order of the phrases. In all of them, [action verb + object] occurs before [action verb 得 **de**], and AV occurs at the end of the sentence.

Variation 1

NP₁ [action verb + object] [action verb 得] 比 NP₂ AV
NP₁ [action verb + object] [action verb de] **bǐ** NP₂ AV

NP₁ performs the action verb more AV than NP₂

他吃饭吃得比我多。
他吃飯吃得比我多。

Tā *chī* fàn *chī de* bǐ wǒ duō.

He *eats* more food than me

弟弟写字写得比妹妹快。
弟弟寫字寫得比妹妹快。

Dìdi *xiě* zì *xiě de* bǐ mèimei kuài.

Younger brother *writes* characters faster than younger sister.

Variation 2

object, NP₁ [action verb 得] 比 NP₂ AV
object, NP₁ [action verb **de**] **bǐ** NP₂ AV

As for the object, NP₁ performs the action verb more AV than NP₂

中国字，弟弟写得比妹妹快。
中國字，弟弟寫得比妹妹快。

Zhōngguo zì, dìdi xiě de bǐ mèimei kuài.

As for Chinese characters, younger brother writes them faster than younger sister.

Variation 3

> NP$_1$ + object [action verb 得]　　比　　NP$_2$　AV
> NP$_1$ + object [action verb **de**]　**bǐ**　NP$_2$　AV
> NP$_1$ performs the action verb more AV than NP$_2$
>> 弟弟的中国字，写得比妹妹快。
>> 弟弟的中國字，寫得比妹妹快。
>> **Dìdi de Zhōngguó zì, xiě de bǐ mèimei kuài.**
>> Younger brother's Chinese characters, (he) writes them faster than younger sister.

Be careful to repeat the verb if you include the object of the verb.

Say this	*Not this*
他吃饭吃得比我多。	*他吃饭得比我多。
他吃飯吃得比我多。	他吃飯得比我多。
Tā chī fàn chī de bǐ wǒ duō.	**Tā chī fàn de bǐ wǒ duō.**
He eats more than I do.	
弟弟写字写得比妹妹快。	*弟弟写字得比妹妹快。
弟弟寫字寫得比妹妹快。	弟弟寫字得比妹妹快。
Dìdi xiě zì xiě de bǐ mèimei kuài.	**Dìdi xiě zì de bǐ mèimei kuài.**
Younger brother writes faster than	
younger sister.	

⇨　27.1.1, 29.1.6, 29.4.3

29.4　Less than

The following patterns indicate the relationship of 'less than.'

29.4.1　Indicating 'less than' with 没有 *méi yǒu*

> NP$_1$　没有　　　　NP$_2$　AV
> NP$_1$　**méi yǒu**　NP$_2$　AV
> NP$_1$ is not as AV as NP$_2$
>> 我没有他<u>高</u>。
>> **Wǒ méi yǒu tā *gāo*.**
>> I am not as *tall* as he.

>> 我没有他<u>用功</u>。
>> **Wǒ méi yǒu tā *yònggōng*.**
>> I am not as *hardworking* as he.

>> 我没有他(那么)<u>高</u>。
>> 我沒有他(那麼)<u>高</u>。
>> **Wǒ méi yǒu tā (nàme) *gāo*.**
>> I am not as *tall* as he.

>> 他没有你(这么)<u>用功</u>。
>> 他沒有你(這麼)<u>用功</u>。
>> **Tā méi yǒu nǐ (zhème) *yònggōng*.**
>> He is not as *hardworking* as you.

Indicating 'less than' with 不如 *bùrú*

不如 **bùrú** can be used when comparing two noun phrases, or when comparing noun phrases in terms of some property. It is used in formal, literary contexts.

> NP₁   不如   NP₂
> NP₁   **bùrú**   NP₂
> NP₁ is not as good as NP₂
>> 论学问，谁都不如赵教授。
>> 論學問，誰都不如趙教授。
>> **Lùn xuéwen, shéi dōu bùrú Zhào jiàoshòu.**
>> As for scholarship, no one is the equal to Professor Zhao.
>>
>> 我的嗓子不如我妹妹。
>> **Wǒ de sǎngzi bùrú wǒ mèimei.**
>> My voice is not as good as my younger sister's.

> NP₁   不如   NP₂   AV
> NP₁   **bùrú**   NP₂   AV
> NP₁ is not as AV as NP₂
>> 弟弟不如哥哥用功。
>> **Dìdi bùrú gēge *yònggōng*.**
>> Younger brother is not as *hardworking* as older brother.
>>
>> 走路不如骑自行车快。
>> 走路不如騎自行車快。
>> **Zǒu lù bùrú qí zìxíngchē *kuài*.**
>> Walking is not as *fast* as riding a bike.

Indicating performance that is less than another's in some way

To indicate that one noun phrase does *not* perform some action *as AV* as another noun phrase, say:

> NP₁   没有   NP₂   [action verb 得]   AV
> NP₁   **méi yǒu**   NP₂   [action verb **de**]   AV
> NP₁ does not perform the action verb as AV as NP₂
>> 我没有他吃得多。
>> **Wǒ méi yǒu tā chī de duō.**
>> I don't eat as much as him.
>>
>> 妹妹没有弟弟写得快。
>> 妹妹沒有弟弟寫得快。
>> **Mèimei méi yǒu dìdi xiě de kuài.**
>> Younger sister doesn't write as fast as younger brother.

那么/那麼 **nàme** and 这么/這麼 **zhème** optionally occur before the AV.

>> 我没有他吃得那么多。
>> 我沒有他吃得那麼多。
>> **Wǒ méi yǒu tā chī de nàme duō.**
>> I don't eat as much as him.
>>
>> 妹妹没有弟弟写得这么快。
>> 妹妹沒有弟弟寫得這麼快。
>> **Mèimei méi yǒu dìdi xiě de zhème kuài.**
>> Younger sister doesn't write as fast as younger brother.

If the object of the action verb is included in the sentence, the action verb is said twice, once followed by the object, and once followed by AV.

NP₁ 没有   NP₂ [action verb + object] [action verb 得] (那么/那麼) AV
NP₁ **méi yǒu** NP₂ [action verb + object] [action verb **de**] (**nàme**)   AV
NP₁ does not perform the action verb as AV as NP₂

> 我没有他吃饭吃得多。
> 我沒有他吃飯吃得多。
> **Wǒ méi yǒu tā chī fàn chī de duō.**
> I don't eat as much food as younger brother.

> 妹妹没有弟弟写字写得(那么)快。
> 妹妹沒有弟弟寫字寫得(那麼)快。
> **Mèimei méi yǒu dìdi xiě zì xiě de (nàme) kuài.**
> Younger sister doesn't write characters as fast as younger brother.

Here are several variations in this pattern. They differ in the order of the phrases. In all of them, [action verb + object] occurs before [action verb 得 **de**], and AV occurs at the end of the sentence.

Variation 1

NP₁ [action verb + object] [action verb 得]   没有   NP₂ (那么/那麼) AV
NP₁ [action verb + object] [action verb **de**] **méi yǒu** NP₂ (**nàme**)   AV
NP₁ does not perform the action verb as AV as NP₂

> 我吃饭吃得没有他多。
> 我吃飯吃得沒有他多。
> **Wǒ chī fàn chī de méi yǒu tā duō.**
> I don't eat as much food as he does.

> 妹妹写字写得没有弟弟(那么)快。
> 妹妹寫字寫得沒有弟弟(那麼)快。
> **Mèimei xiě zì xiěde méi yǒu dìdi (nàme) kuài.**
> Younger sister doesn't write characters as fast as younger brother.

Variation 2

object, NP₁ [action verb 得]   没有   NP₂ (那么/那麼) AV
object, NP₁ [action verb **de**] **méi yǒu** NP₂ (**nàme**)   AV
As for the object, NP₁ does not perform the action verb as AV as NP₂

> 中国字，妹妹写得没有弟弟那么快。
> 中國字，妹妹寫得沒有弟弟那麼快。
> **Zhōngguó zì, mèimei xiě de méi yǒu dìdi nàme kuài.**
> (As for) Chinese characters, younger sister doesn't write them as fast as younger brother.

Be careful to repeat the action verb if you include its object.

Say this	*Not this*
我没有他吃饭吃得多。	*我没有他吃饭得多。
我沒有他吃飯吃得多。	我沒有他吃飯得多。
Wǒ méi yǒu tā chī fàn chī de duō.	**Wǒ méi yǒu tā chī fàn de duō.**
I do not eat as much as he does.	

Say this	Not this
妹妹没有弟弟写字写得(那么)快。 妹妹沒有弟弟寫字寫得(那麼)快。 **Mèimei méi yǒu dìdi xiě zì xiě de (nàme) kuài.** Younger sister doesn't write as fast as younger brother.	*妹妹没有弟弟写字得(那么)快。 妹妹沒有弟弟寫字得(那麼)快。 **Mèimei méi yǒu dìdi xiě zì de (nàme) kuài.**

⇨ 27.1.2, 29.1.6, 29.3.5

29.5 Comparative degree

To indicate the comparative form in Mandarin, place the intensifier 更 **gèng** or the expression 还(要)/還(要) **hái (yào)** before the stative verb or adjectival verb.

哥哥喜欢看电影。妹妹更喜欢。(SV)
哥哥喜歡看電影。妹妹更喜歡。
Gēge xǐhuan kàn diànyǐng. Mèimei *gèng xǐhuan*.
Older brother likes to watch movies. Younger sister *likes to even more*.

日本车很贵。德国车更贵。(AV)
日本車很貴。德國車更貴。
Rìběn chē hěn guì. Déguó chē *gèng guì*.
Japanese cars are very expensive. German cars are *even more expensive*.

日本车很贵。德国车还(要)贵。(AV)
日本車很貴。德國車還(要)貴。
Rìběn chē hěn guì. Déguó chē *hái (yào) guì*.
Japanese cars are very expensive. German cars are *even more expensive*.

更 **gèng** and 还要/還要 **hái yào** may be used in 比 **bǐ** comparison sentences.

德国车比日本车更贵。
德國車比日本車更貴。
Déguó chē bǐ Rìběn chē *gèng guì*.
German cars are *even more expensive* than Japanese cars.

天气预报说明天比今天还要冷。
天氣預報説明天比今天還要冷。
Tiānqì yùbào shuō míngtiān bǐ jīntiān *hái yào lěng*.
The weather report says tomorrow will be *even colder* than today.

⇨ 10.5

29.6 Superlative degree

The intensifier 最 **zuì** indicates a superlative degree: *most stative verb/most adjectival verb*. Sentence final -了 **le** is sometimes used at the end of the sentence to emphasize that the information is new for the addressee. The superlative form is also used for exaggeration.

万里长城是世界上<u>最长</u>的城了。(AV)
萬裏長城是世界上<u>最長</u>的城了。
Wànlǐ Chángchéng shì shìjiè shàng *zuì cháng* de chéng le.
The Great Wall is the *longest* wall in the world.

我妹妹<u>最喜欢</u>吃冰激凌了。(SV)
我妹妹<u>最喜歡</u>吃冰激凌了。
Wǒ mèimei *zuì xǐhuan* chī bīngjilíng le.
My younger sister *loves* to eat ice cream *the most*.

⇨ 10.6

29.7 Relative degree

The following intensifiers may occur before a stative verb or adjectival verb to indicate relative degree.

| 比较/比較 | **bǐjiào** | relatively |
| 相当/相當 | **xiāngdāng** | relatively, quite |

⇨ 10, 11

今天<u>比较热</u>。 (AV)
今天<u>比較熱</u>。
Jīntiān *bǐjiào rè*.
Today is *relatively hot*.

那个女孩子<u>相当高</u>。(AV)
那個女孩子<u>相當高</u>。
Nàge nǚ háizi *xiāngdāng gāo*.
That girl is *quite tall*.

我<u>比较喜欢</u>喝法国酒。 (SV)
我<u>比較喜歡</u>喝法國酒。
Wǒ *bǐjiào xǐhuan* hē Fǎguó jiǔ.
I *prefer to drink French wine*.

四川人<u>比较喜欢</u>吃辣的。 (SV)
四川人<u>比較喜歡</u>吃辣的。
Sìchuān rén *bǐjiào xǐhuan* chī là de.
People from Sichuan *prefer to eat spicy food*.

30

Talking about the present

Here are the expressions and structures most often used to indicate that a state exists at the present time or that an action is occurring at the present time.

30.1 Time expressions that indicate present time

现在/現在 **xiànzài** *'now'*

> 你现在去哪儿?
> 你現在去哪兒?
> **Nǐ xiànzài qù nǎr?**
> Where are you going now?

目前 **mùqián** *'at present'*

> 他目前在学中文。
> 他目前在學中文。
> **Tā mùqián zài xué Zhōngwén.**
> He is presently studying Chinese.

今天 **jīntiān** *'today'*

> 他今天很忙。
> **Tā jīntiān hěn máng.**
> He is very busy today.

这个星期/這個星期 **zhège xīngqī** *'this week'*
or
这个礼拜/這個禮拜 **zhège lǐbài** *'this week'*

> 这个星期很冷。
> 這個星期很冷。
> **Zhège xīngqī hěn lěng.**
> This week it is very cold.

这个月/這個月 **zhège yuè** *'this month'*

> 她这个月在纽约。
> 她這個月在紐約。
> **Tā zhège yuè zài Niǔyuē.**
> She is in New York this month.

今年 **jīnnián** 'this year'

今年是二零零六年。
Jīnnián shì èr líng líng liù nián.
This year is 2006.

30.2 Using 在 *zài* and 正在 *zhèngzài* to indicate ongoing actions in present time

在 **zài** or 正在 **zhèngzài** can occur before action verbs that have duration to indicate that the action is ongoing at the present time.

哥哥在打球。
哥哥在打球。
Gēgē zài dǎ qiú.
Elder brother is playing ball.

他正在洗澡，不能接电话。
他正在洗澡，不能接電話。
Tā zhèngzài xǐ zǎo, bù néng jiē diànhuà.
He's bathing right now (and) can't get the phone.

NOTE   在 **zài** and 正在 **zhèngzài** are only used when talking about actions. They are not used when the main verb of the sentence is an adjectival verb, a stative verb, or a modal verb. 现在/現在 **xiànzài** 'now' can be used when talking about states or actions that occur in the present time.

Say this	*Not this*
汽油现在贵了。(AV)	*汽油正在贵了。
汽油現在貴了。	汽油正在貴了。
Qìyóu xiànzài guì le.	**Qìyóu zhèngzài guì le.**
Gasoline is expensive now.	
他现在很高兴。(AV)	
他現在很高興。	
Tā xiànzài hěn gāoxìng.	
He is happy right now.	
她现在喜欢那个男的。(SV)	*她正在喜欢那个男的。
她現在喜歡那個男的。	她正在喜歡那個男的。
Tā xiànzài xǐhuan nàge nán de.	**Tā zhèngzài xǐhuan nàge nán de.**
She likes that boy now.	

➪   13.4.1, 35.2

30.3 Using the final particle 呢 *ne* to indicate ongoing situations in present time

The final particle 呢 **ne** may be used at the end of a sentence when an action is ongoing in the present time. 呢 **ne** often co-occurs with 在 **zài** and 正在 **zhèngzài**.

他跳舞呢。
Tā tiào wǔ ne.
He is dancing.

你在想什么呢？
你在想甚麼呢？
Nǐ zài xiǎng shénme ne?
What are you thinking?

他们正在开会呢。
他們正在開會呢。
Tāmen zhèng zài kāi huì ne.
They are having a meeting now.

Using 着/著 *zhe* to emphasize ongoing duration or an ongoing state in the present time

Open-ended action verbs may be suffixed with 着/著 **zhe** to emphasize ongoing duration at the present time. 着/著 **zhe** often co-occurs with 在 **zài**, 正在 **zhèngzài** and/or 呢 **ne**.

他在说着话呢。
他在説著話呢。
Tā zài shuōzhe huà ne.
He is speaking.

Change-of-state verbs that describe posture or placement such as 站 **zhàn** 'to stand,' 坐 **zuò** 'to sit,' 躺 **tǎng** 'to lie,' 存 **cún** 'to save/to deposit,' 放 **fàng** 'to put/to place,' 挂/掛 **guà** 'to hang,' and 停 **tíng** 'to park' may be suffixed with 着/著 **zhe** to indicate that the state is ongoing in present time. 呢 **ne** may occur at the end of the sentence.

谁在门口站着？
誰在門口站著？
Shéi zài ménkǒu zhànzhe?
Who is standing at the door?

客人在客厅里坐着呢。
客人在客廳裡坐著呢。
Kèren zài kètīng lǐ zuòzhe ne.
The guests are sitting in the living room.

病人在床上躺着。
病人在床上躺著。
Bìngrén zài chuángshàng tǎngzhe.
The patient is lying on the bed.

我们的钱都在银行里存着呢。
我們的錢都在銀行裏存著呢。
Wǒmen de qián dōu zài yínháng lǐ cúnzhe ne.
All of our money is (saved) in the bank.

那张画在墙上挂着呢。
那張畫在牆上掛著呢。
Nà zhāng huà zài qiáng shàng guàzhe ne.
That painting is hanging on the wall.

我的书在哪儿放着呢？
我的書在哪兒放著呢？
Wǒ de shū zài nǎr fàngzhe ne?
Where is my book? (Where is my book placed?)

我的车在停车场停着呢。
我的車在停車場停著呢。
Wǒ de chē zài tíngchēchǎng tíngzhe ne.
My car is parked in the parking lot.

⇨ | 25.3.3, 35.2

30.5 Indicating present time by context

Time expressions are optional when the context makes it clear that the sentence refers to a present time situation. For example, in the following conversation, 现在/现在 **xiànzài** 'now' can be included, but it is not necessary, because the question and response clearly refer to the present time.

妈妈：你(现在)作什么功课？
媽媽：你(現在)作甚麼功課？
Māma: Nǐ (xiànzài) zuò shénme gōngkè?
Mom: What homework are you doing (now)?

孩子：我(现在)作数学。
孩子：我(現在)作數學。
Háizi: Wǒ (xiànzài) zuò shùxué.
Child: I am doing math (now).

30.6 Negation in present time situations

Present time situations are negated with 不 **bù** with one exception. The verb 有 **yǒu** is always negated with 没 **méi**.

他今天不来上课。
他今天不來上課。
Tā jīntiān bù lái shàng kè.
He is not coming to class today.

我没有钱。
我沒有錢。
Wǒ méi yǒu qián.
I don't have money.

⇨ | 23.1

Action verbs may be negated with 没 **méi** or 没有 **méi yǒu**, but when so negated, they do not refer to present time. Instead, they indicate that the action did not happen in the past.

你为什么没来上课？
你為甚麼沒來上課？
Nǐ wèi shénme méi lái shàng kè?
Why didn't you come to class?

⇨ | 13.3, 33.3

30.7 Talking about actions that begin in the past and continue to the present

To indicate that an action began in the past and continues to the present, end the sentence with sentence final - 了 **le**. If the verb is followed by an object or a duration expression, the sentence will have two instances of 了 **le**, one following the verb, and the other at the end of the sentence. Sentences like these are sometimes described as having 'double 了 le.' The sentence final -了 le is sometimes described as indicating the 'present relevance' of the situation.

➪ 34.1.3

> 我看了两本书了。
> 我看了兩本書了。
> **Wǒ kàn le liǎng běn shū le.**
> I've read two books (so far).

> 他在美国住了十年了。
> 他在美國住了十年了。
> **Tā zài Měiguó zhù le shínián le.**
> He has lived in America for 10 years (and is still there).

The adverb 已经/已經 **yǐjing** 'already' often occurs in these sentences to emphasize the fact that the situation has been ongoing from some time in the past up to the present time.

> 她已经学了三年的中文了。
> 她已經學了三年的中文了。
> **Tā yǐjing xué le sān nián de Zhōngwén le.**
> She has already studied three years of Chinese.

> 我教中文已经有二十多年了。
> 我教中文已經有二十多年了。
> **Wǒ jiào Zhōngwén yǐjing yǒu èrshí duō nián le.**
> I've already taught Chinese for over twenty years.

30.8 Describing situations that are generally true

To indicate that a situation is generally true, the verb is presented without any modifiers that indicate time phrase: no time phrases, no adverbs, no verb suffixes.

> 中国人口很多。
> 中國人口很多。
> **Zhōngguó rénkǒu hěn duō.**
> China has a very large population.

> 这儿的天气很热。
> 這兒的天氣很熱。
> **Zhèr de tiānqì hěn rè.**
> The weather is very hot here.

31

Talking about habitual actions

Habitual actions are actions that occur regularly. The following time expressions and adverbs are used to express habitual actions in Chinese.

Expressing habitual time with the word 每 *měi* 'every/each'

Time expressions that indicate habitual action include the word 每 **měi** 'every/each.' As with other expressions that indicate the time when an action occurs, these expressions occur right after the subject, at the beginning of the predicate. Commonly used time expressions include:

每个小时/每個小時	**měi gè xiǎoshí**	every hour
每个钟头/每個鐘頭	**měi gè zhōngtóu**	every hour
每天	**měitiān**	every day
每天晚上	**měitiān wǎnshang**	every evening
每个礼拜/每個禮拜	**měi gè lǐbài**	every week
每个星期/每個星期	**měi gè xīngqī**	every week
每个月/每個月	**měi gè yuè**	every month
每年	**měi nián**	every year

The adverb 都 **dōu** may also occur with these expressions, right before the verb or, if there is a prepositional phrase, right before the prepositional phrase.

我每天八点半去上班。
我每天八點半去上班。
Wǒ měitiān bādiǎn bàn qù shàng bān.
I go to work every day at 8:30.

她每个星期都回家看父母一次。
她每個星期都回家看父母一次。
Tā měi gè xīngqī dōu huí jiā kàn fùmǔ yīcì.
She goes home once every week to see her parents.

我每个月都跟朋友去看电影。
我每個月都跟朋友去看電影。
Wǒ měi gè yuè dōu gēn péngyou qù kàn diànyǐng.
Every month I go with my friends to see a movie.

Expressing habitual time with 天天 *tiāntiān* and 年年 *niánnián*

天 **tiān** and 年 **nián** may also occur in the following phrases to indicate habitual action.

天天	**tiāntiān**	every day
年年	**niánnián**	every year

大学生天天都很忙。
大學生天天都很忙。
Dàxuéshēng tiāntiān dōu hěn máng.
University students are busy every day.

Adverbs that describe habitual action

Adverbs that describe habitual action include:

常常 *chángcháng* 'often'

我们常常去网吧上网。
我們常常去網吧上網。
Wǒmen chángcháng qù wǎngbā shàng wǎng.
We frequently go to an internet café to surf the web.

平常 *píngcháng* 'ordinarily, usually'

学生平常在周末跟朋友玩儿。
學生平常在週末跟朋友玩兒。
Xuésheng píngcháng zài zhōumò gēn péngyou wár.
Students often have fun with their friends on the weekend.

经常/經常 *jīngcháng* 'usually, often'

弟弟经常上课迟到。
弟弟經常上課遲到。
Dìdi jīngcháng shàng kè chídào.
My younger brother is often late for class.

时常/時常 *shícháng* 'regularly'

你得时常运动运动，锻链身体。
你得時常運動運動，鍛鍊身體。
Nǐ děi shícháng yùndòng yùndòng, duànliàn shēntǐ.
You should exercise regularly and strengthen your body.

总/總 *zǒng* 'always'

她总跟男朋友在一起，不愿意一个人出去。
她總跟男朋友在一起，不願意一個人出去。
Tā zǒng gēn nán péngyou zài yīqǐ, bù yuànyi yī gè rén chūqu.
She's always with her boyfriend; (she's) not willing to go out by herself.

总是/總是 **zǒngshì** *'always'*

> 他真是好人，总是帮助朋友。
> 他真是好人，總是幫助朋友。
> **Tā zhēn shì hǎo rén, zǒngshì bāngzhù péngyou.**
> He really is a good person; (he) always helps his friends.

都 **dōu** *'all/always'*

> 我每天都看报。
> 我每天都看報。
> **Wǒ měitiān dōu kàn bào.**
> I read the news every day.

老 **lǎo** *'always'*

> 我不要老待在家。
> **Wǒ bù yào lǎo dāi zài jiā.**
> I don't want to always stay home.

向来/向來 **xiànglái** *'always in the past'*

> 他向来都听父母的话。
> 他向來都聽父母的話。
> **Tā xiànglái dōu tīng fùmǔ de huà.**
> He always listened to his parents.

一向 **yīxiàng** *'always in the past'*

> 他一向很可靠。我们一定可以信任他。
> 他一向很可靠。我們一定可以信任他。
> **Tā yīxiàng hěn kěkào. Wǒmen yīdìng kéyǐ xìnrèn tā.**
> He has always been very reliable. We can certainly trust him.

NOTE | 向来/向來 xiànglái and 从来/從來 cónglái are opposites.

- 向来/向來 **xiànglái** is used to indicate that an action *habitually occurred* in the past.
- 从来/從來 **cónglái** indicates that an action *does not happen* or *has not happened*. 从来/從來 **cónglái** always occurs with negation:

> 从来/從來 **cónglái** + 不 **bù** indicates that an action never occurs.
> 从来/從來 **cónglái** + 没 **méi** indicates that an action has never occurred in the past.
>> 他从来不喝酒。
>> 他從來不喝酒。
>> **Tā cónglái bù hē jiǔ.**
>> He never drinks alcohol.
>>
>> 我从来没给他打过电话。
>> 我從來沒給他打過電話。
>> **Wǒ cónglái méi gěi tā dǎguo diànhuà.**
>> I have never called him on the phone before.

⇨ | 23.3.1

32

Talking about the future

Mandarin has no distinct future tense. Instead, future time is expressed by words and phrases that refer to the future.

32.1 Time words that refer to future time

Here are some common time words that refer to future time.

今天下午	**jīntiān xiàwǔ**	this afternoon
今天晚上	**jīntiān wǎnshang**	tonight
明天	**míngtiān**	tomorrow
后天/後天	**hòutiān**	the day after tomorrow
大后天/大後天	**dà hòutiān**	three days from now
下个星期/下個星期	**xià gè xīngqī**	next week
下个礼拜/下個禮拜	**xià gè lǐbài**	next week
下个月/下個月	**xià gè yuè**	next month
明年	**míngnián**	next year
将来/將來	**jiānglái**	in the future

The neutral position for 'time when' expressions is after the subject, at the beginning of the predicate. To emphasize the time when a situation occurs, put the 'time when' expression at the beginning of the sentence, before the subject.

我们今天晚上去看电影。
我們今天晚上去看電影。
Wǒmen *jīntiān wǎnshang* qù kàn diànyǐng.
We are going to see a movie *tonight*.

今天晚上我们去看电影。
今天晚上我們去看電影。
***jīntiān wǎnshang* wǒmen qù kàn diànyǐng.**
Tonight we are going to see a movie.

⇨ 4.5, 53.3.2

32.2 Adverbs that refer to future time

Common adverbs that refer to the future include the following. (Note that adverbs always occur before the [prepositional phrase +] verb phrase.)

就要 *jiù yào* 'soon will'

> 他<u>就要</u>结婚了。
> 他<u>就要</u>結婚了。
> **Tā *jiù yào* jiéhūn le.**
> He *is going to* get married soon.

再 *zài* '(do) again in the future'

> <u>再</u>见！
> <u>再</u>見！
> ***Zài* jiàn!**
> See you *again*! (Goodbye)

> 我没听清楚，请你<u>再</u>说一次。
> 我沒聽清楚，請你<u>再</u>説一次。
> **Wǒ méi tīng qīngchu, qǐng nǐ *zài* shuō yīcì.**
> I didn't hear clearly, please say it *again*.

可能 *kěnéng* 'possible'

> 她<u>可能</u>不学中文了。
> 她<u>可能</u>不學中文了。
> **Tā *kěnéng* bù xué Zhōngwén le.**
> She *may* not study Chinese any more.

⇨ | 15

Notice that the adverb 再 **zài** is closely related to the adverb 又 **yòu**. The adverb 再 **zài** means (to do) again in the future, and the adverb 又 **yòu** means (to do) again in the past.

> 你前天迟到了。昨天又迟到了。
> 你前天遲到了。昨天又遲到了。
> **Nǐ qiántiān chídào le. Zuótiān yòu chídào le.**
> You were late the day before yesterday. Yesterday you were late again.

⇨ | 33.5

32.3 Indicating future time with the modal verb 会/會 *huì*

The modal verb 会/會 **huì** can be used to indicate future time. The meaning of 'future' is associated with the meanings of 'possibility' and 'prediction' conveyed by 会/會 **huì**.

> 我想他不<u>会</u>来了。
> 我想他不<u>會</u>來了。
> **Wǒ xiǎng tā bù *huì* lái le.**
> I don't think he *will* come.

Sometimes, 会/會 **huì** simply indicates future.

> 天气预报说，明天一定会下雨。
> 天氣預報説，明天一定會下雨。
> **Tiānqì yùbào shuō, míngtiān yīdìng *huì* xià yǔ.**
> The weather report says tomorrow it *will* definitely rain.

⇨ | 12.1

32.4 Verbs that refer to the future

Verbs involving thinking or planning refer to future time. The most common include the following:

要 *yào* 'to want'

> 我要出去买东西。
> 我要出去買東西。
> **Wǒ yào chūqu mǎi dōngxi.**
> I want to go out to buy some things.

想 *xiǎng* 'to think'

> 我今天想早一点回家。
> 我今天想早一點回家。
> **Wǒ jīntiān xiǎng zǎo yīdiǎn huí jiā.**
> I want to return home a little earlier today.

愿意/願意 *yuànyi* 'to be willing'

> 我愿意跟他结婚。
> 我願意跟他結婚。
> **Wǒ yuànyi gēn tā jiéhūn.**
> I am willing to marry him.

准备/準備 *zhǔnbèi* 'to prepare to, to get ready to'

> 请你准备下车。
> 請你準備下車。
> **Qǐng nǐ zhǔnbèi xià chē.**
> Please get ready to get off the bus.

打算 *dǎsuan* 'to plan to'

> 我将来打算住在日本。
> 我將來打算住在日本。
> **Wǒ jiānglái dǎsuan zhù zài Rìběn.**
> I plan to live in Japan in the future.

33

Indicating completion and talking about the past

Mandarin has no grammatical structure that is entirely equivalent to past tense in English. Instead, it has structures that signal the completion of an event or that indicate that an event occurred or did not occur at some time in the past, or that a situation existed at some time in the past. The primary strategies for indicating completion and talking about the past are presented in this chapter.

33.1 Completion: V -了 *le*

Mandarin uses the verb suffix 了 **le** to mark an action as complete. When an action is marked as complete with respect to now (speech time), completion also indicates that the action happened in the past.

Only action verbs can be marked as complete. If a stative verb, adjectival verb, or modal verb is followed by 了 **le**, the meaning is one of *change* rather than *completion*.

⇨ 10, 11, 12, 13.1

Ordinarily, when -了 **le** marks completion it occurs right after the verb.

> Q: 你跟谁看了电影?
> 你跟誰看了電影?
> **Nǐ gēn shéi *kàn* le diànyǐng?**
> With whom did you see the movie?
> A: 我跟我女朋友看了电影。
> 我跟我女朋友看了電影。
> **Wǒ gēn wǒ nǚ péngyou *kàn* le diànyǐng.**
> I saw the movie with my girlfriend.

Notice that these sentences refer to situations that are both completed and past. If the verb takes an object and the object is only one syllable in length, 了 **le** may occur after the *verb + object*. Some speakers of Mandarin prefer to put 了 **le** after the object regardless of the length of the object noun phrase.

> 我昨天晚上八点钟回家了。
> 我昨天晚上八點鐘回家了。
> **Wǒ zuótiān wǎnshang bādiǎn zhōng *huí jiā* le.**
> Last night I returned home at 8 p.m.

The use of 了 **le** to mark completed actions is not obligatory. However, it is commonly used when the verb takes an object that includes a number phrase. In these sentences, 了 **le** occurs right after the verb.

> 他男朋友给他买了一本中文词典。
> 他男朋友給他買了一本中文詞典。
> **Tā nán péngyou gěi tā mǎi le yī běn Zhōngwén cídiǎn.**
> Her boy friend bought *a Chinese dictionary* for her.

> 上个周末我们跳了两个钟头的舞。
> 上個週末我們跳了兩個鐘頭的舞。
> **Shàng gè zhōumò wǒmen tiào le liǎng gè zhōngtóu de wǔ.**
> We danced for *two hours* last weekend. (here: two hours of dance)

The adverb 已经/已經 **yǐjing** 'already' often occurs before a completed action to indicate that an action is already concluded:

> 我已经吃了晚饭。
> 我已經吃了晚飯。
> **Wǒ yǐjing chī le wǎnfàn.**
> I already ate dinner.

or

> 我已经吃晚饭了。
> 我已經吃晚飯了。
> **Wǒ yǐjing chī wǎnfàn le.**
> I already ate dinner.

> Q: 那件事，你什么时候做完？
> 那件事，你甚麼時候做完？
> **Nà jiàn shì, nǐ shénme shíhòu zuòwán?**
> When will you finish that matter?
> A: 我已经做完了。
> 我已經做完了。
> **Wǒ yǐjing zuòwán le.**
> I've already finished.

33.2 Talking about sequence in the past

To indicate that two actions occur in sequence, follow the first action verb with 了 **le**.

> 他吃了饭就走。
> 他吃了飯就走。
> **Tā chī le fàn jiù zǒu.**
> He will eat and then leave. (After he eats, he will leave.)

As the translation of this sentence indicates, this sentence refers to a sequence that will take place in the future: 了 **le** indicates that 吃 **chī** 'to eat' occurs before 走 **zǒu** 'to leave.'

To indicate that a *sequence* occurred in the *past*, follow the second verb or the object of the second verb with -了 **le**.

他吃了饭就走了。
他吃了飯就走了。
Tā chī le fàn jiù zǒu le.
After he ate, he left.

学生做完了功课就交给老师了。
學生做完了功課就交給老師了。
Xuésheng zuòwán le gōngkè jiù jiāo gěi lǎoshī le.
After the students finished their work they handed it to the teacher.

These sentences have two instances of 了 **le**. The one that follows the first verb indicates sequence. The one that follows the second verb or its object indicates that the sequence is complete, that is, that it happened in the past.

33.3 Indicating that an action did not occur in the past

To indicate that an action did not occur in the past, negate the verb with 没 **méi** or 没有 **méi yǒu**. Do not use 不 **bù** as the marker of negation, and do not use 了 **le** after the verb when talking about an action that did not occur.

我寒假没回家。
Wǒ hánjià méi huí jiā.
I didn't go home for winter break.

我昨天一天都没看见他。
我昨天一天都沒看見他。
Wǒ zuótiān yī tiān dōu méi kànjian tā.
I didn't see him at all yesterday.

他没(有)买那本书。
他沒(有)買那本書。
Tā méi (yǒu) mǎi nà běn shū.
He didn't buy that book.

The adverb 还/還 **hái** may occur in sentences negated with 没(有) **méi (yǒu)**. 还没(有)/還沒(有) **hái méi (yǒu)** means *not yet*.

我还没吃早饭。
我還沒吃早飯。
Wǒ hái méi chī zǎofàn.
I haven't yet eaten breakfast.

他才十三岁。当然还没结婚。
他才十三歲。當然還沒結婚。
Tā cái shísān suì. Dāngrán hái méi jiéhūn.
He's only 13. Of course he hasn't yet married.

⇨ 13.3, 23.1.2

33.4 Asking whether an action has occurred

To ask whether an action has occurred, use a yes–no question:

S-吗/嗎/*ma*

Q: 你买了飞机票了吗?　　　or　　Q: 你买飞机票了吗?
你買了飛機票了嗎?　　　　　　　　你買飛機票了嗎?
Nǐ mǎi le fēijī piào le ma?　　　**Nǐ mǎi fēijī piào le ma?**
Did you buy the airplane　　　　　Did you buy the airplane
ticket?　　　　　　　　　　　　　ticket?

verb 了 *le (object)* 没有 **méi yǒu**

Q: 你买了飞机票了没有?　　or　　Q: 你买飞机票了没有?
你買了飛機票了沒有?　　　　　　　你買飛機票了沒有?
Nǐ mǎi le fēijī piào le　　　　**Nǐ mǎi fēijī piào le**
méi yǒu?　　　　　　　　　　　**méi yǒu?**
Have you bought (the)　　　　　　Have you bought (the)
airplane ticket yet?　　　　　　　airplane ticket yet?
A: 买了。　　　　　　　　　　　A: 买了。
買了。　　　　　　　　　　　　　買了。
Mǎi le.　　　　　　　　　　　**Mǎi le.**
[I] bought [it].　　　　　　　　　[I] bought [it].

有没有 **yǒu méi yǒu** + [*prepositional phrase* +] *verb phrase*

Q: 你有没有买飞机票?
你有沒有買飛機票?
Nǐ yǒu méi yǒu mǎi fēijī piào?
Have you bought the airplane ticket?
A: 买了。
買了。
Mǎi le.
[I] bought [it].

For any form of yes–no question, a 'yes' answer includes 了 **le** after the verb.

A: 买了。
買了。
Mǎi le.
[I] bought [it].

A 'no' answer does not have 了 **le**.

A: 没(有)买。
沒(有)買。
Méi (yǒu) mǎi
[I] haven't.

⇨ | 24.1

33.5 Indicating that an action occurred again in the past: 又 *yòu* verb 了 *le*

To indicate that an action occurred *again* in the past, precede the [prepositional phrase +] verb phrase with the adverb 又 **yòu** and follow the verb with 了 **le**.

他前天来了。今天早上又来了。
他前天來了。今天早上又來了。
Tā qiántiān lái le. Jīntiān zǎoshang *yòu* lái *le*.
He came the day before yesterday. This morning he came *again*.

Notice that the adverb 又 **yòu** '(to do) again in the past' is closely related to the adverb 再 **zài** '(to do) again in the future.'

我昨天晚上又吃饺子了。明天不要再吃。
我昨天晚上又吃餃子了。明天不要再吃。
Wǒ zuótiān wǎnshang yòu chī jiǎozi le. Míngtiān bù yào zài chī.
I ate dumplings again last night. I don't want to eat them again tomorrow.

⇨ | 32.2

NOTE | 又 **yòu** . . . 又 **yòu** . . . means 'both . . . and . . .' and can be used to link stative verbs or adjectival verbs.

他们又饿又渴。
他們又餓又渴。
Tāmen yòu è yòu kě.
They are hungry and thirsty.

⇨ | 10.8, 36.9, 39.4

33.6 Talking about past experience: verb suffix -过/過 *guo*

To indicate that an action has been experienced at least once in the indefinite past, follow the verb with the verb suffix -过/過 **guo**.

我吃过中国饭。
我吃過中國飯。
Wǒ chīguo Zhōngguó fàn.
I've eaten Chinese food (before).

The verb suffix 过/過 **guo** is appropriate in the following circumstances:

• when talking about actions that the subject does not perform on a regular basis,
• when talking about actions that happened in the remote past,
• when talking about actions that are repeatable. Actions that are not repeatable cannot be suffixed with 过/過 **guo**.

> *Do not say*

> *她大学毕业过。
> 她大學畢業過。
> **Tā dàxué bìyè guò.**
> intended: She has graduated from university before.

⇨ | 13.2

小英以前是大明的女朋友。(stative verb)
Xiǎoyīng yǐqián *shì* Dàmíng de nǚ péngyou.
Xiaoying used to *be* Daming's girlfriend.

我以前很喜欢他。(stative verb)
我以前很喜歡他。
Wǒ yǐqián hěn *xǐhuan* tā.
I used to *like* him a lot.

石油以前很便宜。(adjectival verb)
Shíyóu yǐqián hěn *piányi*.
In the past, gasoline was *cheap*.

过去/過去 *guòqù* 'in the past'

他过去是英文老师。(stative verb)
他過去是英文老師。
Tā guòqù *shì* Yīngwén lǎoshī.
He used to *be* an English teacher.

从前/從前 *cóngqián* 'previously'

中国从前有很多人不识字。(stative verb)
中國從前有很多人不識字。
Zhōngguó cóngqián *yǒu* hěn duō rén bù shí zì.
In the past, China *had* a lot of people who were illiterate.

These adverbs may also be used when talking about situations that customarily occurred in the past.

我从前天天去公园散步。
我從前天天去公園散步。
Wǒ cóngqián tiāntiān qù gōngyuán sànbù.
I used to take a walk in the park every day.

我过去每年都带孩子到海边去玩。
我過去每年都帶孩子到海邊去玩。
Wǒ guòqù měi nián dōu dài háizi dào hǎibiān qù wán.
In the past, every year I used to take the children to the ocean to play.

33.9 Focusing on a detail of a past event with 是...的 *shì...de*

To focus on a specific detail of an event such as the time or place of the event, use 是...的 **shì...de**.

是 **shì** occurs right before the phrase that is being focused.
的 **de** occurs right after the verb or at the end of the sentence.

是...的 **shì...de** is used to focus on:

- the time when an event occurred:

> 他是一年以前去中国的。
> 他是一年以前去中國的。
> **Tā shì *yīnián yǐqián* qù Zhōngguó de.**
> He went to China *a year ago*.

> 你的新车是什么时候买的？
> 你的新車是甚麼時候買的？
> **Nǐ de xīn chē shì *shénme shíhòu* mǎi de?**
> *When* did you buy your new car?

- the one who performed the activity:

> 这本书是谁写的？
> 這本書是誰寫的？
> **Zhè běn shū shì *shéi* xiě de?**
> *Who* wrote this book?

- location:

> 你的大衣是在哪儿买的？
> 你的大衣是在哪兒買的？
> **Nǐ de dàyī shì *zài nǎr* mǎi de?**
> *Where* did you buy your coat?

> 这张磁碟是在哪儿买的？
> 這張磁碟是在哪兒買的？
> **Zhè zhāng cí dié shì *zài nǎr* mǎi de?**
> *Where* did you buy this CD?

- a prepositional phrase:

> 他是跟谁结婚的？
> 他是跟誰結婚的？
> **Tā shì *gēn shéi* jiéhūn de?**
> Who (*with whom*) did he marry?

If the verb has an object and the object is not a pronoun, 的 **de** can come either after the verb or at the end of the sentence.

> 昨天晚上是谁给你做的晚饭？
> 昨天晚上是誰給你做的晚飯？
> **Zuótiān wǎnshàng shì *shéi* gěi nǐ zuò de wǎnfàn?**
> *Who* cooked dinner for you last night?

or

> 昨天晚上是谁给你做晚饭的？
> 昨天晚上是誰給你做晚飯的？
> **Zuótiān wǎnshàng shì *shéi* gěi nǐ zuò wǎnfàn de?**
> *Who* cooked dinner for you last night?

If the object of the verb is a pronoun, 的 **de** can only occur after the pronoun, at the end of the sentence.

Say this	*Not this*
你是在<u>哪儿</u>认识他的？	*你是在哪儿认识的他？
你是在<u>哪兒</u>認識他的？	你是在哪兒認識的他？
Nǐ shì zài *nǎr* rènshi tā de?	**Nǐ shì zài nǎr rènshi de tā?**
Where did you meet him?	

是 **shì** may be omitted in affirmative sentences.

这张磁碟(是)在书店买的。
這張磁碟(是)在書店買的。
Zhè zhāng cí dié (shì) zài shū diàn mǎi de.
This CD was bought at the bookstore.

是 **shì** may not be omitted in negated sentences.

Say this	*Not this*
这张磁碟不是在书店买的。	*这张磁碟不在书店买的。
這張磁碟不是在書店買的。	這張磁碟不在書店買的。
Zhè zhāng cídié bù shì zài	**Zhè zhāng cídié bù zài**
shūdiàn mǎi de.	**shūdiàn mǎi de.**
This CD was not bought at the bookstore.	

⇨ 11.4, 26.4, 53.2.4

34

Talking about change, new situations, and changing situations

Mandarin has a number of ways to indicate that a situation represents a change from the past or that it is in the process of change. **34.1** and **34.3** present grammatical patterns that are used to talk about change. **34.4** presents words that are used to talk about change.

34.1 Indicating that a situation represents a change

To indicate that a situation represents a change, add the particle 了 **le** to the end of the sentence that describes the situation. We refer to this use of 了 **le** as 'sentence final -了 **le**.' Here are the most common types of change associated with sentence final -了 **le**. Notice that in English, this sense of change is sometimes expressed with the word 'become' (verb) or (verb) 'now' or 'gotten' (verb).

34.1.1 New information for the addressee

他们订婚了！
他們訂婚了！
Tāmen dìng hūn le!
They have become engaged!

我有两个孩子了。
我有兩個孩子了。
Wǒ yǒu liǎng gè háizi le.
I have two children now.

34.1.2 Change of state

When the main verb of sentence is a stative verb, sentence final -了 **le** indicates a change of state.

东西都贵了。
東西都貴了。
Dōngxi dōu guì le.
Things have become expensive.

他有女朋友了。
Tā yǒu nǚ péngyou le.
He has a girlfriend now. (He didn't have one before.)

34.1.3 Actions that continue into the future: double -了 *le* sentences

Sentence final -了 **le** can be used with the verb suffix -了 **le** to signal that a certain portion of an action is complete but that the action is continuing into the future. Sentences like these are sometimes described as having 'double -了 **le**,' and the function of the sentence final -了 **le** is sometimes described as indicating the 'present relevance' of the situation.

他已经睡了十个钟头了。
他已經睡了十個鐘頭了。
Tā yǐjing shuì le shí gè zhōngtóu le.
He has already slept for ten hours.

⇨ 30.7

34.1.4 Situations that do not exist anymore

To indicate that a situation does not exist anymore, add sentence final -了 **le** to the end of a negated sentence:

negated sentence + sentence final -了 le

她不吃肉了。
Tā bù chī ròu le.
She doesn't eat meat anymore.

太阳出来了。不冷了。
太陽出來了。不冷了。
Tàiyáng chūlái le. Bù lěng le.
The sun has come out. (It) isn't cold anymore.

34.1.5 Imminent occurrences and imminent change

Sentence final -了 **le** can be used to indicate that a situation will happen soon. Often, an adverb or adverbial phrase such as 快 **kuài**, 快要 **kuài yào**, or 就要 **jiù yào** occurs before the [prepositional phrase +] verb phrase to emphasize the fact that the situation will happen soon.

我们快到了。
我們快到了。
Wǒmen kuài dào le.
We will be arriving soon.

我快要做完了。
我快要做完了。
Wǒ kuài yào zuòwán le.
I'm just about done.

34.2 ## Comparing sentences with and without sentence final -了 *le*

Notice how sentence final -了 **le** changes the meaning of the sentence. Without sentence final -了 **le**, the sentence is a description of a situation. With sentence final -了 **le**, the sentence focuses on a change.

No sentence final -了 le	*Sentence final -了 le*
我会看中文报。	我会看中文报了。
我會看中文報。	我會看中文報了。
Wǒ huì kàn Zhōngwén bào.	**Wǒ huì kàn Zhōngwén bào le.**
I can read Chinese newspapers.	I can read Chinese newspapers now.
汽油很贵。	汽油很贵了。
汽油很貴。	汽油很貴了。
Qìyóu hěn guì.	**Qìyóu hěn guì le.**
Gasoline is very expensive.	Gasoline has become very expensive.
我不喜欢吃肉。	我不喜欢吃肉了。
我不喜歡吃肉。	我不喜歡吃肉了。
Wǒ bù xǐhuan chī ròu.	**Wǒ bù xǐhuan chī ròu le.**
I don't like to eat meat.	I don't like to eat meat anymore.

34.3 ## Indicating change over time

34.3.1 ### More and more of some situation

越来越　**yuè lái yuè**　AV/SV/MV
more and more AV/SV/MV

This pattern is used to indicate that something is becoming *more and more* adjectival verb (AV), stative verb (SV), or modal verb (MV) over time.

Sentence final -了 **le** can optionally occur with this pattern to emphasize the sense of change that the pattern conveys.

'more and more' adjectival verb

东西越来越贵(了)。
東西越來越貴(了)。
Dōngxi yuè lái yuè guì (le).
Things are getting more and more expensive.

天气越来越冷(了)。
天氣越來越冷(了)。
Tiānqì yuè lái yuè lěng (le).
The weather is getting colder and colder.

'more and more' stative verb

他长大了，越来越懂事(了)。
他長大了，越來越懂事(了)。
Tā zhǎng dà le, yuè lái yuè dǒng shì (le).
He has grown up. More and more he knows how to behave.

中国的生活，我越来越习惯了。
中國的生活，我越來越習慣了。
Zhōngguó de shēnghuó, wǒ yuè lái yuè xíguàn le.
(As for) Life in China, I am getting used to it.

'more and more' modal verb

你越来越会做饭(了)。
你越來越會做飯(了)。
Nǐ yuè lái yuè huì zuò fàn (le).
You are getting better and better at cooking.

他们越来越会说中文(了)。
他們越來越會説中文(了)。
Tāmen yuè lái yuè huì shuō Zhōngwén (le).
They are getting more and more proficient in speaking Chinese.

越來越 **yuè lái yuè** can be used to express negative situations.

我越来越不喜欢他了。
我越來越不喜歡他了。
Wǒ yuè lái yuè bù xǐhuan tā le.
I dislike him more and more.

他们家越来越没有钱了。
他們家越來越沒有錢了。
Tāmen jiā yuè lái yuè méi yǒu qián le.
Their family has less and less money.

34.3.2 Indicating change caused by changing events

To indicate that one change causes another change, say:

越	VP	越	AV/SV/MV
yuè	**VP**	**yuè**	AV/SV/MV
the more VP		the more	AV/SV/MV

越 *yuè* VP 越 *yuè adjectival verb*

我越吃冰淇淋越胖。
Wǒ yuè chī bīngqilín yuè pàng.
The more I eat ice cream, the fatter I get.

越 *yuè* VP 越 *yuè stative verb*

我越吃豆腐，越喜欢吃。
我越吃豆腐，越喜歡吃。
Wǒ yuè chī dòufu, yuè xǐhuan chī.
The more I eat beancurd, the more I like to eat it.

越 *yuè* VP 越 *yuè modal verb*

我越学中文越会说中国话。
我越學中文越會説中國話。
wǒ yuè xué Zhōngwén yuè huì shuō Zhōngguó huà.
The more I study Chinese the more I am able to speak Chinese.

Note that this pattern indicates both change and result.

⇨ | 10.9, 12.6.4

34.4 Nouns and verbs that express change

Noun

变化/變化 *biànhuà* 'a change'

> 最近十年来，北京变化很大。
> 最近十年來，北京變化很大。
> **Zuìjìn shínián lái, Běijīng biànhuà hěn dà.**
> In the past ten years, Beijing has had a lot of changes.
> (In the past ten years, Beijing's changes have been big.)

> 这附近没有什么变化。
> 這附近沒有甚麼變化。
> **Zhè fùjìn méi yǒu shénme biànhuà.**
> The area around here hasn't had much change.

Verbs

变/變 *biàn* 'to change' [does not take an object]

> 情况变了。
> 情況變了。
> **Qíngkuàng biàn le.**
> The circumstances have changed.

换 *huàn* 'to change (something)' [takes an object]

> 这句话不容易懂，请你换一个说法。
> 這句話不容易懂，請你換一個說法。
> **Zhè jù huà bù róngyì dǒng, qǐng nǐ huàn yī gè shuōfa.**
> This sentence is difficult to understand. Please put it another way.

成 *chéng* 'to change into (something), to turn into (something), to become (something)'
[takes an object]

> 他成了一个很有名的人了。
> 他成了一個很有名的人了。
> **Tā chéng le yī gè hěn yǒu míng de rén le.**
> He has become a very famous person.

Some common expressions with 成 *chéng*:

成名	**chéng míng**	become famous
成年	**chéng nián**	grow up, become an adult; to come of age

改变/改變 *gǎibiàn* 'to change' [does not take an object]

> 他的样子改变了。
> 他的樣子改變了。
> **Tā de yàngzi gǎibiàn le.**
> His appearance has changed.

变成/變成 **biànchéng** 'to turn into (something), to change into (something)' [takes an object]

> 你觉得坏人能变成好人吗？
> 你覺得壞人能變成好人嗎？
> **Nǐ juéde huàirén néng biànchéng hǎorén ma?**
> Do you think that bad people can turn into good people?

成为/成為 **chéngwéi** 'to become (something), to turn into (something)' [takes an object]

> 他成为一个科学家了。
> 他成為一個科學家了。
> **Tā chéngwéi yī gè kēxuéjiā le.**
> He became a scientist.

改 **gǎi** 'to change (something), to reform (something), to correct (something)' [takes an object]

> 请你帮我改我的文章。
> 請你幫我改我的文章。
> **Qǐng nǐ bāng wǒ gǎi wǒ de wénzhāng.**
> Please help me correct my essay.

改 **gǎi** is also used as the first part of the following verbs:

改写/改寫 **gáixiě** 'to rewrite'

> 这本书，我已经改写三次了。你还不满意吗？
> 這本書，我已經改寫三次了。你還不滿意嗎？
> **Zhè běn shū, wǒ yǐjing gáixiě sāncì le. Nǐ hái bù mǎnyì ma?**
> I've rewritten this book three times. Are you still not satisfied?

改正 **gǎizhèng** 'to correct, to rectify'

> 请你改正我的错误。
> 請你改正我的錯誤。
> **Qǐng nǐ gǎizhèng wǒ de cuòwù.**
> Please correct my mistakes.

改造 **gǎizào** 'to remodel, to reform' [this expression has political overtones]

> 你的思想意识太旧，真应该改造改造。
> 你的思想意識太舊，真應該改造改造。
> **Nǐ de sīxiǎng yìshi tài jiù, zhēn yīnggāi gǎizào gǎizào.**
> Your ideological awareness is out of date and needs to be reformed.

改善 **gǎishàn** 'to improve'

> 政府应该设法改善人民的生活。
> 政府應該設法改善人民的生活。
> **Zhèngfǔ yīnggāi shèfǎ gǎishàn rénmín de shēnghuó.**
> (The) Government should think of ways to improve people's livelihood.

改良 *gǎiliáng* 'to improve'

中国帮助非洲国家改良农业。
中國幫助非洲國家改良農業。
Zhōngguó bāngzhù Fēizhōu guójiā gǎiliáng nóngyè.
China has helped African nations improve their agriculture.

改换(成)/改換(成) *gǎihuàn (chéng)* 'to change (something)'; 'to exchange for some equivalent item'

现在朝代已经改换了。
現在朝代已經改換了。
Xiànzài cháodài yǐjing gǎihuàn le.
The dynasty has changed (to another dynasty).

改进/改進 *gǎijìn* 'to improve'

我们的税收制度，仍得改进。
我們的税收制度，仍得改進。
Wǒmen de shuìshōu zhìdù, réng děi gǎijìn.
Our tax system still needs to be improved.

35

Talking about duration and frequency

When we talk about duration, we can specify the length of an action ('we walked *for an hour*'), or we can focus on the ongoing duration of the action without reference to its length ('while *we were walking*, it started to rain'). When we talk about frequency we indicate how often an action occurs. This chapter will show you how to express both duration and frequency in Mandarin.

35.1 Specifying the length of an action with a duration phrase

Duration phrases can be used to indicate *how long* an action occurs. To indicate the duration of an action, follow the verb with a time phrase:

> *subject + verb + duration*

Only open-ended actions have duration. Open-ended actions include 买/買 **mǎi** 'to shop,' 学/學 **xué** 'to study,' 看 **kàn** 'to look at,' 'to watch,' 'to read,' 吃 **chī** 'to eat,' 睡 **shuì** 'to sleep,' 唱 **chàng** 'to sing,' 洗 **xǐ** 'to wash,' etc.

⇨ 13.4

35.1.1 Indicating duration when there is no object noun phrase

When the action verb does not have an object noun phrase, the duration phrase simply follows the verb. If the verb is suffixed with 了 **le**, the duration phrase follows verb -了 **le**.

> 我想在中国住一年。
> 我想在中國住一年。
> **Wǒ xiǎng zài Zhōngguó *zhù* yīnián.**
> I plan to live in China for a year.

> 他病了三天。
> **Tā *bìng* le sāntiān.**
> He was *sick* for three days.

35.1.2 **Indicating duration when the verb takes an object**

When the verb takes an object noun phrase, duration may be indicated using the following sentence patterns. In all of these patterns, the verb is followed by its object or by a duration phrase. A single verb is never followed directly by both an object and a duration phrase, with one exception. If the object is a pronoun, the pronoun may occur after the verb and before the duration phrase.

> 我等了他三个小时了。
> 我等了他三個小時了。
> **Wǒ děng le tā sān gè xiǎoshí le.**
> I've been waiting for him for three hours.

Pattern 1: verb + object verb + duration

The verb occurs twice in the verb phrase. First it is followed by the object, then it is followed by the duration phrase.

Say this	*Not this*
我每天晚上看书看四个小时。	*我每天晚上看书四个小时。
我每天晚上看書看四個小時。	我每天晚上看書四個小時。
Wǒ měitiān wǎnshang *kàn* shū *kàn* sì gè xiǎoshí.	**Wǒ měitiān wǎnshang *kàn* shū sì gè xiǎoshí.**
Every night I read (books) for four hours.	

If the sentence refers to a past event, the second occurrence of the verb is followed by 了 **le**.

> 我睡觉睡了八个钟头。
> 我睡覺睡了八個鐘頭。
> **Wǒ shuì jiào *shuì* le bā gè zhōngtóu.**
> I slept for eight hours.

> 我等他等了三个小时。
> 我等他等了三個小時。
> **Wǒ děng tā *děng* le sān gè xiǎoshí.**
> I waited for him for three hours.

⇨ 33.1

Pattern 2: verb + object 有 *yǒu* + duration

The verb and its object are stated first, followed by 有 **yǒu** and the duration phase. 有 **yǒu** is not directly followed by 了 **le**, though sentence final -了 **le** may occur at the end of the sentence.

> 我等王明有三个小时了。
> 我等王明有三個小時了。
> **Wǒ *děng* Wáng Míng *yǒu* sān gè xiǎoshí le.**
> I have been waiting for Wang Ming for three hours.

Pattern 3: verb + duration 的 *de* object noun phrase

The duration phrase plus 的 **de** occurs immediately before the object noun phrase. This pattern cannot be used when the object noun phrase is a pronoun.

我学了两年的中文。
我學了兩年的中文。
Wǒ *xué* le liǎng nián de Zhōngwén.
I studied Chinese for two years.

我睡了八个钟头的觉。
我睡了八個鐘頭的覺。
Wǒ *shuì* le bā gè zhōngtóu de jiào.
I slept for eight hours.

的 **de** is sometimes omitted.

那个学生已经学了两年(的)中文了。
那個學生已經學了兩年(的)中文了。
Nàge xuésheng yǐjing xué le liǎng nián (de) Zhōngwén le.
That student has been studying Chinese for two years already.

Pattern 4: object noun phrase, verb + duration

The object noun phrase may occur at the beginning of the sentence, before the subject, as a topic. The verb is then directly followed by the duration phrase. This pattern cannot be used when the object noun phrase is a pronoun or a default object.

这个问题，我已经想了很久了。
這個問題，我已經想了很久了。
Zhège wèntí, wǒ yǐjing xiǎng le hěn jiǔ le.
This problem, I have already thought about (it) for a long time.

中文，我已经学了四年了。
中文，我已經學了四年了。
Zhōngwén, wǒ yǐjing xué le sìnián le.
Chinese, I've already studied (it) for four years.

中文，我至少会学两年。
中文，我至少會學兩年。
Zhōngwén, wǒ zhìshǎo huì xué liǎng nián.
Chinese, at the very least I will study (it) for two years.

➪ 53.1.2.1

35.1.3 **Duration vs. time when**

Note the difference between phrases that indicate duration and those that indicate time when.

Time phrases that indicate the *duration* of a situation always occur after the verb.

我学了两个小时了。
我學了兩個小時了。
Wǒ xué le liǎng gè xiǎoshí le.
I studied for two hours.

Time phrases that indicate the *time when* a situation takes place always occur before the verb:

我昨天学了中文。
我昨天學了中文。
Wǒ zuótiān xué le Zhōngwén.
I studied Chinese yesterday.

A sentence may include a 'time when' phrase and a duration phrase.

我昨天学了两个小时。
我昨天學了兩個小時。
Wǒ zuótiān xué le liǎng gè xiǎoshí.
Yesterday I studied for two hours.

35.1.4 Indicating how long it has been that something has not occurred

In Mandarin, only situations that occur can be described in terms of their duration. If a situation *does not occur*, the duration pattern cannot be used to describe it. To indicate the length of time that something has not occurred, put the time phrase before the [prepositional phrase +] verb or verb phrase.

我两天没睡觉。
我兩天沒睡覺。
Wǒ liǎng tiān méi shuì jiào.
I haven't slept for two days.

他三年没有抽烟。
他三年沒有抽菸。
Tā sān nián méi yǒu chōu yān.
He hasn't smoked for three years.

35.2 Emphasizing ongoing duration

35.2.1 Emphasizing the ongoing duration of an action

To emphasize the ongoing duration of an action without specifying the length of the duration, follow the verb with the suffix 着/著 **zhe**. To indicate that an action is ongoing at the moment of speaking, 在 **zài** or 正在 **zhèngzài** may also precede the verb. 呢 **ne** may occur at the end of the sentence.

他在说着话呢。
他在說著話呢。
Tā zài shuōzhe huà ne.
He is speaking.

她正在吃着早饭呢。
她正在吃著早飯呢。
Tā zhèngzài chīzhe zǎofàn ne.
She is eating breakfast right now.

在 **zài** before the verb may also mark duration without the verb suffix 着/著 **zhe**.

他在说话呢。
他在說話呢。
Tā zài shuō huà ne.
He is speaking.

我们在吃饭呢。
我們在吃飯呢。
Wǒmen zài chī fàn ne.
We are eating right now. (We are right in the middle of eating.)

⇨ 13.4, 30.2, 30.3

The duration suffix 着/著 **zhe** is often used with verbs that refer to the placement or location of an object.

街上站着很多人。
街上站著很多人。
Jiēshàng zhànzhe hěn duō rén.
There are a lot of people standing in the street.

公共汽车上坐着很多人。
公共汽車上坐著很多人。
Gōnggòng qìchē shàng zuòzhe hěn duō rén.
There are a lot of people sitting on the bus.

⇨ 30.4

This use of 着/著 **zhe** is similar to the use of the present progressive verb suffix '-ing' in English in its focus on ongoing actions. However, 着/著 **zhe** and '-ing' are not always equivalent. For example, 着/著 **zhe** can be used in Mandarin to emphasize the duration of an adjectival verb. The English equivalent does not typically use '-ing.'

她的脸红着呢。(AV)
她的臉紅著呢。
Tā de liǎn hóngzhe ne.
Her face is red. (Not 'Her face is being red.')

汤热着呢。(AV)
湯熱著呢。
Tāng rèzhe ne.
The soup is hot. (Not 'The soup is being hot.')

In Mandarin, 着/著 **zhe** may also be suffixed to certain verbs in commands. The English equivalent does not ordinarily involve verb '-ing.'

拿着！/拿著！	**Názhe!**	Hold it!/Take it!
记着！/記著！	**Jìzhe!**	Remember!
等着！/等著！	**Děngzhe!**	Wait!
坐着！/坐著！	**Zuòzhe!**	Sit!

⇨ 47.1.1

35.2.2 Emphasizing the ongoing duration of a situation or state

To emphasize the ongoing duration of a situation or state, use the adverb 还/還 **hái** before the [prepositional phrase +] verb or verb phrase. In affirmative sentences and questions, this use of 还/還 **hái** can often be translated into English with the word 'still.'

他还在中国。
他還在中國。
Tā hái zài Zhōngguó.
He is still in China.

你还喜欢他吗?
你還喜歡他嗎?
Nǐ hái xǐhuan tā ma?
Do you still like him?

In negative sentences, this use of 还/還 **hái** can often be translated into English with the phrase 'not yet.'

他还没结婚。
他還沒結婚。
Tā hái méi jiéhūn.
He has not yet gotten married. (He still hasn't gotten married.)

我还没看那个电影。
我還沒看那個電影。
Wǒ hái méi kàn nàge diànyǐng.
I have not yet seen that movie. (I still haven't seen that movie.)

⇨ 15.2.3, 36.2

35.3 Indicating the ongoing duration of a background event

When two events occur at the same time, we sometimes consider one event to be the main event and the other to be the background event. To signal that a background event is ongoing as the main event occurs, follow the verb of the background event with the verb suffix 着/著 **zhe.**

我们喝着咖啡谈话。
我們喝著咖啡談話。
Wǒmen hēzhe kāfēi tán huà.
We talked while drinking coffee. ('drinking coffee' is the background event.)

他看着电视吃早饭。
他看著電視吃早飯。
Tā kànzhe diànshì chī zǎofàn.
He eats breakfast while watching television. ('watching television' is the background event.)

To indicate that an event is a background event without focusing on its duration, use 的时候/的時候 **de shíhou** 'when, while.'

我在中国的时候认识他了。
我在中國的時候認識他了。
Wǒ zài Zhōngguó de shíhou rènshi tā le.
While I was in China I met him.

⇨ 39.1

35.4 Indicating frequency

35.4.1 Words used to indicate frequency

The classifiers 次 **cì** 'number of times' and 遍 **biàn** 'a time' are used to indicate frequency. They are always preceded by a number or the question words 几/幾 **jǐ** or 多少 **duōshǎo** 'how many.' 次 **cì** can be used to refer to the frequency of any kind of action. 遍 **biàn** is more restricted in its use and refers only to actions that have been performed from beginning to end.

35.4.2 The grammar of the frequency expression

To indicate the frequency of an action, follow the action verb with the phrase number + 次 **cì** 'number of times.' If the verb is suffixed with suffix 了 **le** or 过/過 **guo**, the frequency phrase occurs after the verb suffix.

> 我已经说了三次，你怎么还不懂？
> 我已經説了三次，你怎麼還不懂？
> **Wǒ yǐjing shuō le sān cì, nǐ zěnme hái bù dǒng?**
> I've already said it three times, how can you still not understand?
> (遍 **biàn** can be used instead of 次 **cì** in this sentence.)

A verb may be followed by both a frequency expression and an object. The frequency expression always precedes the object.

There are several ways to indicate frequency.

Pattern 1: verb + object, verb + frequency
If the verb takes an object, the verb may be repeated, once followed by the object, and once followed by the frequency expression.

> 我去年<u>坐</u>飞机<u>坐</u>了<u>三次</u>。
> 我去年<u>坐</u>飛機<u>坐</u>了<u>三次</u>。
> **Wǒ qùnián _zuò_ fēijī _zuò_ le _sān cì_.**
> Last year I _rode_ airplanes _three times_.
> (遍 **biàn** cannot be used here.)

Pattern 2: verb + frequency + object noun phrase
The frequency expression can occur between the verb and its object.

> 她坐过一次飞机。(遍 **biàn** cannot be used here.)
> 她坐過一次飛機。
> **Tā zuòguo yī cì fēijī.**
> She's ridden on a plane once.

> 我给他打了两次电话。(遍 **biàn** cannot be used here.)
> 我給他打了兩次電話。
> **Wǒ gěi tā dǎ le liǎng cì diànhuà.**
> I called him on the phone twice.

Pattern 3: object noun phrase, verb + frequency
If the verb takes an object, the object may be topicalized, and presented first in the sentence:

那个电影，我看过<u>两次</u>。
那個電影，我看過<u>兩次</u>。
Nàge diànyǐng, wǒ kànguo *liǎng cì*.
That movie, I have seen it twice.

西安，我去过一次。(遍 **biàn** can be used here)
西安，我去過一次。
Xī'ān, wǒ qùguo yīcì.
Xi'an, I've been there once.

⇨ 53.1.2.1

36

Expressing additional information

Mandarin uses the following expressions to provide additional information.

36.1 ## 也 *yě* 'also'

也 **yě** is an adverb and is always followed by a [prepositional phrase +] verb or verb phrase.

也 **yě** can be used to introduce additional information about the subject of the sentence.

> 张美丽学英文。她也学日文。
> 張美麗學英文。她也學日文。
> **Zhāng Měilì xué Yīngwén. Tā yě xué Rìwén.**
> Zhang Meili studies English. She also studies Japanese.

也 **yě** can be used to indicate that two different subjects share similar characteristics or perform the same action.

> 张美丽很高。她妹妹也很高。
> 張美麗很高。她妹妹也很高。
> **Zhāng Měilì hěn gāo. Tā mèimei yě hěn gāo.**
> Zhang Meili is very tall. Her younger sister is also very tall.

> 张美丽学英文。她妹妹也学英文。
> 張美麗學英文。她妹妹也學英文。
> **Zhāng Měilì xué Yīngwén. Tā mèimei yě xué Yīngwén.**
> Zhang Meili studies English. Her younger sister also studies English.

⇨ 15.2.1

36.2 ## 还/還 *hái* 'in addition, also'

还/還 **hái** is an adverb and is always followed by a [prepositional phrase +] verb or verb phrase. 还/還 **hái** overlaps in meaning with 也 **yě**, but they are not identical in function. 也 **yě** introduces any kind of new information. 还/還 **hái** only introduces new actions or situations.

还/還 **hái** can be used to introduce additional actions performed by the subject.

> 他要学中文，还要学日文。
> 他要學中文，還要學日文。
> **Tā yào xué Zhōngwén, hái yào xué Rìwén.**
> He wants to study Chinese, (and) he also wants to study Japanese.

> 她买了字典，还买了本子。
> 她買了字典，還買了本子。
> **Tā mǎi le zìdiǎn, hái mǎi le běnzi.**
> She bought a dictionary, (and she) also bought notebooks.

还/還 **hái** is also used to indicate the continuation of a situation.

> 他还在这儿。
> 他還在這兒。
> **Tā hái zài zhèr.**
> He is still here.

⇨ | 15.2.3, 35.2.2

36.3 还有/還有 *hái yǒu* 'in addition'

还有/還有 **hái yǒu** begins a new sentence or clause. It introduces additional information related to the topic of the conversation.

> 别忘了明天考试。还有，可以用字典。
> 別忘了明天考試。還有，可以用字典。
> **Bié wàng le míngtiān kǎo shì. Hái yǒu, kéyǐ yòng zìdiǎn.**
> Don't forget we have a test tomorrow. In addition, you can use a dictionary.

36.4 并且/並且 *bìngqiě* 'moreover'

并且/並且 **bìngqiě** begins a new sentence and provides additional information to support a preceding statement.

> 我觉得那个电影的故事没有意思。并且，太长。
> 我覺得那個電影的故事沒有意思。並且，太長。
> **Wǒ juéde nàge diànyǐng de gùshì méi yǒu yìsi. Bìngqiě, tài cháng.**
> I think that movie's story wasn't interesting. Moreover, it was too long.

36.5 再说/再說 *zài shuō* 'besides, moreover, to put it another way'

再說 **zài shuō** begins a new sentence and presents information that continues and clarifies information presented in the preceding sentence.

> 我们很喜欢去中国旅行。再说在那儿也可以练习说中文。
> 我們很喜歡去中國旅行。再說在那兒也可以練習説中文。
> **Wǒmen hěn xǐhuan qù Zhōngguó lǚxíng. Zài shuō zài nàr yě kéyǐ liànxí shuō Zhōngwén.**
> We like to go to China to travel. Moreover, we can practice speaking Chinese there.

36.6 而 *ér* 'and, but'

而 **ér** joins adjectival verbs and introduces additional though contrasting information. It is literary in usage.

> 办奥运是一个艰辛而光荣的任务。
> 辦奧運是一個艱辛而光榮的任務。
> **Bàn ào yùn shì yī gè jiānxīn ér guāngróng de rènwu.**
> Organizing the Olympics is a difficult but prestigious responsibility.

36.7 和 *hé* and 跟 *gēn* 'and'

和 **hé** and 跟 **gēn** are conjunctions, and they are identical in meaning. They join nouns or noun phrases.

> 哥哥和弟弟都很像爸爸。
> **Gēge hé dìdi dōu hěn xiàng bàba.**
> Older brother and younger brother both resemble dad.

For more on these and related conjunctions, see

⇨ 16.1

跟 **gēn** is also a preposition.

⇨ 14

36.8 不但 . . . 而且 . . . *búdàn . . . érqiě . . .* 'not only . . . but also . . .'

This expression introduces related information about a subject. 不但 **búdàn** and 而且 **érqiě** are always followed by a [prepositional phrase +] verb or verb phrase or clause.

> 那个饭馆，不但菜好吃，而且服务也很好。
> 那個飯館，不但菜好吃，而且服務也很好。
> **Nàge fànguǎn, búdàn cài hǎo chī, érqiě fúwù yě hěn hǎo.**
> (As for) that restaurant, not only is the food good, but so is the service.
> (lit. 'That restaurant, not only is the food good, but the service is also good'.)

不但 **búdàn** can occur without 而且 **érqiě**. In the following examples, it occurs with the adverbs 还/還 **hái** and 也 **yě**.

> 哈佛大学不但录取了他，还给了他一笔很大的奖学金。
> 哈佛大學不但錄取了他，還給了他一筆很大的獎學金。
> **Hāfó dàxué búdàn lùqǔ le tā, hái gěi le tā yī bǐ hěn dà de jiǎngxuéjīn.**
> Harvard University not only admitted him but also gave him a big scholarship.

> 那个饭馆，不但菜好吃，服务也很好。
> 那個飯館，不但菜好吃，服務也很好。
> **Nàge fànguǎn, búdàn cài hǎo chī, fúwù yě hěn hǎo.**
> (As for) that restaurant, not only is the food good, so is the service.

36.9 又 . . . 又 . . . *yòu . . . yòu . . .* 'both . . . and . . .'

This expression is used to indicate two similar properties about a subject. Each instance of 又 **yòu** must be followed by an adjectival verb.

> 中国梨，又甜又脆，特别好吃。
> 中國梨，又甜又脆，特別好吃。
> **Zhōngguó lí, yòu tián yòu cuì, tèbié hǎo chī.**
> Chinese pears (are) both sweet and crisp. (They are) especially delicious.

➪ 10.8, 39.4

36.10 除了 . . . 以外 *chúle . . . yǐwài* 'besides . . .'

This expression can be used to introduce additional information or it can be used to introduce an exception. When it introduces additional information, the additional information is always related in meaning to the phrase that occurs between 除了 **chúle** and 以外 **yǐwài**.

The phrase that occurs between 除了 **chúle** and 以外 **yǐwài** can be a subject noun phrase, an object noun phrase, or a time phrase.

Subject noun phrase

> 除了妹妹以外，弟弟也想去中国留学。
> 除了妹妹以外，弟弟也想去中國留學。
> **Chúle mèimei yǐwài, *dìdi* yě xiǎng qù Zhōngguó liúxué.**
> Besides younger sister, *younger brother* also wants to go to China to study.

Object noun phrase

> 除了中国以外，弟弟也想去越南旅行。
> 除了中國以外，弟弟也想去越南旅行。
> **Chúle Zhōngguó yǐwài, dìdi yě xiǎng qù *Yuènán* lǚxíng.**
> Besides China, younger brother also wants to go to *Vietnam* to travel.

Time phrase

> 除了夏天以外，我们冬天也放假。
> 除了夏天以外，我們冬天也放假。
> **Chúle xiàtiān yǐwài, wǒmen *dōngtiān* yě fàng jià.**
> Besides the summer, we also have (a) vacation in the *winter*.

除了 **chúle** and 以外 **yǐwài** need not both occur in the same sentence. One or the other may be omitted.

> 除了中国，弟弟也想去越南旅行。
> 除了中國，弟弟也想去越南旅行。
> **Chúle Zhōngguó, dìdi yě xiǎng qù *Yuènán* lǚxíng.**
> Besides China, younger brother also wants to go to *Vietnam* to travel.

妹妹以外，<u>弟弟</u>也想去中国留学。
妹妹以外，<u>弟弟</u>也想去中國留學。
Mèimei yǐwài, *dìdi* yě xiǎng qù Zhōngguó liúxué.
Besides younger sister, *younger brother* also wants to go to China to study.

⇨ | 53.2.2

36.11 另外 *lìngwài* 'in addition,' '(an)other'

另外 **lìngwài** functions as an adverb, occurring before the verb phrase to indicate an additional action:

她买了裙子，另外(也)买了毛衣。
她買了裙子，另外(也)買了毛衣。
Tā mǎi le qúnzi, lìngwài (yě) mǎi le máoyī.
She bought a skirt, and in addition also bought a sweater.

It can also occur before a *number + classifier phrase + noun* to indicate 'another' (number of nouns).

那是另外一种方法。
那是另外一種方法。
Nà shì lìngwài yī zhǒng fāngfǎ.
That is another method.

我还有另外几个问题。
我還有另外幾個問題。
Wǒ hái yǒu lìngwài jǐ gè wèntí.
I still have several other questions.

37

Expressing contrast

37.1 ## Expressing contrast with paired connecting words

Mandarin uses the following paired connecting words to express contrast.

虽然 . . . 可是	or	虽然 . . . 但是	or	虽然 . . . 不过
雖然 . . . 可是		雖然 . . . 但是		雖然 . . . 不過
suīrán . . . kěshì		**suīrán . . . dànshì**		**suīrán . . . búguò**
although . . . but		although . . . but		although . . . however

可是 **kěshì** and 但是 **dànshì** are identical in meaning and are interchangeable. 不过/ 不過 **búguò** conveys a slightly stronger sense of contrariness to expectation.

The Chinese connecting words occur at the beginning of their clauses or right before the predicate. Both members of the pair can occur in the same sentence. Although English permits only a single contrast connector in a sentence, in order to best illustrate the usage of the Mandarin words, the English translations in this section translate each connector in the Mandarin sentences.

虽然他是中国人，可是他还喜欢吃日本菜。
雖然他是中國人，可是他還喜歡吃日本菜。
Suīrán tā shì Zhōngguó rén, kěshì tā hái xǐhuan chī Rìběn cài.
Although he is Chinese, but he still likes to eat Japanese food.

虽然他是中国人，但是他没去过北京。
雖然他是中國人，但是他沒去過北京。
Suīrán tā shì Zhōngguó rén, dànshì tā méi qùguo Běijīng.
Although he is Chinese, but he has never been to Beijing.

虽然他很有钱，可是我还不愿意嫁给他。
雖然他很有錢，可是我還不願意嫁給他。
Suīrán tā hěn yǒu qián, kěshì wǒ hái bù yuànyi jiàgěi tā.
Although he has a lot of money, but I'm still not willing to marry him.

37.1.1 ### The placement of connecting words

If the subjects of the two clauses are identical in reference and the second one is not omitted, 虽然/雖然 **suīrán** typically occurs before the subject.

虽然我哥哥已经三十岁了，但是他还没结婚。
雖然我哥哥已經三十歲了，但是他還沒結婚。
Suīrán wǒ gēge yǐjing sānshí suì le, dànshì tā hái méi jiéhūn.
Although my older brother is already 30 years old, but he still hasn't married.

When subjects of the two clauses in contrast sentences are identical in reference, the second one is sometimes omitted. When this is the case, the connecting word 虽然/雖然 **suīrán** typically occurs after the subject of the first clause.

> 我哥哥虽然已经三十岁了可是还没结婚。
> 我哥哥雖然已經三十歲了可是還沒結婚。
> **Wǒ gēge suīrán yǐjing sānshí suì le kěshì hái méi jiéhūn.**
> Although my older brother is already 30 years old but (he) still hasn't married.

37.1.2 **Relative order of the clauses in contrast sentences**

The position of the clauses is fixed. The 虽然/雖然 **suīrán** clause comes first. The 可是 **kěshì**, 但是 **dànshì**, or 不过/不過 **búguò** clause comes second.

Say this

> 虽然他认识很多人，
> 可是他没有很好的朋友。
> 雖然他認識很多人，
> 可是他沒有很好的朋友。
> **Suīrán tā rènshi hěn duō rén,**
> **kěshì tā méiyǒu hěn hǎo**
> **de péngyou.**
> Although he knows a lot of people
> he doesn't have any very good friends.

> 虽然他很小不过他胆子很大。
> 雖然他很小不過他膽子很大。
> **Suīrán tā hěn xiǎo búguò tā**
> **dǎnzi hěn dà.**
> Although he is little he is very brave
> (his courage is big).

Not this

> *(可是)他没有很好的朋友，
> 虽然他认识很多人。
> (可是)他沒有很好的朋友，
> 雖然他認識很多人。
> **(Kěshì) tā méi yǒu hěn hǎo de**
> **péngyou, suīrán tā rènshi**
> **hěn duō rén.**

> *他胆子很大虽然他很小。
> 他膽子很大雖然他很小。
> **Tā dǎnzi hěn dà suīrán**
> **tā hěn xiǎo.**

37.1.3 **Omission of the connecting words**

虽然/雖然 **suīrán** can be freely omitted:

> 他很有钱，可是我还不愿意嫁给他。
> 他很有錢，可是我還不願意嫁給他。
> **Tā hěn yǒu qián, kěshì wǒ hái bù yuànyi jiàgěi tā.**
> He has a lot of money, but I'm still not willing to marry him.

可是 **kěshì**, 但是 **dànshì**, or 不过 **búguò** can be omitted when the second clause contains the adverb 还/還 **hái** or an adverb that indicates contrast. Adverbs that indicate contrast are presented in **37.2**.

> 虽然他很有钱，我还不愿意嫁给他。
> 雖然他很有錢，我還不願意嫁給他。
> **Suīrán tā hěn yǒu qián, wǒ hái bù yuànyi jiàgěi tā.**
> Although he has a lot of money, I'm still not willing to marry him.

37.2 Adverbs that indicate contrast

37.2.1 Adverbs that must occur before the [prepositional phrase +] verb or verb phrase

却 *què 'in contrast'*

却 **què** may occur with other contrast connectors.

> 虽然他很有钱，可是我却不愿意嫁给他。
> 雖然他很有錢，可是我卻不願意嫁給他。
> **Suīrán tā hěn yǒu qián, kěshì wǒ què bù yuànyi jiàgěi tā.**
> Although he is rich, I am not willing to marry him.

> 他很有钱，我却不愿意嫁给他。
> 他很有錢，我卻不願意嫁給他。
> **Tā hěn yǒuqián, wǒ què bù yuànyi jiàgěi tā.**
> He is rich but I am still not willing to marry him.

倒是 *dǎoshì 'contrary to one's expectations'*

> 房子不大，布置得倒是很讲究。
> 房子不大，佈置得倒是很講究。
> **Fángzi bù dà, bùzhì de dǎoshì hěn jiǎngjiu.**
> The house isn't big, but it is fixed up really nicely.

37.2.2 Contrast adverbs that can occur at the beginning of a sentence or before a verb or very phrase

不过/不過 *búguò 'however, nevertheless'*

> 中国字很难写，不过文法比较简单。
> 中國字很難寫，不過文法比較簡單。
> **Zhōngguó zì hěn nán xiě, búguò wénfǎ bǐjiào jiǎndān.**
> Chinese characters are very difficult to write, but the grammar is relatively easy.

> 吃四川菜可以，不过不能太辣。
> 吃四川菜可以，不過不能太辣。
> **Chī Sìchuān cài kéyǐ, búguò bù néng tài là.**
> It is okay (with me) to eat Sichuan food, but it can't be too hot.

然而 *rán'ér 'however, nevertheless'*

> 他虽然没考上大学，然而他并不灰心。
> 他雖然沒考上大學，然而他並不灰心。
> **Tā suīrán méi kǎoshàng dàxué, rán'ér tā bìng bù huīxīn.**
> Although he didn't pass the college entrance exam, he did not lose heart.

> 他小的时候体弱多病，然而长大后却非常强壮。
> 他小的時候體弱多病，然而長大後卻非常強壯。
> **Tā xiǎo de shíhòu tǐruò duō bìng, rán'ér zháng dà hòu què fēicháng qiáng zhuàng.**
> When he was young he was weak and sickly, but after he grew up he was extremely strong.

反而 *fǎn'ér* 'on the contrary, in contrast'

> 难的字他都记住了，容易的反而忘了。
> 難的字他都記住了，容易的反而忘了。
> **Nán de zì tā dōu jìzhù le, róngyì de fǎn'ér wàng le.**
> He remembers all of the difficult characters; the easy characters he forgets.

> 你不但不帮我忙，反而批评我。
> 你不但不幫我忙，反而批評我。
> **Nǐ búdàn bù bāng wǒ máng, fǎn'ér pīpíng wǒ.**
> Not only don't you help me, but on the contrary you criticize me.

反过来/反過來 *fǎnguòlái* 'conversely'

> 有的人认为学数学快的人学语言学也快，反过来也一样。
> 有的人認為學數學快的人學語言學也快，反過來也一樣。
> **Yǒu de rén rènwéi xué shùxué kuài de rén xué yǔyánxué yě kuài, fǎnguolái yě yīyàng.**
> Some people think that people who learn math quickly also learn linguistics quickly. The converse is also true. (The converse is the same.)

> 你们是好朋友，看到他做错了就应该跟他说。反过来，如果不跟他说就不是真正的朋友了。
> 你們是好朋友，看到他做錯了就應該跟他説。反過來，如果不跟他説就不是真正的朋友了。
> **Nǐmen shì hǎo péngyǒu, kàndào tā zuòcuò le jiù yìnggāi gēn tā shuō. Fǎnguolái, rúguǒ bù gēn tā shuō jiù bù shì zhēnzhèng de péngyǒu le.**
> You are good friends. When you see him do something wrong you should speak with him. Conversely, if you don't speak with him, you are not a real friend.

37.3 Qualifying a statement with an adjectival verb or stative verb

To qualify a statement involving an adjectival verb or stative verb, use this pattern:

> AV/SV 是 **shì** AV/SV, 可是 **kěshì** . . .
> 　　　　　　　　　　但是 **dànshì**
> 　　　　　　　　　　不过/不過 **búguò**
> 　　　　　　　　　　就是 **jiù shì**

AV/SV 'all right, but . . .'

> 那个电影好是好，就是太长。(AV)
> 那個電影好是好，就是太長。
> **Nàge diànyǐng hǎo shì hǎo, jiù shì tài cháng.**
> That movie is *good all right* but it is too long.

> 那个女孩子好看是好看，就是太瘦。(AV)
> 那個女孩子好看是好看，就是太瘦。
> **Nàge nǚ háizi hǎo kàn shì hǎo kàn, jiù shì tài shòu.**
> That girl is *pretty all right*, but she is too thin.

> 我喜欢是喜欢他，就是他有一点太无聊。(SV)
> 我喜歡是喜歡他，就是他有一點太無聊。
> **Wǒ xǐhuan shì xǐhuan tā, jiùshì tā yǒu yīdiǎn tài wúliáo.**
> I *like him all right*, he's just a little boring.

38

Expressing sequence

Expressing the relationship 'before'

The structure of the 以前 yǐqián 'before' sentence

以前 **yǐqián** is used to indicate the relationship 'before one event occurs, another event occurs.'

event$_1$ 以前 **yǐqián**, event$_2$
before event$_1$, event$_2$

> 我上大学以前，想去澳大利亚旅游。
> 我上大學以前，想去澳大利亞旅遊。
> **Wǒ shàng dàxué yǐqián, xiǎng qù Aòdàlìyà lǚyóu.**
> Before I attend university, I want to go to Australia to travel.

> 妈妈上班以前，都吃早饭。
> 媽媽上班以前，都吃早飯。
> **Māma shàng bān yǐqián, dōu chī zǎofàn.**
> Before mom goes to work, she always eats breakfast.

To indicate that a sequence occurred in the past, follow the verb of the second clause with the verb suffix -了 **le**.

> 我来中国以前，在日本住了一年。
> 我來中國以前，在日本住了一年。
> **Wǒ lái Zhōngguó yǐqián, zài Rìběn zhùle yīnián.**
> Before I came to China, I lived in Japan for a year.

NOTE | The more literary form of 以前 **yǐqián** is 之前 **zhīqián**.

⇨ | 9.6

Comparing 以前 yǐqián with 'before'

以前 **yǐqián** signals the same relationship of sequence as the English word 'before.' However, there are important differences between 以前 **yǐqián** and 'before.'

- 以前 **yǐqián** occurs at the end of the first clause:

> 妈妈上班以前
> 媽媽上班以前
> **Māma shàng bān yǐqián**

260

Before occurs at the beginning of the first clause:

before mom goes to work

- In Mandarin, the clause that ends with 以前 **yǐqián** must come first in the sentence. In English, the order of the clauses in the 'before' sentence is not fixed. Either can come first in the sentence. Compare the following sentences.

Good English	*Good Mandarin*
Before mom went to work she ate breakfast.	妈妈上班以前吃了早饭。 媽媽上班以前吃了早飯。 ***Māma shàng bān yǐqián** chī le zǎofàn.*

Good English	*Bad Mandarin*
Mom ate breakfast *before* she went to work.	*妈妈吃了早饭上班以前。 媽媽吃了早飯上班以前。 ***Māma chī le zǎofàn *shàng bān yǐqián*.*

38.2 Expressing the relationship 'after' in a single sentence

In Mandarin, the relationship of 'after' is expressed using some combination of the word 以后/以後 **yǐhòu** 'after,' the verb suffix 了 **le**, and adverbs, usually 就 **jiù** or 才 **cái**.

These markers of sequence can occur together in a single sentence to express the relationship of sequence, or they can occur independently.

Native speakers of Mandarin differ in their preference for the use of these markers of sequence.

⇨ 6.9, 33.2, 38.2.2

38.2.1 Indicating sequence with 以后/以後 *yǐhòu* 'after'

以后/以後 **yǐhòu** 'after' is used to express the following relationship: 'after an event occurs, another event occurs.'

event₁ 以后/以後 **yǐhòu**, event₂
after event₁, event₂

我们吃了饭以后，就去看电影。
我們吃了飯以後，就去看電影。
Wǒmen chī le fàn *yǐhòu*, jiù qù kàn diànyǐng.
After we eat, we will go to a movie.

我下了课以后，就回家。
我下了課以後，就回家。
Wǒ xià le kè *yǐhòu*, jiù huí jiā.
After I get out of class, I go home.

孩子睡了觉以后，父母就看电视。
孩子睡了覺以後，父母就看電視。
Háizi shuì le jiào *yǐhòu*, fùmǔ jiù kàn diànshì.
After the children go to sleep, the parents watch television.

To signal that a sequence occurred in the past, follow the verb of the second clause with 了 **le**. If the verb takes a one-syllable object, 了 **le** may also follow the object.

> 他吃了饭以后就看了电视。
> 他吃了飯以後就看了電視。
> **Tā chī le fàn *yǐhòu* jiù kàn le diànshì.**
> *After* he ate he watched television.

> 他吃了饭以后就睡觉了。
> 他吃了飯以後就睡覺了。
> **Tā chī le fàn *yǐhòu* jiù shuì jiào le.**
> *After* he ate he went to sleep.

以后/以後 **yǐhòu** signals the same relationship of sequence as the English word 'after.' However, there are important differences between 以后/以後 **yǐhòu** and 'after.'

- 以后/以後 **yǐhòu** occurs at the end of the first clause:

  > 我下了课以后
  > 我下了課以後
  > **wǒ xià le kè *yǐhòu***

  After occurs at the beginning of the clause:

  > *after* I get out of class

- In Mandarin, the clause that ends with 以后/以後 **yǐhòu** must come first in the sentence. In English, the order of the clauses in the 'after' sentence is not fixed. Either can come first in the sentence. Compare the following sentences.

Good English	*Good Mandarin*
After I get out of class I go home.	我下了课以后回家。 我下了課以後回家。 ***Wǒ xià le kè yǐhòu* huí jiā.**

Good English	*Bad Mandarin*
I go home *after I get out of class*.	*我回家下了课以后。 我回家下了課以後。 **Wǒ huí jiā xià le kè *yǐhòu*.**

NOTE | The more literary form of 以后/以後 **yǐhòu** is 之后/之後 **zhīhòu**.

⇨ | 9.6

38.2.2 **Adverbs that occur in sequence sentences**

38.2.2.1 **就 *jiù***

The adverb 就 **jiù** has several functions. One function is to signal a relationship of sequence between events that occur in a series. The relationship of sequence indicated by 就 **jiù** reinforces the meaning of sequence indicated by 以后/以後 **yǐhòu**. Therefore, 就 **jiù** often occurs with 以后/以後 **yǐhòu** in sequence sentences.

> 我学了中国历史以后就想去中国。
> 我學了中國歷史以後就想去中國。
> **Wǒ xué le Zhōngguó lìshǐ yǐhòu jiù xiǎng qù Zhōngguó.**
> After I studied Chinese history I wanted to go to China.

The meaning of 就 **jiù** is related to the meaning of 以后/以後 **yǐhòu**, but the two words are independent. 就 **jiù** may occur without 以后/以後 **yǐhòu**, and 以后/以後 **yǐhòu** may occur without 就 **jiù**.

The following two sentences, one with 就 **jiù** and the other with 以后/以後 **yǐhòu**, are equivalent in meaning. Compare them to the sentence above in which 就 **jiù** and 以后/以後 **yǐhòu** both occur.

> 我学了中国历史就想去中国。
> 我學了中國歷史就想去中國。
> **Wǒ xué le Zhōngguó lìshǐ jiù xiǎng qù Zhōngguó.**
> After I studied Chinese history I wanted to go to China.

> 我学了中国历史以后想去中国。
> 我學了中國歷史以後想去中國。
> **Wǒ xué le Zhōngguó lìshǐ yǐhòu xiǎng qù Zhōngguó.**
> After I studied Chinese history I wanted to go to China.

⇨ 15.2.4

38.2.2.2 Indicating that one event happens 'only after' another event: sequence with the adverb 才 *cái*

To indicate that some event happens 'only after' another event, use the adverb 才 **cái** before the second verb of a sequence. 才 **cái** can occur with 以后/以後 **yǐhòu** and 了 **le**. 才 **cái** and 就 **jiù** cannot both occur before the same verb.

> 她在中国住了两年才会说中国话。
> 她在中國住了兩年才會說中國話。
> **Tā zài Zhōngguó zhù le liǎng nián cái huì shuō Zhōngguó huà.**
> She lived in China for two years and only then was able to speak Chinese.
> (After she lived in China for two years, only then was she able to speak Chinese.)

> 你长大了以后才懂这种事情。
> 你長大了以後才懂這種事情。
> **Nǐ zhǎng dà le yǐhòu cái dǒng zhè zhǒng shìqing.**
> After you grow up, only then will you understand this kind of situation.

⇨ 15.2.6

Pay attention to the difference between the adverbs 才 **cái** and 就 **jiù** in the following sentences. Since 就 **jiù** indicates simleple sequence, it is used much more frequently than 才 **cái**. For many speakers of Mandarin, a verb phrase with 才 **cái** cannot include 了 **le**.

就 *jiù*	才 *cái*
他吃了药就好了。	他吃了药才好(了)。
他吃了藥就好了。	他吃了藥才好(了)。
Tā chī le yào jiù hǎo le.	**Tā chī le yào cái hǎo (le).**
After he ate the medicine he recovered.	Only after he ate the medicine did he recover.
	(He ate the medicine and only then recovered.)

就 *jiù*	才 *cái*
他开了空调就舒服了。	他开了空调才舒服。
他開了空調就舒服了。	他開了空調才舒服。
Tā kāi le kōngtiáo jiù shūfu le.	**Tā kāi le kōngtiáo cái shūfu.**
After he turned on the air conditioner he was comfortable.	Only after he turned on the air conditioner was he comfortable.
	(He turned on the air conditioner and only then was comfortable.)

⇨ | 33.2

38.2.2.3 **便** *biàn*

便 **biàn**, like 就 **jiù**, is used to reinforce a relationship of sequence between two events.

> 每天一下课他便到图书馆去工作。
> 每天一下課他便到圖書館去工作。
> **Měitiān yī xià kè tā biàn dào túshūguǎn qù gōngzuò.**
> Every day, as soon as he gets out of class he goes to the library to work.

便 **biàn** is largely restricted to formal, literary contexts.

> 自从毕业以后，我们便没有来往。
> 自從畢業以後，我們便沒有來往。
> **Zìcóng bì yè yǐhòu, wǒmen biàn méi yǒu láiwǎng.**
> Since we've graduated, we haven't had any contact.

38.2.3 **Indicating sequence with the verb suffix 了 *le***

Like the adverbs 就 **jiù**, 才 **cái**, and 便 **biàn**, the verb suffix 了 **le** can be used to signal a relationship of sequence between two events. 了 **le** is optional, but when it occurs, it normally follows the first verb in a series of verb phrases. Notice that 就 **jiù** or 才 **cái** often occurs with 了 **le** and 以后/以後 **yǐhòu** in sequence sentences that indicate the relationship 'after.'

> 她买了照相机以后就照了很多照片。
> 她買了照相機以後就照了很多照片。
> **Tā mǎi le zhàoxiàngjī yǐhòu jiù zhào le hěn duō zhàopiàn.**
> After she bought a camera she took a lot of pictures.

> 我做完了功课以后才睡觉。
> 我做完了功課以後才睡覺。
> **Wǒ zuòwán le gōngkè yǐhòu cái shuì jiào.**
> Only after I finish my homework will I go to sleep.
> (I will finish my homework and only then go to sleep.)

When the object of the first verb is one syllable in length, some speakers of Mandarin prefer to put after 了 **le** the object. Both of the following sentences are acceptable.

他每天下了班就回家。	他每天下班了就回家。
Tā měitiān xià le bān jiù huí jiā.	**Tā měitiān xià bān le jiù huí jiā.**
Every day after he gets out of work he goes home.	Every day after he gets out of work he goes home.

⇨ | 33.2

38.2.4 **Indicating 'after' in a single sentence: a summary of the use of 以后/以後 yǐhòu, 了 le, and sequence adverbs**

- 以后/以後 **yǐhòu**, 了 **le**, and sequence adverbs all signal a sequence of events within a single sentence.
- Sequence sentences can contain any combination of 以后/以後 **yǐhòu**, 了 **le**, and sequence adverbs.
- None of these markers of sequence is obligatory, and native speakers of Mandarin differ in their preferences in using them.
- Events that are related in terms of sequence need not have any of these sequence markers.

> 我每天下课回家。
> 我每天下課回家。
> **Wǒ měitiān xià kè huí jiā.**
> Every day, after I get out of class I return home.
> (Every day I get out of class and return home.)

38.3 # Indicating that one event happens first and another event happens afterwards

The following pairs of adverbs are used to indicate that one event happens first and another event happens afterwards. The adverbs always occur before [prepositional phrases +] verb phrases. The order of the adverbs and their following verb phrases is fixed. They are often used when giving instructions and describing processes.

38.3.1 ### Indicating the relationship 'first . . . then . . .'

The following pairs of adverbs are commonly used to indicate the relationship 'first . . . then . . .'

> 先 **xiān** VP$_1$ 再 **zài** VP$_2$
> first VP$_1$ then VP$_2$
> > 你先买票，再上公共汽车。
> > 你先買票，再上公共汽車。
> > **Nǐ xiān mǎi piào, zài shàng gōnggòng qì chē.**
> > You first buy a ticket, then get on the bus.

> 先 **xiān** VP$_1$ 然后/然後 **ránhòu** VP$_2$
> first VP$_1$ then/afterwards VP$_2$
> > 我们得先去换钱，然后再去买东西。
> > 我們得先去換錢，然後再去買東西。
> > **Wǒmen děi xiān qù huàn qián, ránhòu zài qù mǎi dōngxi.**
> > We have to first change money and then go shopping.

> 先 **xiān** VP$_1$ 以后/以後 **yǐhòu** VP$_2$
> first VP$_1$ then/afterwards VP$_2$
> > 我们先吃饭，以后再讨论那件事情。
> > 我們先吃飯，以後再討論那件事情。
> > **Wǒmen xiān chī fàn, yǐhòu zài tǎolùn nà jiàn shìqing.**
> > We will eat first and discuss this matter afterwards.

38.3.2 Indicating the relationship 'first . . . only then . . .'

To indicate that some event occurs 'only after' another event, say:

先 **xiān** VP₁ 才 **cái** VP₂
first VP₁ only then VP₂

> 你先买票，才上公共汽车。
> 你先買票，才上公共汽車。
> **Nǐ xiān mǎi piào, cái shàng gōnggòng qìchē.**
> You first buy a ticket and only then get on the bus.

⇨ 15.2.6

38.3.3 Indicating the relationship 'as soon as . . . then . . .'

To indicate that some event occurs 'as soon as' another event occurs, say:

一 **yī** VP₁ 就 **jiù** VP₂
as soon as VP₁ then VP₂

> 我们一到北京，就去爬长城。
> 我們一到北京，就去爬長城。
> **Wǒmen yī dào Běijīng, jiù qù pá chángchéng.**
> As soon as we get to Beijing we will go climb the Great Wall.

NOTE When 一 **yī** occurs immediately before a [prepositional phrase +] verb or verb phrase, it always means *as soon as*. When 一 **yī** occurs immediately before a classifier, it is always the number 'one.'

38.4 Indicating 'afterwards' in a separate sentence

Mandarin has a number of *sentence adverbs*, adverbs that occur at the beginning of a sentence, to introduce an event that happens afterwards. The most common are 以后/以後 **yǐhòu**, 然后/然後 **ránhòu**, and 后来/後來 **hòulái**.

以后/以後 yǐhòu 'afterwards, later'

以后/以後 **yǐhòu** is the most neutral of the sentence adverbs used to indicate 'afterwards.'

> 请先喝点茶吧！以后我们出去吃晚饭。
> 請先喝點茶吧！以後我們出去吃晚飯。
> **Qǐng xiān hē diǎn chá ba! Yǐhòu wǒmen chūqu chī wǎnfàn.**
> Drink a little tea first. Afterwards we will go out to eat dinner.

然后/然後 ránhòu 'afterwards/after that'

然后/然後 **ránhòu** can only be used to indicate sequence between two events that occur in close temporal sequence to each other.

> 我们看了电影。然后我们去了咖啡店喝咖啡。
> 我們看了電影。然後我們去了咖啡店喝咖啡。
> **Wǒmen kàn le diànyǐng. Ránhòu wǒmen qù le kāfēi diàn hē kāfēi.**
> We saw a movie. Afterwards, we went to a coffee shop and drank coffee.

后来/後來 hòulái 'afterwards'

后来/後來 **hòulái** can only be used to indicate sequence between two events that have already occurred.

> 我昨天早上考了中文。后来我回宿舍睡觉了。
> 我昨天早上考了中文。後來我回宿舍睡覺了。
> **Wǒ zuótiān zǎoshang kǎo le Zhōngwén. Hòulái wǒ huì sùshè shuì jiào le.**
> Yesterday morning I had a Chinese test. Afterwards I went back to the dormitory and went to sleep.

38.5   Comparing 以前 *yǐqián* 'before' with 以后/以後 *yǐhòu* 'after'

In some ways, the uses of 以前 **yǐqián** 'before' and 以后/以後 **yǐhòu** 'after' are parallel. Both must occur in the first clause of a sequence sentence, and both words occur at the end of their clause.

However, the words are different in their occurrence with the verb suffix 了 **le**. The verb suffix 了 **le** may occur in the 以后/以後 **yǐhòu** clause but it may not occur in the 以前 **yǐqián** clause. Compare these sentences.

Say this	*Not this*
我去中国以前学了两年的中文。 我去中國以前學了兩年的中文。 **Wǒ qù Zhōngguó yǐqián xué le liǎng nián de Zhōngwén.** Before I went to China I studied two years of Chinese.	*我去了中国以前学了两年的中文。 我去了中國以前學了兩年的中文。 **Wǒ qù *le* Zhōngguó yǐqián xué le liǎng nián de Zhōngwén.**
他考试以前复习了功课。 他考試以前復習了功課。 **Tā kǎo shì yǐqián fùxí le gōngkè.** Before he took the test he reviewed the lessons.	*他考试了以前复习了功课。 他考試了以前復習了功課。 **Tā kǎo shì *le* yǐqián fùxí le gōngkè.**

For many Mandarin speakers, the sequence use of 就 **jiù** is also not acceptable in 以前 **yǐqián** sentences. For these speakers, if 就 **jiù** occurs in an 以前 **yǐqián** sentence, it has the sense of 'only,' and not of sequence.

> 我去中国以前就学了两年的中文。
> 我去中國以前就學了兩年的中文。
> **Wǒ qù Zhōngguó yǐqián *jiù* xué le liǎng nián de Zhōngwén.**
> Before I went to China I *only* studied two years of Chinese.

39

Expressing simultaneous situations

Indicating that one situation is the background for another situation

To indicate that one situation is the background for another situation, say:

S₁ 的时候 S₂/S₁ 的時候 S₂
S₁ de shíhou S₂
while, when S₁, S₂

S₁ and S₂ can be actions or states.

S₁ and S₂ are states

我小的时候，生活很苦。
我小的時候，生活很苦。
Wǒ xiǎo de shíhou, shēnghuó hěn kǔ.
When I was young, life was very hard (bitter).

S₁ and S₂ are actions

我看书的时候，常听音乐。
我看書的時候，常聽音樂。
Wǒ kàn shū de shíhou, cháng tīng yīnyuè.
When I read, I often listen to music.

的时候/的時候 **de shíhou** can be used when one situation overlaps with the start of another one.

你来的时候，我们正在上课。
你來的時候，我們正在上課。
Nǐ lái de shíhou, wǒmen zhèngzài shàng kè.
When you arrived, we were in class.

However, 的时候/的時候 **de shíhou** cannot be used when the relationship between S₁ and S₂ is that of sequence. When S₁ and S₂ are related in terms of sequence, use 以后/以後 **yǐhòu**.

⇨ 38.2

The events in the following sentence are related in terms of sequence. Therefore, they should be connected by 以后/以後 **yǐhòu** 'after' and not 的时候/的時候 **de shíhou** 'when.' Notice that in English, 'when' can be used with sequential situations or with simultaneous situations.

Say this

你吃(完)了晚饭以后请给我打电话。
你吃(完)了晚飯以後請給我打電話。
**Nǐ chī(wán) le wǎnfàn yǐhòu
qǐng gěi wǒ dǎ diànhuà.**
After (when) you arrive home,
please call me.

Not this

*你吃完了晚饭的时候请给我打电话。
 你吃完了晚飯的時候請給我打電話。
 **Nǐ chīwán le wán fàn de shíhou
 qǐng gěi wǒ dǎ diànhuà.**

39.2 Indicating that two actions occur at the same time

39.2.1 Focusing on each action separately

(subject) 一边/邊 VP₁ 一边/邊 VP₂
(subject) **yībiān** VP₁ **yībiān** VP₂
subject does both VP₁ and VP₂ at the same time
一边/一邊 **yībiān** must occur before each verb phrase:

我儿子一边听音乐，一边作功课。
我兒子一邊聽音樂，一邊作功課。
Wǒ érzi yìbiān tīng yīnyuè, yìbiān zuò gōngkè.
My son listens to music and does homework at the same time.

39.2.2 Focusing on the shared time

(subject) 同时/同時 VP₁ VP₂
(subject) **tóngshí** VP₁ VP₂
subject simultaneously does VP₁ and VP₂
同时/同時 **tóngshí** occurs before the list of actions that occur at the same time:

你为什么同时听音乐作功课？
你為甚麼同時聽音樂作功課？
Nǐ wèi shénme tóngshí tīng yīnyuè zuò gōngkè?
Why do you listen to music and do your homework at the same time?

39.3 Indicating that two actions occur in the same time frame

To indicate that two actions occur in the same time frame, though not necessarily at the same time, say:

又 action VP₁ 又 action VP₂
yòu VP₁ **yòu** VP₂
(subject) does both VP₁ and VP₂

他特别忙，又念书，又做事。
Tā tèbié máng, yòu niàn shū, yòu zuò shì.
He is really busy. He both studies and has a job.

39.4 Describing a subject in terms of two qualities that exist at the same time

(subject) 又 AV/SV$_1$ 又 AV/SV$_2$
(subject) **yòu** AV/SV$_1$ **yòu** AV/SV$_2$
(subject) is both AV/SV$_1$ and AV/SV$_2$

那个男的又高又大。
那個男的又高又大。
Nàge nán de yòu gāo yòu dà.
That guy is both tall and big.

⇨ 10.8, 36.9

39.5 Indicating that a situation is reached at a specific point in time

到 **dào** + time phrase/S$_1$, S$_2$
when/by that time that time phrase/S$_1$, S$_2$

到六月，我就在这儿教了十五年书了。
到六月，我就在這兒教了十五年書了。
Dào liù yuè, wǒ jiù zài zhèr jiào le shíwǔ nián shū le.
In June, I will have been teaching here for fifteen years.

到三月，我就三十岁了。
到三月，我就三十歲了。
Dào sānyuè, wǒ jiù sānshí suì le.
When March comes I will be 30.

等 **děng** + S$_1$, S$_2$
when/by that time that S$_1$, S$_2$

等你学完这本书，你就学了很多中文了。
等你學完這本書，你就學了很多中文了。
Děng nǐ xuéwán zhè běn shū, nǐ jiù xué le hěn duō Zhōngwén le.
By the time you finish this book, you will have studied a lot of Chinese.

等菜来了我们都饿死了。
等菜來了我們都餓死了。
Děng cài lái le wǒmen dōu è sǐ le.
By the time the food arrived we were all starving to death.

等到 **děngdào** + S$_1$, S$_2$
when/by that time that S$_1$, S$_2$

等到你毕业，你的中国话一定会说得很好。
等到你畢業，你的中國話一定會説得很好。
Děngdào nǐ bìyè, nǐ de Zhōngguó huà yīdìng huì shuō de hěn hǎo.
By the time you graduate, your spoken Chinese will be very good.

等到爸爸回家了，孩子都睡觉了。
等到爸爸回家了，孩子都睡覺了。
Děngdào bàba huí jiā le, háizi dōu shuìjiào le.
By the time that dad returned home, the children were already asleep.

39.6 Presenting simultaneous situations

To present two parallel circumstances that exist at the same time and describe the same situation, say:

一方面 S₁ 一方面 S₂
yī fāngmiàn S₁ yī fāngmiàn S₂
on the one hand S₁, on the other hand S₂

> 她一定考得上大学。一方面她很聪明，一方面她很用功。
> 她一定考得上大學。一方面她很聰明，一方面她很用功。
> **Tā yīdìng kǎodeshàng dàxué. Yīfāngmiàn tā hěn cōngming, yīfāngmiàn tā hěn yònggōng.**
> She will certainly pass the college entrance exam. On the one hand, she is very smart, on the other hand, she is very hardworking.

> 他的体重不会减轻。一方面，他吃得太多，一方面他不愿意运动。
> 他的體重不會減輕。一方面，他吃得太多，一方面他不願意運動。
> **Tā de tǐzhòng bù huì jiǎnqīng. Yīfāngmiàn, tā chī de tài duō, yīfāngmiàn tā bù yuànyi yùndòng.**
> He can't lose weight. On the one hand, he eats too much. On the other hand, he isn't willing to exercise.

40

Expressing cause and effect or reason and result

Expressing cause and effect or reason and result in a single sentence

Mandarin uses the paired connecting words 因为/因為 **yīnwei** 'because/since' . . . 所以 **suóyǐ** 'therefore' . . . to express cause and effect or reason and result. 因为/因為 **yīnwei** and 所以 **suóyǐ** occur at the beginning of their clauses or right before the predicate. They can occur in the same sentence.

> 因为他没有很多钱，所以他不随便买东西。
> 因為他沒有很多錢，所以他不隨便買東西。
> **Yīnwéi tā méi yǒu hěn duō qián, suóyǐ tā bù suíbiàn mǎi dōngxi.**
> Because he doesn't have a lot of money, therefore he doesn't casually buy things.

40.1.1 **Omission of subjects in 因为/因為 *yīnwei* . . . 所以 *suóyǐ* . . . sentences**

When the subjects of the 因为/因為 **yīnwei** clause and the 所以 **suóyǐ** clause are identical, the subject is often omitted in the second (所以 **suóyǐ**) clause. In that case, 因为/因為 **yīnwei** is usually placed after the subject of the first clause.

> 我最近因为忙，所以没给你打电话。
> 我最近因為忙，所以沒給你打電話。
> **Wǒ zuìjìn yīnwei máng, suóyǐ méi gěi nǐ dǎ diànhuà.**
> Because I have been busy recently, I haven't called you.

When the subjects of the two clauses are identical, the subject may also be omitted from the first clause. This sentence is acceptable with or without 所以 **suóyǐ**.

> 因为有事，(所以)王先生请假了。
> 因為有事，(所以)王先生請假了。
> **Yīnwei yǒu shì, (suóyǐ) Wáng xiānsheng qǐng jià le.**
> Because he had business to attend to, Mr. Wang asked for time off.

40.1.2 **Relative order of the 因为/因為 *yīnwei* and 所以 *suóyǐ* clauses**

The position of the 所以 **suóyǐ** clause is fixed. It must come second in the sentence, after a clause that introduces the cause.

Say this	Not this
因为他是中国人，所以他会说中国话。 因為他是中國人，所以他會説中國話。 **Yīnwéi tā shì Zhōngguó rén, suóyǐ tā huì shuō Zhōngguó huà.** *Because* he is Chinese, (*therefore*) he can speak Chinese.	*所以他会说中国话，因为他是中国人。 所以他會説中國話，因為他是中國人。 *Suóyǐ tā huì shuō Zhōngguó huà, yīnwéi tā shì Zhōngguó rén.*

However, the 因为/因為 **yīnwei** clause may occur either first or second in the sentence. As the sentences above illustrate, when 因为/因為 **yīnwei** occurs in the second clause, 所以 **suóyǐ** cannot be included in the first clause.

他会说中国话，因为他是中国人。
他會説中國話，因為他是中國人。
Tā huì shuō Zhōngguó huà, yīnwéi tā shì Zhōngguó rén.
He can speak Chinese *because* he is Chinese.

王先生请假了，因为他有事。
王先生請假了，因為他有事。
Wáng xiānsheng qǐng jià le, yīnwéi tā yǒu shì.
Mr. Wang asked for time off, *because* he had a matter (to attend to).

40.1.3 Omission of the connecting words

Although you can include 因为/因為 **yīnwei** and 所以 **suóyǐ** in the same sentence, it is often possible to have only 因为/因為 **yīnwei** or only 所以 **suóyǐ** in a cause and effect sentence.

所以 **suóyǐ** and not 因为/因為 **yīnwei**:

我最近忙，所以没给你打电话。
我最近忙，所以沒給你打電話。
Wǒ zuì jìn máng, suóyǐ méi gěi nǐ dǎ diànhuà.
I have been busy recently, so I haven't called you.

因为/因為 **yīnwei** and not 所以 **suóyǐ**:

他因为病了，没来上课。
他因為病了，沒來上課。
Tā yīnwéi bìng le, méi lái shàng kè.
Because he was sick, he didn't come to class.

40.2 Introducing the cause or reason

The following expressions introduce a cause or reason for some situation.

因为 (noun phrase) 的关系, . . .
因為 (noun phrase) 的關係, . . .
yīnwei (noun phrase) **de guānxi**, . . .
because of/due to (noun phrase), . . .

因为他朋友的关系，汽车的价格减少了。
因為他朋友的關係，汽车的價格減少了。
***Yīnwéi* tā péngyou *de guānxi*, qìchē de jiàgé jiǎnshǎo le.**
Because of his friend, the price of the car was reduced.

(noun phrase) (之)所以 situation₁, 是因为 situation₂
(noun phrase) (之)所以 situation₁, 是因為 situation₂
(noun phrase) **(zhī) suóyǐ** situation₁, **shì yīnwei** situation₂
(nouns phrase's) reason for situation₁ is situation₂

有些人之所以对工作不认真，是因为缺乏责任感。
有些人之所以對工作不認真，是因為缺乏責任感。
Yǒu xiē rén *zhī suóyǐ* duì gōngzuò bù rènzhēn, *shì yīnwei* quēfá zérèngǎn.
The reason why some people don't work conscientiously *is because* they lack a sense of responsibility.

我之所以不去美国，是因为身体不好。
我之所以不去美國，是因為身體不好。
Wǒ *zhī suóyǐ* bù qù Měiguó, *shì yīnwéi* shēntǐ bù hǎo.
The reason why I am not going to America *is that* my health isn't good.

由于/由於 (situation)
yóu yú (situation)
owing to, due to, because of, as a result of (situation)
由于/由於 **yóu yú** may be placed before or after the subject.

由于我的粗心大意，这次考试的成绩不好。
由於我的粗心大意，這次考試的成績不好。
***Yóuyú* wǒ de cūxīn dàyì, zhè cì kǎoshì de chéngjī bù hǎo.**
Because of my carelessness, my grade on this exam was not good.

他由于不了解情况，造成了一个大错误。
他由於不瞭解情況，造成了一個大錯誤。
Tā *yóuyú* bù liáojiě qíngkuàng, zàochéng le yī gè dà cuòwù.
Because he did not understand the situation, he made a big mistake.

由于/由於 (situation₁), 所以 (situation₂)
yóu yú (situation₁), suóyǐ (situation₂)

or

由于/由於 (situation₁), 因而 (situation₂)
yóu yú (situation₁), yīn'ér (situation₂)
due to/because of (situation₁), therefore (situation₂)

The inclusion of 所以 **suóyǐ** 'therefore', or 因而 **yīn'ér** 'therefore', etc., makes the relationship between cause and effect or reason and result clearer.

由于买不到票，所以我们上不了火车。
由於買不到票，所以我們上不了火車。
***Yóuyú* mǎibudào piào, *suóyǐ* wǒmen shàngbuliǎo huǒchē.**
Because we could not get tickets, we couldn't get on the train.

由于各自坚持自己的意见，因而无法达成协议。
由於各自堅持自己的意見，因而無法達成協議。
***Yóuyú* gèzì jiānchí zìjǐ de yìjiàn, *yīn'ér* wú fǎ dáchéng xiéyì.**
Owing to the fact that everyone held onto his own opinion, there was no way to reach an agreement.

The result may be stated first in the sentence. The reason is then introduced with 由于/由於 **yóu yú**. 由于/由於 **yóu yú** must be preceded by 是 **shì**:

(situation₂) 是由于/由於 (situation₁)
(situation₂) **shì yóu yú** (situation₁)
situation₂ is because of situation₁

碰到一点儿困难就退缩，这都是由于你缺乏信心。
碰到一點兒困難就退縮，這都是由於你缺乏信心。
Pèngdào yīdiǎr kùnnan jiù tuìsuō, zhè dōu shì *yóuyú* nǐ quēfá xìnxīn.
(If) you retreat when you meet a little difficulty, this is *because of* your lack of confidence.

为了/為了 (noun phrase)
wéi le (noun phrase)
because of/for the sake of (noun phrase)

为了/為了 **wéi le** can be used to identify some noun phrase as the reason for performing some action.

我这样作，完全是为了你。
我這樣作，完全是為了你。
Wǒ zhèyàng zuò, wánquán shì *wéi le* nǐ.
My doing this is completely *for* you. (I'm doing this all *for* you.)

40.3 Introducing the effect or result

In this pattern, 为了/為了 **wéi le** introduces a desired effect or result.

为了 situation 起见…,
為了 situation 起見…,
wéi le situation **qǐjiàn**, . . .
in order to, for the purpose of (obtaining the situation)

为了安全起见，绝对禁止司机酒后开车。
為了安全起見，絕對禁止司機酒後開車。
***Wéi le* ānquán *qǐjiàn*, juéduì jìnzhǐ sījī jiǔ hòu kāi chē.**
For the sake of safety, drivers are absolutely forbidden to drink and drive.

40.4 Inquiring about cause or reason

To inquire about the cause or reason for something, use the following expressions:

为什么/為甚麼? *wèi shénme?* 'why?'
为什么/為甚麼 **wèi shénme** is the most common and neutral expression used to inquire about the cause or reason for something.

你昨天为什么没来上课？
你昨天為甚麼沒來上課？
Nǐ zuótiān *wèi shénme* méi lái shàng kè?
Why didn't you come to class yesterday?

你为什么还在这儿？
你為甚麼還在這兒？
Nǐ *wèi shénme* hái zài zhèr?
Why are you still here?

怎么?/怎麼? *zěnme?* 'Why? How come?'

怎么/怎麼 **zěnme** is used to inquire about the reason for something, at the same time conveying surprise or disapproval. It may not require an answer.

他说今天来，怎么没来？
他説今天來，怎麼沒來？
Tā shuō jīntiān lái, *zěnme* méi lái?
He said he was coming today. *Why* hasn't he come?

你不说，我怎么知道？
你不説，我怎麼知道？
Nǐ bù shuō, wǒ *zěnme* zhīdao?
If you don't say (if you don't tell me), how can I know?

什么理由?/甚麼理由? *shénme lǐyóu?* 'What is the reason?'

什么理由/甚麼理由 **shénme lǐyóu** is used to inquire about the reason for something. When the speaker uses this expression, he or she expects an answer.

你有什么理由要跟我离婚？
你有甚麼理由要跟我離婚？
Nǐ yǒu *shénme lǐyóu* yào gēn wǒ lí hūn?
What is the reason why you want to divorce me?

什么理由你不给我们工钱？
甚麼理由你不給我們工錢？
***Shénme lǐyóu* nǐ bù gěi wǒmen gōngqian?**
What is the reason why you haven't given us our wages?

凭什么?/憑甚麼? *píng shénme?* 'On what basis?' 'By what right?'

凭什么/憑甚麼 **píng shénme** is a colloquial expression, most often used in speaking.

你凭什么打人？
你憑甚麼打人？
Nǐ *píng shénme* dǎ ren?
What right do you have to hit me?

你凭什么逮捕我？
你憑甚麼逮捕我？
Nǐ *píng shénme* dàibǔ wǒ?
On what grounds are you arresting me?

何故 *hégù?* and 为何/為何 *wéi hé* 'For what reason?' 'Why?'

何故 **hégù** and 为何/為何 **wéi hé** are used only in formal (usually written) language.

他何故杀人？
他何故殺人？
Tā *hégù* shā rén?
Why did he kill someone?

为何惊慌？
為何驚慌？
Wéi hé jīnghuāng?
Why are (you) so frightened?

 24.6

41

Expressing conditions

41.1 'If . . . then' conditional sentences

Mandarin uses the following words to express 'if' in conditional sentences.

> 要是 **yàoshi**
> 如果 **rúguǒ**
> 假如 **jiǎrú**
> 假使 **jiáshǐ**
> 倘若 **tǎngruò**
> 倘使 **tángshǐ**

要是 **yàoshi** and 如果 **rúguǒ** are commonly used in formal and informal speech or writing.

假如 **jiǎrú** is used in more formal speech or writing.

假使 **jiáshǐ**, 倘若 **tǎngruò**, and 倘使 **tángshǐ** are most commonly used in formal, written Chinese.

The 'if' word is placed before or after the subject in the first clause of a sentence.

Mandarin does not have a word that specifically corresponds to 'then' in conditional sentences. Instead, the adverb 就 **jiù** typically occurs in the second clause, immediately before the [prepositional phrase +] verb phrase.

➡ 15.2.4

NOTE | 便 **biàn** or 则/則 **zé** are sometimes used instead of 就 **jiù** before the [prepositional phrase +] verb phrase of the second clause.

Here are examples of conditional sentences.

要是 *yàoshi*

> 要是你不给他钱，他就不会给你做事。
> 要是你不給他錢，他就不會給你做事。
> **Yàoshi nǐ bù gěi tā qián, tā jiù bù huì gěi nǐ zuò shì.**
> If you don't pay him he won't work for you.

如果 *rúguŏ*

> 如果你是我，你也不会同意他的看法的。
> 如果你是我，你也不會同意他的看法的。
> **Rúguŏ nǐ shì wŏ, nǐ yě bù huì tóngyì tā de kànfa de.**
> If you were I, you wouldn't agree with his viewpoint either.

假如 *jiǎrú*

> 这篇文章写得不错，假如再短一点儿那就更好了。
> 這篇文章寫得不錯，假如再短一點兒那就更好了。
> **Zhè piān wénzhāng xiě de bù cuò, jiǎrú zài duǎn yīdiǎr nà jiù gèng hǎo le.**
> This essay is very good; if it were a little shorter it would be even better.

假使 *jiáshǐ*

> 假使人人都骑自行车或坐公共汽车，环境污染的问题就容易解决了。
> 假使人人都騎自行車或坐公共汽車，環境污染的問題就容易解決了。
> **Jiáshǐ rénrén dōu qí zìxíngchē huò zuò gōnggòng qìchē, huánjìng wūrǎn de wèntí jiù róngyì jiějué le.**
> If everyone rode a bicycle or took the bus, the pollution problem would be easy to solve.
>
> 假使我是老师，我每天都给学生考试。
> 假使我是老師，我每天都給學生考試。
> **Jiáshǐ wŏ shì lǎoshī, wŏ měitiān dōu gěi xuéshēng kǎo shì.**
> If I were a teacher, I would give students a test every day.

倘若/儻若 *tǎngruò*

> 倘若学生都一看就懂，那老师还有什么用呢？
> 儻若學生都一看就懂，那老師還有甚麼用呢？
> **Tǎngruò xuéshēng dōu yī kàn jiù dǒng, nà lǎoshī hái yǒu shénme yòng ne?**
> If students understood as soon as they looked at something, then what use would there be for teachers?

倘使 *tángshǐ*

> 倘使放假不能回家，请及时写信告知。
> 儻使放假不能回家，請及時寫信告知。
> **Tángshǐ fàng jiǎ bù néng huí jiā, qǐng jí shí xiě xìn gào zhī.**
> If you have a vacation and cannot return home, please write me right away to let me know.

则/則 *zé*

> 大家共同努力则一定能把事情作好。
> 大家共同努力則一定能把事情作好。
> **Dàjiā gòngtóng nǔlì zé yīdìng néng bǎ shìqíng zuòhǎo.**
> (If) everyone works hard together, we certainly can take care of this matter.
>
> 坚持不懈则会成功。
> 堅持不懈則會成功。
> **Jiānchí bù xiè zé huì chénggōng.**
> (If)(we) persist (we) can definitely succeed.

'if . . . then' sentences with . . . 的话/的話 de huà

The 'if' clause may end with 的话/的話 **de huà**. Here are examples with 要是 **yàoshi** . . . 的话/的話 **de huà** and 如果 **rúguǒ** . . . 的话/的話 **de huà**.

> 要是你愿意的话，我们可以今天去市场。
> 要是你願意的話，我們可以今天去市場。
> **Yàoshi nǐ yuànyì de huà, wǒmen kéyǐ jīntiān qù shìchǎng.**
> If you are interested, we can go to the market today.

> 要是方便的话，就请你给我买一份人民日报。
> 要是方便的話，就請你給我買一份人民日報。
> **Yàoshi fāngbiàn de huà, jiù qǐng nǐ gěi wǒ mǎi yī fèn rénmín rìbào.**
> If it is convenient, could you buy me a copy of today's *People's Daily.*

> 如果不是你帮助他的话，他是不会成功的。
> 如果不是你幫助他的話，他是不會成功的。
> **Rúguǒ bù shì nǐ bāngzhù tā de huà, tā shì bù huì chénggōng de.**
> If you hadn't helped him, he wouldn't have succeeded.

41.2 'even if'

就是 **jiùshì** situation, (subject) 也/ **yě** [prepositional phrase +] verb phrase

就是 **jiùshì** situation, (subject) 还/還 **hái** [prepositional phrase +] verb phrase

Even if (situation), (subject) still ([prepositional phrase +] verb phrase)

> 就是你去我也不去。
> **Jiùshì nǐ qù wǒ yě bù qù.**
> Even if you go I still won't go.

> 那本字典特别好。就是很贵我还要买。
> 那本字典特別好。就是很貴我還要買。
> **Nà běn zìdiǎn tèbié hǎo. Jiùshì hěn guì wǒ hái yào mǎi.**
> That dictionary is particularly good. Even if it is expensive I still want to buy it.

> 我爱她。就是她不爱我我还爱她。
> 我愛她。就是她不愛我我還愛她。
> **Wǒ ài tā. Jiùshì tā bù ài wǒ wǒ hái ài tā.**
> I love her. Even if she doesn't love me, I still love her.

41.3 'as long as'

Use 只要 **zhǐyào** to express this meaning:

> 只要我们一起努力合作，我们一定会成功。
> 只要我們一起努力合作，我們一定會成功。
> **Zhǐyào wǒmen yīqǐ nǔlì hézuò, wǒmen yīdìng huì chénggōng.**
> As long as we work hard together, we will definitely succeed.

41.4 'only if', 'unless'

Use 除非 **chúfēi** to express this meaning.

除非你是百万富翁，要不然你最好别去看那边的房子。
除非你是百萬富翁，要不然你最好別去看那邊的房子。
Chúfēi nǐ shì bǎiwàn fùwēng, yàobùrán nǐ zuì hǎo bié qù kàn nàbian de fángzi.
Unless you are a millionaire, you'd best not go look at the houses over there.

除非多修几个水库，否则无法解决饮水的问题。
除非多修幾個水庫，否則無法解決飲水的問題。
Chúfēi duō xiū jǐ gè shuǐkù, fǒuzé wúfǎ jiějué yǐnshuǐ de wèntí.
Unless we build more reservoirs, there is no way to solve the drinking water problem.

41.5 'otherwise'

Use the following words to express this meaning. Notice that they occur before the subject of the second clause or sentence.

要不然 *yàoburán* 'otherwise'

快一点走吧，要不然上课又要迟到了。
快一點走吧，要不然上課又要遲到了。
Kuài yīdiǎn zǒu ba, yàobùrán shàng kè yòu yào chídào le.
Hurry up, otherwise we will be late for class.

我的汽车坏了，要不然我不会不来上班。
我的汽車壞了，要不然我不會不來上班。
Wǒ de qìchē huài le, yàobùrán wǒ bù huì bù lái shàng bān.
My car is broken, otherwise I wouldn't miss work.

不然 *bùrán* 'otherwise'

他让我跟他一起去买东西，不然他不帮我练习中文。
他讓我跟他一起去買東西，不然他不幫我練習中文。
Tā ràng wǒ gēn tā yīqǐ qù mǎi dōngxī, bùrán tā bù bāng wǒ liànxí Zhōngwén.
He makes me go with him to buy things (to go shopping with him). Otherwise, he won't help me study Chinese.

幸亏我的身体好，不然一定会生病。
幸虧我的身體好，不然一定會生病。
Xìngkuī wǒ de shēntǐ hǎo, bùrán yīdìng huì shēng bìng.
It is a good thing I am healthy. Otherwise I would get sick.

否则 *fǒuzé* 'otherwise'

幸亏我多带了点钱，否则我们就回不去了。
幸虧我多帶了點錢，否則我們就回不去了。
Xìngkuī wǒ duō dài le diǎn qián, fǒuzé wǒmen jiù huí bù qù le.
Luckily I brought a little extra money with me. Otherwise we wouldn't be able to get back.

要走人行横道，否则撞死了也是白撞。
要走人行橫道，否則撞死了也是白撞。
Yào zǒu rén xíng héng dào, fǒuzé zhuàngsǐ le yě shì bái zhuàng.
You should walk in the crosswalk. Otherwise, if you get killed it's your fault.
(lit. 'Otherwise, if you get killed (by being hit) it would have been avoidable.')

42

Expressing 'both,' 'all,' 'every,' 'any,' 'none,' 'not any,' and 'no matter how'

42.1 Expressing 'both' and 'all'

42.1.1 Expressing 'both' and 'all' with 都 *dōu*

Mandarin does not have separate words for 'both' and 'all.' It uses the same word, 都 **dōu**, to indicate that a situation is true for the entire plural subject or object. 都 **dōu** is an adverb and always occurs before the verb. When the sentence occurs in neutral *subject-verb-object* form, 都 **dōu** usually indicates 'both' or 'all' of the subject.

> 我们都喜欢他。
> 我們都喜歡他。
> **Wǒmen dōu xǐhuan tā.**
> We all like him.

To indicate 'both' or 'all' of the object noun phrase using 都 **dōu**, 'topicalize' the object noun phrase by placing it before the subject.

> 那样的音乐，我都喜欢听。
> 那樣的音樂，我都喜歡聽。
> **Nà yàng de yīnyuè, wǒ dōu xǐhuan tīng.**
> That kind of music, I like to listen to all of it.

> 中国菜我都喜欢吃。
> 中國菜我都喜歡吃。
> **Zhōngguó cài wǒ dōu xǐhuan chī.**
> (As for) Chinese food, I like to eat everything.

⇨ 53.1.2

Mandarin does not have a distinct word for 'both.' To specify that a situation is true for precisely *two* nouns, your noun phrase must include the number two:

> 那两本书都很有意思。
> 那兩本書都很有意思。
> **Nà liǎng běn shū dōu hěn yǒu yìsī.**
> Those two books are both very interesting.

42.1.2 Expressing 'all' with 所有的 *suóyǒu de*

所有的 **suóyǒu de** occurs before any noun with plural reference to indicate *all of the noun*. It generally refers to nouns that represent a relatively large number of objects.

所有的车都太贵。
所有的車都太貴。
Suóyǒu de chē dōu tài guì.
All of the cars are too expensive.

那个饭馆，所有的菜都太咸。
那個飯館，所有的菜都太鹹。
Nàge fànguǎn, suóyǒu de cài dōu tài xián.
(In) that restaurant, all of the dishes are too salty.

我校的足球队，所有的男的都很帅。
我校的足球隊，所有的男的都很帥。
Wǒ xiào de zúqiú duì, suóyǒu de nán de dōu hěn shuài.
(In) Our school's football team, all of the guys are really cute.

42.1.3 Expressing the concept 'all' with 全 *quán*

全 **quán** occurs before certain nouns to indicate *all of the noun* or *the entire noun*.

Commonly occurring phrases with 全 **quán** include:

全家	**quán jiā**	all of the family/the whole family
全班	**quán bān**	all of the class/the whole class
全国/全國	**quán guó**	the whole country
全民	**quánmín**	all of the people
全年	**quán nián**	the whole year

上个星期我们全家人都去法国旅行了。
上個星期我們全家人都去法國旅行了。
Shàng gè xīngqī wǒmen quán jiā rén dōu qù Fǎguó lǚxíng le.
Last week, our whole family went to France for vacation.

全班都考得很好。
Quán bān dōu kǎo de hěn hǎo.
The whole class did well on the exam.

42.1.4 Expressing 'double' or 'both' with 双/雙 *shuāng*

双/雙 **shuāng** 'pair' is a classifier:

一双鞋子/一雙鞋子
yī shuāng xiézi
a pair of shoes

双/雙 **shuāng** also occurs before a noun to indicate *double noun* or *both nouns*. It is often used to describe objects that come in pairs:

双面/雙面	**shuāngmiàn**	both sides; reversible
双方/雙方	**shuāngfāng**	both parties (both people)
双亲/雙親	**shuāngqīn**	both parents
双姓/雙姓	**shuāngxìng**	two-character family name

双人床/雙人牀	**shuāngrén chuáng**	double bed
双胞胎/雙胞胎	**shuāngbāotāi**	twins

42.2 Expressing 'none'

Mandarin does not have a single word for 'none.' Instead, 'none' is expressed as:

都 *dōu* + negation all not = none

> 孩子都不愿意睡觉。
> 孩子都不願意睡覺。
> **Háizi dōu bù yuànyi shuì jiào.**
> The children are all not willing to sleep. = None of the children is willing to sleep.

> 我的朋友都没上过大学。
> 我的朋友都沒上過大學。
> **Wǒ de péngyou dōu méi shàngguo dàxué.**
> All of my friends have not attended college. = None of my friends has attended college.

42.3 Expressing 'every'

42.3.1 Expressing 'every' with 每 *měi*

每 **měi** + number + classifier (+ noun).
every + number + classifier (+ noun)
If the number is 'one,' it is usually omitted.

> 那些书，每(一)本都很贵。
> 那些書，每(一)本都很貴。
> **Nà xiē shū, měi (yī) běn dōu hěn guì.**
> Those books, every volume is expensive.

> 每(一)个学生都考得很好。
> 每(一)個學生都考得很好。
> **Měi (yī) gè xuésheng dōu kǎo de hěn hǎo.**
> Every student did well on the exam.

> 我每天都上课。
> 我每天都上課。
> **Wǒ měitiān dōu shàng kè.**
> I attend class every day.

> 你每两天可以借一本书。
> 你每兩天可以借一本書。
> **Nǐ měi liǎng tiān kéyǐ jiè yī běn shū.**
> Every two days you can borrow one book.

42.3.2 Expressing 'every' with double negatives

没有 **méi yǒu** + noun phrase + negation
there is no noun phrase that is not = every noun phrase

没有人不喜欢她。
沒有人不喜歡她。
Méi yǒu rén bù xǐhuan tā.
There is no one who doesn't like her. = Everyone likes her.

那个学生没有一天不迟到。
那個學生沒有一天不遲到。
Nàge xuésheng méi yǒu yī tiān bù chídào.
That student, there is not one single day that he is not late. = That student, he is late every day.

42.3.3 Expressing 'every' with reduplication

Certain nouns and classifiers can be reduplicated (repeated) to mean *every noun* or *every classifier*. The most common of these include the following.

人人 *rénrén* 'everyone'

人人都喜欢吃好吃的东西。
人人都喜歡吃好吃的東西。
Rénrén dōu xǐhuan chī hǎo chī de dōngxi.
Everyone likes to eat delicious food.

个个/個個 *gègè* 'everyone'

他们的孩子，个个都很聪明。
他們的孩子，個個都很聰明。
Tāmen de háizi, gègè dōu hěn cōngming.
All their children are very bright.

年年 *niánnián* 'every year'

他们的生活不变。年年都一样。
他們的生活不變。年年都一樣。
Tāmen de shēnghuó bù biàn. Niánnián dōu yīyàng.
Their lives do not change. Every year is the same.

本本 *běnběn* 'every volume'

他写的书，本本都很好。
他寫的書，本本都很好。
Tā xiě de shū, běn běn dōu hěn hǎo.
The books that he writes, every volume (every one) is very good.

天天 *tiāntiān* 'everyday'

我们天天吃中国饭。
我們天天吃中國飯。
Wǒmen tiāntiān chī Zhōngguó fàn.
We eat Chinese food every day.

42.4 Expressing 'every,' 'any,' 'not any,' and 'no matter how' with question words

42.4.1 Expressing 'every' and 'any' with question words

In Mandarin, questions words + 都 **dōu** or 也 **yě** are commonly used to convey the meaning 'every' or 'any.'

Here is a list of question words + 都 **dōu** or 也 **yě** with translations and examples. Note that in some expressions, the question word is part of a larger noun phrase.

谁/誰 + 都 or 也
shéi + **dōu** or **yě**
everyone

> 谁都会作这个工作。
> 誰都會作這個工作。
> **Shéi dōu huì zuò zhège gōngzuò.**
> Anyone can do this job.

> 谁都要跟张三做生意。
> 誰都要跟張三做生意。
> **Shéi dōu yào gēn Zhāng Sān zuò shēngyì.**
> Everyone wants to do business with Zhang San.

什么/甚麼 + 都 or 也
shénme + **dōu** or **yě**
everything, anything

> 他什么事情都懂。
> 他甚麼事情都懂。
> **Tā shénme shìqing dōu dǒng.**
> He understands everything.

> 弟弟什么书都喜欢看。
> 弟弟甚麼書都喜歡看。
> **Dìdi shénme shū dōu xǐhuan kàn.**
> Little Brother enjoys reading everything.

哪 + classifier + 都 or 也
nǎ + classifier + **dōu** or **yě**
everything, anything

> 这儿的天气很好。哪天都很舒服。
> 這兒的天氣很好。哪天都很舒服。
> **Zhèr de tiānqì hěn hǎo. Nǎ tiān dōu hěn shūfu.**
> The weather here is very good. Every day is very comfortable.

> 我特别喜欢看王老师的书。他写的书，哪本都很有意思。
> 我特別喜歡看王老師的書。他寫的書，哪本都很有意思。
> **Wǒ tèbié xǐhuan kàn Wáng lǎoshī de shū. Tā xiě de shū, nǎ běn dōu hěn yǒu yìsī.**
> I especially like to read Professor Wang's books. Of the books that he has written, every book is very interesting.

哪儿/哪兒 + 都 or 也
nǎr + dōu or yě
everywhere

> 他妹妹哪儿都想去。
> 他妹妹哪兒都想去。
> **Tā mèimei nǎr dōu xiǎng qù.**
> His little sister wants to go everywhere.

> Q: 你想去哪儿吃饭？
>   你想去哪兒吃飯？
> **Nǐ xiǎng qù nǎr chī fàn?**
> Where do you want to go to eat?

> A: 哪儿都行。
>   哪兒都行。
> **Nǎr dōu xíng.**
> Any place is okay.

什么地方/甚麼地方 + 都 or 也
shénme dìfang + dōu or yě
everywhere/anywhere

> 中国人口很多。什么地方都是人。
> 中國人口很多。甚麼地方都是人。
> **Zhōngguó rénkǒu hěn duō. Shénme dìfang dōu shì rén.**
> China's population is very big. There are people everywhere.
> (. . . Every place is full of people.)

> 我听说意大利什么地方都很漂亮。
> 我聽説意大利甚麼地方都很漂亮。
> **Wǒ tīngshuō Yìdàlì shénme dìfang dōu hěn piàoliang.**
> I've heard it said that in Italy, every place is very pretty.

几点钟/幾點鐘 + 都 or 也
jǐdiǎn zhōng + dōu or yě
always/at any hour

> Q: 我们几点钟去看电影？
>   我們幾點鐘去看電影？
> **Wǒmen jǐdiǎn zhōng qù kàn diànyǐng?**
> What time should we go to see a movie?

> A: 几点钟都可以。
>   幾點鐘都可以。
> **Jǐdiǎn zhōng dōu kéyǐ.**
> Anytime is okay.

什么时候/甚麼时候 + 都 or 也
shénme shíhòu + dōu or yě
always/any time/whenever

> 爸爸什么时候都很忙。
> 爸爸甚麼時候都很忙。
> **Bàba shénme shíhòu dōu hěn máng.**
> Dad is always busy.

> Q: 你什么时候有空？
>   你甚麼時候有空？
> **Nǐ shénme shíhòu yǒu kòng?**
> When do you have free time?

> A: 我什么时候都有空。
>   我甚麼時候都有空。
> **Wǒ shénme shíhòu dōu yǒu kòng.**
> I always have free time.

The following expressions with 多 **duō** also express the meaning 'no matter how.'
Note that they do not occur with 都 **dōu** or 也 **yě**.

多么/多麼 + adjectival verb
duóme + adjectival verb
no matter how adjectival verb

> 那件衣服多么贵我还想买。
> 那件衣服多麼貴我還想買。
> **Nà jiàn yīfú duóme guì wǒ hái xiǎng mǎi.**
> No matter how expensive that item of clothing is I still want to buy it.

多少
duōshǎo
however many

> 我跟你说了多少次你还不听。
> 我跟你説了多少次你還不聽。
> **Wǒ gēn nǐ shuō le duōshǎo cì nǐ hái bù tīng.**
> No matter how many times I've told you, you still don't listen.

42.4.2 Expressing 'not any' with question words

Question words with 都 **dōu** or 也 **yě** and negation are used to express the concept 'not any.'

Here is a list of question words + 都 **dōu** or 也 **yě** + negation, with translations and examples. 也 **yě** is much more commonly used than 都 **dōu** when expressing 'not any.'

谁/誰 + 都 or 也 + negation
shéi + **dōu** or **yě** + negation
no one/not anyone

> 谁也不会作这个工作。
> 誰也不會作這個工作。
> **Shéi yě bù huì zuò zhège gōngzuò.**
> No one can do this job.

> 谁都不要跟张三做生意。
> 誰都不要跟張三做生意。
> **Shéi dōu bù yào gēn Zhāng Sān zuò shēngyì.**
> No one wants to do business with Zhang San.

什么/甚麼 + 都 or 也 + negation
shénme + **dōu** or **yě** + negation
nothing/not anything

> 他什么事情也不懂。
> 他甚麼事情也不懂。
> **Tā shénme shìqing yě bù dǒng.**
> He doesn't understand anything.

> 弟弟什么书都不喜欢看。
> 弟弟甚麼書都不喜歡看。
> **Dìdi shénme shū dōu bù xǐhuan kàn.**
> Little Brother doesn't like to read any book.

哪/哪 + classifier + 都 or 也 + negation
nǎ + classifier + **dōu** or **yě** + negation
nothing/not anything

> 他哪个菜也不喜欢吃。
> 他哪個菜也不喜歡吃。
> **Tā nǎge cài yě bù xǐhuan chī.**
> He doesn't like to eat any dish.

> 他哪个车都没买。
> 他哪個車都沒買。
> **Tā nǎge chē dōu méi mǎi.**
> He didn't buy a car.

哪儿/哪兒 + 都 or 也 + negation
nǎr + **dōu** or **yě** + negation
nowhere/not anyplace

> 他妹妹哪儿也不想去。
> 他妹妹哪兒也不想去。
> **Tā mèimei nǎr yě bù xiǎng qù.**
> His little sister doesn't want to go anywhere.

> 我哪儿都没去过。
> 我哪兒都沒去過。
> **Wǒ nǎr dōu méi qùguo.**
> I haven't been anywhere.

什么地方/甚麼地方 + 都 or 也 + negation
shénme dìfang + **dōu** or **yě** + negation
nowhere/not anyplace

> 我刚到这儿来。什么地方都不认识。
> 我剛到這兒來。甚麼地方都不認識。
> **Wǒ gāng dào zhèr lái. Shénme dìfang dōu bù rènshi.**
> I've just come here. (I'm new here.) I don't recognize any place.

> 怎么了？什么地方都没有人。
> 怎麼了？甚麼地方都沒有人。
> **Zěnme le? Shénme dìfang dōu méi yǒu rén.**
> What's going on? There aren't any people anywhere.

什么时候/甚麼時候 + 都 or 也 + negation
shénme shíhòu + **dōu** or **yě** + negation
never/not anytime

> Q: 你什么时候有空？
> 你甚麼時候有空？
> **Nǐ shénme shíhòu yǒu kòng?**
> When do you have free time?

> A: 我什么时候也没有空。
> 我甚麼時候也沒有空。
> **Wǒ shénme shíhòu yě méi yǒu kòng.**
> I never have free time.

Q: 你什么时候看电视？
你甚麼時候看電視？
Nǐ shénme shíhòu kàn diànshì?
When do you watch television?

A: 我什么时候都不看电视。
我甚麼時候都不看電視。
Wǒ shénme shíhòu dōu bù kàn diànshì.
I never watch television.

Expressing 'no matter how' with 怎么/怎麼 *zěnme*

怎么/怎麼 verb₁ 也 + verb₂
zěnme verb₁ yě + verb₂
no matter how much one does verb₁ (the anticipated goal or result is not attained)

When 怎么/怎麼 **zěnme** is used, verb₂ is often a resultative verb.

这个字，我怎么写，也写不对。
這個字，我怎麼寫，也寫不對。
Zhège zì, wǒ zěnme xiě, yě xiě bù duì.
This character, no matter how I write it, I write it incorrectly.

这件事，我怎么作也不好。
這件事，我怎麼作也不好。
Zhè jiàn shì, wǒ zěnme zuò yě bù hǎo.
This situation, no matter how I handle it, it is not good.

你做的菜太多了！怎么吃，也吃不完。
你做的菜太多了！怎麼吃，也吃不完。
Nǐ zuò de cài tài duō le! Zěnme chī, yě chībuwán.
You made too much food! No matter how we eat we can't finish it.

这个谜语，怎么猜也猜不着。
這個謎語，怎麼猜也猜不著。
Zhège míyǔ, zěnme cāi yě cāibuzháo.
This riddle, no matter how I guess I can't figure it out.

The expression 不论/不論 **búlùn** 'regardless/no matter how' may occur before 怎么/怎麼 **zěnme**. The meaning of the expression is the same.

这个字，我不论怎么写，也写错。
這個字，我不論怎麼寫，也寫錯。
Zhège zì, wǒ búlùn zěnme xiě yě xiěcuò.
This character, no matter how I write it, I write it wrong.

这件事，我不论怎么作也不好。
這件事，我不論怎麼作也不好。
Zhè jiàn shì, wǒ búlùn zěnme zuò yě bù hǎo.
This situation, no matter how I handle it, it is not good.

⇨ 24.6, 28

43

Expressing location and distance

43.1 Location

43.1.1 Words that indicate location and compass direction

43.1.1.1 Location words

Mandarin location words consist of a base form and a location suffix. Base forms never occur alone. Some base forms occur with several different suffixes with no change in meaning. Here are the Mandarin location words and their English equivalents.

Base form	Mandarin location words			English
里/裏	里头/裏頭	里面/裏面	里边/裏邊	
lǐ	**lǐtou**	**lǐmiàn**	**lǐbiān**	in
外	外头/外頭	外面	外边/外邊	
wài	**wàitou**	**wàimian**	**wàibian**	out
上	上头/上頭	上面	上边/上邊	
shàng	**shàngtou**	**shàngmian**	**shàngbian**	over
下	下头/下頭	下面	下边/下邊	
xià	**xiàtou**	**xiàmian**	**xiàbian**	under
前	前头/前頭	前面	前边/前邊	
qián	**qiántou**	**qiánmian**	**qiánbian**	in front of
后/後	后头/後頭	后面/後面	后边/後邊	
hòu	**hòutou**	**hòumian**	**hòubian**	behind
左		左面	左边/左邊	
zuǒ		**zuǒmiàn**	**zuǒbian**	left
右		右面	右边/右邊	
yòu		**yòumiàn**	**yòubian**	right
对/對		对面/對面		
duì		**duìmiàn**		across from
旁		对面/對面	旁边/旁邊	
páng		**duìmiàn**	**pángbiān**	next to
中	中间/中間			
zhōng	**zhōngjiān**			between

NOTES

1 In traditional characters, the character 裏 **lǐ** is also written as 裡.
2 The choice of suffix is determined by the region of China and the personal preference of the speaker.
3 Mandarin has a second word for 'in,' 内 **nèi**. 内 **nèi** does not occur with suffixes and has very restricted in usage. It is used in fixed expressions such as:

国内/國内	**guónèi**	domestic (vs. 国外/國外 **guówài** foreign)
内部	**nèibù**	internal
内人	**nèiren**	my wife

43.1.1.2 Compass direction

The words for north, east, south, and west are also formed with a base form and a suffix. The suffix can be 面 **miàn** or 边/邊 **biān**.

The combination compass direction words (northeast, southwest, etc.) usually occur without a suffix. If a suffix occurs, it is 面 **miàn** or 边/邊 **biān**.

Base form	*Mandarin compass direction words*		*English*
东/東	东面/東面	东边/東邊	
dōng	**dōngmiàn**	**dōngbian**	east
南	南面	南边/南邊	
nán	**nánmiàn**	**nánbian**	south
西	西面	西边/西邊	
xī	**xīmiàn**	**xībian**	west
北	北面	北边/北邊	
běi	**běimiàn**	**běibian**	north
	东南(面)/東南(面)	东南(边)/東南(邊)	
	dōngnán (miàn)	**dōngnán (bian)**	southeast
	东北(面)/東北(面)	东北(边)/東北(邊)	
	dōngběi (miàn)	**dōngběi (bian)**	northeast
	西南(面)	西南(边)/西南(邊)	
	xīnán (miàn)	**xīnán (bian)**	southwest
	西北(面)	西北(边)/西北(邊)	
	xīběi (miàn)	**xīběi (bian)**	northwest

43.1.2 Spatial orientation with respect to a reference point

43.1.2.1 Indicating location with respect to a reference using location words

To indicate that something is 'inside,' 'outside,' 'over,' 'under,' etc. a reference point, use the following structure:

reference point 的 ***de*** *location word*

In the following phrases, the reference point is the house. Note that 的 **de** may be omitted.

房子(的)里头/房子(的)裏頭
fángzi (de) lǐtou
inside the house

房子(的)外头/房子(的)外頭
fángzi (de) wàitou
outside the house

房子(的)上头/房子(的)上頭
fángzi (de) shàngtou
on the house/over the house

房子(的)下头/房子(的)下頭
fángzi (de) xiàtou
below the house/under the house

房子(的)前头/房子(的)前頭
fángzi (de) qiántou
in front of the house

房子(的)后头/房子(的)後頭
fángzi (de) hòutou
behind the house

房子(的)左边/房子(的)左邊
fángzi (de) zuǒbian
to the left of the house

房子(的)右边/房子(的)右邊
fángzi (de) yòubian
to the right of the house

房子(的)对面/房子(的)對面
fángzi (de) duìmiàn
across from the house

房子(的)中间/房子(的)中間
fángzi (de) zhōngjiān
between the houses

房子的旁边/房子的旁邊
fángzi (de) pángbiān
next to the house

The location base forms 里/裏 **lǐ** 'inside,' 外 **wài** 'outside,' 上 **shàng** 'above,' and 下 **xià** 'below' can directly follow the reference point. When they occur this way, 的 **de** does not occur.

reference point + location base form

房子(的)里头/房子(的)裏頭	or	房子里/房子裏
fángzi (de) lǐtou		**fángzi lǐ**
inside the house		inside the house
房子(的)外头/房子(的)外頭	or	房子外
fángzi (de) wàitou		**fángzi wài**
outside the house		outside the house
房子(的)上头/房子(的)上頭	or	房子上
fángzi (de) shàngtou		**fángzi shàng**
on top of the house		on top of the house
房子(的)下头/房子(的)下頭	or	房子下
fángzi (de) xiàtou		**fángzi xià**
below the house		below the house

43.1.2.2 | **Indicating location with compass direction words**

To indicate that something is 'east of,' 'west of,' 'north of,' or 'south of' a reference point, use the following structure. Keep in mind that compass direction words can be used with the 面 **miàn** or 边/邊 **biān** suffix.

reference point 的 **de** *compass direction word*

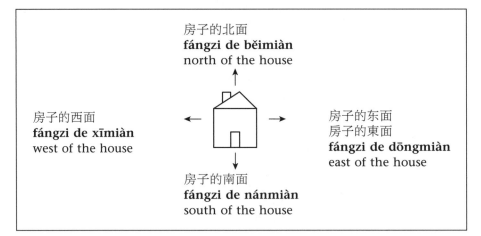

43.1.3 | **Describing the location of an object**

To describe the location of an object with respect to a reference point, say:

object 在 **zài** *reference point* 的 **de** *location word*

In these examples, the object is the cat, and the reference point is the house.

猫在房子(的)里头。
貓在房子(的)裏頭。
Māo zài fángzi (de) lǐtou.
The cat is inside the house.

猫在房子(的)外头。
貓在房子(的)外頭。
Māo zài fángzi (de) wàitou.
The cat is outside the house.

猫在房子(的)上头。
貓在房子(的)上頭。
Māo zài fángzi (de) shàngtou.
The cat is on the house/over the house.

猫在房子(的)下头。
貓在房子(的)下頭。
Māo zài fángzi (de) xiàtou.
The cat is below the house/under the house.

猫在房子(的)前头。
貓在房子(的)前頭。
Māo zài fángzi (de) qiántou.
The cat is in front of the house.

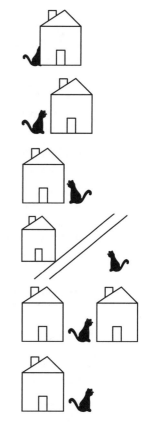

猫在房子(的)后头。
貓在房子(的)後頭。
Māo zài fángzi (de) hòutou.
The cat is behind the house.

猫在房子(的)左边。
貓在房子(的)左邊。
Māo zài fángzi (de) zuǒbian.
The cat is to the left of the house.

猫在房子(的)右边。
貓在房子(的)右邊。
Māo zài fángzi (de) yòubian.
The cat is to the right of the house.

猫在房子(的)对面。
貓在房子(的)對面。
Māo zài fángzi (de) duìmiàn.
The cat is across from the house.

猫在房子(的)中间。
貓在房子(的)中間。
Māo zài fángzi (de) zhōngjiān.
The cat is between the houses.

猫在房子(的)旁边。
貓在房子(的)旁邊。
Māo zài fángzi (de) pángbiān.
The cat is next to the house.

Use the same pattern to indicate location in terms of compass direction:

object 在 **zài** *reference point* 的 **de** *compass location word*

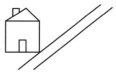

房子在路(的)西北(边)。
房子在路(的)西北(邊)。
Fángzi zài lù (de) xīběi (biān).
The house is to the northwest of the road.

路在房子(的)东南(边)。
路在房子(的)東南(邊)。
Lù zài fángzi (de) dōngnán (biān).
The road is to the southeast of the house.

43.2 Indicating that an object exists or does not exist at a location

To indicate that an object exists at a location, use the following pattern. Note that 在 **zài** is optional at the beginning of the sentence.

(在 **zài**) location 有 **yǒu** object。
At location there is object (there are objects).

(在)桌子上有书。
(在)桌子上有書。
(Zài) zhuōzi shàng yǒu shū.
On the table there is a book (there are books).

(在)房子后边有猫。
(在)房子後邊有貓。
(Zài) fángzi hòubian yǒu māo.
Behind the house there is a cat (there are cats).

有 **yǒu** object 在 **zài** location。
There is object (there are objects) at location.

有两本书在桌子上。
有兩本書在桌子上。
Yǒu liǎng běn shū zài zhuōzi shàng.
There are two books on the table.

有一只猫在房子的后边。
有一只貓在房子的後邊。
Yǒu yīzhī māo zài fángzi de hòubian.
There is a cat behind the house.

To indicate that an object does not exist at a location, use the following structure:

(在 **zài**) location 没有 **méi yǒu** object
At location there is no object.

(在)房子里没有人。
(在)房子裏沒有人。
(Zài) fángzi lǐ méi yǒu rén.
There are no people in the house.
(lit. 'In the house there are no people.')

(在)屋子里没有桌子。
(在)屋子裏沒有桌子。
(Zài) wūzi lǐ méi yǒu zhuōzi.
There aren't any tables in the room.
(lit. 'In the room there aren't any tables.')

or

没有 **méi yǒu** object 在 **zài** location

没有人在房子里。
沒有人在房子裏。
Méi yǒu rén zài fángzi lǐ.
There are no people in the house.

没有桌子在屋子里。
沒有桌子在屋子裏。
Méi yǒu zhuōzi zài wūzi lǐ.
There aren't any tables in the room.

43.3 Using location as a description

Location phrases may also be used to describe a noun. When used as a description, the location phrase precedes the noun, as follows:

> Location phrase 的 **de** noun
> the noun at this location [or] the noun in this direction

To help you to understand this structure, the location phrase in each of the following examples is presented in square brackets. Notice that the words 'that,' 'who,' and 'which' that occur in the description in English are not translated into Mandarin. In Mandarin, the noun can be understood as singular or plural.

> [沙发上] 的猫
> [沙發上] 的貓
> **[shāfā shàng] de māo**
> the cat [(that is) on the sofa]

> [房子里] 的人
> [房子裏] 的人
> **[fángzi lǐ] de rén**
> the person [(who is) in the house]

> [北边] 的湖
> [北邊] 的湖
> **[běibiān] de hú**
> the lake [(that is) in the north]

> [左边] 的人
> [左邊] 的人
> **[zuǒbian] de rén**
> the person [(who is) on the left]

The location phrase may itself include a noun with a description:

> [房子(的)后头] 的人
> [房子(的)後頭] 的人
> **[fángzi de hòutou] de rén**
> the person [(who is) behind the house]

> [图书馆(的)对面] 的学校
> [圖書館(的)對面] 的學校
> **[túshūguǎn (de) duìmiàn] de xuéxiào**
> the school [(that is) across from the library]

⇨ 9.2, 26.3

Compare the use of the location phrase as a description of a noun, with the use of the location phrase to indicate the location of a noun. Keep in mind that location phrases follow the noun and description phrases precede the noun.

Location: noun 的 *de location phrase*	*Description: location phrase* 的 *de noun*
房子的后头 房子的後頭 **fángzi de hòutou** behind the house	后头的房子 後頭的房子 **hòutou de fángzi** the house that is behind
房子的北面 **fángzi de běimiàn** to the north of the house	北面的房子 **běimiàn de fángzi** the house to the north
孩子的右边 孩子的右邊 **háizi de yòubian** to the right of the child	右边的孩子 右邊的孩子 **yòubian de háizi** the child on the right
前头的人 前頭的人 **qiántou de rén** the person who is in front	人的前头 人的前頭 **rén de qiántou** in front of the person
书的上头 書的上頭 **shū de shàngtou** on top of the book	上头的书 上頭的書 **shàngtou de shū** the book on top

43.4 Talking about distance

In Mandarin, distance is always expressed with the word 离/離 **lí** 'to be separated from.' All expressions of distance use the following structure. The noun phrases refer to objects or locations.

> noun phrase₁ 离/離 **lí** noun phrase₂ close/far/x distance
> noun phrase₁ is close/far/x distance from noun phrase₂

43.4.1 Talking about 'near' and 'far'

To say that one object or place is (very) far from another object or place, say:

noun phrase₁ 离/離 noun phrase₂ (很) 远/遠
noun phrase₁ **lí**   noun phrase₂ **(hěn) yuǎn**

> 我家离图书馆很远。
> 我家離圖書館很遠。
> **Wǒ jiā lí túshūguǎn hěn yuǎn.**
> My house is very far from the library.

To say that one object or place is (very) close to another object or place, say:

noun phrase₁ 离/離 noun phrase₂ (很) 近
noun phrase₁ **lí**   noun phrase₂ **(hěn) jìn**

> 公园离学校(很)近。
> 公園離學校(很)近。
> **Gōngyuán lí xuéxiào (hěn) jìn.**
> The park is very close to the school.

To say that an object or place is close to your present location, say:

noun phrase₁ 离/離 这儿/這兒 (很) 近
noun phrase₁ **lí**　　**zhèr**　　**(hěn) jìn**

or

noun phrase₁ 离/離 这里/這裏 (很) 近
noun phrase₁ **lí**　　**zhèlǐ**　　**(hěn) jìn**

> 公园离这儿(很)近。
> 公園離這兒(很)近。
> **Gōngyuán lí zhèr (hěn) jìn.**
> The park is (very) close to here.

> 学校离这里(很)近。
> 學校離這裏(很)近。
> **Xuéxiào lí zhèlǐ (hěn) jìn.**
> The school is (very) close to here.

To say that an object or place is far from your present location, say:

noun phrase₁ 离/離 这儿/這兒 (很) 远/遠
noun phrase₁ **lí**　　**zhèr**　　**(hěn) yuǎn**

or

noun phrase₁ 离/離 这里/這裏 (很) 远/遠
noun phrase₁ **lí**　　**zhèlǐ**　　**(hěn) yuǎn**

> 公园离这儿(很)远。
> 公園離這兒(很)遠。
> **Gōngyuán lí zhèr (hěn) yuǎn.**
> The park is (very) far from here.

> 学校离这里(很)远。
> 學校離這裏(很)遠。
> **Xuéxiào lí zhèlǐ (hěn) yuǎn.**
> The school is (very) far from here.

Be careful to use 离/離 **lí** 'to be separated from,' and not the prepositions 到 **dào** 'from' or 从/從 **cóng** 'from' when talking about distance.

Say this	*Not this*
我家离图书馆近。	*我家到图书馆近。
我家離圖書館近。	我家到圖書館近。
Wǒ jiā lí túshūguǎn jìn.	**Wǒ jiā dào túshūguǎn jìn.**
My house is close to the library.	
	*我家近到图书馆。
	我家近到圖書館。
	Wǒ jiā jìn dào túshūguǎn.

43.4.2　Talking about specific distance

To indicate the specific distance between two objects or places, say:

noun phrase₁ 离/離 noun phrase₂ (有) distance
noun phrase₁ **lí**　　noun phrase₂ **(yǒu)** distance

公园离图书馆(有)三里(路)。
公園離圖書館(有)三里(路)。
Gōngyuán lí túshūguǎn (yǒu) sān lǐ (lù).
The park is three miles from the library.

Commonly used distance words include:

里	**lǐ**	Chinese mile (.5 kilometers)
公里	**gōnglǐ**	kilometer
米	**mǐ**	meter
英里	**Yīng lǐ**	English mile
哩	**lǐ**	English mile

43.5 Asking about distance

43.5.1 Asking about 'near' and 'far'

To ask if an object or place is far from another object or place, say:

noun phrase₁	离	noun phrase₂	远吗?
noun phrase₁	離	noun phrase₂	遠嗎?
noun phrase₁	**lí**	noun phrase₂	**yuǎn ma?**

or

noun phrase₁	离	noun phrase₂	远不远?
noun phrase₁	離	noun phrase₂	遠不遠?
noun phrase₁	**lí**	noun phrase₂	**yuǎn bù yuǎn?**

你家离图书馆远吗?
你家離圖書館遠嗎?
Nǐ jiā lí túshūguǎn yuǎn ma?
Is your house far from the library?

or

你家离图书馆远不远?
你家離圖書館遠不遠?
Nǐ jiā lí túshūguǎn yuǎn bù yuǎn?
Is your house far from the library?

To ask if an object or place is near to another object or place, say:

noun phrase₁	离	noun phrase₂	近吗?
noun phrase₁	離	noun phrase₂	近嗎?
noun phrase₁	**lí**	noun phrase₂	**jìn ma?**

你家离图书馆近吗?
你家離圖書館近嗎?
Nǐ jiā lí túshūguǎn jìn ma?
Is your house close to the library?

NOTE As in English, the question 'is it far?' is more neutral than the question 'is it close?' When the speaker asks 'is it far?' he or she typically does not necessarily expect the answer to be 'far.' However, when the question is 'is it close?' the speaker often expects the answer to be 'close.'

To ask if an object or place is far from your present location, say:

> 图书馆离这儿远吗?
> 圖書館離這兒遠嗎?
> **Túshūguǎn lí zhèr yuǎn ma?**
> Is the library far from here?

or

> 图书馆离这里远吗?
> 圖書館離這裏遠嗎?
> **Túshūguǎn lí zhèlǐ yuǎn ma?**
> Is the library far from here?

⇨ | 24.1

43.5.2 Asking about specific distances

To ask how far one object or place is from another object or place, say:

> 你家离图书馆多(么)远?
> 你家離圖書館多(麼)遠?
> **Nǐ jiā lí túshūguǎn duō(me) yuǎn?**
> How far is your house from the library?

or

> 你家离图书馆有多远?
> 你家離圖書館有多遠?
> **Nǐ jiā lí túshūguǎn yǒu duō yuǎn?**
> How far is your house from the library?

⇨ | 24.6

44

Talking about movement, directions, and means of transportation

44.1 Talking about 'going' and 'coming'

Expressions used to talk about going and coming usually involve a preposition indicating 'to,' 'from,' or 'towards,' and a verb indicating 'going' or 'coming.' The structures used to indicate going and coming are presented here. In Mandarin, the prepositional phrase always occurs before the verb.

⇨ 14

Note the difference between 走 **zǒu** and 去 **qù**.

The verb 走 **zǒu** 'to go' is used with movement *towards* a direction.
The verb 去 **qù** is used with movement that *terminates* at a location.

44.1.1 Talking about 'going towards' a direction

[往/向/朝   (direction)] 走
[wǎng/xiàng/cháo (direction)] zǒu

往东走。	朝南走。	向西走。
往東走。		
Wǎng dōng zǒu.	**Cháo nán zǒu.**	**Xiàng xī zǒu.**
Go east.	Go south.	Go west.

To say that you are 'going straight', say:

一直走。
Yī zhí zǒu.
Go straight ahead.

To say that you are 'going straight towards' a direction, say:

[一直] [往/向/朝   (direction)] 走
[yī zhí] [wǎng/xiàng/cháo (direction)] zǒu

or

[往/向/朝   (direction)] [一直] 走
[wǎng/xiàng/cháo (direction)] [yī zhí] zǒu
go straight towards (direction)

  一直往北走。   or 往北一直走。
  Yīzhí wǎng běi zǒu.   **Wǎng běi yīzhí zǒu.**
  Go straight north.   Go straight north.

44.1.2 Talking about 'going to' a destination

到 destination 去
dào destination qù
to [a destination] go = go to a destination

or

去 **qù** destination
go (to) a destination

  我想到图书馆去。   or 我想去图书馆。
  我想到圖書館去。   我想去圖書館。
  Wǒ xiǎng dào túshūguǎn qù. **Wǒ xiǎng qù túshūguǎn.**
  I want to go to the library. I want to go to the library.

44.1.3 Talking about 'coming to' a destination

到 destination 来/來
dào destination lái
to [a place] come (come to a place)

or

来/來 **lái** destination
come to a destination

  你什么时候到我家来? or 你什么时候来我家?
  你甚麼時候到我家來?   你甚麼時候來我家?
  Nǐ shénme shíhòu dào wǒ jiā lái? **Nǐ shénme shíhòu lái wǒ jiā?**
  When are you coming to my house? When are you coming to my house?

44.1.4 Talking about 'coming from' a location

从/從 location 来/來
cóng location lái
from location come (come from a location)

  她刚从美国来。
  她剛從美國來。
  Tā gāng cóng Měiguó lái.
  She just came from America.

44.2 ## Talking about turning

Turning is a type of movement *towards* a direction. Therefore, it may be expressed with the prepositions 往 **wǎng**, 向 **xiàng**, and 朝 **cháo**.

To talk about turning, say:

> [往/向/朝]　　　　　(direction) 拐
> **[wǎng/xiàng/cháo]** (direction) **guǎi**
> turn towards (direction)

[往]左拐。	[向]右拐。	[朝]北拐。
[Wǎng] zuǒ guǎi.	**[Xiàng] yòu guǎi.**	**[Cháo] běi guǎi.**
Turn left.	Turn right.	Turn north.

or
> 拐 (direction)
> **guǎi** (direction)

> 拐北。
> **Guǎi běi.**
> Turn left.

44.3 ## Talking about crossing

> 过一条街。
> 過一條街。
> **Guò yī tiáo jiē.**
> Cross one street or go one block.

> 过两个红绿灯。
> 過兩個紅綠燈。
> **Guò liǎng gè hóng lǜ dēng.**
> Pass two traffic lights.

> 过一个路口。
> 過一個路口。
> **Guò yī gè lùkǒu.**
> Cross one intersection.

44.4 ## Talking about arriving

The verb 到 **dào** means *to arrive*.

> 我们到了。
> 我們到了。
> **Wǒmen dào le.**
> We've arrived (at our destination.)

> 你到了奶奶家请给我打电话。
> 你到了奶奶家請給我打電話。
> **Nǐ dào le nǎinai jiā qǐng gěi wǒ dǎ diànhuà.**
> After you arrive at (get to) grandma's house please call me.

这个包裹，今天寄，什么时候到。
這個包裹，今天寄，什麼時候到。
Zhège bāoguǒ, jīntiān jì, shémo shíhòu dào?
This package, if I mail it today, when will it arrive?

44.5 Talking about means of transportation

44.5.1 Describing means of transportation

Means of transportation includes locomotion: 走 **zǒu** 'to walk,' 跑 **pǎo** 'to run,' 跳 **tiào** 'to hop/to jump,' 游 **yóu** 'to swim,' 飞/飛 **fēi** 'to fly'; or transportation by a vehicle: 车/車 **chē** 'car,' 出租车/出租車 **chūzū chē** 'taxi cab,' 火车/火車 **huǒchē** 'train,' 地铁/地鐵 **dìtiě** 'subway,' 公共汽车/公共汽車 **gōnggòng qìchē** 'public bus,' 飞机/飛機 **fēijī** 'plane,' 摩托车/摩托車 **mótuōchē** 'motorcycle,' or 自行车/自行車 **zìxíngchē** (in Taiwain: 脚踏车/腳踏車 **jiǎotàchē**) 'bicycle.'

The expression used to describe riding on a vehicle depends upon the vehicle.

For vehicles in which you sit on a seat, the verb is 坐 **zuò** 'sit.'

坐 **zuò** sit	车/車 **chē** 出租车/出租車	ride in a car (go by car)
	chūzū chē 火车/火車	ride in a taxi cab/take a cab/(go) by cab
	huǒchē 地铁/地鐵	take a train/by train
	dìtiě 飞机/飛機	take the subway
	fēijī 公共汽车/公共汽車	take an airplane/by plane
	gōnggòng qìchē or 公车/公車 **gōngchē**	take a bus/(go)by bus

For things that you ride astraddle such as bicycles, motorcycles, and horses, the verb is 骑/騎 **qí**:

骑/騎 **qí** ride	自行车/自行車	
	zìxíngchē	ride a bicycle
	摩托车/摩托車	
	mótuōchē	ride a motorcycle
	马/馬	
	mǎ	ride a horse

The expression used to get on or into a vehicle is 上 **shàng** [vehicle]:

上飞机/上飛機　**shàng fēijī**　get on the plane; board the plane

The expression used to get off or out of a vehicle is 下 **xià** [vehicle]:

> 下火车/下火車　**xià huǒchē**　get off the train

To indicate that you wish to get off a public vehicle, you say:

> 下车/下車!
> **Xià chē!**
> Getting off!

44.5.2　Including the means of transportation in a directional expression

The means of transportation normally occurs before the verb, or before the prepositional phrase and the verb.

> 他想坐船到中国去。
> 他想坐船到中國去。
> **Tā xiǎng *zuò chuán* dào Zhōngguo qù.**
> He's thinking about *taking a boat* to China.
> (He's thinking about going to China *by boat*.)

> 你可以坐地铁去天安门。
> 你可以坐地鐵去天安門。
> **Nǐ kéyǐ *zuò dìtiě* qù Tiān'ānmén.**
> You can take the subway to Tian'an Men.

⇨ | 14.2.4

44.6　Asking about locations and asking for directions

44.6.1　Asking about locations

To ask where a place is located, say:

(place)在哪儿? 　　　　or	(place) 在哪里?
(place)在哪兒?	(place) 在哪裏?
(place) **zài nǎr?**	(place) **zài nálǐ?**
Where is (the place)?	Where is (the place)?
图书馆在哪儿?	图书馆在哪里?
圖書館在哪兒?	圖書館在哪裏?
Túshūguǎn zài nǎr?	**Túshūguǎn zài nálǐ?**
Where is the library?	Where is the library?

44.6.2　Asking how to go from one place to another

To ask how to get from one place to another place, say:

> 怎么走?
> 怎麼走?
> **Zěnme zǒu?**
> How do you go?

(从 place₁) 到 place₂ 怎么走?
(從 place₁) 到 place₂ 怎麼走?
(cóng place₁) dào place₂ zěnme zǒu?
How do you go (from place₁) to place₂?

> (从这儿)到图书馆怎么走?
> (從這兒)到圖書館怎麼走?
> **(Cóng zhèr) dào túshūguǎn zěnme zǒu?**
> How do you go (from here) to the library?

Asking about alternative directions

To ask about alternative directions, use 还是/還是 **háishi** 'or':

> 往北拐<u>还是</u>往南拐?
> 往北拐<u>還是</u>往南拐?
> **Wǎng běi guǎi *háishi* wǎng nán guǎi?**
> (Do you) turn north *or* turn south?

⇨ 24.3

What to say when you do not know the way

> 我不太清楚。
> **Wǒ bù tài qīngchu.**
> I am not too clear (about this).

> (对不起,) 我不知道怎么去。
> (對不起,) 我不知道怎麼去。
> **(Duìbuqǐ,) wǒ bù zhīdao zěnme qù.**
> (Sorry,) I don't know how to go.

> (对不起,) 我不认识这个地方。
> (對不起,) 我不認識這個地方。
> **(Duìbuqǐ,) wǒ bù rènshi zhèige dìfang.**
> (Sorry,) I don't know this place.

> (对不起,) 我不知道。
> (對不起,) 我不知道。
> **(Duìbuqǐ,) wǒ bù zhīdao.**
> (Sorry,) I don't know.

Asking for and giving directions: sample conversations

Notice that the adverb 再 **zài** can be used to connect a series of directions.

⇨ 32.2

Conversation 1

> A: 请问,火车站在哪儿?
> 請問,火車站在哪兒?
> **Qǐngwèn, huǒchēzhàn zài nǎr?**
> May I ask, where is the train station?

B: 从这儿一直往前走，过三条街，向右拐就可以看见了。
从這兒一直往前走，過三條街，向右拐就可以看見了。
Cóng zhèr yī zhí wǎng qián zǒu, guò sān tiáo jiē, xiàng yòu guǎi, jiù kéyǐ kànjiàn le.
Go straight ahead, pass three blocks, turn right and you will see it.

Conversation 2

A: 劳驾，去邮政局怎么走？
勞駕，去郵政局怎麼走？
Láojià, qù yóuzhèngjú zěnme zǒu?
May I trouble you? How does one get to the post office?

B: 从这儿往东走，过一个十字路口，往南拐，再走几分钟，在左边有一个红房子就是邮政局。
從這兒往東走，過一個十字路口，往南拐，再走幾分鐘，在左邊有一個紅房子就是郵政局。
Cóng zhèr wǎng dōng zǒu, guò yī gè shí zì lùkǒu, wǎng nán guǎi, zài zǒu jǐ fēn zhōng, zài zuǒ biān yǒu yī gè hóng fángzi jiù shì yóuzhèngjú.
Go east, pass one intersection, turn south, then walk for a few minutes. On your left there is a red building; that is the post office.

Conversation 3

A: 请您告诉我去地铁站怎么走？
請您告訴我去地鐵站怎麼走？
Qǐng nín gàosu wǒ qù dìtiě zhàn zěnme zǒu?
Please tell me how to get to the subway station.

B: 对不起，我也不知道。你问别人吧！
對不起，我也不知道。你問別人吧！
Duìbuqǐ, wǒ yě bù zhīdao. Nǐ wèn biéren ba!
Sorry, I don't know either. You'd better ask someone else.

44.8 Talking about directional movement

Action verbs that refer to movement such as 跑 **pǎo** 'to run,' 走 **zǒu** 'to walk,' 跳 **tiào** 'to jump,' 开/開 **kāi** 'to drive,' 飞/飛 **fēi** 'to fly,' 划 **huá** 'to row,' 游 **yóu** 'to swim,' and even 穿 **chuān** 'to put on,' 吃 **chī** 'to eat,' and 喝 **hē** 'to drink' may be suffixed with directional phrases that indicate the direction of the movement.

The directional suffix always ends in 来/來 **lái** 'to come' or 去 **qù** 'to go.' 来/來 **lái** 'to come' is used when the movement is towards the speaker or addressee. 去 **qù** 'to go' is used when the movement is away from the speaker or addressee.

我们走进来了。
我們走進來了。
Wǒmen zǒujìnlái le.
We walked in.

他跑出去了。
Tā pǎochūqù le.
He ran out.

These directional suffixes behave like resultative endings. 得 **de** and 不 **bu** may occur between the action verb and the direction suffix to indicate that the subject was able or unable to move to the direction indicated by the suffix.

> 你开得进去吗？
> 你開得進去嗎？
> **Nǐ kāidejìnqu ma?**
> Can you drive in?

> 车太大。我开不进去。
> 車太大。我開不進去。
> **Chē tài dà. Wǒ kāibujìnqu.**
> The car is too big. I can't drive in.

⇨ 28.2

The object of the action verb may also be included in these directional endings. When it is included, it occurs between the direction word and 来/來 **lái** 'to come' or 去 **qù** 'to go.'

> 她走进屋子来了。
> 她走進屋子來了。
> **Tā zǒujìn wūzi lái le.**
> She walked into the room.

> 我们开进城里去了。
> 我們開進城裏去了。
> **Wǒmen kāijìn chénglǐ qù le.**
> We drove into the city.

45

Talking about clock time and calendar time

45.1 Clock time

45.1.1 Talking about hours

There are two Mandarin words for hour 钟头/鐘頭 **zhōngtóu** and 小时/小時 **xiǎoshí**. Speakers in different regions of China prefer one or the other word, but the meanings are identical. Hours are counted with the classifier 个/個 **gè**:

one hour	一个钟头/一個鐘頭 **yī gè zhōngtóu**	or	一个小时/一個小時 **yī gè xiǎoshí**
two hours	两个钟头/兩個鐘頭 **liǎng gè zhōngtóu**	or	两个小时/兩個小時 **liǎng gè xiǎoshí**
three hours	三个钟头/三個鐘頭 **sān gè zhōngtóu**	or	三个小时/三個小時 **sān gè xiǎoshí**

To say 'half an hour,' place 半 **bàn** *before* the classifier 个/個 **gè**.

半个钟头/半個鐘頭 **bàn gè zhōngtóu** half an hour	or	半个小时/半個小時 **bàn gè xiǎoshí** half an hour

To indicate one or more hours and a half, place 半 **bàn** *after* the classifier 个/個 **gè**.

一个半钟头/一個半鐘頭 **yī gè bàn zhōngtóu** one and a half hours	or	一个半小时/一個半小時 **yī gè bàn xiǎoshí** one and a half hours
两个半钟头/兩個半鐘頭 **liǎng gè bàn zhōngtóu** two and a half hours	or	两个半小时/兩個半小時 **liǎng gè bàn xiǎoshí** two and a half hours

⇨ 6.6.4

45.1.2 Talking about minutes and seconds

The word for minute is 分 **fēn**. The word for second is 秒 **miǎo**. 分 **fēn** and 秒 **miǎo** are classifiers and are directly preceded by a number. A phrase indicating the number of minutes or seconds may optionally end with the noun 钟/鐘 **zhōng** 'clock.'

		or	
一分(钟/鐘)	两分(钟)/兩分(鐘)		二分(钟)/二分(鐘)
yī fēn (zhōng)	**liǎng fēn (zhōng)**		**èr fēn (zhōng)**
one minute	two minutes		two minutes
一秒(钟/鐘)	两秒(钟)/兩秒(鐘)	or	二秒(钟)/二秒(鐘)
yī miǎo (zhōng)	**liǎng miǎo (zhōng)**		**èr miǎo (zhōng)**
one second	two seconds		two seconds

To indicate half a minute or half a second, place 半 **bàn** before the word for minute or second.

半分	半秒
bàn fēn	**bàn miǎo**
half an hour	half a second

To indicate one or more minutes or seconds and a half, place 半 **bàn** immediately after the word for minute/second.

Minutes	*Seconds*
一分半	一秒半
yī fēn bàn	**yī miǎo bàn**
one and a half minutes	one and a half seconds
两分半/兩分半	两秒半/兩秒半
liǎng fēn bàn	**liǎng miǎo bàn**
two and a half minutes	two and a half seconds

⇨ | 6.6.4

45.1.3 Telling time

45.1.3.1 o'clock: time on the hour

o'clock time is expressed as follows. 钟/鐘 **zhōng** is optional and is often not used. The '(X) o'clock' phrase literally means '(X) dots of the clock.'

1 o'clock	一点钟/一點鐘 **yī diǎn zhōng**		7 o'clock	七点钟/七點鐘 **qī diǎn zhōng**
2 o'clock	两点钟/兩點鐘 **liǎng diǎn zhōng** or 二点钟/二點鐘 **èr diǎn zhōng**		8 o'clock	八点钟/八點鐘 **bā diǎn zhōng**
3 o'clock	三点钟/三點鐘 **sān diǎn zhōng**		9 o'clock	九点钟/九點鐘 **jiǔ diǎn zhōng**
4 o'clock	四点钟/四點鐘 **sì diǎn zhōng**		10 o'clock	十点钟/十點鐘 **shí diǎn zhōng**
5 o'clock	五点钟/五點鐘 **wǔ diǎn zhōng**		11 o'clock	十一点钟/十一點鐘 **shí'yī diǎn zhōng**
6 o'clock	六点钟/六點鐘 **liù diǎn zhōng**		12 o'clock	十二点钟/十二點鐘 **shí'èr diǎn zhōng**

45.1.3.2 Reciting time as digital time

The most common way to tell time is to say it the way it appears on a digital clock.

3:50	三点五十分(钟)
	三點五十分(鐘)
	sān diǎn wǔ shí fēn (zhōng)
4:27	四点二十七分(钟)
	四點二十七分(鐘)
	sì diǎn èr shí qī fēn (zhōng)

Reciting time with 零 *líng* 'zero'

When time is recited as digial time, if the number of minutes is smaller than ten, minutes may optionally begin with 零 **líng** 'zero.' 零 **líng** 'zero' is also written as 〇.

2:02	两点零二分
	兩點零二分
	liǎng diǎn líng èr fēn

To indicate half past the hour, use 半 **bàn**.

6:30	六点半
	六點半
	liù diǎn bàn

The phrases 一刻 **yī kè** 'one quarter' and 三刻 **sān kè** 'three quarters' can be used to express a quarter after or a quarter to and 45 minutes after the hour.

7:15	七点一刻(钟)
	七點一刻(鐘)
	qī diǎn yī kè (zhōng)
7:45	七点三刻(钟)
	七點三刻(鐘)
	qī diǎn sān kè (zhōng)

Telling time specifying 'minutes to' and 'minutes past' the hour

过/過 **guò** 'pass' introduces minutes past the hour. When reciting time with 过/過 **guò**, the order of information is as follows. 钟/鐘 **zhōng** is optional and is often omitted.

| x hour | past | x minutes | |
| x 点/點 **diǎn** | 过/過 **guò** | x 分 **fēn** | 钟/鐘 **zhōng** |

3:10	三点过十分(钟)
	三點過十分(鐘)
	sān diǎn guò shí fēn (zhōng)

4:27	四点过二十七分(钟)
	四點過二十七分(鐘)
	sì diǎn guò èr shí qī fēn (zhōng)

7:15	七点过一刻(钟)
	七點過一刻(鐘)
	qī diǎn guò yī kè (zhōng)

7:45	七点过三刻(钟)
	七點過三刻(鐘)
	qī diǎn guò sān kè (zhōng)

NOTE | 过/過 **guò** cannot be used with 半 **bàn** half.

差 **chà** 'lack' introduces minutes before the hour. 差 **chà** + minutes can occur either before or after the hour phrase, as follows. 钟/鐘 **zhōng** is optional and is often omitted.

Pattern 1

x 点/點 **diǎn**   差 **chà**   x 分 **fēn**   (钟/鐘 **zhōng**)
(lit. 'x o'clock lacking x minutes')

6:50	七点差十分(钟)
	七點差十分(鐘)
	qī diǎn chà shífēn (zhōng)

7:45	八点差一刻(钟)
	八點過一刻(鐘)
	bā diǎn chà yī kè (zhōng)

Pattern 2

差 **chà**   x 分 **fēn**   x 点/點 **diǎn**   (钟/鐘 **zhōng**)
(lit. 'lacking x minutes, x o'clock')

6:50	差十分七点(钟)
	差十分七點(鐘)
	chà shífēn qī diǎn (zhōng)

7:45	差一刻八点(钟)
	過一刻八點(鐘)
	chà yī kè bā diǎn (zhōng)

45.1.4 Indicating a.m. and p.m.

In Mandarin, instead of the two-way distinction between a.m. and p.m., time is categorized as follows:

morning (the early hours, approximately 6–8 or 9 a.m.)	早上 **zǎoshang** or 早晨 **zǎochén**
before noon (approximately 8 or 9 a.m. until noon)	上午 **shàngwǔ**
midday (12 noon or the time around noon.)	中午 **zhōngwǔ**
afternoon (approximately 1 p.m. to 6 p.m.)	下午 **xiàwǔ**
evening (beginning approximately 6 p.m.)	晚上 **wǎnshang**
midnight – middle of the night (approximately midnight to 3 a.m.)	半夜 **bàn yè**

These expressions occur at the beginning of the clock time phrase:

下午三点钟
下午三點鐘
xiàwǔ sān diǎn zhōng
3 o'clock in the afternoon (3 p.m.)

早上六点半
早上六點半
zǎoshang liù diǎn bàn
6:30 in the morning (6:30 a.m.)

上午十点
上午十點
shàngwǔ shí diǎn
10 in the morning (10 a.m.)

晚上七点三刻
晚上七點三刻
wǎnshang qī diǎn sānkè
7:45 in the evening (7:45 p.m.)

半夜两点
半夜兩點
bàn yè liǎng diǎn
2 o'clock in the morning

45.1.5 The location of clock time phrases in the sentence

Clock time, like all phrases that indicate the time when a situation takes place, occurs at the beginning of the predicate, right after the subject.

他每天中午十二点钟吃饭。
他每天中午十二點鐘吃飯。
Tā měitiān zhōngwǔ shí'èr diǎn zhōng chī fàn.
He eats every day around 12:00 noon.

The position of the clock time phrase in the sentence is the same whether the sentence is a statement or a question.

Q: 什么时候吃晚饭？
甚麼時候吃晚飯？
Shénme shíhòu chī wǎnfàn?
When will we have dinner?

A: 我们六点吃晚饭。
我們六點吃晚飯。
Wǒmen liù diǎn chī wǎnfàn.
We will eat dinner at 6:00.

Q: 我们什么时候见？
我們甚麼時候見？
Wǒmen shénme shíhòu jiàn?
When shall we meet?

A: 我们明天上午九点见。
我們明天上午九點見。
Wǒmen míngtiān shàngwǔ jiǔ diǎn jiàn.
We will meet at 9:00 tomorrow morning.

➪ 4.5, 4.11

45.1.6 Asking about time

To ask for the present hour of the day, say:

现在几点钟?
現在幾點鐘?
Xiànzài jǐ diǎn zhōng?
What time (hour) is it now?

More general questions about the present time are the following:

现在(是)什么时候?	or　现在(是)什么时间?
現在(是)甚麼時候?	現在(是)甚麼時間?
Xiànzài (shì) shénme shíhòu?	**Xiànzài (shì) shénme shíjiān?**
What time is it now?	What time is it now?

⇨ 24.6

45.2 Calendar time

China uses two different calendar systems. The Western calendar, called 阳历/陽曆 **yánglì**, is used in nearly all official and public contexts, such as school, business, publishing, civil administration, military affairs, and politics. The 阴历/陰曆 **yīnlì** (lunar calendar), sometimes called 农历/農曆 **nónglì** (agricultural calendar), is used to mark birthdays, and traditional Chinese holidays such as the Chinese New Year, the Dragon Festival, the Mid-Autumn festival, etc. Until the nineteenth century, the lunar calendar was the primary calendar. Nowadays, the Western calendar is more widely used than the lunar calendar, especially in urban China.

45.2.1 Years

45.2.1.1 Counting years and asking about the number of years

To count years, precede the word 年 **nián** 'year' by a number. No additional classifier occurs between the number and the word for year.

one year	一 年	**yī nián**
two years	两年/兩年	**liǎng nián**
three years	三年	**sān nián**

To ask how many years, say:

几年?/幾年?
jǐ nián?
how many years?

or

多少年?
duōshǎo nián?
how many years?

⇨ 24.6

45.2.1.2 **Referring to years**

this year	今年	**jīnnián**
next year	明年	**míngnián**
two years from now	后年/後年	**hòunián**
three years from now	大后年/大後年	**dà hòunián**
four years from now	四年以后/四年以後	**sì nián yǐhòu**
last year	去年	**qùnián**
the year before last	前年	**qiánnián**
three years ago	大前年	**dà qiánnián**
four years ago	四年以前	**sì nián yǐqián**

45.2.1.3 **Reciting years**

To recite a year, read the year as a series of single numbers followed by 年 **nián**:

2004	二零零四年	**èr líng líng sì nián**
1976	一九七六年	**yī jiǔ qī liù nián**

To indicate BC and AD, say:

公元 **gōngyuán** or 公历/公曆 **gōnglì**, AD
公元前 **gōngyuánqián** or 前 **qián** BC

> 公元 2002 年
> **gōngyuán 2002 nián**
> 2002 AD

> 公元前 146 年
> **gōngyuánqián 146 nián**
> 146 BC

In Taiwan, years are counted from the founding of the Republic of China in 1911:

民國 47 年 **Mínguó 47 nián** = 1958
民國 93 年 **Mínguó 93 nián** = 2004

45.2.1.4 **Asking about years**

To ask about a year say:

哪年?
něi nián? or nǎ nián?
which year?

你是哪年毕业的?
你是哪年畢業的?
Nǐ shì nǎ nián bì yè de?
In what year did you graduate?

这个大学是哪年建立的?
這個大學是哪年建立的?
Zhège dàxué shì nǎ nián jiànlì de?
In what year was this university established?

45.2.2 **Months**

月 **yuè** is the word for month and it is also part of the name of the months. When months are counted or referred to in expressions such as 'one month,' 'this month,' or 'next month,' the classifier 个/個 **gè** occurs between the specifier and/or number and 月 **yuè** 'month.' The names of the months do not include a classifier.

45.2.2.1 Counting months and asking about the number of months

To count months, precede the word 月 **yuè** 'month' by a number and the classifier 个/個 **gè**:

one month	一个月/一個月	**yī gè yuè**
two months	两个月/兩個月	**liǎng gè yuè**
three months	三个月/三個月	**sān gè yuè**

To ask how many months, say:

几个月？ or 多少月？
幾個月？
jǐ gè yuè? **duōshǎo yuè?**
how many months? how many months?

一年有几个月？
一年有幾個月？
Yī nián yǒu jǐ gè yuè?
One year has how many months? (How many months are there in a year?)

你已经学了多少月了？
你已經學了多少月了？
Nǐ yǐjing xué le duōshǎo yuè le?
How many months have you studied already?

45.2.2.2 Referring to months with respect to 'now'

To refer to the months, use these expressions:

this month	这个月/這個月	**zhège yuè**
next month	下个月/下個月	**xià gè yuè**
last month	上个月/上個月	**shàng gè yuè**

45.2.2.3 The names of the months

January	一月	**yīyuè**
February	二月	**èryuè**
March	三月	**sānyuè**
April	四月	**sìyuè**
May	五月	**wǔyuè**
June	六月	**liùyuè**
July	七月	**qīyuè**
August	八月	**bāyuè**
September	九月	**jiǔyuè**
October	十月	**shíyuè**
November	十一月	**shíyī yuè**
December	十二月	**shí'èryuè**

To ask which month it is, say 几月？ 幾月？ **jǐ yuè?** 'which month?'

你是几月生的？
你是幾月生的？
Nǐ shì jǐ yuè shēng de?
In which month were you born?

45.2.3 **Weeks**

Mandarin has two words for week: 礼拜/禮拜 **lǐbài** and 星期 **xīngqī**.

礼拜/禮拜 **lǐbài** was originally associated with religious services, but no longer has religious connotations. Different regions of China have different preferences in the choice of the word for week. 星期 **xīngqī** is the word used in calendars, newspapers, and formal documents.

45.2.3.1 **Counting weeks and asking about the number of weeks**

To count weeks use the classifier 个/個 **gè**:

one week	一个星期/一個星期	or	一个礼拜/一個禮拜
	yī gè xīngqī		**yī gè lǐbài**
two weeks	两个星期/兩個星期	or	两个礼拜/兩個禮拜
	liǎng gè xīngqī		**liǎng gè lǐbài**
three weeks	三个星期/三個星期	or	三个礼拜/三個禮拜
	sān gè xīngqī		**sān gè lǐbài**

To ask how many weeks, say:

几个星期?/幾個星期?	or	几个礼拜?/幾個禮拜?
jǐ gè xīngqī?		**jǐ gè lǐbài?**
how many weeks?		how many weeks?

45.2.3.2 **Referring to weeks and weekends with respect to 'now'**

Expressions that refer to weeks:

this week	这个星期/這個星期	**zhège xīngqī**
next week	下个星期/下個星期	**xià gè xīngqī**
last week	上个星期/上個星期	**shàng gè xīngqī**

Expressions that refer to weekends:

this weekend	这个周末/這個週末	**zhège zhōumò**
next weekend	下个周末/下個週末	**xià gè zhōumò**
last weekend	上个周末/上個週末	**shàng gè zhōumò**

45.2.4 **Days**

45.2.4.1 **Counting days and asking about the number of days**

To count days, put the number right before the word for day. No additional classifier is used:

one day	一天	**yī tiān**
two days	两天/兩天	**liǎng tiān**
three days	三天	**sān tiān**

To ask about the number of days, say:

几天? 幾天?	**jǐ tiān?**	how many days? (small number expected)
多少天?	**duōshǎo tiān?**	how many days?

45.2.4.2 **Referring to days of the week and asking about days of the week**

There are two sets of words for the days of the week. One is based on the word 礼拜/禮拜 **lǐbài** and the other is based on the word 星期 **xīngqī**. In both sets, the names of the days of the week from Monday to Saturday include a number. Pay attention to the words for Sunday.

Sunday	礼拜天/禮拜天 **lǐbài tiān** or 礼拜日/禮拜日 **lǐbài rì**	星期天 **xīngqī tiān** or 星期日 **xīngqī rì**
Monday	礼拜一/禮拜一 **lǐbài yī**	星期一 **xīngqī yī**
Tuesday	礼拜二/禮拜二 **lǐbài èr**	星期二 **xīngqī èr**
Wednesday	礼拜三/禮拜三 **lǐbài sān**	星期三 **xīngqī sān**
Thursday	礼拜四/禮拜四 **lǐbài sì**	星期四 **xīngqī sì**
Friday	礼拜五/禮拜五 **lǐbài wǔ**	星期五 **xīngqī wǔ**
Saturday	礼拜六/禮拜六 **lǐbài liù**	星期六 **xīngqī liù**

To say 'last Tuesday,' say:

上(个)星期二 or 上(个)礼拜二
上(個)星期二 or 上(個)禮拜二
shàng (gè) xīngqī èr or **shàng (gè) lǐbài èr**

To say 'next Saturday,' say:

下(个)星期六 or 下(个)礼拜六
下(個)星期六 or 下(個)禮拜六
xià (gè) xīngqī liù or **xià (gè) lǐbài liù**

To ask about days of the week, say:

星期几? 星期幾? **xīngqī jǐ?** what day of the week?	or	礼拜几? 禮拜幾? **lǐbài jǐ?** what day of the week?

今天(是)星期几?
今天(是)星期幾?
Jīntiān (shì) xīngqī jǐ?
What day of the week is it today?

明天(是)礼拜几?
明天(是)禮拜幾?
Míngtiān (shì) lǐbài jǐ?
What day of the week is it tomorrow?

45.2.4.3 | **Referring to days before and after today**

大前天	**dà qiántiān**	three days ago
前天	**qiántiān**	the day before yesterday
昨天	**zuótiān**	yesterday
今天	**jīntiān**	today
明天	**míngtiān**	tomorrow
后天/後天	**hòutiān**	the day after tomorrow
大后天/大後天	**dà hòutiān**	three days from now

45.2.4.4 | **Referring to the date of the month (the first, second, third of the month, etc.)**

There are two words for date that are used when referring to the date of the month, 号/號 **hào** and 日 **rì**. 日 **rì** is more formal than 号/號 **hào** and is used in calendars and other written documents. To indicate the date, put the number directly before 日 **rì** or 号/號 **hào**:

the 5th (of the month)	五号/五號	or	五日
	wǔ hào		**wǔ rì**
the 22nd (of the month)	二十二号	or	二十二日
	二十二號		
	èrshí'èr hào		**èrshí'èr rì**

To ask about the date, say:

几号?	or	几日?
幾號?		幾日?
jǐ hào?		**jǐ rì?**
what is the date?		what is the date?

今天几号?	or	今天几月几号?
今天幾號?		今天幾月幾號?
Jīntiān jǐ hào?		**Jīntiān jǐ yuè jǐ hào?**
What is today's date?		What is today's date?
		(What is today's month and date?)

45.2.4.5 | **Reciting complete days and asking about dates**

In Mandarin, complete dates are presented from the largest unit of time to the smallest unit of time as follows:

year + month + date

一九九八年，七月，三十一日
yī jiǔ jiǔ bā nián, qīyuè, sānshí yī rì
July 31, 1998

二零零零年一月一日
èr líng líng líng nián yī yuè yī rì
January 1, 2000

一九八二年十月五号
一九八二年十月五號
yī jiǔ bā èr nián shí yuè wǔ hào
October 5, 1982

To ask about complete dates, say:

哪年几月几日？	or	哪年几月几号？
哪年幾月幾日？		哪年幾月幾號？
nǎ nián jǐ yuè jǐ rì?		**nǎ nián jǐ yuè jǐ hào?**
which year which month which date		which year which month which date

你是哪年几月几号生的？
你是哪年幾月幾號生的？
Nǐ shì nǎ nián jǐ yuè jǐ hào shēng de?
You were born in which year, which month, which date?
(When were you born?)

他们是哪年几月几日结婚的？
他們是哪年幾月幾日結婚的？
Tāmen shì nǎ nián jǐ yuè jǐ rì jiéhūn de?
In which year, which month, and on which date were they married?
(When were they married?)

45.2.5 Talking about semesters

学期/學期 **xuéqī** means a semester (of a school year).

45.2.5.1 Counting semesters

To count semesters, put the classifier 个/個 **gè** after the number and before the word 学期/學期 **xuéqī** semester.

one semester	一个学期/一個學期	**yī gè xuéqī**
two semesters	两个学期/兩個學期	**liǎng gè xuéqī**
three semesters	三个学期/三個學期	**sān gè xuéqī**

45.2.5.2 Referring to semesters

学期/學期 **xuéqī** are referred to in the same way as weeks, weekends, and months.

this semester	这个学期/這個學期	**zhège xuéqī**
next semester	下个学期/下個學期	**xià gè xuéqī**
last semester	上个学期/上個學期	**shàng gè xuéqī**

46

Expressing obligations and prohibitions

46.1 Expressing obligations

46.1.1 Expressing strong obligations: must

Here are the words used to express 'strong obligations' in Mandarin with sentences illustrating their use. All of these words can be translated with the English 'must.'

得 *děi*

> 明天你得早点儿起来。
> 明天你得早點兒起來。
> **Míngtiān nǐ *děi* zǎo diǎr qǐlái.**
> You *have to* get up earlier tomorrow morning.

必得 *bìděi*

> 你必得按时来上课。
> 你必得按時來上課。
> **Nǐ *bìděi* ànshí lái shàng kè.**
> You *must* come to class on time.

必须/必須 *bìxū*

> 去中国以前你必须申请签证。
> 去中國以前你必須申請簽証。
> **Qù Zhōngguó yǐqián nǐ *bìxū* shēnqǐng qiānzhèng.**
> Before you go to China you *must* apply for a visa.

必得 **bìděi** and 必须/必須 **bìxū** are more formal and stronger than 得 **děi**. 必须/必須 **bìxū** is also used in legal pronouncements and in other formal spoken and written contexts.

> 经济合同用货币履行义务时，。。。必须用人民币计算和支付。
> 經濟合同用貨幣履行義務時，。。。必須用人民幣計算和支付。
> **Jīngjì hétóng yòng huòbì lǚxíng yìwù shí, ... *bìxū* yòng rénmínbì jìsuàn hé zhīfù.**
> When economic contracts provide for the performance of obligations through money, ... Rénminbi *must* be used for calculating and paying obligations.

⇨ 12.4.1

Expressing 'weak' social and moral obligations: should, shall, ought to

Here are the words used in Mandarin to express the kind of 'weak obligations' associated with the English words 'should' and 'ought to' with sentences illustrating their use. In Mandarin, these words are also used to express moral obligations such as the responsibilities of parents to children or children to parents, and social obligations involving the things that a good person should do.

应当/應當 **yīngdāng** is more formal than 应该/應該 **yīnggāi** and can be used in formal texts including legal documents. 该/該 **gāi** is used in informal speech. 应/應 **yīng** is used in formal texts including legal documents.

应该/應該 *yīnggāi*

> 父母应该照顾他们的孩子。
> 父母應該照顧他們的孩子。
> **Fùmǔ *yīnggāi* zhàogù tāmen de háizi.**
> Parents *should* take care of their children.

应当/應當 *yīngdāng*

> 你有错误就应当改正。
> 你有錯誤就應當改正。
> **Nǐ yǒu cuòwù jiù *yīngdāng* gǎizhèng.**
> When you make a mistake, you *should* correct it.

该/該 *gāi*

> 我该去上班了。
> 我該去上班了。
> **Wǒ *gāi* qù shàngbān le.**
> I *should* go to work.

In legal documents, 应/應 **yīng** often means shall.

> 经济合同被确认无效后，当事人依据该合同所取得的财产，应返还给对方。
> 經濟合同被確認無效後，當事人依據該合同所取得的財產，應返還給對方。
> **Jīngjì hétóng bèi quèrèn wúxiào hòu, dāngshìrén yījù gāi hétong suǒ qǔ dé de cáichǎn, *yìng* fǎnhuán gěi duìfāng.**
> After an economic contract has been confirmed to be invalid, the parties *shall* return to each other any property that they have acquired pursuant to the contract.

应/應 **yìng** may occur in legal texts to specify moral, though non-legal obligations. The following is an excerpt from Section 1, Article 3, of the Child Welfare Law of Taiwan.

> 父母、养父母或监护人对其儿童应负保育之责任。
> 父母、養父母或監護人對其兒童應負保育之責任。
> **Fùmǔ, yǎng fùmǔ huò jiānhù rén duì qí értóng *yìng* fù bǎoyù zhī zérèn.**
> Parents, foster parents, or legal guardians *should* bear the responsibility of rearing the children in the household.

⇨ 12.4.2

46.1.3   Expressing negative obligations: need not, do not have to

The Mandarin words used to indicate that an action need not be done are 不必 **bù bì**, 不用 **bù yòng**, 甭 **béng**, 不须/不須 **bù xū**, and 无须/無須 **wú xū**.

不必 *bù bì*

> 他们明天不必来上课。
> 他們明天不必來上課。
> **Tāmen míngtiān bù bì lái shàng kè.**
> They don't have to come to class tomorrow.

不用 *bù yòng*

> 你不用谢我。谢她。
> 你不用謝我。謝她。
> **Nǐ bù yòng xiè wǒ. Xiè tā.**
> You don't have to thank me. Thank her.

甭 *béng*

甭 **béng** is the contraction of 不用 **bù yòng**. It is used in informal speech.

> 我们都是自己人。甭那么客气。
> 我們都是自己人。甭那麼客氣。
> **Wǒmen dōu shì zìjǐ rén. Béng nàme kèqi.**
> We are all friends. You don't have to be so polite.

不须/不須 *bù xū*

> 去中国以前不须打针。
> 去中國以前不須打針。
> **Qù Zhōngguó yǐqián bù xū dǎ zhēn.**
> Before going to China it is not necessary to get vaccinations.

无须/無須 *wú xū*

> 这件事无须告诉你父母。
> 這件事無須告訴你父母。
> **Zhè jiàn shì wú xū gàosu nǐ fùmǔ.**
> There is no need to tell your parents about this matter.
> (As for this matter, there is no need to tell your parents.)

46.1.4   Asking questions about obligations

To ask if there is an obligation to do something, use a yes–no question. 吗/嗎 **ma** questions can be used with all obligation words.

> 我们得看那本书吗?
> 我們得看那本書嗎?
> **Wǒmen děi kàn nà běn shū ma?**
> Do we have to read that book?

应该/應該 **yīnggāi** and 应当/應當 **yīngdāng** can also occur in *verb-not-verb* questions.

我应该不应该给他道歉？
我應該不應該給他道歉？
Wǒ yīnggāi bù yīnggāi gěi tā dàoqiàn?
Do I have to apologize to him?

我应当/不应当给他道歉？
我應當不應當給他道歉？
Wǒ yīngdāng bù yīngdāng gěi tā dàoqiàn?
Should I apologize to him?

得 **děi**, 必得 **bìděi**, and 必须/必須 **bìxū** cannot occur in *verb-not-verb* questions.

⇨ 24.1.2

46.2 Expressing prohibitions: must not, should not

46.2.1 Expressing strong prohibitions: must not

The words used to express strong prohibitions in Mandarin are 不许/不許 **bù xǔ** 'must not,' 不要 **bù yào** 'don't,' and 别 **bié** 'don't.'

医院里不许抽烟。
醫院裏不許抽菸。
Yīyuàn lǐ bù xǔ chōu yān.
Smoking is not permitted in the hospital.

别开玩笑。
別開玩笑。
Bié kāi wánxiào.
Don't joke. (Be serious.)

考试以前不要紧张。
考試以前不要緊張。
Kǎoshì yǐqián bù yào jǐnzhāng.
Before a test don't be nervous.

⇨ 12.5

46.2.2 Expressing weak prohibitions: should not

The Mandarin words used to indicate that an action should not be done are 不应该/ 應該 **bù yīnggāi** and 不应当/應當 **bù yīngdāng**.

你不应该/应当打人。
你不應該/應當打人。
Nǐ bù yīnggāi/yīngdāng dǎ rén.
You shouldn't hit people.

不应该/應該 **bù yīnggāi** 'should not' and 不应当/應當 **bù yīngdāng** 'should not' sometimes carry negative expectations. Both of the following sentences can be used after the fact, when we have seen that the medicine had side effects, or that Zhang San is a bad person.

这个药不应该有副作用啊。
這個藥不應該有副作用啊。
Zhège yào bù yīnggāi yǒu fù zuòyòng a.
This drug is not supposed to have any side effects.

张三不应该是坏人啊。
張三不應該是壞人啊。
Zhāng Sān bù yīnggāi shì huài rén a.
Zhang San is not supposed to be a bad person.

46.2.3 Formal written words that specify prohibited activities

Here are some commonly used expressions in formal written texts that indicate prohibited activities. They are always followed by a verb phrase.

禁止	**jìnzhǐ** + verb phrase	prohibited from
免	**miǎn** + verb phrase	prohibited from
勿	**wù** + verb phrase	do not
严禁/嚴禁	**yánjìn** + verb phrase	strictly prohibited from
不准	**bù zhǔn** + verb phrase	not permitted to

Here are the texts of actual signs posted in Chinese cities indicating prohibited activities. They illustrate the use of formal written words for prohibitions.

各种车辆禁止进入
各種車輛禁止進入
Gè zhǒng chēliàng jìnzhǐ jìnrù
No entry
(lit. 'All vehicles prohibited
from entering')

严禁酒后开车
嚴禁酒後開車
Yánjìn jiǔ hòu kāi chē
Don't drink and drive
(lit. 'Driving after drinking is
strictly prohibited')

自行车汽车摩托车禁止入内
自行車汽車摩托車禁止入內
**Zìxíng chē qìchē mótuōchē
jìnzhǐ rù nèi**
Bicycles, cars and motorcycles
prohibited from entering

车辆行人严禁穿行
車輛行人嚴禁穿行
**Chēliàng xíngrén yánjìn
chuānxíng**
No crossing
(lit. 'Vehicles and pedestrians are
strictly prohibited from crossing')

禁止拍照
Jìnzhǐ pāi zhào
No photographs
(lit. 'Taking photographs is
prohibited')

不准乱扔瓜果皮核
不准亂扔瓜果皮核
Bùzhǔn luàn rēng guāguǒ píhé
It is not permitted to throw away
melon and fruit peels and pits

禁止吸烟
禁止吸菸
Jìnzhǐ xī yān
No smoking
(lit. 'Smoking is prohibited')

闲人免进
閒人免進
Xiánrén miǎn jìn
No admission except on business
(lit. 'Persons with no business here are
prohibited from entering')

禁止停车
禁止停車
Jìnzhǐ tíng chē
No parking
(lit. 'Parking is prohibited')

请勿停车
請勿停車
Qǐng wù tíng chē
No parking
(lit. 'Please don't park')

禁止摘花

Jìnzhǐ zhāi huā
Do not pick the flowers
(lit. 'Picking flowers is prohibited')

不准随地吐痰
不准隨地吐痰
Bù zhǔn suídì tǔtán
No spitting
(lit. 'Spitting on the ground is
not permitted')

禁止随地吐痰
禁止隨地吐痰
jìnzhǐ suídì tǔtán
No spitting
(lit. 'Spitting is prohibited')

请勿随地吐痰
請勿隨地吐痰
Qǐng wù suídì tǔtán
No spitting
(lit. 'Please don't spit')

47

Expressing commands and permission

Commands

Making a command

There is no specific command form in Mandarin, but there are several ways to make a command.

The simplest way is simply to state the verb:

吃！	说！/說！	坐！
Chī!	**Shuō!**	**Zuò!**
Eat!	Speak!	Sit!

The verb may sometimes be suffixed with 着/著 **zhe**:

吃着！/吃著！	拿着！/拿著！	坐着！/坐著！
Chīzhe!	**Názhe!**	**Zuòzhe!**
Eat!	Hold it!/Take it!	Sit!

 35.2.1

Commands may also take the form of a statement followed by 吧 **ba**.

吃吧！	给我吧！ 給我吧！	坐吧！
Chī ba!	**Gěi wǒ ba!**	**Zuò ba!**
Eat!	Give (it) to me!	Sit!

Note that the particle 吧 **ba** at the end of the sentence may also convey suggestion:

我们看电影吧！
我們看電影吧！
Wǒmen kàn diànyǐng ba!
Let's see a movie!

or supposition:

你是王老师吧。
你是王老師吧。
Nǐ shì Wáng lǎoshī ba.
You must be professor Wang.

Context will make the function of 吧 **ba** clear in any given sentence.

➪ | 52.2

47.1.2 **Negative commands: prohibitions**

To command someone not to do something, use 不要 **bù yào** 'don't,' 别 **bié** 'don't,' or 不许/不許 **bù xǔ** 'not allow.'

> 不要在屋里吸烟！
> 不要在屋裡吸菸！
> **Bù yào zài wūlǐ xī yān!**
> Don't smoke in the house!

> 别出去！
> **Bié chūqu!**
> Don't go out!

> 喝酒以后不许开车。
> 喝酒以後不許開車。
> **Hē jiǔ yǐhòu bù xǔ kāi chē.**
> After you drink alcohol you are not allowed to drive a car.

➪ | 46.2.1

47.1.3 **Reporting a command**

To report a command, use the verb 叫 **jiào** 'to order,' 'to call,' 'to tell.'

> 他叫我走。
> **Tā jiào wǒ zǒu.**
> He ordered me to leave. (He told me to leave.)

> 谁叫你这样做的？
> 誰叫你這樣做的？
> **Shéi jiào nǐ zhèyàng zuò de?**
> Who told you to do it this way?

> Q: 妈妈叫你去买什么？
> 媽媽叫你去買甚麼？
> **Māma jiào nǐ qù mǎi shénme?**
> What did mom tell you to buy?
> A: 妈妈叫我去买一瓶可口可乐。
> 媽媽叫我去買一瓶可口可樂。
> **Māma jiào wǒ qù mǎi yī píng kěkǒukělè.**
> Mom made me (told me to) buy a bottle of Coke.

Note that 叫 **jiào** has other meanings and functions that are not associated with commands. They include 'to call/to be called':

> 我叫郭美玲。
> **Wǒ jiào Guō Měilíng.**
> I am called Meiling Guo.

➪ | 18.5

and the passive marker 'by':

> 饼干都叫孩子吃完了。
> 餅乾都叫孩子吃完了。
> **Bǐnggān dōu jiào háizi chīwán le.**
> The cookies were all eaten up by the children.

⇨ 17

47.2 Permission

47.2.1 Giving permission

To give permission use the modal verb 可以 **kéyǐ** 'can/permitted.' To deny permission, say 不可以 **bù kéyǐ** 'cannot/not permitted.'

> Q: 妈妈，今天晚上，我可以不可以跟朋友去看电影？
> 媽媽，今天晚上，我可以不可以跟朋友去看電影？
> **Māma, jīntiān wǎnshang, wǒ kéyǐ bù kéyǐ gēn péngyou qù kàn diànyǐng?**
> Mom, may I go to see a movie with my friends tonight?
>
> A: 你可以去看电影，可是不可以太晚回家。
> 你可以去看電影，可是不可以太晚回家。
> **Nǐ kéyǐ qù kàn diànyǐng, kěshì bù kéyǐ tài wǎn huí jiā.**
> Yes, you may go to see a movie, but you can't come home too late.
>
> Q: 这里可以不可以抽烟？
> 這裡可以不可以抽菸？
> **Zhèli kéyǐ bù kéyǐ chōu yān?**
> Can one smoke here?
>
> A: 这里不可以抽烟。
> 這裡不可以抽菸。
> **Zhèli bù kéyǐ chōu yān.**
> No, one can't smoke here.
>
> Q: 我们今天不能来，可以明天来吗？
> 我們今天不能來，可以明天來嗎？
> **Wǒmen jīntiān bù néng lái, kéyǐ míngtiān lái ma?**
> We can't come today. Can we come tomorrow instead?
>
> A: 当然可以。
> 當然可以。
> **Dāngrán kéyǐ.**
> Of course you can.

⇨ 12.2.3

47.2.2 Reporting permission

To report that someone is allowed to do something, use 让/讓 **ràng** 'to let/to permit/to allow,' or 许/許 **xǔ** 'to permit/to allow.'

> 我父母让我去中国学习。
> 我父母讓我去中國學習。
> **Wǒ fùmǔ ràng wǒ qù Zhōngguó xuéxí.**
> My parents let me go to China to study.

政府许我出国。
政府許我出國。
Zhèngfǔ xǔ wǒ chū guó.
The government has allowed me to leave the country.

让/讓 **ràng** also functions as the passive marker 'by':

我的行李让人拿走了。
我的行李讓人拿走了。
Wǒ de xíngli ràng rén názǒu le.
My suitcase was taken away by someone.

⇨ | 17

To indicate that someone is not allowed to do something, say 不叫 **bù jiào**, 不让/ 不讓 **bù ràng**, or 不许/不許 **bù xǔ**.

老师不叫我们出去。
老師不叫我們出去。
Lǎoshī bù jiào wǒmen chūqu.
The teacher won't allow us to go out.

妈妈不让我看电视。
媽媽不讓我看電視。
Māma bù ràng wǒ kàn diànshì.
Mom won't let me watch television.

你不许喝酒以后开车。
你不許喝酒以後開車。
Nǐ bù xǔ hē jiǔ yǐhòu kāi chē.
You are not allowed to drive after drinking alcohol.

48

Expressing ability and possibility

48.1 Expressing ability

48.1.1 Expressing a learned ability

To express a learned or acquired ability or skill, something that you *know how* to do or have *learned how* to do, use the modal verb 会/會 **huì**.

Q: 你会说英文吗?
你會説英文嗎?
Nǐ huì shuō Yīngwén ma?
Do you know how to speak English?

A: 我会说一点儿英文。
我會説一點兒英文。
Wǒ huì shuō yīdiǎr Yīngwén.
I know how to speak a little English.

Q: 你会开车吗?
你會開車嗎?
Nǐ huì kāi chē ma?
Do you know how to drive?

A: 我还不会开车呢。
我還不會開車呢。
Wǒ hái bù huì kāi chē ne.
I don't know how to drive yet.

48.1.2 Expressing an innate ability or talent

To express a skill or talent or an innate ability, use the modal verb 会/會 **huì**. When expressing this meaning, 会/會 **huì** may be preceded by the intensifiers 很 **hěn** 'very,' 真 **zhēn** 'really,' or 最 **zuì** 'the most.'

我妹妹很会跳舞。你请她跳吧。
我妹妹很會跳舞。你請她跳吧。
Wǒ mèimei hěn huì tiào wǔ. Nǐ qǐng tā tiào ba.
My little sister dances very well. Ask her to dance with you.

王教授最会教数学了。
王教授最會教數學了。
Wáng jiàoshòu zuì huì jiāo shùxué le.
Professor Wang is the best at teaching math.

王: 来,干杯!
來,乾杯!
Wáng: Lái, gānbēi!
Wang: Bottoms up!

林: 我真不会喝酒。
我真不會喝酒。
Lín: Wǒ zhēn bù huì hē jiǔ.
Lin: I really can't drink.

⇨ 10.3, 12.2.1

Expressing physical ability

To express physical ability or the unobstructed ability to perform an action use 能 **néng**.

> 我的身体不好。大夫说我不能游泳。
> 我的身體不好。大夫説我不能游泳。
> **Wǒ de shēntǐ bù hǎo. Dàifu shuō wǒ bù néng yóu yǒng.**
> My health is not so good. The doctor said I cannot swim.

> 他一天能作十几个小时的事。
> 他一天能作十幾個小時的事。
> **Tā yītiān néng zuò shí jǐ gè xiǎoshí de shì.**
> He can work more than ten hours a day.

When used to express ability, 能 **néng**, like 会/會 **huì**, can be modified by intensifiers such as 很 **hěn** 'very,' 真 **zhēn** 'really,' or 太 **tài** 'too.'

> 中国人很能吃苦。
> 中國人很能吃苦。
> **Zhōngguórén hěn néng chī kǔ.**
> Chinese can endure a lot of hardship.

> 我的女儿真会花钱。
> 我的女兒真會花錢。
> **Wǒ de nǚ'ér zhēn huì huā qián.**
> My daughter can really spend money.

⇨ 10.3, 12.2.2

48.2 Expressing possibility

48.2.1 **Expressing the likely occurrence of an event**

To express possibility or the likelihood of the occurrence of an event, as in 'will, could possibly,' or 'would probably,' use the modal verb 会/會 **huì**.

Q: 明天会不会下雪？
明天會不會下雪？
Míngtiān huì bù huì xià xuě?

Is it going to snow tomorrow?

A: 天气预报说明天不会下雪。
天氣預報説明天不會下雪。
Tiānqì yùbào shuō míngtiān bù huì xià xuě.

According to the weather report, it won't snow tomorrow.

Q: 你想我们要坐的飞机会不会误点？

你想我們要坐的飛機會不會誤點？

Nǐ xiǎng wǒmen yào zuò de fēijī huì bù huì wùdiǎn?

Do you think the plane we are going to take will be late?

A: 航空公司说，我们要坐的飞机不会误点。
航空公司説，我們要坐的飛機不會誤點。

Hángkōng gōngsī shuō, wǒmen yào zuò de fēijī bù huì wùdiǎn.

The airline company says the plane we are going to take won't be late.

⇨ 12.1, 32.3

48.2.2 **Expressing feasibility**

The modal 可以 **kéyǐ** is also sometimes used to express the feasibility of an event.

我们今天可以不考试吗？ 不可以。
我們今天可以不考試嗎？
Wǒmen jīntiān kéyǐ bù kǎo shì ma? **Bù kéyǐ.**
Can we not have a test today? No, not possible.

The most common function of 可以 **kéyǐ** is to express permission.

➪ 47.2

48.2.3 **Describing circumstances that may influence the occurrence of an event**

To specify circumstantial factors that favor or obstruct the occurrence of an event use 能 **néng**.

中国孩子都能上中学吗？
中國孩子都能上中學嗎？
Zhōngguó háizi dōu néng shàng zhōngxué ma?
Can all Chinese children go to high school?

今天我的车坏了，所以不能去接你了。
今天我的車壞了，所以不能去接你了。
Jīntiān wǒ de chē huài le, suóyi bù néng qù jiē nǐ le.
I can't pick you up today because my car has broken down.

49

Expressing desires, needs, preferences, and willingness

Expressing desires

To express a desire for something to happen, say:

希望 *xīwàng* 'to hope'

> 我希望我们有机会再见。
> 我希望我們有機會再見。
> **Wǒ xīwàng wǒmen yǒu jīhuì zài jiàn.**
> I hope we have the chance to meet again.

要 *yào* 'to want'

> 她要看她母亲。
> 她要看她母親。
> **Tā yào kàn tā mǔqīn.**
> She wants to see her mother.

> 她要回家。
> **Tā yào huí jiā.**
> She wants to go home.

盼望 *pànwang* 'hope for, long for' (+ VP)

> 母亲天天盼望哥哥回来。
> 母親天天盼望哥哥回來。
> **Mǔqīn tiāntiān pànwàng gēge huí lai.**
> Mother hopes every day that older brother will come back.

期望 *qīwàng* 'to expect'

> 我期望能早日回国。
> 我期望能早日回國。
> **Wǒ qīwàng néng zǎorì huí guó.**
> I hope I can return to my home country soon.

期望 **qīwàng** can also be used as a noun:

> 父母对孩子的期望很大。
> 父母對孩子的期望很大。
> **Fùmǔ duì háizi de qīwàng hěn dà.**
> Parents have great hopes and expectations for their children.
> (The expectations of parents regarding their children are very big.)

To express a desire for something, say:

要 *yào 'to want'*

> 他要一辆新车。
> 他要一輛新車。
> **Tā yào yī liàng xīn chē.**
> He wants a new car.

> 小狗饿了，要吃东西。
> 小狗餓了，要吃東西。
> **Xiǎo gǒu è le, yào chī dōngxi.**
> The little dog is hungry and wants to eat something.

49.2 Expressing needs

To indicate that you need something, say:

需要 *xūyào 'to need'*

> 他需要安慰和了解。
> **Tā xūyào ānwèi hé liáojiě.**
> He needs comfort and understanding.

> 我需要你的帮助。
> 我需要你的幫助。
> **Wǒ xūyào nǐ de bāngzhù.**
> I need your help.

得 *děi [+ verb] 'to need [to do]'*

> 这个汤得多加点盐。
> 這個湯得多加點鹽。
> **Zhège tāng děi duō jiā diǎn yán.**
> This soup needs a little more salt.
> (This soup needs (for us) to add a little more salt.)

> 我们得晚上十点到家。
> 我們得晚上十點到家。
> **Wǒmen děi wǎnshang shí diǎn dào jiā.**
> We need to be home by 10 p.m.

⇨ 12.4, 46.1

Expressing preferences

To indicate a preference, say:

宁可/寧可 *níngkě 'to prefer'*

> 我们宁可在家吃饭，不愿意去饭馆吃。
> 我們寧可在家吃飯，不願意去飯館吃。
> **Wǒmen níngkě zài jiā chī fàn, bù yuànyi qù fànguǎn chī.**
> We'd prefer to eat at home. We do not want to go to a restaurant to eat.

> 他宁可死，也不愿意屈服。
> 他寧可死，也不願意屈服。
> **Tā níngkě sǐ, yě bù yuànyi qūfú.**
> He'd prefer to die, and he is not ready to surrender.

偏爱/偏愛 *piān'ài 'favor, be partial to somebody or something'*

> 老师不应该偏爱某一个学生。
> 老師不應該偏愛某一個學生。
> **Lǎoshī bù yīnggāi piān'ài mǒu yī gè xuésheng.**
> The teacher should not be partial to any student.

情愿/情願 *qíngyuàn 'would rather'*

> 我情愿一辈子不结婚，也不要跟他结婚。
> 我情願一輩子不結婚，也不要跟他結婚。
> **Wǒ qíngyuàn yī bèizi bù jiéhūn, yě bù yào gēn tā jiéhūn.**
> I'd rather be single all my life than marry him.

Expressing willingness

To indicate willingness, say:

愿意/願意 *yuànyi 'to be willing'*

> 我愿意嫁给他。
> 我願意嫁給他。
> **Wǒ yuànyi jiàgěi tā.**
> I am willing to marry him.

> 我不愿意嫁给别人。
> 我不願意嫁給別人。
> **Wǒ bù yuànyi jiàgěi biéren.**
> I don't want to marry anyone else.

> 我愿意跟你合作。
> 我願意跟你合作。
> **Wǒ yuànyi gēn nǐ hézuò.**
> I am willing to cooperate with you.

50

Expressing knowledge, advice, and opinions

Expressing knowledge

To express knowledge, use the following verbs:

知道	**zhīdao**	to know
认识/認識	**rènshi**	to recognize/to know
会/會	**huì**	to be able to, to know

Expressing knowledge with 知道 *zhīdao* and 认识/認識 *rènshi*

知道 **zhīdao** and 认识/認識 **rènshi** can both be translated into English as 'to know.' They are sometimes interchangeable, but they often have distinct uses.

- 知道 **zhīdao** means *to know information.*
- 认识/認識 **rènshi** means *to know of* or *to recognize.* It is used to talk about recognizing Chinese characters and locations, as well as people.

The following examples illustrate the differences between 知道 **zhīdao** and 认识/認識 **rènshi**.

Conversation 1

Q: 你认识他吗?
你認識他嗎?
Nǐ *rènshi* tā ma?

Do you *know* him?

A: 我知道他是谁,可是我不认识他。
我知道他是誰,可是我不認識他。
Wǒ *zhīdao* tā shì shéi, kěshì wǒ bù *rènshi* tā.

I *know* who he is, but I don't *know* him.

Do not say

*你知道他吗?
你知道他嗎?
Nǐ *zhīdao* tā ma?

Conversation 2

Q: 你知道火车站在哪儿吗？
你知道火車站在哪兒嗎？
**Nǐ zhīdao huǒchēzhàn
zài nǎr ma?**
Do you *know* where the
train station is?

A: 我不知道。对不起。
我不知道。對不起。
Wǒ bù zhīdao. Duìbuqǐ.

I don't *know*. Sorry.

Do not say

*你认识火车站在哪儿吗？
你認識火車站在哪兒嗎？
**Nǐ rènshi huǒchēzhàn zài
nǎr ma?**

Do not say

*我不认识。对不起。
我不認識。對不起。
Wǒ bù rènshi. Duìbuqǐ.

Conversation 3

Q: 你认识中国字吗？
你認識中國字嗎？
**Nǐ rènshi Zhōngguó
zì ma?**
Do you *know* Chinese
characters?

A: 我认识，可是我不知道怎么写。
我認識，可是我不知道怎麼寫。
**Wǒ rènshi, kěshì wǒ bù zhīdao
zěnme xiě.**
I recognize them, but I don't
know how to write them.

Do not say

*你知道中国字吗？
你知道中國字嗎？
Nǐ zhīdao Zhōngguó zì ma?

Do not say

*我知道，可是我不认识怎么写。
我知道，可是我不認識怎麼寫。
**Wǒ zhīdao, kěshì wǒ bù rènshi
zěnme xiě.**

Conversation 4

Q: 请问，到图书馆怎么走？
請問，到圖書館怎麼走？
**Qǐngwèn, dào túshūguǎn
zěnme zǒu?**
Excuse me, how do you go
to the library?

A: 对不起，我不认识路。
對不起，我不認識路。
Duìbuqǐ, wǒ bù rènshi lù.

Sorry, I don't know the way.

Do not say

*我不知道路。
Wǒ bù zhīdao lù.

Expressing knowledge with 会/會 huì

One meaning conveyed by the modal verb 会/會 **huì** is that of ability associated
with knowledge. In the following sentences, 会/會 **huì** means *to be able to* or *to know*.

Q: 你会说英文吗？
你會說英文嗎？
Nǐ huì shuō Yīngwén ma?
Do you speak English?

A: 我会说一点儿。
我會說一點兒。
Wǒ huì shuō yìdiǎr.
I can speak a little.

Q: 你会不会开车？
你會不會開車？
Nǐ huì bù huì kāi chē?
Do you know how to drive?

A: 我十八岁就会开车了。
我十八歲就會開車了。
Wǒ shíbā suì jiù huì kāi chē le.
I have known how to drive since I was eighteen.

Q: 美国人都会跳舞吧？
美國人都會跳舞吧？
Měiguórén dōu huì tiào wǔ ba?
All Americans know how to dance, right?

A: 不一定。我就不会。
不一定。我就不會。
Bù yídìng. Wǒ jiù bù huì.
Not necessarily. I for one cannot dance.

⇨ | 12.1

50.2 Advice and opinions

50.2.1 Requesting and giving advice and opinions

To give your opinion or your advice, or to ask another for their opinion or advice use these expressions.

想 *xiǎng* 'to think'

Q: 你想我们是坐飞机好，还是坐火车好？
你想我們是坐飛機好，還是坐火車好？
Nǐ xiǎng wǒmen shì zuò fēijī hǎo, háishi zuò huǒchē hǎo?
Do you think we should fly or take the train?

A: 我想我们坐飞机比较好。
我想我們坐飛機比較好。
Wǒ xiǎng wǒmen zuò fēijī bǐjiào hǎo.
I think it is better to fly.

The Mandarin equivalent of the English expression 'I don't think . . . ' is 我想 . . . 不 **wǒ xiǎng . . . bù** 'I think . . . not . . .' and not 我不想 **wǒ bù xiǎng . . .**

我想他不聪明。
我想他不聰明。
Wǒ xiǎng tā bù cōngming.
I don't think he is smart.

我想他不会来。
我想他不會來。
Wǒ xiǎng tā bù huì lái.
I don't think he is going to come.

看 *kàn* 'to look at, consider, think'

Q: 你看这件事应该怎么办？
你看這件事應該怎麼辦？
Nǐ kàn zhè jiàn shì yīnggāi zěnme bàn?
How do you think we should handle this matter?

> A: 我看我们得先看看大家的意见。
> 我看我們得先看看大家的意見。
> **Wǒ kàn wǒmen děi xiān kànkan dàjiā de yìjiàn.**
> I think we should consider everybody's opinion first.

觉得/覺得 **juéde** 'to feel, to consider, think'

> 他们都觉得这样作比较妥当。
> 他們都覺得這樣作比較妥當。
> **Tāmen dōu juéde zhèyàng zuò bǐjiào tuǒdang.**
> They all feel that doing it this way is more appropriate.

说/説 **shuō** 'say'

> 你说我应该选哪门课?
> 你説我應該選哪門課?
> **Nǐ shuō wǒ yīnggāi xuǎn nǎ mén kè?**
> Which courses do you say I should take?

认为/認為 **rènwéi** 'to believe, to suppose, to consider'

以为/以為 **yǐwéi** 'to believe, to suppose, to consider'

以为/以為 **yǐwéi** and 认为/認為 **rènwéi** overlap in meaning and usage. Both mean *to consider, to suppose*.

> 我以为这次的旅行很有意思。(认为/認為 **rènwéi** can be used)
> 我以為這次的旅行很有意思。
> **Wǒ yǐwéi zhècì de lǚxíng hěn yǒu yìsi.**
> I *consider* this trip to be very interesting.

> 大家都以为他是一个好人。(认为/認為 **rènwéi** can be used)
> 大家都以為他是一個好人。
> **Dàjiā dōu yǐwéi tā shì yī gè hǎorén.**
> Everyone *believes* he is a good person.

以为/以為 **yǐwéi** also means *to mistakenly assume* something. This meaning is not shared by 认为/認為 **rènwéi**. It is illustrated in the following sentences:

> 我以为你是日本人,原来你是韩国人。
> 我以為你是日本人,原來你是韓國人。
> **Wǒ yǐwéi nǐ shì Rìběn rén, yuánlái nǐ shì Hánguó rén.**
> I thought you were Japanese, but you are Korean.

> 我以为今天不会下雨。没想到下了这么大的雨。
> 我以為今天不會下雨。沒想到下了這麼大的雨。
> **Wǒ yǐwéi jīntiān bù huì xià yǔ. Méi xiǎngdào xià le zhème dà de yǔ.**
> I assumed that it wouldn't rain today. I had no idea that it would rain this much.

When giving or requesting advice, you can make reference to obligations.

> 我想你应该多用功一些。
> 我想你應該多用功一些。
> **Wǒ xiǎng nǐ yīnggāi duō yònggōng yīxiē.**
> I think you *should* be a little more diligent.

⇨ 12.4, 46.1

50.2.2 **Making your request polite**

To make your request for an opinion or advice polite, use these expressions.

请问/請問 *qǐng wèn* 'may I ask, excuse me'

> 请问，我应该送他什么礼物？
> 請問，我應該送他甚麼禮物？
> **Qǐngwèn, wǒ yīnggāi sòng tā shénme lǐwù?**
> May I ask, what kind of gift should I give him?

请教/請教 *qǐng jiào* 'please teach me/(I) request instruction'

> 我有一个问题跟您请教。
> 我有一個問題跟您請教。
> **Wǒ yǒu yī gè wèntí gēn nín qǐng jiào.**
> I'd like some advice from you on a question.

请指教/請指教 *qǐng zhǐjiào* 'please provide instruction'

> 我写了一篇文章请你多指教。
> 我寫了一篇文章請你多指教。
> **Wǒ xiě le yī piān wénzhāng qǐng nǐ duō zhǐjiào.**
> I've written an essay that I would like your comments on.

50.2.3 **Telling someone their best or only option**

These expressions can be used when giving strong, direct advice.

最好 *zuì hǎo* (+ verb phrase) 'the best thing to do is' (verb phrase)

> Q: 下雨呢！怎么办啊？
> 下雨呢！怎麼辦啊？
> **Xià yǔ ne! Zěnme bàn a?**
> It's raining. What should we do?

> A: 那，我们最好不去。
> 那，我們最好不去。
> **Nà, wǒmen zuì hǎo bù qù.**
> Well then, we'd best not go.

只好 *zhǐ hǎo* (+ verb phrase) 'the only thing to do is' (verb phrase)

> 要是你要考得好，只好认真的学习。
> 要是你要考得好，只好認真的學習。
> **Yàoshi nǐ yào kǎo de hǎo, zhǐ hǎo rènzhēn de xuéxí.**
> If you want to do well on the exam, the only thing you can do is study hard.

50.2.4 **Telling someone to do as they please**

To tell someone to do as they please, use the following expression:

subject	怎么	verb	就	怎么	verb
subject	怎麼	verb	就	怎麼	verb
subject	zěnme	verb	jiù	zěnme	verb

do whatever the subject pleases

Conversation 1

Q: 这件事我怎么作好？
這件事我怎麼作好？
Zhè jiàn shì wǒ zěnme zuò hǎo?
How should I best do this?

A: 这我可不知道，你想怎么作就怎么作吧。
這我可不知道，你想怎麼作就怎麼作吧。
Zhè wǒ kě bù zhīdào, nǐ xiǎng zěnme zuò jiù zěnme zuò ba.
I don't know. Do it the way you think it should be done.

Conversation 2

Q: 你想这个周末我们去哪儿好？
你想這個週末我們去哪兒好？
Nǐ xiǎng zhège zhōumò wǒmen qù nǎr hǎo?
Where do you think we should go this weekend?

A: 你想去哪儿我们就去哪儿吧，我没意见。
你想去哪兒我們就去哪兒吧，我沒意見。
Nǐ xiǎng qù nǎr wǒmen jiù qù nǎr ba, wǒ méi yìjiàn.
We will go wherever you think we should go. I don't have an opinion.

Conversation 3

Q: 姐姐，你说我跟谁出去玩儿好？
姐姐，你説我跟誰出去玩兒好？
Jiějie, nǐ shuō wǒ gēn shéi chūqu wár hǎo?
Older sister, who do you think I should go out with?

A: 你想跟谁玩儿就跟谁玩儿。不必问我。
你想跟誰玩兒就跟誰玩兒。不必問我。
Nǐ xiǎng gēn shéi wár jiù gēn shéi wár. Bù bì wèn wǒ.
Go out with whomever you want. You don't have to ask me.

51

Expressing fear, worry, and anxiety

Expressing fear of something

To express fear of something, say:

subject 怕 **pà** something
subject is afraid of something

> 我怕狗。
> **Wǒ pà gǒu.**
> I am afraid of dogs.

> 我们不要怕困难。
> 我們不要怕困難。
> **Wǒmen bù yào pà kùnnán.**
> We shouldn't be afraid of difficulty.

> 我妈妈怕胖，不敢多吃。
> 我媽媽怕胖，不敢多吃。
> **Wǒ māma pà pàng, bù gǎn duō chī.**
> My mother is afraid of getting fat. She doesn't dare eat much.

> 这个人真是天不怕，地不怕。
> 這個人真是天不怕，地不怕。
> **Zhège rén zhēn shì tiān bù pà, dì bù pà.**
> This person is not afraid of anything.

To tell someone not to be afraid of something, say:

别怕！ *Bié pà!* 'Don't be afraid!'

> 别怕我的狗。
> **Bié pà wǒ de gǒu.**
> Don't be afraid of my dog.

不要怕！ *Bù yào pà!* 'Don't be afraid!'

> 不要怕他。他人很好。
> **Bù yào pà tā. Tā rén hěn hǎo.**
> Don't be afraid of him. He means well.

To indicate that someone is afraid use these expressions:

怕死(了) **pàsǐ le** 'to be scared to death'

> 我怕死了。
> **Wǒ pàsǐ le.**
> I am scared to death.

害怕 **hàipà** 'to be afraid'

> 我很害怕。
> **Wǒ hěn hàipà.**
> I'm very afraid.

恐惧/恐懼 **kǒngjù** 'to be terrified' (literary expression used in formal speech and writing)

> 听到 SARS 流行的报道，大家都很恐惧。
> 聽到 SARS 流行的報道，大家都很恐懼。
> **Tīngdào SARS liúxíng de bàodào, dàjiā dōu hěn kǒngjù.**
> When people heard the report about the spread of SARS, they were filled with terror.

恐惧/恐懼 **kǒngjù** is also used as a noun, meaning *fear* or *terror*.

> 一想到战争的可能性，我心里就充满了恐惧。
> 一想到戰爭的可能性，我心裏就充滿了恐懼。
> **Yī xiǎngdào zhànzhēng de kěnéng xìng, wǒ xīnli jiù chōngmǎn le kǒngjù.**
> When I think about the possibility of war, my heart fills with fear.

⇨ 38.3.3

51.2 Expressing nervousness or anxiety

To indicate that someone is nervous, say:

紧张/緊張 **jǐnzhāng** 'to be nervous'

> 考试以前我很紧张。
> 考試以前我很緊張。
> **Kǎoshì yǐqián wǒ hěn jǐnzhāng.**
> Before I take a test I am very nervous.

To indicate that someone is worried or anxious, say:

着急/著急 **zháojí** 'to be worried or anxious'

> 他找不着飞机票了。非常着急。
> 他找不著飛機票了。非常著急。
> **Tā zhǎobuzháo fēijī piào le. Fēicháng zháojí.**
> He can't find the airplane ticket(s). (He is) extremely anxious.

To indicate worry about someone or something, say:

担心/擔心 **dānxīn** *'worry about'*

> 我担心我的儿子。
> 我擔心我的兒子。
> **Wǒ dānxīn wǒ de érzi.**
> I am worried about my son.

为 something 着急
為 something 著急
worried about something

> 我为后果着急。
> 我為後果著急。
> **Wǒ wéi hòuguǒ zháojí.**
> I am worried about the results.

To tell someone not to worry or be nervous, say:

> 别着急。　　　　　别紧张。
> 　　　　　　　　　别緊張。
>
> **Bié zháojí.**　　**Bié jǐnzhāng.**
> Don't worry.　　Don't be nervous.

To ask someone in an informal context what they are worried about, say:

> 你着什么急啊？
> 你著什麼急啊？
> **Nǐ zháo shénme jí a?**
> What are you worried about?

51.3 **Indicating that something is scary**

To indicate that something is scary or frightening, say:

something 可怕 **kěpà**

> 今天看的这个电影真可怕
> 今天看的這個電影真可怕。
> **Jīntiān kàn de zhège diànyǐng zhēn kěpà.**
> The movie we saw today was very scary.

> 战争真可怕。
> 戰爭真可怕。
> **Zhànzhēng zhēn kěpà.**
> War is very frightening.

To describe something as scary, say:

恐怖 的 noun
kǒngbù de noun
scary noun

我不喜欢看恐怖的电影。
我不喜歡看恐怖的電影。
Wǒ bù xǐhuan kàn kǒngbù de diànyǐng.
I don't like to watch horror movies.

⇨ | 9.2

51.4 Indicating that something scares someone

something 吓/嚇 *xià someone*

别吓着孩子。
別嚇著孩子。
Bié xiàzhe háizi.
Don't scare the child.

你别吓我好不好?
你別嚇我好不好?
Nǐ bié xià wǒ hǎo bù hǎo?
Don't scare me, okay?

你吓死我了。
你嚇死我了。
Nǐ xiàsǐ wǒ le.
You scared me to death.

52

Expressing speaker attitudes and perspectives

Mandarin uses interjections at the beginning of the sentence and syllables at the end of the sentence (*sentence-final particles*) to indicate the attitude of the speaker towards the situation expressed in the sentence. Attitudes expressed by interjections and sentence final particles include surprise, disgust, agreement, pity, etc.

Interjections and sentence final particles stand outside of the grammar of the sentence. Their omission or inclusion never affects the grammatical status of the sentence. However, their appropriate use contributes to the naturalness of the sentence, making it sound more authentically Mandarin.

52.1 Interjections

Syllables serving as interjections always have tones. Here are some common interjections and their associated meanings.

哈 *hā satisfaction*

> 哈哈！还是我对吧！
> 哈哈！還是我對吧！
> **Hā hā! Hái shì wǒ duì ba!**
> Well (ha), so I was right after all!

嗐 *hài sorrow, regret*

> 嗐，你怎么能跟这种人结婚？
> 嗐，你怎麼能跟這種人結婚？
> **Hài, nǐ zěnme néng gēn zhè zhǒng rén jiéhūn?**
> Why, how can you marry this kind of person?

啊 *ā surprise*

> 啊！他死了？
> **Ā! tā sǐ le?**
> What? He passed away?

啊 *á doubt, surprise*

> 啊，你会说英文！
> 啊，你會說英文！
> **Á, nǐ huì shuō Yīngwén!**
> Oh! You speak English!

啊 *ǎ puzzled surprise*

> 啊，你把飞机票弄丢了？
> 啊，你把飛機票弄丢了？
> **Ǎ, nǐ bǎ fēijī piào nòngdiū le?**
> What! You lost your airplane ticket?

啊 *à agreement, approval, acknowledgement*

> 啊，你说得很对。
> 啊，你説得很對。
> **À, nǐ shuō de hěn duì.**
> Yes. What you said was right.

哎 *āi surprise, dissatisfaction*

> 哎，火车怎么还没来啊？
> 哎，火車怎麼還沒來啊？
> **Āi, huǒchē zěnme hái méi lái a?**
> Oh! Why isn't the train here yet?

哎哟/哎唷 *āiyō surprise, pain*

> 哎哟/哎唷！把我疼死了。
> **Āiyō! Bǎ wǒ téngsǐ le.**
> Ouch! It hurts so much.

哎呀 *āiyā wonder, admiration, shock*

> 哎呀！太晚了。我得走了。
> **Āiyā! Tài wǎn le. Wǒ děi zǒu le.**
> Gosh! It is already so late. I have to go now.

啊呀 *āyā pained surprise*

> 啊呀！我的钱包不见了。
> 啊呀！我的錢包不見了。
> **Āyā! Wǒ de qiánbāo bù jiàn le.**
> Oh no! My wallet is missing.

唉 *āi regret*

> 唉，真没想到他的车出事了。
> 唉，真沒想到他的車出事了。
> **Āi, zhēn méi xiǎngdào tā de chē chūshì le.**
> How awful. I never thought that his car would be in an accident.

噢 *ō sudden realization*

> 噢，我忘了给你钱了。
> 噢，我忘了給你錢了。
> **Ō, wǒ wàng le gěi nǐ qián le.**
> Oh, I forgot to pay you.

哦 *ó suspicion, not fully believing*

> 哦，你们认识？
> 哦，你們認識？
> **Ó, nǐmen rènshi?**
> Oh, you know each other?

喔 *ō surprise, sudden realization*

> 喔，原来你是警察啊！
> 喔，原來你是警察啊！
> **Ō, yuánlái nǐ shì jǐngchá a!**
> Oh, so you are a policeman!

52.2 Sentence final particles

Sentence final particles occur in neutral tone. Here are some common sentence final particles that are used to express speaker attitude.

嘛 *ma indicates that something is obviously true*

> 我早就告诉你他不是好人嘛。
> 我早就告訴你他不是好人嘛。
> **Wǒ zǎo jiù gàosu nǐ tā bù shì hǎo rén ma.**
> Didn't I tell you from the start that he wasn't a good person?

啊 *a obviousness, impatience*

> 你要多注意身体啊。
> 你要多注意身體啊。
> **Nǐ yào duō zhùyì shēntǐ a.**
> You should pay more attention to your health.

咯 *lo obviousness*

> 我们该走了。再不走就晚咯。
> 我們該走了。再不走就晚咯。
> **Wǒmen gāi zǒu le. Zài bù zǒu jiù wǎn lo.**
> We'd better go now. If we don't go we will be late.

啦 *la exclamation*

> 好啦，好啦，别再说啦！
> 好啦，好啦，別再說啦！
> **Hǎo la, hǎo la, bié zài shuō la!**
> Okay, okay, don't say it again!

NOTE 啦 **la** is a combination of the sentence final particles 了 **le** and 啊 **a**. Its meaning varies depending upon the sentence.

吧 **ba** *suggestions; suppositions*

> 多吃一点吧！
> 多吃一點吧！
> **Duō chī yīdiǎn ba!**
> Eat a little more!

> 您是王教授吧！
> **Nín shì Wáng jiàoshòu ba!**
> You must be Professor Wang!

For discussion of the sentence final particles 吗/嗎 **ma**, 呢 **ne**, and 了 **le**, see

⇨ 24.1.1, 24.5, 30.3, 34.1

53

Topic, focus, and emphasis

53.1 ## Introducing a topic

The topic is the thing that is being discussed or written about. Mandarin has a variety of ways to introduce and identify the topic. Here are the most common.

53.1.1 ### Expressions that introduce the topic of a sentence

Mandarin uses the following expressions to introduce the topic of a sentence.

至于/至於 *zhìyú* *'concerning, regarding, as for'*

> 至于我们两个人的事情，你就不要管了。
> 至於我們兩個人的事情，你就不要管了。
> **Zhìyú wǒmen liǎng gè rén de shìqing, nǐ jiù bù yào guǎn le.**
> As for the matter between the two of us, you don't have to pay attention to it.

对于/對於 *duìyú* *'concerning, regarding, as for (topic)'*

> 对于中国的情形，我也不太清楚。
> 對於中國的情形，我也不太清楚。
> **Duìyú Zhōngguó de qíngxing, wǒ yě bù tài qīngchu.**
> Regarding China's state of affairs, I am also not too clear (about it).

关于/關於 *guānyú* *'concerning, regarding, as for (topic)'*

> 关于国家大事，我们都应该注意。
> 關於國家大事，我們都應該注意。
> **Guānyú guójiā dà shì, wǒmen dōu yīnggāi zhùyì.**
> As for the major events of (our) country, we all should pay attention.

对 *(topic)* 来说/對*(topic)*來說 *duì (topic) lái shuō* *'as for (topic) . . .'*

> 对我来说，教书是一件很快乐的事。
> 對我來說，教書是一件很快樂的事。
> **Duì wǒ lái shuō, jiāo shū shì yī jiàn hěn kuàilè de shì.**
> As for me, teaching is a very enjoyable task.

论(到)/論(到) *lùn (dào)* *'speaking about (topic)'*

> 论到足球，我是一窍不通。
> 論到足球，我是一竅不通。

> Lùn dào zúqiú, wǒ shì yīqiào bù tōng.
> Speaking about football, I am completely ignorant.

提(到) *tí (dào)* 'speaking about (topic)'

> 提到奥运，你觉得那个裁判公平不公平？
> 提到奧運，你覺得那個裁判公平不公平？
> **Tí dào Àoyùn, nǐ juéde nàge cáipàn gōngpíng bù gōngpíng?**
> Speaking about the Olympics, do you think that decision was fair?

谈(到)/談(到) *tán (dào)* 'speaking about (topic)'

> 谈到中英两国的历史，他比谁都有兴趣。
> 談到中英兩國的歷史，他比誰都有興趣。
> **Tán dào Zhōng Yīng liǎng guó de lìshǐ, tā bǐ shéi dōu yǒu xìngqu.**
> Speaking about the history of China and England, he is more interested than anyone.

至于/至於 **zhìyú**, 对于/對於 **duìyú**, and 关于/關於 **guānyú** are interchangeable, as are 提到 **tí dào** and 谈到/談到 **tán dào**.

53.1.2 Structures that identify the topic of a sentence

53.1.2.1 Topicalization

In Mandarin, a noun phrase may be identified as the topic of a sentence when it occurs at the beginning of the sentence. If another noun phrase in the sentence has the same reference as the topic, it is typically omitted. In the following sentences, the first noun phrase is the topic. The omitted phrase is indicated as ( ).

> 那个饭馆，服务不好。
> 那個飯館，服務不好。
> *Nàge fànguǎn*, fúwù bù hǎo.
> *That restaurant*, the service is not good.

> 美国大学，学费很贵。
> 美國大學，學費很貴。
> *Měiguó dàxué*, xuéfèi hěn guì.
> (In) *American universities*, tuition is very expensive.

> 中国长城，我听说 ( )冬天最美。
> 中國長城，我聽説 ( )冬天最美。
> *Zhōngguó* Chángchéng, wǒ tīngshuō ( ) dōngtiān zuì měi.
> *The Great Wall of China*, I hear (it) is prettiest in the winter.

> 汉字，我怎么写( )也写不好。
> 漢字，我怎麼寫( )也寫不好。
> *Hànzì*, wǒ zěnme xiě ( ) yě xiě bù hǎo.
> *Chinese characters*, no matter how I write them I don't write ( ) well.

English also topicalizes noun phrases in this way, but topicalization is much more common in Mandarin than in English.

53.1.2.2 Noun phrase omission

In English, when a series of noun phrases refer to the same entity, all instances after the first reference typically occur as pronouns. In Mandarin, noun phrase omission is more common than pronominalization as a way to mark identity of reference. Noun phrase omission is one way that Mandarin identifies a noun phrase as a topic. As we saw in the previous section, noun phrases are typically omitted if they refer to the topic of the discourse.

Noun phrases are omitted when they occur in the same grammatical role as the first noun phrase.

In this example, the first reference and the omitted noun phrases are subjects of the verb:

> 张美丽每天都很忙。(_)早上六点起床，(_)七点出门，(_)晚上九点才回家。
> 張美麗每天都很忙。(_)早上六點起牀，(_)七點出門，(_)晚上九點才回家。
> **Zhāng Měilì měitiān dōu hěn máng. (_) Zǎoshang liùdiǎn qǐchuáng, (_) qīdiǎn chūmén, (_) wǎnshang jiǔdiǎn cái huí jiā.**
> Meili Zhang is very busy every day. *She* gets up at 6 o'clock, (*she*) leaves the house by 7 o'clock, and *she* doesn't get home at night until 9 o'clock.

In this example, the first reference and the omitted noun phrase are objects of the verb:

> 她买了裙子，到家以后马上穿上了(_)。
> 她買了裙子，到家以後馬上穿上了(_)。
> **Tā mǎi le qúnzi, dào jiā yǐhòu mǎshàng chuānshàng le (_).**
> She bought a skirt; when she got home she immediately put *it* on.

When a noun phrase with identical reference occurs in a different grammatical role from the first instance, it occurs as a pronoun and is not omitted. In this example, the first reference is the object of 喜欢/喜歡 **xǐhuan** 'to like.' In the second reference, it is the subject of the sentence.

> 我们都喜欢那个孩子。她又可爱又乖。
> 我們都喜歡那個孩子。她又可愛又乖。
> **Wǒmen dōu xǐhuan *nàge háizi. Tā* yòu kě'ài yòu guāi.**
> We all like that child. She is both cute and well-behaved.

53.2 Focus

Mandarin uses the following expressions to *focus* or highlight a phrase. This section presents the structure and purpose of the most common focusing constructions in Mandarin.

53.2.1 把 *bǎ*

把 **bǎ** is used to indicate what a subject does to some object, while focusing on the object. 把 **bǎ** sentences can always be used to answer the question: 'What did the subject do to the object?' 把 **bǎ** sentences are sometimes called the 'disposal construction.' The structure of 把 **bǎ** sentences is as follows.

subject 把 **bǎ** object [prepositional phrase +] verb phrase

> 弟弟把饺子吃完了。
> 弟弟把餃子吃完了。
> **Dìdi bǎ jiǎozi chīwán le.**
> Younger brother ate up the dumplings.
> (Younger brother took the dumplings and ate them up.)

他把桌子擦干净了。
他把桌子擦乾淨了。
Tā bǎ zhuōzi cā gānjìng le.
He wiped the table clean.
(He took the table and wiped it clean.)

The object of 把 **bǎ** must refer to something specific and definite.

The action must have a conclusion or completion. Therefore, 把 **bǎ** is often used with change-of-state verbs and verbs with resultative endings.

我把他的地址忘了。 (*change-of-state verb*)
Wǒ bǎ tā de dìzhǐ *wàng* le.
I forgot his address.
(I took his address and forgot it.)

他把窗户打破了。(*verb with resultative ending*)
Tā bǎ chuānghu *dǎpò* le.
He broke the window.
(He took the window and broke it.)

她把论文写完了。(*verb with resultative ending*)
她把論文寫完了。
Tā bǎ lùnwén *xiěwán* le.
She *finished writing* her thesis.
(She took her thesis and finished writing it.)

他把每个字都写错了。(*verb with resultative ending*)
他把每個字都寫錯了。
Tā bǎ měi gè zì dōu *xiěcuò* le.
He *wrote* every character *wrong*.
(He took every character and *wrote* it *wrong*.)

⇨ 13.5, 28.1

Mandarin often uses 把 **bǎ** when English would use a passive sentence.

⇨ 17

53.2.2 **Indicating exception or addition with 除了 *chúle* ... 以外 *yǐwài***

除了 **chúle** noun phrase 以外 **yǐwài**
except for noun phrase; in addition to (noun phrase)

This expression introduces an exception to a situation or an additional example of a situation. The structure itself is the same whether it focuses on an exception or an example. The context of the sentence makes it clear whether the sentence is providing an exception or an additional example.

- The noun phrase that follows 除了 **chúle** may be the subject, a 'time when' expression, or the object of the verb.
- The full expression includes both 除了 **chúle** and 以外 **yǐwài**. However, either phrase may be omitted.
- 也 **yě** or 都 **dōu** typically occurs in the predicate.

除了 *chúle* . . . 以外 *yǐwài* marking exception: 'except for noun phrase'

除了 *chúle* + *subject*

> 除了爷爷以外，我们全家都去中国旅游。
> 除了爺爺以外，我們全家都去中國旅遊。
> *Chúle yéye yǐwài, wǒmen quánjiā dōu qù Zhōngguó lǚyóu.*
> *Except for grandfather*, our whole family is going to China to travel.

除了 *chúle* + *time when*

> 除了星期天以外，他每天都复习中文。
> 除了星期天以外，他每天都復習中文。
> *Chúle xīngqītiān yǐwài, tā měitiān dōu fùxí Zhōngwén.*
> *Except for Sunday*, he reviews Chinese every day.

除了 *chúle* + *object*

> 除了苦瓜以外，我弟弟什么都吃。
> 除了苦瓜以外，我弟弟甚麼都吃。
> *Chúle kǔguā yǐwài, wǒ dìdi shénme dōu chī.*
> Except for bitter melon, my younger brother eats everything.

除了 *chúle* . . . 以外 *yǐwài* marking an additional example: 'In addition to noun phrase'

In this use of 除了 *chúle* . . . 以外 *yǐwài*, the adverb 也 *yě* usually occurs in the predicate.

除了 *chúle* + *subject*

> 除了爷爷以外，奶奶也去中国旅游。
> 除了爺爺以外，奶奶也去中國旅遊。
> *Chúle yéye yǐwài, nǎinai yě qù Zhōngguó lǚyóu.*
> Besides grandfather, grandmother will also go to China to travel.

除了 *chúle* + *time when*

> 除了晚上以外，他白天也上网。
> 除了晚上以外，他白天也上網。
> *Chúle wǎnshang yǐwài, tā báitiān yě shàng wǎng.*
> In addition to the evening, he also surfs the web during the day.

除了 *chúle* + *object*

> 除了苦瓜以外，我弟弟也吃辣椒。
> *Chúle kǔguā yǐwài, wǒ dìdi yě chī làjiāo.*
> Besides bitter melon, my younger brother also eats hot peppers.

53.2.3 Indicating inclusion with 连/連 *lián*

连/連 **lián** noun phrase 也/都 **yě/dōu** [+ prepositional phrase +] verb phrase

even noun phrase does verb phrase [+ prepositional phrase]

连/連 **lián** is used to indicate that a noun phrase is included in the situation described by the verb phrase. The noun phrase that follows 连/連 **lián** may be the subject, a 'time when' expression, or the object of the verb. 也 **yě** or 都 **dōu** typically occurs in the predicate.

连/連 **lián** + *subject noun phrase*

> 人人都喜欢吃中国饭。连外国人也喜欢。
> 人人都喜歡吃中國飯。連外國人也喜歡。
> **Rén rén dōu xǐhuan chī Zhōngguó fàn. *Lián wàiguórén* yě xǐhuan.**
> Everyone likes to eat Chinese food. *Even foreigners* like to (eat Chinese food).

> 我们全家都去中国旅游。连爷爷也去。
> 我們全家都去中國旅遊。連爺爺也去。
> **Wǒmen quánjiā dōu qù Zhōngguó lǚyóu. *Lián yéye* yě qù.**
> Our whole family is going to China to travel. *Even grandpa* will go.

连/連 **lián** + *'time when' expression*

> 他每天都复习中文。连周末也复习。
> 他每天都復習中文。連週末也復習。
> **Tā měitiān dōu fùxí Zhōngwén. *Lián zhōumò* yě fùxí.**
> He reviews Chinese every day. He *even* reviews *on the weekend*.

> 他每天都很忙。连礼拜天都很忙。
> 他每天都很忙。連禮拜天都很忙。
> **Tā měitiān dōu hěn máng. *Lián lǐbàitiān* dōu hěn máng.**
> He is busy every day. He is *even* busy *on Sunday*.

连/連 **lián** + *object noun phrase*

> 我弟弟什么都吃。连苦瓜也吃。
> 我弟弟甚麼都吃。連苦瓜也吃。
> **Wǒ dìdi shénme dōu chī. *Lián kǔguā* yě chī.**
> My younger brother eats anything. He *even* eats *bitter melon*.

> 谁都喜欢这个电影。连爸爸也喜欢。
> 誰都喜歡這個電影。連爸爸也喜歡。
> **Shéi dōu xǐhuan zhège diànyǐng. *Lián bàba* yě xǐhuan.**
> Everyone likes that movie. Even dad likes it.

53.2.4 Focusing with 是 *shì* or 是 . . . 的 *shì . . . de*

是 **shì**, or 是 . . . 的 **shì . . . de** together, focus on some detail of an event: the time, the place, the actor, etc.

The phrase that is focused occurs immediately after 是 **shì**.

If the sentence refers to a situation in past time, 的 **de** occurs at the very end of the sentence, or immediately after the verb. In the following examples, the phrase that is focused is emphasized.

⇨ 11.4, 26.4

Focus on the subject

> 是他给我们介绍的。
> 是他給我們介紹的。
> **Shì *tā* gěi wǒmen jièshào de.**
> It was *he* who introduced us.

Focus on the place

> 我是在中国学中文的。
> 我是在中國學中文的。
> **Wǒ shì *zài Zhōngguó* xué Zhōngwén de.**
> It was *in China* where I studied Chinese.

> 你们是在哪儿认识的?
> 你們是在哪兒認識的?
> **Nǐmen shì *zài nǎr* rènshi de?**
> Where did you meet?

Focus on the 'time when'

> 他是去年买的那本书。
> 他是去年買的那本書。
> **Tā shì *qùnián* mǎi de nà běn shū.**
> It was *last year* when he bought that book.

Focus on the prepositional phrase

> 我是跟朋友看电影的。
> 我是跟朋友看電影的。
> **Wǒ shì *gēn péngyou* kàn diànyǐng de.**
> It was *with friends* that I saw the movie.

是 **shì** may be omitted, unless it is negated.

> 这张磁碟(是)在书店买的。
> 這張磁碟(是)在書店買的。
> **Zhè zhāng cídié (shì) *zài shūdiàn* mǎi de.**
> This CD was bought *at the bookstore*.

> 这张磁碟不是在书店买的。
> 這張磁碟不是在書店買的。
> **Zhè zhāng cídié bù shì *zài shūdiàn* mǎi de.**
> This CD was not bought *at the bookstore*.

If the object of the verb is a pronoun, 的 **de** can only occur after the pronoun, at the end of the sentence.

Say this	*Not this*
你是在哪儿认识他的?	*你是在哪儿认识的他?
你是在哪兒認識他的?	你是在哪兒認識的他?
Nǐ shì *zài nǎr* rènshi tā de?	**Nǐ shì *zài nǎr* rènshi de tā?**
Where did you meet him?	

When the sentence refers to a non-past event, 是 **shì** alone can be used to focus a phrase.

我是<u>明年</u>毕业，不是<u>今年</u>毕业。
我是<u>明年</u>畢業，不是<u>今年</u>畢業。
Wǒ shì *míngnián* bìyè, bù shì *jīnnián* bìyè.
It is *next year* when I graduate, not *this year*.

是 **shì** and 的 **de** are often used to indicate contrastive focus. They contrast some situation with another situation. 是 **shì** or 不是 **bù shì** occurs before each of the phrases that is being contrasted.

这件衣服，我不是<u>在西班牙</u>买的。我是<u>在法国</u>买的。
這件衣服，我不是<u>在西班牙</u>買的。我是<u>在法國</u>買的。
Zhè jiàn yīfu, wǒ bù shì *zài Xībānyá* mǎi de. Wǒ shì *zài Fǎguó* mǎi de.
This article of clothing, I didn't buy it *in Spain*. I bought it *in France*.

这个字不是<u>我</u>写的。是<u>王老师</u>写的。
這個字不是<u>我</u>寫的。是<u>王老師</u>寫的。
Zhège zì bù shì *wǒ* xiě de. Shì *Wáng lǎoshī* xiě de.
This character, it wasn't *I* who wrote it. It was *Professor Wang* who wrote it.

53.3 Emphasis

53.3.1 Using 是 *shì* for emphasis

Mandarin uses the word 是 **shì** to emphasize words or phrases in the sentence, especially when the sentence is used to confirm some previously mentioned situation. 是 **shì** may be added before a 'time when' phrase, a location phrase, or a [prepositional phrase +] verb phrase to emphasize the following phrase.

In English, words that are emphasized usually receive heavy stress and falling pitch. Because Mandarin is a tone language, pitch contour cannot be used for emphasis. However, 是 **shì** often receives heavy stress when it is used for emphasis, and the emphasis used in the following examples is intended to convey heavy stress.

Neutral	*With emphasis*
那本书很贵。	那本书<u>是</u>很贵。
那本書很貴。	那本書<u>是</u>很貴。
Nà běn shū hěn guì.	**Nà běn shū *shì* hěn guì.**
That book is expensive.	That book *is* expensive. (just like you said)
我明天走。	我<u>是</u>明天走。
Wǒ míngtiān zǒu	**Wǒ *shì* míngtiān zǒu.**
I'm leaving tomorrow.	I *am* going tomorrow.
他很会唱歌。	他<u>是</u>很会唱歌。
他很會唱歌。	他<u>是</u>很會唱歌。
Tā hěn huì chàng gē.	**Tā *shì* hěn huì chàng gē.**
He can sing well.	He really *can* sing.
我们在小王家吃饭。	我们<u>是</u>在小王家吃饭。
我們在小王家吃飯。	我們<u>是</u>在小王家吃飯。
Wǒmen zài Xiǎo Wáng jiā chī fàn.	**Wǒmen *shì* zài Xiǎo Wáng jiā chī fàn.**
We are eating at Little Wang's house.	We *are* eating at Little Wang's house.

⇨ 10, 11.4

53.3.2 **Emphasizing the time when a situation occurs**

To emphasize the time when a situation occurs, you can also put the 'time when' expression before the subject. This phrase order is typically used to contrast one time phrase with another time phrase.

> 昨天他很忙。今天他不忙。
> **Zuótiān tā hěn máng. Jīntiān tā bù máng.**
> Yesterday he was very busy. Today he is not busy.

54

Guest and host

The present day roles of guest and host are based on centuries of tradition. In their simplest form, the roles are as follows: the host must take care of the guest, and the guest must accept the hospitality of the host without being a burden to the host. In practice, this means that the host must offer food and drink to the guest, must make the guest comfortable, and must escort the guest when he/she departs, and the guest must reject the hospitality of the host several times before eventually accepting it. Here are some general rules of behavior for guest and host.

- When visiting a Chinese host, the guest should bring a small gift. Items such as tea, fruit, flowers, and candy are usually appropriate. The host does not ordinarily open a gift in the presence of the guest.
- When a host invites a guest to participate in an activity for which there is a fee (dinner in a restaurant, coffee or ice cream in a café, attendance at a movie or show, transportation by taxi or train, etc.), it is understood that the host pays the bill.
- In most social situations, one of the participants typically assumes the role of host, paying the bill, ordering food or drink, paying for transportation, etc. It is expected that today's guest will be tomorrow's host, and the obligations (financial and otherwise) associated with the host will be reciprocated on later occasions by other members of the group. This creates a network of mutual obligations among participants and solidifies their identity as a group. It is rare for people to split the bill in China, or for individuals to pay for themselves when participating in some entertainment as part of a group. It is common for individuals to have a good natured fight over a bill to establish the host for the occasion.

Many common interactions between guest and host are conducted using ritual expressions and behavior. The most common of these are presented here. Expressions used in welcoming a guest and in saying goodbye are also used towards customers in restaurants.

54.1 Welcoming the guest

To welcome a guest, say:

> 欢迎！
> 歡迎！
> **Huānyíng!**
> Welcome!

54.2 Offering food and drink

When the host offers the guest something to eat or drink, he or she either serves something or gives the guest a choice of beverages or food. For example:

请喝茶。
請喝茶。
Qǐng hē chá.
Have some tea.

or

你喝可乐喝茶？
你喝可樂喝茶？
Nǐ hē kělè hē chá?
Do you drink cola or tea?

It is not polite to ask the guest *whether* he or she wants something to eat or drink (Would you like something to drink?), or if he or she is thirsty (Are you thirsty?). These kind of questions allow a response of 'no,' and imply that the host does not wish to provide food. A good Chinese host does not give the guest the opportunity to refuse hospitality.

54.3 Inviting the guest to get comfortable

To invite a guest to get comfortable, say:

请坐。
請坐。
Qǐng zuò.
Have a seat.

休息一会儿。
休息一會兒。
Xiūxi yīhuìr.
Rest for awhile.

54.4 Saying goodbye and seeing the guest off

When it is time for guests to leave, the host has a ritual obligation to encourage them to stay. Guests have a ritual obligation to insist upon leaving. Expressions used in this ritual are presented below.

When guests leave, the host is expected to 送 **sòng** the guests, that is, to see them off. When you see guests off, you are expected to walk them a portion of the way home. Modern day interpretation requires accompanying guests at least to the doorway if not to their car or bus or train, and staying with them until they depart. Even if the host does not accompany the guest beyond the doorway, he or she does not close the door when guests walk out of the house. Instead, the host stands in view of the guests, waving, until they are out of sight.

54.4.1 Expressions that the host can say to the guest at the end of a visit

再来玩。
再來玩。
Zài lái wán.
Come again. (informal)

有空再来。
有空再來。
Yǒu kòng zài lái.
Come again when you have time.

(请)慢走。
(請)慢走。
(Qǐng) màn zǒu.
(Please) Don't hurry off.

(请)好走。
(請)好走。
(Qǐng) hǎo zǒu.
(Please) take care.

➪ 20.2.2

54.4.2 Expressions that guests can say to the host at the end of a visit

请留步。
請留步。
Qǐng liú bù.
Don't bother to see me out.

别送。
Bié sòng.
There's no need to see me off.

54.5 Additional expressions involving guest and host

The opposite of *seeing a guest off* is *picking a guest up*. The verb used is 接 **jiē**.

我今天晚上到机场去接白经理。
我今天晚上到機場去接白經理。
Wǒ jīntiān wǎnshang dào jīchǎng qù jiē Bái jīnglǐ.
Tonight I am going to the airport to pick up Manager Bai.

The verb that is used for a formal visit to someone is 拜访/拜訪 **bàifǎng**.

我们明天拜访王教授。
我們明天拜訪王教授。
Wǒmen míngtiān bàifǎng Wáng jiàoshòu.
Tomorrow we will visit Professor Wang.

55

Giving and responding to compliments

55.1 Cultural conventions regarding praise

Traditionally, Chinese people do not say 谢谢/謝謝 **xièxiè** 'thank you' in response to a personal compliment of any kind. In Chinese culture, accepting a personal compliment can be interpreted as showing conceit. Thus, it is customary in China for people to reject rather than to accept compliments. To a Westerner, 谢谢/謝謝 **xièxiè** is merely thanks for the compliment. However, in Chinese culture, it is often interpreted as a boastful agreement with someone's assessment of the quality of your abilities or possessions.

55.2 Expressions used in deflecting praise

You are expected to reject compliments and deflect praise of your accomplishments, abilities, and possessions, and to deflect praise of the accomplishments and abilities of those close to you. The following expressions are commonly used to deflect praise:

Deflecting praise in neutral or informal situations

哪里，哪里。
哪裏，哪裏。
Nálǐ, nálǐ.
I have done nothing to deserve
your compliments.
(lit. 'where? where?')

哪儿的话?
哪兒的話?
Nǎr de huà?
What kind of talk is that?
What are you talking about?

没什么。
沒甚麼。
Méi shénme.
It is nothing.

不好，不好。
Bù hǎo, bù hǎo.
Not good, not good.

真的吗?
真的嗎?
Zhēnde ma?
Really?

More formal expressions used to deflect praise

过奖了。
過獎了。
Guò jiǎng le.
You are excessive in your praise.

不敢当。
不敢當。
Bùgǎndāng.
I cannot accept your praise.

55.3 Compliments and appropriate responses

The type of compliment determines the type of response. Here are some examples of compliments and appropriate responses.

Compliment	*Appropriate response*
你的孩子很聪明。 你的孩子很聰明。 **Nǐ de háizi hěn cōngming.** Your child is very intelligent.	不聪明。不聪明。 不聰明。不聰明。 **Bù cōngming. Bù cōngming.** (She/he) is not intelligent.
你的中国字写得真好。 你的中國字寫得真好。 **Nǐ de Zhōngguó zì xiě de zhēn hǎo.** You write Chinese characters really well.	我写得不好。 我寫得不好。 **Wǒ xiě de bù hǎo.** I do not write well.
您的讲演太精彩了。 您的講演太精彩了。 **Nín de jiángyǎn tài jīngcǎi le.** You gave an outstanding speech.	过奖了。 過獎了。 **Guò jiǎng le.** You are excessive in your praise.
你的医术真高明。 你的醫術真高明。 **Nǐ de yīshù zhēn gāomíng.** Your medical skill is brilliant.	不敢当。 不敢當。 **Bùgǎndāng.** I cannot accept your praise.
今天的菜太丰富了。 今天的菜太豐富了。 **Jīntiān de cài tài fēngfù le.** Today's meal is so bountiful.	没什么菜。便饭。 沒甚麼菜。便飯。 **Méi shénme cài. Biàn fàn.** There isn't anything special. It is just ordinary food.
你太太做的菜真好吃。 你太太做的菜真好吃。 **Nǐ tàitai zuò de cài zhēn hǎo chī.** The dishes that your wife made are really good.	哪里，哪里。便饭。 哪裏，哪裏。便飯。 **Nálǐ, nálǐ. Biàn fàn.** There is nothing worth praising. It is ordinary food.
你这件毛衣很漂亮。 你這件毛衣很漂亮。 **Nǐ zhè jiàn máoyī hěn piàoliang.** Your sweater is very pretty.	真的吗？很便宜。 真的嗎？很便宜。 **Zhēnde ma? Hěn piányi.** Really? It was very inexpensive.

56

Expressing satisfaction and dissatisfaction

56.1 Expressing satisfaction

56.1.1 Expressions used to indicate satisfaction

The following expressions are used to express satisfaction. They are arranged here according to approximate intensity ranging from least to most enthusiastic.

马马虎虎
馬馬虎虎
mámǎ hūhū
so-so

还不错	还行	还可以
還不錯	還行	還可以
hái bù cuò	**hái xíng**	**hái kéyǐ**
it's okay	it's okay	it's okay

可以
kéyǐ
fine

不错	相当好
不錯	相當好
bù cuò	**xiāngdāng hǎo**
not bad	pretty good

很好	挺好
hěn hǎo	**tǐng hǎo**
very good	very good

满意
mǎnyì
satisfied, pleased

很满意	很喜欢
	很喜歡
hěn mǎnyì	**hěn xǐhuan**
very satisfied	like it very much

非常好	好极了
	好極了
fēicháng hǎo	**hǎojíle**
excellent	excellent

⇨ 10.3, 11.2

56.1.2 ### Situations in which satisfaction is expressed

Question	*Response indicating satisfaction*
这个菜的味道怎么样?	马马虎虎。
這個菜的味道怎麼樣?	馬馬虎虎。
Zhège cài de wèidao zěnmeyàng?	**Mámǎ hūhū.**
How is the flavor of this dish?	So-so.
这本书有意思吗?	还不错。
這本書有意思嗎?	還不錯。
Zhè běn shū yǒu yìsī ma?	**Hái bù cuò.**
Is this book interesting?	It's okay.
你们住的旅馆好吗?	不错。
你們住的旅館好嗎?	不錯。
Nǐmen zhù de lǚguǎn hǎo ma?	**Bù cuò.**
How is the hotel that you are staying in?	Not bad.
旅行社的服务怎么样?	还行。
旅行社的服務怎麼樣?	還行。
Lǚxíngshè de fúwù zěnmeyàng?	**Hái xíng.**
How is that travel agency's service?	It's okay.
这个车可以吗?	可以。
這個車可以嗎?	
Zhège chē kéyǐ ma?	**Kéyǐ.**
Is this car okay?	It's okay.
那个电影怎么样?	相当好。
那個電影怎麼樣?	相當好。
Nàge diànyǐng zěnmeyàng?	**Xiāngdāng hǎo.**
How is that movie?	Rather good.
这本书好不好?	很好。
這本書好不好?	
Zhè běn shū hǎo bù hǎo?	**Hěn hǎo.**
How is this book?	Very good.
这个博物馆怎么样?	好极了。
這個博物館怎麼樣?	好極了。
Zhège bówùguǎn zěnmeyàng?	**Hǎojíle.**
How is this art museum?	Extremely good.
您对我们的服务满意吗?	很满意。
您對我們的服務滿意嗎?	
Nín duì wǒmen de fúwù mǎnyì ma?	**Hěn mǎnyì.**
Are you satisfied with our service?	Very satisfied.

56.2 Expressing dissatisfaction

56.2.1 Expressions used to indicate dissatisfaction

These expressions are arranged from mild to strong dissatisfaction.

不太好
bù tài hǎo
not too good

不好 **bù hǎo** not good	不行 **bù xíng** not okay

不合格
bù hé gé
not up to standard

很差
hěn chà
very inferior

太差了
tài chà le
too inferior

非常不好
fēicháng bù hǎo
extremely bad

非常坏 非常壞 **fēicháng huài** extremely bad	坏极了 壞極了 **huàijíle** extremely bad
完全不行 **wánquán bù xíng** completely unacceptable	完全不好 **wánquán bù hǎo** completely bad

糟透了
糟透了
zāotòu le
it's a mess

56.2.2 Situations in which dissatisfaction is expressed

Question	*Response indicating dissatisfaction*
这个医院怎么样? 這個醫院怎麼樣? **Zhège yīyuàn zěnmeyàng?** How is this hospital?	不太好。 **Bù tài hǎo.** Not too good.
餐厅的饭怎么样? 餐廳的飯怎麼樣? **Cāntīng de fàn zěnmeyàng?** How is the food in the cafeteria?	很差。 **Hěn chà.** Really inferior.

Question	*Response indicating dissatisfaction*
他们的服务还好吧？ 他們的服務還好吧？ **Tāmen de fúwù hái hǎo ba?** Is their service okay?	太差了。 **Tài chà le.** It's really inferior.
这儿的空气怎么样？ 這兒的空氣怎麼樣？ **Zhèr de kōngqì zěnmeyàng?** How is the air here?	非常不好。 **Fēicháng bù hǎo.** It is extremely bad.
那儿的天气怎么样？ 那兒的天氣怎麼樣？ **Nàr de tiānqì zěnmeyàng?** How is the weather here?	坏极了。 壞極了。 **Huàijíle.** Extremely bad.
那儿的交通怎么样？ 那兒的交通怎麼樣？ **Nàr de jiāotōng zěnmeyàng?** How is the transportation there?	糟透了。 **Zāotòu le.** It's a mess./It's terrible.

57

Expressing gratitude and responding to expressions of gratitude

Expressing gratitude

In Chinese culture, you thank others for actions that benefit you or show you respect. Such actions include doing something for you, taking the time to visit or write you, or helping you in some way. In Chinese culture, you do not thank others for compliments or invitations.

⇨ 54

57.1.1 **Direct expressions of thanks**

Gratitude is expressed in Chinese with the following expressions:

谢谢/謝謝 *xièxiè 'thank you'*

> 谢谢你帮我忙。
> 謝謝你幫我忙。
> **Xièxiè nǐ bāng wǒ máng.**
> *Thank you* for helping me.

感谢/感謝 *gǎnxiè 'gratefully thank; appreciate'*

> 非常感谢您的建议。
> 非常感謝您的建議。
> **Fēicháng gǎnxiè nín de jiànyì.**
> I greatly *appreciate* your suggestions.

表示感谢/表示感謝 *biǎoshì gǎnxiè 'to express thanks'*

> 这点小礼物表示我们的感谢。请笑纳。
> 這點小禮物表示我們的感謝。請笑納。
> **Zhè diǎn xiǎo lǐwù biǎoshì wǒmen de gǎnxiè. Qǐng xiàonà.**
> This little gift expresses our *thanks*. Please accept our humble gift.

道谢/道謝 **dàoxiè** 'to thank, to express thanks'

> 我代表我们公司向您道谢。
> 我代表我們公司向您道謝。
> **Wǒ dàibiǎo wǒmen gōngsī xiàng nín dàoxiè.**
> I represent our company in *expressing our thanks* to you.

57.1.2 **Indirect expressions of gratitude**

To express gratitude without saying 'thank you,' use the following expressions:

> 太麻烦你了。
> 太麻煩你了。
> **Tài máfan nǐ le.**
> This caused you too much trouble. (I've troubled you too much.)

> 太辛苦了。
> **Tài xīnkǔ le.**
> or
> 辛苦你了。
> **Xīnkǔ nǐ le.**
> This was really a lot of work for you.

> 真不好意思。
> **Zhēn bù hǎo yìsi.**
> I'm really embarrassed.

57.2 **Replying to expressions of gratitude**

In Chinese, it is considered presumptuous or rude to accept compliments, praise, and expressions of gratitude. Chinese does not have an expression equivalent to 'you're welcome' in English. Common appropriate responses to expressions of gratitude include the following:

不谢。 不謝。 **Bù xiè.** Don't thank me.	没事。 **Méi shì.** It wasn't anything. (It was nothing.)	没什么。 沒甚麼。 **Méi shénme.** It wasn't anything. (It was nothing.)
不客气。 不客氣。 **Bù kèqi.** Don't be polite.	不必客气。 不必客氣。 **Bù bì kèqi.** Don't be polite.	你太客气了。 你太客氣了。 **Nǐ tài kèqi le.** You are too polite.
哪里。 哪裏。 **Nálǐ.** It was nothing.	哪儿的话? 哪兒的話? **Nǎr de huà** What kind of talk is that?	

⇨ | 55.2

58

Invitations, requests, and refusals

In Chinese culture, people are connected through a web of obligations and mutual social debt often referred to as 关系/關係 **guānxi**, 'relationships' or 'connections.'

This social debt is created by invitations, favors, and requests, big and small, that have been offered and accepted by others. They include buying small items for someone such as coffee, soft drinks, or ice cream, helping someone complete a task, inviting someone to dinner, or facilitating an introduction. By accepting an invitation or favor, or by making or agreeing to a request, you enter into a relationship that obliges you to reciprocate at some time in the future.

The Chinese expression that captures this social obligation is 来往/來往 **lái wǎng**, as in the expression:

> 有来有往。
> 有來有往。
> **Yǒu lái yǒu wǎng.**
> To have give and take.

A friendship is based on giving and taking, and one expects a regular exchange of giving and receiving favors and assistance with a Chinese friend. When taking is not balanced with giving, the behavior is described by the Chinese expression:

> 有来无往，非礼也。
> 有來無往，非禮也。
> **Yǒu lái wú wǎng, fēi lǐ yě.**
> Taking without giving is ill-mannered and uncivil.

In many Western cultures, the relationship between favors and social obligations is not so strong. One may accept favors without creating any obligation towards the giver. English has an expression that captures this: 'no strings attached.' The expression means that a gift or favor comes with no obligations to the recipient. In Chinese, where relationships are built on *give and take*, favors often come with the expectation of reciprocation. A Chinese friend may be more generous with you than a Western friend, but will expect more from you in return.

This chapter provides the basic strategies for negotiating invitations and requests in Chinese and for forming socially acceptable refusals.

58.1 Invitations

58.1.1 Offering invitations

In English, invitations are often expressed in terms of a choice about whether or not to participate:

> Would you like to have coffee with me?

In Chinese, giving the listener a choice about whether or not to participate is considered rude. It implies that the speaker does not want the listener to accept the invitation. Therefore, invitations are often worded as suggestions.

> 我们去喝一杯咖啡吧！
> 我們去喝一杯咖啡吧！
> **Wǒmen qù hē yī bēi kāfēi ba!**
> Let's go drink a cup of coffee!

An invitation may also imply that the speaker will assume the role of 'host' and pay for any expenses involved in the activity. If the speaker specifically *invites* the addressee with the word 请/請 **qǐng** 'please' (lit. 'invite'), he or she expects to pay for the activity.

> 我请你去喝咖啡，好吗？
> 我請你去喝咖啡，好嗎？
> **Wǒ qǐng nǐ qù hē kāfēi, hǎo ma?**
> Please have coffee with me.
> (lit. 'I invite you to go with me to drink coffee, okay?')

⇨ 47.1.1, 54

58.1.2 Accepting and refusing invitations

Words and phrases used to accept invitations include:

好。	行。	可以。
Hǎo.	**Xíng.**	**Kéyǐ.**
Okay.	Okay.	I can.

Invitations between friends are accepted or rejected without ceremony. However, in more formal circumstances, it is often not considered polite to accept an invitation at its first offer. Typically, people refuse an invitation once or twice before accepting, even if they intend to accept all along. In the same way, the one who gives an invitation does not give up after an initial refusal, but offers a second or a third time before being certain that the refusal is genuine. This cycle of refusal and re-invitation is a social ritual in which you are expected to participate.

Expressions that are commonly used for the *ritual refusal* of an invitation to eat or drink include:

不要客气。	你太客气了。	我不(吃)/(喝) 。
不要客氣。	你太客氣了。	
Bù yào kèqi.	**Nǐ tài kèqi le.**	**Wǒ bù (chī)/(hē).**
Don't be polite.	You are too polite.	I am not (eating)/(drinking).

If you are a guest, you cannot ultimately refuse an offer of a snack or a non-alcoholic drink. After the ritual refusal, you must accept it, though you need not eat or drink it. If you accept an invitation for a meal, however, you must eat.

It is acceptable to provide a direct refusal to an invitation to drink an alcoholic beverage or to smoke. If you do not or cannot drink, say:

	or	
我不喝酒。		我不会喝酒。
我不喝酒。		我不會喝酒。
Wǒ bù hē jiǔ.		**Wǒ bù huì hē jiǔ.**
I do not drink alcohol.		I am not able to drink alcohol.

If you do not smoke, you can refuse a cigarette by saying:

我不抽烟。
我不抽菸。
Wǒ bù chōu yān.
I do not smoke.

In general, appropriate refusals for most other kinds of invitations are indirect and involve face-saving strategies. See section 58.3 for polite ways to refuse invitations.

⇨ 54

58.1.3 Formal written invitations

Written invitations are issued for weddings and formal dinners and events. Formal Chinese events have a fixed ending time as well as a fixed beginning time. Guests come on time and the event ends at the predetermined time. Formal events typically begin with a short formal speech announcing the commencement and end with a short formal speech announcing the conclusion.

The cover of the invitation often includes one of the following expressions that identify it as an invitation.

	or	
邀请(书/信)		请帖
邀請(書/信)		請帖
yāoqǐng (shū/xìn)		**qǐngtiě**
invitation		invitation (lit. 'a written submission')

The body of the invitation includes the following expressions.

- Expressions that say 'formally invite':

敬约/敬約	敬邀	诚邀/誠邀
jìng yuē	**jìng yāo**	**chéng yāo**
respectfully arrange an appointment/ respectfully invite	respectfully invite	respectfully invite

恭请/恭請	光临/光臨	恭请光临
		恭請光臨
gōng qǐng	**guānglín**	**gōng qǐng guānglín**
formally request	(your) presence	formally request your presence

呈送
chéngsòng
formally send a
report or petition
(to a higher authority)

- Expressions that identify the recipient(s) of the invitation:

    (family name) 台启 **táiqǐ**
    respectfully submitted to (family name)

  or (less formal)

    致 **zhì** (the names of the invited guests)

- Expressions that identify the type of event:

    举行/舉行 **jǔxíng** (the type of event)
    hold (a ceremony)

  or (less formal)

    参加 (the type of event)
    cānjiā
    to attend an event

- Expressions that indicate the location of the event:

    在 **zài** (location of event)
    or
    地点/地點 (location of event)
    dìdiǎn
    place

- Expressions that indicate the date and time of the event:

    谨订于 (2002 年 10 月 5 日)
    謹訂於 (2002 年 10 月 5 日)
    jǐndìng yǔ (2002 nián shí yuè wǔ rì)
    respectfully reserve the date of (October 5, 2002)

    晚上六点举行
    晚上六點舉行
    wǎnshang liù diǎn jǔxíng
    begin at (6 p.m.)

  or (less formal)

    时间/時間 (the time)
    shíjiān
    time

晚上九点散会	or	晚上九点散会闭幕
晚上九點散會		晚上九點散會閉幕
Wǎnshang jiǔ diǎn sàn huì		**Wǎnshang jiǔ diǎn sàn huì bì mù**
the event concludes at 9 p.m.		the curtain falls at 9 p.m.
		(the event concludes at 9 p.m.)

58.2 Requests

58.2.1 Making requests of close relatives and close friends

Close relatives and close friends have an obligation to help you. Therefore, requests to close relatives and close friends are often indistinguishable from commands.

> 给我那本字典。
> 給我那本字典。
> **Gěi wǒ nà běn zìdiǎn.**
> Give me that dictionary.

> 我借用一下你的笔。
> 我借用一下你的筆。
> **Wǒ jiè yòng yī xià nǐ de bǐ.**
> Let me borrow your pen for a minute.

> 给我笔用一下。
> 給我筆用一下。
> **Gěi wǒ bǐ yòng yī xià.**
> Lend me a pen for a minute.

To make a request more polite, you may preface it with 请/請 **qǐng** 'please.'

> 请给我笔用一下。
> 請給我筆用一下。
> **Qǐng gěi wǒ bǐ yòng yī xià.**
> Please lend me a pen for a minute.

58.2.2 Requesting information or assistance from teachers

Teachers have an obligation to help you with learning so requests to teachers for information can be direct. However, they should always be polite. You can preface a request with 请教/請教 **qǐng jiào** 'please teach me,' or 请问/請問 **qǐng wèn** 'may I ask.'

> 老师，请教。。。(这个字怎么用?)
> 老師，請教。。。(這個字怎麼用?)
> **Lǎoshī, qǐng jiào . . . (zhège zì zěnme yòng?)**
> Professor, may I ask . . . (literally: please teach me)

> 王教授，请问，您的意思是。。。
> 王教授，請問，您的意思是。。。
> **Wáng jiàoshòu, qǐng wèn, nín de yìsi shì . . .**
> Professor Wang, may I ask, do you mean . . .

58.2.3 Face-saving strategies used in requests

When making a request to someone outside of your close personal circle, you should leave him or her room for a graceful refusal. That is, you should allow him or her the opportunity to 留面子 **liú miànzi** 'save face' if he or she has to refuse you. Here are some face-saving ways to phrase requests.

- Ask if he or she has time.

你忙吗?	你有空吗?	你有工夫吗?
你忙嗎?	你有空嗎?	你有工夫嗎?
Nǐ máng ma?	**Nǐ yǒu kōng ma?**	**Nǐ yǒu gōngfu ma?**
Are you busy?	Do you have free time?	Do you have free time?

- Ask if he or she has the ability to help.

  你能不能帮我一点忙?
  你能不能幫我一點忙?
  Nǐ néng bu néng bāng wǒ yīdiǎn máng?
  Can you help me?

- Be humble
  The use of to 求 **qiú** 'beg' makes this request more humble.

  我有一点事要求你。
  我有一點事要求你。
  Wǒ yǒu yīdiǎn shì yào qiú nǐ.
  May I ask you a favor? (Lit: I have a little matter that I seek your help with.)

⇨ 12.1, 48.1.3

58.3 Refusals

It is not always possible to grant a request, but it is important to phrase a refusal in such a way that it saves face for all parties involved. Here are common ways to do so.

- Promising to try
  A promise to try leaves open the possibility that your request may be granted at some point. Here are some responses that promise to try.

我试试看。	我试一试。	我尽力做。
我試試看。	我試一試。	我盡力做。
Wǒ shì shì kàn.	**Wǒ shì yī shì.**	**Wǒ jìnlì zuò.**
I'll see what I can do.	I'll try.	I'll try my best.

This promise to try is more formal:

  尽力而为。
  盡力而為。
  Jìnlì' ér wéi.
  I will do everything possible. (formal)

- Pleading a lack of understanding
  This kind of response is a common way to avoid answering a request for information.

  我不太清楚。
  Wǒ bù tài qīngchu.
  I'm not too clear about that.

- Postponing the decision
  These responses are used to postpone a decision to another time.

我们考虑考虑。
我們考慮考慮。
Wǒmen kǎolǜ kǎolǜ.
We'll think about it.

以后再说。
以後再説。
Yǐhòu zài shuō.
Let's talk about it again another time.

现在有一点不方便。
現在有一點不方便。
Xiànzài yǒu yīdiǎn bù fāngbiàn.
It's a little inconvenient right now.

- Pleading an inability to perform the task

我做不了。
Wǒ zuòbuliǎo.
I am unable to do it.

我恐怕帮不了你的忙。
我恐怕幫不了你的忙。
Wǒ kǒngpà bāngbùliǎo nǐ de máng.
I am afraid I am unable to help you.

我没做过那样的事。
我沒做過那樣的事。
Wǒ méi zuòguo nèi yàng de shì.
I've never done this kind of thing before.

无能为力。
無能為力。
Wúnéng wéilì.
I am powerless to help. (formal)

- Pleading a time conflict

我现在有别的事。
我現在有别的事。
Wǒ xiànzài yǒu biéde shì.
I've got something else I have to do right now.

恐怕我太忙。
Kǒngpà wǒ tài máng.
I'm afraid I'm too busy.

我没有时间。
我沒有時間。
Wǒ méi yǒu shíjiān.
I don't have time.

对不起，我(那天)有事。
對不起，我(那天)有事。
Duìbuqǐ, wǒ (nà tiān) yǒu shì.
Sorry, I have something to do (that day).

To indicate that your explanation is genuine, and that you really do not have the knowledge, ability, time, or connections required to comply with a request, add 真的 **zhēnde** to your refusal.

> 我真的不会。
> 我真的不會。
> **Wǒ zhēnde bù huì.**
> I really can't do it.

> 我真的不懂。
> **Wǒ zhēnde bù dǒng.**
> I really don't understand.

You can soften a refusal with an apology by saying:

> 不好意思。
> **Bù hǎo yìsi.**
> I'm embarrassed about this.

or

> 对不起。
> 對不起。
> **Duìbuqǐ.**
> Excuse me.

不好意思 **bùhǎoyìsi** indicates the speaker's discomfort at not being able to comply with a request.

58.4 Abandoning a request

To abandon a request and indicate that you will not ask anymore, say:

算了 (吧)。	不要紧。 不要緊。	没关系。 沒關係。
Suànle (ba).	**Bù yàojǐn.**	**Méi guānxi.**
Forget it.	It is not important.	It is not important.

59

Expressing apologies, regrets, sympathy, and bad news

Apologies and regrets

Cultures differ in the kinds of things that people are expected to apologize for. This chapter presents the types of situations for which an apology is expected and provides expressions of apology that can be used in these situations.

Note that in Chinese culture, you are not expected to apologize for or otherwise acknowledge bodily functions such as coughs, sneezes, belches, flatulence, etc. In response to someone's sneeze, you can say:

> 百岁。/ 百歲。
> **Bǎi suì.**
> (May you live to be) 100 years old.

If someone sneezes a second time, you can say:

> 千岁。/ 千歲。
> **Qiān suì.**
> (May you live to be) 1000 years old.

59.1.1 **Apologizing for showing disrespect:** 对不起/對不起 *duìbuqǐ*

对不起/對不起 **duìbuqǐ** is the appropriate apology for actions that show disrespect towards another, including:

- Physical actions: bumping into someone, stepping on someone's foot, spilling something on someone, etc.
- Inappropriate behavior: interrupting someone, ending a conversation, etc.
- Imperfect performance: work done poorly, language spoken poorly, comprehension difficulty, etc.

> 对不起。我中文说得不好。
> 對不起。我中文說得不好。
> **Duìbuqǐ. Wǒ Zhōngwen shuō de bù hǎo.**
> Excuse me. I speak Chinese poorly.

对不起。我不懂。
對不起。我不懂。
Duìbuqǐ. Wǒ bù dǒng.
I'm sorry. I don't understand.

对不起。我耽误了你。
對不起。我耽誤了你。
Duìbuqǐ. Wǒ dānwu le nǐ.
Excuse me. I've caused you to be delayed.

Reply to 对不起/對不起 **duìbuqǐ** by saying:

没事。	没关系。	不要紧。
	沒關係。	不要緊。
Méi shì.	**Méi guānxi.**	**Bù yàojǐn.**
It's nothing.	It's not important.	It's not important.

Apologizing for refusals: 不好意思 *bù hǎo yìsi*

不好意思 **bù hǎo yìsi** acknowledges embarrassment on the part of the speaker. It is commonly used when the speaker refuses an invitation or turns down a request for assistance.

王：今天下午跟我去喝咖啡吧。
Wáng: Jīntiān xiàwǔ gēn wǒ qù hē kāfēi ba.
Wang: Have coffee with me this afternoon.

林：不好意思。我今天下午有事。
Lín: Bù hǎo yìsi. Wǒ jīntiān xiàwǔ yǒu shì.
Lin: How embarrassing. This afternoon I've got something to do.

There is no formulaic response to 不好意思 **bù hǎo yìsi**.

⇨ | 58.3

Apologizing for mistakes or wrongs: 抱歉 *bàoqiàn* and 道歉 *dàoqiàn*

抱歉 **bàoqiàn** and 道歉 **dàoqiàn** acknowledge a wrong to another and acknowledge personal responsibility for the wrong. Formal and written contexts often call for 抱歉 **bàoqiàn** or 道歉 **dàoqiàn**. Many speakers of Mandarin use these two words interchangeably. Here are expressions in which these words are used.

抱歉。	抱歉。我来晚了。
	抱歉。我來晚了。
Bàoqiàn.	**Bàoqiàn. Wǒ lái wǎn le.**
I apologize.	I'm sorry. I've arrived late.

真抱歉。	我向你道歉。
Zhēn bàoqiàn.	**Wǒ xiàng nǐ dàoqiàn.**
I really apologize.	I apologize to you.

NOTE   The use of the more formal preposition 向 **xiàng** 'towards' in the prepositional phrase 向你 **xiàng nǐ** 'towards you' makes this structure more formal.

⇨ | 14

The appropriate response to 抱歉 **bàoqiàn** or 道歉 **dàoqiàn** is the same as the response to 对不起/對不起 **duìbuqǐ**:

没事。	没关系。	不要紧。
	沒關係。	不要緊。
Méi shì.	**Méi guānxi.**	**Bù yàojǐn.**
It's nothing.	It's not important.	It's not important.

59.1.4 Asking for forgiveness: 请原谅/請原諒 *qǐng yuánliàng* 'please forgive me'

请原谅我/請原諒我 **qǐng yuánliàng wǒ** is used in an apology acknowledging personal responsibility for an action that negatively affects others.

The response to this kind of apology is the same as for 对不起/對不起 **duìbuqǐ**, 抱歉 **bàoqiàn**, and 道歉 **dàoqiàn**.

59.2 Expressing sympathy

To acknowledge a bad situation that another is experiencing, say:

真可惜。
Zhēn kěxī.
What a pity. What a shame.

To express sympathy when another is ill, say:

多保重身体。
多保重身體。
Duō bǎozhòng shēntǐ.
Take care of your health.

希望你早日康复。
希望你早日康復。
Xīwàng nǐ zǎo rì kāngfù.
I hope your health is soon restored.

59.3 Conveying bad news

To introduce bad news or a negative situation use 怕 **pà** 'to fear' and 恐怕 **kǒngpà** 'to be afraid that.' Notice that 怕 **pà** requires a subject and 恐怕 **kǒngpà** does not take a subject.

(subject) 怕 *pà* situation

这件事，我怕他作不好。
這件事，我怕他作不好。
Zhè jiàn shì, wǒ pà tā zuòbuhǎo.
I am afraid that he won't be able to do this job well.

我怕你这次考得不好。
我怕你這次考得不好。
Wǒ pà nǐ zhècì kǎo de bù hǎo.
I am afraid that this time you didn't do well on the exam.

我怕我帮不了你的忙。
我怕我幫不了你的忙。
Wǒ pà wǒ bāngbuliǎo nǐ de máng.
I am afraid that I can't help you.

恐怕 *kǒngpà situation*

恐怕明天会下雨。
恐怕明天會下雨。
Kǒngpà míngtiān huì xià yǔ.
I'm afraid it will rain tomorrow.

恐怕他们今天不会来了。
恐怕他們今天不會來了。
Kǒngpà tāmen jīntiān bù huì lái le.
I am afraid that they may not come today.

恐怕你这次考得不好。
恐怕你這次考得不好。
Kǒngpà nǐ zhè cì kǎo de bù hǎo.
I'm afraid that this time you did not do well on the exam.

恐怕我帮不了你的忙。
恐怕我幫不了你的忙。
Kǒngpà wǒ bāngbuliǎo nǐ de máng.
I am afraid that I cannot help you.

60

Expressing congratulations and good wishes

60.1 **General expressions of congratulations and good wishes**

The following expressions may be used to extend congratulations in any occasion. Each is followed by an illustration of its use.

恭喜！ *gōngxǐ! 'congratulations'*

> 恭喜！恭喜！
> **Gōngxǐ! Gōngxǐ!**
> Congratulations!
> (As an expression of congratulations, the word is often said twice.)

> 恭喜发财！
> 恭喜發財！
> **Gōngxǐ fācái!**
> Wishing you a prosperous New Year! (standard New Year greeting)

祝贺/祝賀 *zhù hè 'congratulations'*

> 祝贺开张大吉。
> 祝賀開張大吉。
> **Zhù hè kāizhāng dàjí.**
> Wishing you extraordinary good luck on your great business opening.

庆祝/慶祝 *qìngzhù 'celebrate'*

> 庆祝结婚纪念。
> 慶祝結婚紀念。
> **Qìngzhù jiéhūn jìniàn.**
> Congratulations on your wedding anniversary.

> 庆祝新婚。
> 慶祝新婚。
> **Qìngzhù xīn hūn.**
> Congratulations on your wedding. (on your new marriage)

> 庆祝开业。
> 慶祝開業。
> **Qìngzhù kāi yè.**
> Congratulations on your new business.

庆祝毕业典礼。
慶祝畢業典禮。
Qìngzhù bìyè diǎnlǐ.
Congratulations on your graduation.

60.2 Fixed phrases of congratulations and good wishes for special events

Occasion	*Phrase of congratulations and good wishes*
New Year	恭喜发财！ 恭喜發財！(traditional greeting) **Gōngxǐ fā cái!** Congratulations and get rich!
	新春大喜！ **Xīn chūn dà xǐ!** Wishing you great happiness at the new year!
	新年快乐！ 新年快樂！ **Xīnnián kuàilè!** Happy New Year! (Western influenced greeting)
Christmas	圣诞快乐！ 聖誕快樂！ **Shèngdàn kuàilè!** Merry Christmas!
Wedding	恭喜！ **Gōngxǐ!** Congratulations!
	天作之合！ **Tiān zuò zhī hé!** A match made in heaven!
	百年好合！ **Bǎi nián hǎo hé!** A happy union lasting 100 years!
	白头偕老！ 白頭偕老！ **Báitóu xiélǎo!** Growing old together in happiness!
Birthday	恭喜！ **Gōngxǐ!** Congratulations!
	祝你生日快乐！ 祝你生日快樂！ **Zhù nǐ shēngrì kuàilè!** Wishing you a happy birthday! (Western influenced greeting)

Birth of child (a new birth is celebrated when the child is a month old)

长命百岁！
長命百歲！
Chángmìng bǎi suì!
May you live to be 100 years old!

Birthday of someone 60 years old or older

祝你寿比南山，福如东海。
祝你壽比南山，福如東海。
Zhù nǐ shòu bǐ nán shān, fú rú dōng hǎi.
I wish you a long life (live as long as the south mountain) and great fortune (as great as the east sea).

Graduation

祝贺你前途无量。
祝賀你前途無量。
Zhù hè nǐ qiántú wúliàng.
Wishing you boundless prospects.

祝你前途光明。
Zhù nǐ qiántú guāngmíng.
Wishing you a bright future.

祝你鹏程万里。
祝你鵬程萬裏。
Zhù nǐ péngchéng wànlǐ.
Wishing you a promising future.

Good wishes for a business

开市大吉！
開市大吉！
Kāi shì dà jí!
开张大吉！
開張大吉！
Kāi zhāng dà jí!
开业大吉！
開業大吉！
Kāi yè dàjí!
Wishing you great luck in your new business!

祝贺生意兴隆！
祝賀生意興隆！
Zhù hè shēngyi xīnglóng!
Wishing you booming business!

祝贺财源茂盛！
祝賀財源茂盛！
Zhù hè cáiyuán màoshèng!
Wishing you abundant wealth!

⇨ 20.3

60.3 ## Replying to expressions of congratulations and good wishes

When someone congratulates you, you can reply by saying:

谢谢。	or	多谢。	or	谢谢你的好意。
謝謝。		多謝。		謝謝你的好意。
Xièxiè.		**Duō xiè.**		**Xièxie nǐ de hǎoyì.**
Thanks.		Thanks.		Thank you for your good wishes.

To give a more formal reply, say:

多谢你的吉言。
多謝你的吉言。
Duō xiè nǐ de jíyán.
Thank you for your good wishes.

Index

Index

Related titles from Routledge

Chinese:
A Comprehensive Grammar

Yip Po-Ching and Don Rimmington

Chinese: A Comprehensive Grammar is a complete reference guide to Chinese grammar.

It presents a fresh and accessible description of the language, concentrating on the real patterns of use in modern Chinese. The *Grammar* is an essential reference source for the learner and user of Chinese, irrespective of level. It is ideal for use in schools, colleges, universities and adult classes of all types, and will remain the standard reference work for years to come.

This volume is organized to promote a thorough understanding of Chinese grammar. It offers a stimulating analysis of the complexities of the language, and provides full and clear explanations. Throughout, the emphasis is on Chinese as used by present-day native speakers.

An extensive index and numbered paragraphs provide readers with easy access to the information they require.

Features include:
- Thorough and comprehensive coverage of the modern language
- Use of script and romanization throughout
- Detailed treatment of common grammatical sructures and parts of speech
- Extensive and wide-ranging use of examples
- Particular attention to areas of confusion and difficulty

Yip Po-Ching was Lecturer in Chinese at Leeds University and **Don Rimmington** is Emeritus Professor of Chinese, formerly at Leeds University.

ISBN10: 0-415-15031-0 (hbk)
ISBN10: 0-415-15032-9 (pbk)
ISBN13: 978-0415-15031-6 (hbk)
ISBN13: 978-0415-15032-3 (pbk)

Available at all good bookshops
For ordering and further information please visit:
www.routledge.com